RECUERDOS

Recuerdos
Basque Children Refugees in Great Britain

Published by Mousehold Press
for
Basque Children of '37 Association UK
Secretary: Natalia Benjamin,
8, Hernes Road,
Oxford, OX2 7PU
www.basquechildren.org

Published 2007
Reprinted 2009

Cover design: Dawn Velasco
Cover photograph: courtesy The Birmingham Post and Mail

ISBN 978-1-874739-44-9

Printed by Barnwell's, Aylsham, Norfolk

RECUERDOS

Basque Children Refugees in Great Britain

edited by

Natalia Benjamin

Editor's Acknowledgements:

I wish to thank the many people who have helped to produce this book, helped with typing, transcribing, translating the material, read drafts and proof read. Without their stalwart assistance, freely given, this book could not have been published.

They are:
Isabel Anjarwalla-Jones, Germán Ferrer, Jen Gardner, Tere Gautrey, Penny Harper, Anne Harrap, Gerald Hoare, Norman Jones, Shirley Jordan, Pilar McGillycuddy, Monique Moreton, Irina Nelson, Jesús Nieto, Patrick O'Kane, Alicia Pozo-Gutierrez, Ana Reynoso, Laura Román, Helen Sawyer.

And special thanks are due to the *niños* themselves who provided their life stories for the book.

I am grateful to the Ministerio de la Presidencia in Spain for a grant towards the costs of publication.

In particular, I want to thank Adrian Bell for his support. He has been extraordinarily helpful at all stages, sending me proofs, doing the typesetting and making sure the project would come to fruition.

Last but not least I wish to record my gratitude to my daughter, Victoria, who was always supportive and encouraging, helping me sort out all the texts I was being sent and generally organising me.

FOREWORD

On 21 May 1937 some 4000 children along with their teachers and helpers left the war-torn Basque country and set sail for Southampton on the *SS Habana*. On arrival they were cared for by an *ad hoc* committee, first in an encampment at Eastleigh and then in temporary homes across Britain. The arrival of the children, their dispersal to often remote corners of the United Kingdom, and their participation in fundraising cultural events did much to hring home the human cost of the Spanish Civil War within Britain. Many of the children eventually returned to their homes following the fall of the Basque country, but some, including those whose families were by now in exile, remained and settled in this country.

I first encountered the story of the Basque refugees when I was working on my doctoral research in the 1980s. At that time – approaching the subject as I did principally through the official papers of the British government and the Trades Union Congress – the subject seemed a very remote one. Admittedly scholars, notably Jim Fyrth and Dorothy Legarreta, were just beginning to publish the first detailed research into the experiences of the children and the networks of volunteers that sustained them in Britain. However, the *niños* seemed to have been largely forgotten beyond the academic world. Their own personal narratives had often not yet been recorded, and there was little public commemoration of their time in Britain.

Today the situation is very different, and this is in great measure due to the remarkable work of Natalia Benjamin and her colleagues in the Basque Children of '37 Association UK. Natalia, the daughter of one of the teachers, set up the association in November 2002 as a means of reuniting the surviving *niños* and ensuring that their story was preserved. Since then the association has erected numerous plaques and organised a series of exhibitions and lectures, as well as acting as the focal point for the collection of a wealth of historical material, shortly to be deposited at Southampton University for the benefit of future scholars. As a result, the remarkable story of the *niños* has finally begun to receive the public recognition that it deserves in Britain. For this 70th anniversary year the association embarked on an ambitious project to elicit written memoirs (*Recuerdos)* from the surviving *niños* and others who played a part in these events. The response was almost overwhelming, and this volume is testimony to the desire of so many of the *niños* to tell their story. It should also be noted that in order to bring the project to fruition, many have generously volunteered their time to translate the memoirs.

This edited collection is a magnificent monument to the children's remarkable journey and the warmth of the reception that they received from many ordinary British citizens. To read the memoirs collected here is fascinating for me, as a historian, but also intensely moving. For here one is reading – through the eyes of "children" now often in their eighties – about the most painful experiences of separation, dislocation and anxiety. Fortunately, one also encounters tremendous loyalty (especially between siblings), incredible resilience in the face of much uncertainty, and unanticipated, enduring friendships with British supporters. Despite the suffering and insecurity that they must have often felt, it is touching to read that so many of the *niños* have a warm and positive recollection of their time in Britain. This is surely due to the great support that they received from the many volunteers in Britain, but it also reflects the excitement that they experienced on arriving in such a new and different society. Indeed, this collection is something of a social history of Britain in the late 1930s: a vanished world of gas lighting, double-decker buses and the coronation of George VI. In particular, we encounter the social conventions and associational life of the small-town, suburban British middle classes, who were the best-placed to take the Basque children into their homes and had the leisure time to take them away on holidays. But above all we learn about how the children learned to adapt to their abrupt change in circumstances – often sent to old country mansions set in spacious grounds – and how they kept alive memories of their families and the hope of eventual reunion.

Tom Buchanan
Kellogg College, Oxford

INTRODUCTION

We are all familiar with public or collective remembrance after a war – soldiers are remembered in ceremonies, documentary films, in narrative and verse, on public monuments. But what of the others? Those who were forced to leave their country at a young age and who had no say in their future? In 1937, some 33,000 *niños* were evacuated from Spain during the Civil War, many of whom never returned to their own country. The war shattered their familiar world. They left their country to escape the bombings, hunger and fear; deprived of a normal childhood spent with their parents and siblings, uprooted at a very young age and were sent to countries whose language they didn't speak and whose cultural heritage they had to try and assimilate. These forgotten exiles are equally victims of the Civil War.

May 2007 marks the 70th anniversary of the evacuation of the Basque children to Great Britain. In spite of the reluctance of   the British government to admit 4,000 children, the British public responded magnificently: armies of dedicated volunteers rallied round immediately to care for them. "You can't help liking them" was the headline on a leaflet sent out by the Basque Children's Committee asking people to "adopt" a Basque refugee by giving ten shillings a week for his upkeep. The leaflet went on to say: " He becomes peculiarly yours. You can send him presents, take him out for the day and for the week-end," and continued: "They are small, dark little people with straight black hair and merry dancing eyes". These small and dark little people are now grandparents and are conscious of belonging to a historic group, *"los niños de la guerra"*.

When we were thinking of projects in which to commemorate this anniversary, it immediately came to my mind that we should produce a book of testimonies, so that the *niños de la guerra* would be able to record their story and it shouldn't fall into oblivion. Compelling reasons led me to be confident that the project was certainly worthwhile, especially in the light of the interest that has emerged in Spain in the last few years on the "recuperation of historic memory". There is a general fascination with the past and books on diverse aspects of the Civil War abound in the bookshops. Spaniards are wanting to read what happened to their people during the darkest years of its history. It seemed a unique and timely opportunity to ask the *niños* to tell their story.

So first a letter was sent in May 2006 to *niños* living in England who might be interested in participating. The idea also was to include *niños* who had been evacuated to England but who had later returned to Spain. When I was in Vitoria in September for the *Homenaje a los niños de la guerra* that the Basque government organised, I was fortunate in being able to contact some of those who had been sent to England and hand them copies of the original letter. This was successful, as, in the weeks that followed, testimonies started to come in from Spain. I had specified that although I would obviously have to edit the texts, all would be included. The *niños* were asked for their impressions on coming to this country and what life in the "colonies", as their care homes were called, had been like for them. A few of the English people who had had some experience of living and working with the children were also contacted, and luckily I found a nurse, a teacher and a former university student. Three of the testimonies come from books, two of which are unpublished. Many of the niños were tired of recounting their personal history to research students or documentary film makers, and I thought that the project would be fairly small scale and that, with luck, I would have at the most twenty accounts. I was little prepared for the numbers of testimonies that arrived, 28 written in English and 34 in Spanish. The willingness to join in the venture and the enthusiasm of the *niños* was impressive and the ways in which they remember their British sojourn highlights the personal meaning and significance of their experience.

I decided at an early stage that because many of the *niños* writing now understood only one language, either English or Spanish, that there would have to be translations of the *recuerdos*, so that they could be read and understood by all. This created double the amount of work and I am very grateful to those friends who joined in the task of translating with such dedication. (This symbol * signifies a translation.)

As regards subject matter, we inevitably find certain recurring themes in the collection, such as the sea crossing from Bilbao to Southampton, life in the camp, the reaction to hearing that Bilbao had fallen and the dedication of the British volunteers. So that there shouldn't be too many accounts of the same event, I had, clearly, to edit the texts.

However, what stands out in particular in these accounts is the diversity. For a start, presentation varied greatly. Not surprisingly, many of the stories were handwritten, so there was the problem of deciphering the writing; some were on tape or CD and had to be transcribed; others were typewritten. Furthermore, elderly people don't necessarily find it easy to draft stories and so not all the *niños* wrote their memories themselves. Some talked to me, to their children, to their husbands, and we transcribed what we heard. Some children of *niños* wrote the stories of parents who were no longer alive. The length of the testimonies varied enormously too. Having naively specified "from one to ten pages", I received anything from 350 to 6000 words, and because the response was so much greater than expected, I had to edit in particular the longer texts, simply because the book would have become too unwieldy. Moreover, my directives concerning the content were taken somewhat loosely. This all makes for interesting reading. There is also a vast diversity of experience: details of the horrendous journey to England and of the different colonies, anecdotes of life in England during the war and of being repatriated to Spain, accounts of what it was like returning to Spain after a long period and even a description of joining the Royal Navy.

As for length of stay, experiences were very different. Some *niños* left after less than a year in Britain, others at the end of the Second World War, and a small band remained and made their lives in this country. Many were fortunate enough to stay in only one colony throughout their time in this country; others had the deleterious experience of being sent from one to another as they closed down when repatriation began. We have to remember too that the word "children" has a different interpretation according to age. The youngest were five and had not been to school in Spain and would grow up in Britain, adopting its cultural values as their own, whereas the adolescents had spent their formative years in Spain, had already reached school leaving age and found it more difficult to adapt to English customs. Many of the older boys were older than the cut-off age for the evacuation. Their parents had lied about their age on the registration form as they had wanted them to come to Britain to be safe. Many of them were intensely politicised, having acted as head of their family in Spain because their father was absent, either in hiding, imprisoned, or killed, and they weren't used to being treated as children. Their recollections of Bilbao and the war were of hunger, fear, the exploding of the bombs, schools being closed, endless time spent in shelters. And seeing people killed and dead bodies, gruesome scenes that young people don't usually have to witness. Most of the children were eventually repatriated but some of the children stayed, either through choice (if they were over 17) or because their family couldn't be traced.

The years in Britain are regarded as a period of stability and peace far away from the danger of war. Surrounded for the most part by kindness, the young exiles became children once again; they went to school or had lessons in the colonies, they played games and the older ones were found work. Those who returned to Spain in the post-war period found a fractured country, reeling from the effects of the war, and a return to hunger and misery, with many having lost one or more of their parents.

In a way, however, the stories are not entirely representative of the experiences the *niños* underwent, as for the most part, those who contributed to this book have a very positive recollection of their stay in Britain. Indeed, many actually say that they count their time here as being the happiest period in their lives. There are a few whose remembering is seared by the tragic sadness of families damaged and torn apart through exile. But the single most common way of remembering the years in Britain, amongst children of all ages, is that it was a very positive experience. Though some children only spent less than a year in Great Britain, that time of their life is often remembered in vivid detail and the memories of those years take on a disproportionate significance. And it is natural that those who had good experiences would want to write about them. What comes across in the recollections of so many *niños* is the sense that being evacuated was a great achievement – for some the most important in their lives – and that these memories are particularly special. There are several explanations for this phenomenon: when they left their country, these children did something extraordinary with their lives. They saw the world beyond their homes in Spain and they experienced evacuation as a remarkable adventure. This gave them a new knowledge of the world and a new understanding of themselves. So we can say that their story narrates a rite of passage and in many cases also defines the evacuation experience as a coming of age, a time of self discovery when the boy became a man, the girl a woman. Indeed, personal growth through adventure becomes the main way in which the evacuee experience is remembered and the stay in Britain thus occupies a central place in the *niños'* identity.

We do know, however, that some of the colonies were better than others, and that life was not always as idyllic as it has been painted. The convents in particular seem to have treated the children unnecessarily harshly. Meeting parents again after many years was also a traumatic experience for some: they were no longer their parents' little ones. They had grown up, often they didn't recognise their parents and in quite a few cases, had forgotten the language. But it is evident that the act of writing down their reminiscences has been a cathartic process for some, healing wounds and helping them come to terms with their splintered childhood. Important memories that had been bottled up are recognised and affirmed as significant in their own lives and for the historical record. There is the realisation that 4,000 children arriving in this country is a very significant historical event about which we have heard virtually nothing. It certainly is an event of some significance to Britain. The *niños* can feel liberated as they go through issues that have had an effect on their identity and their life ever since.

My job was to decide how to present the testimonies. How should the material I was receiving be ordered? I could have taken the "storyline" approach, that is, extracted from each contribution parts of the story of the *niños*, such as, leaving Bilbao, the journey to England, North Stoneham camp, the different colonies etc. However, given the constraints, that the book had to be published by May, this was not practicable, so I decided simply to organise it alphabetically. This method has the virtue that it captures a patchwork of collective experience in a way that a more artificially ordered account would not do. As the collector of these *recuerdos*, I didn't want to dictate a plan, but rather leave the reader to find his own way through the multiplicity of narratives.

And then I had to think of the reader of such a book of *recuerdos*. Who is the book intended for? Who is the reader? One of the obvious targets is the children of the *niños* so they can learn more about this period in their parents' life. We don't listen enough to our parents when they talk to us about their childhood, at least I certainly didn't, so here is the chance of filling in many gaps in our knowledge. But this book will also interest social historians, anthropologists and anyone who feels strongly about the recuperation of historic memory. It is vital that these accounts should be published, if only that we should learn lessons from them and place the story of the *niños* in Britain in its rightful historical context. A few of the testimonies end by saying that if similar circumstances occurred today, they would never be parted from their children. In 1937, Basque families wanted to remove their children from danger and wanted them to be fed properly - they only envisaged that the children would be away for three months.

My interest, and indeed the affection, I feel for the Basque children stems from the fact that my mother, from Madrid, left for England alone in July 1937, at the age of 21; her registration form qualified her as an "independent refugee". She was sent to the colony in Langham near Colchester, where she taught the children English. About five years ago, I embarked on an odyssey to find out more about the three years she spent there. I realised that the story of the Basque children was virtually unknown in Britain and that valuable archival material was being lost to posterity. I determined to do something about this and that is how and why the Basque Children of '37 Association UK was set up. Since then I have got to know personally many of the *niños* who are still living in this country as well as some from Spain.

Memories such as these are remarkable and allow us to learn about individuals who might not otherwise appear in historical records. The testimonies have the value of bringing alive an important part of British as well as Spanish history. They help us understand the past in a more personal way and add another dimension to the story of the Spanish Civil War, ensuring that the exiles will not be *los olvidados*.

Natalia Benjamin
March 2007

Josefina Álvarez Álvarez

It was July 1936 and I had just finished my fourth year at the *instituto* and was very happy to have passed my exams – no worries about resits in September. That was just before 18 July. We were getting ready to go on holiday to visit our grandmother when we were told that there were no trains running. Our bags remained packed for a few days until my parents realised that there would be no visit to our grandmother and that the Franco uprising was worse than we thought.

Looking back, it is hard to imagine that a legally elected government could have lost a war through the rebels being helped by two European dictators and the apathy of the European democracies.

As the war progressed and we in the Basque Country suffered the bombings of Guernica and Durango, it was obvious that children had to be evacuated in order to avoid the horrors of war, even to survive. Much has been written about our departure from Bilbao: the terrible sadness of saying goodbye to our parents; the stormy voyage across the Bay of Biscay to Southampton; the arrival at North Stoneham; our dispersal from there to various parts of the British Isles, and finally our settling down in Britain, which would turn out to be for far longer than the three months we had expected.

Fifty-six of us were sent to Caerleon, a small village in South Wales that had once been a Roman fortress. We stayed at Cambria House and life started and continued as probably in every other colony. As friends of the Basque children started to arrive, one of them, a local teacher, took an interest in me and I was allowed to visit her home in order to learn English quickly. It worked. I did learn English quickly!

By the autumn of 1938, I had been offered a place at Badmington School. When I arrived there, I was sad and lonely, missing Cambria House, which had been home for a long time. I also missed my friends, but then I made new friends at the school and became very interested in the work I had to do. It was a wonderful school. It had three large buildings – the senior school, the junior school and the old junior school. There was also a rest room and a kitchen for cookery lessons, playing fields and an open-air swimming pool.

At the *instituto* we had worn ordinary clothes, but here we all wore uniform, a pleasure to me because we were all the same and I have always liked equality! There were girls from different countries and a German girl became my best friend. We had some very interesting lessons: "News of the Day" was a study of the newspapers and "Progress of Civilisation" was a study of history, not through a series of battles, but through peaceful developments. Life at school was made difficult by what was happening in Spain – the defeat of the government – and the outbreak of the Second World War. Some of our School Certificate examinations were taken between visits to the air raid shelter.

Looking back on those days, the kindness of the staff, the discipline and the high standards of teaching, I feel that it was a wonderful experience and a preparation for what would be my higher education. But I still ask myself how could all the various nationalities live happily together because, to this day, the various nationalities cannot live in harmony?

Félix Amat Irazola

My first recollection on arriving at the camp in Southampton was to be called on the loudspeaker to go to the main tent to meet one of the teachers. Her name was Srta Amada Renouard. I learned years later that she was a friend of one of my older brothers in Bilbao and he had asked her to look after us.

With my younger brother and sister we boarded a bus that took us to Langham, near Colchester. The excitement we all felt on arriving at Basque House was incredible, especially as children don't take much notice of their surroundings. The home was enormous, with bedrooms big enough to accommodate up to eight beds. There were about 30 girls and 24 boys, as well as the teachers, Srtas Celia, Berta, Amada, Peque and Deme and an assistant cook, Rafaela. I also remember the first Directors we had, Mr Stirling and Mr Darling. Mr Stirling left within a few months to take up a diplomatic appointment in South America. Later we had Mr Theo Wills as Director. He was a keen photographer and before he left he gave me most of his photographs and negatives to keep because, as he said to me, "I know you'll look after them". To this day I have most of these photos and they have been well used in exhibitions.

But if the house was enormous and comfortable, the gardens were out of this world. We had never seen anything like it and it's no wonder one of the boys shouted: "This is paradise!" There were tennis courts, a full cricket pitch, rose gardens, lawns and borders with beautiful flowers, greenhouses, a gardener's cottage and stables and so on. At first we used the cricket pitch to play football (we didn't know anything about cricket), but on the gardener's orders we had to stop because we were doing too much damage! Later we had the use of an adjoining field, which became our football pitch. We must have had school lessons since that was why the teachers were there, but all I remember is playing football all day, every day.

Basque House closed down in September 1939. I was sent to Nottingham with a group of children and we were fostered by local people, mostly Co-op and Peace Pledge Union members who had supported us financially at Langham. I was very fortunate to be fostered by a school teacher and his parents who kept me at school for 18 months after the school leaving age so that I could learn English. I made many friends at the local school and some of us still meet twice a year.

I have been in the building trade all my working life, including during the Second World War. Even now, at the age of 81, I still do maintenance work at two old peoples' homes.

In 1987 there was a reunion to mark the 50th anniversary of our arrival at Langham. It was our first meeting with our childhood friends who had travelled from the Basque Country. I was quoted in the *Essex County Standard* as having said that our two years in Langham were the best years of our life. From the correspondence that I still have with my friends in Bilbao they express the same opinion.

Mari Carmen de Andrés Elorriaga

Food had become difficult to come by in Bilbao and Mari Carmen's mother was obviously going short herself so that her three children would get enough of whatever was going. Soon there was an opportunity for older children to be sent to France out of harm's way. Only Andrés was within the age limits imposed and off he went with the others to safety.

Later, there was talk that an English lady had organised a ship to take the younger children away from Bilbao to England. Many had already put their children's names down. The ship was due to leave the next day, carrying up to 4,000 children to safety. Mari Carmen's mother would take no chances: her daughter would be on that boat tomorrow.

On that fateful morning, Mari Carmen set off with her mother, hand in hand, towards the docks. Her mother was carrying a case, not much larger than a shopping bag. Soon they stopped by the side of an old white motor van, drawn up at the side of the road. A seaman sitting in the driving seat poked his head out of the window and asked: "Señora de Andrés?" "Yes," Mari Carmen's mother replied. The driver got out, went round to the back and opened the door. Mari Carmen's mother turned to her, bent down so that her face was level with that of her daughter: "You are going for a little trip and I want you to be good and remember us always." With these few words, she pushed her daughter into the back of the van, together with the case she had been carrying and slammed the door. The van, which had had its engine running all the time, started away before the little seven year old had fully taken in her mother's words.

Within ten minutes the van had stopped, the rear door opened and the seaman's friendly face appeared. "Here we are," he said. She saw that she was on the quayside next to the largest ship she had ever seen. "Where are we going?" she asked. "You're going for a little boat ride with lots of other children. You'll enjoy yourself." "Where's my mamá?" she shouted. "I'm not going without her! I want to go home!" The seaman signalled to another man and without another word, they lifted her and the case and carried her up the gangway on to the ship. She screamed, fought and twisted in every direction, but the two men, tears streaming down their faces, held firm and left her in a big state room with what seemed like hundreds of other boys and girls, all of them crying.

The voyage was a nightmare. When they arrived at Southampton they were taken to a place called Eastleigh. England seemed quite nice. At any rate there was no more sickness. The sun shone, which was just as well as they were living and sleeping in tents. Some nice ladies had washed them and helped them to dress in clean clothes, then they had given Mari Carmen some liquid that they called tea. She took a big gulp and immediately spat it out. From that moment on she drank water whilst others had tea. She was much more taken with the milk drink that they were given before bed, either Ovaltine or Horlicks.

After a month, news came that they were to leave Eastleigh and a feeling of excitement and anticipation ran through the canvas camp. Mari Carmen had become friendly with a girl called Elena, who said to Mari Carmen sorrowfully: "You'll be all right, you'll get a nice foster mum somewhere, but I'm an orphan." "What's an orphan?" Mari Carmen asked. When she heard from Hélène what it was, she sighed with relief: "Well, I'll say I'm an orphan too, then we can be sent to a foster home together."

She came to wish that she hadn't been so foolish. Most brothers and sisters went to individual foster homes, others to community homes, but those professing to be orphans were sent to an orphanage in a convent in rainy Manchester. Moreover, Mari Carmen's friendship with Elena had soon ended as she had gone off with other children. Generally, the treatment by the teachers and the nuns was pretty bad at this convent. The children were punished, being made to stand in the corner of the dormitory at night with their hands above their heads if they didn't finish their meal. The terrible food was served up with the pudding slopped on to the remains of the main course. All this led to Mari Carmen sleepwalking, until one night she was found trying to lift a heavy sash window to escape. A kindly nun found her and, after guiding her back to her bedroom, she gently woke her and they talked quietly for a while.

That was the only act of kindness she experienced. One day, one of the nuns, realising that she was in a bad way, took her to see a doctor. When Mari Carmen saw this white-coated person, she screamed and screamed. She was quickly sedated and when she woke up she found herself in hospital amongst children who only spoke English. The terrified little mite never saw those nuns or teachers again. In years to come she would ruefully recall agreeing to be an orphan and wondering what would have happened if she had told the truth. That day she promised herself that she would always tell the truth, whatever the consequences.

When she recovered, she was sent to the colony at Margate, where she joined some 40 or 50 children. The committee organised shows and concerts to raise money for their keep. Mari Carmen knew the Basque songs and dances and soon she played a central role in the shows. She was very happy. No longer were there any wet beds.

By 1939, many of the children had returned to Spain, their parents having asked for them. But Mari Carmen had heard nothing from her parents. One of the teachers at Margate was called Bessie and came from Wales. She had talked about adopting Mari Carmen. War had been declared between England and Germany after the Germans had marched into Poland. As Margate was just over the water from the European coastline, pillboxes were erected on the cliffs and barbed wire was spread across the beaches as a precaution.

At last Bessie came to see Mari Carmen and told her they were leaving for Wales the next day. They arrived at Barry Dock station and made their way to Bessie's family's house. After breakfast, a kindly looking lady, Mary Jones, who turned out to be Bessie's sister, and two little boys came in through the back door. The younger boy, a bright lad about three years old, was introduced as Lynden, his older brother as Morris. The younger boy immediately began to ask a lot of questions and was very puzzled when it was explained that Mari Carmen spoke no English. Later he was to be very proud of his Spanish sister and was always repeating her name, María Carmen de Andrés Elorriaga, to whoever he met. Mari Carmen was very surprised when Mary Jones took her hand and led her out onto the pavement, as she thought she was to stay with Bessie. With Lynden holding her other hand, the three of them walked to the top of a very long hill to the house that she would call home for the next few years. Mary Jones, who was profoundly deaf, became her foster mother. She insisted that Mari Carmen was too long a name and that from then on she would be known as Maria, as she has been to this very day.

Within a month or two she had been introduced to another Spanish girl, Espe, and they became good friends. Soon Mari Carmen started school and, although it was difficult at first to join in the lessons, once the English teacher knew that she was foreign, she made a special effort to help this girl who seemed so anxious to get on and do well. Within two years Maria had grasped the essentials of grammar and spelling and had made some friends.

By this time the war with Germany was two years old and Mari Carmen had got used to being called Maria by everyone. She had become part of the Jones family. Bill Jones was in the Home Guard, and worked in the office at the docks. In his spare time, he tended an allotment which provided the family with fruit and vegetables. Mary looked after the family with Maria's help, and saw that all the children went to Sunday school looking smart.

At the end of term she was top of the class in English and was given a book as a prize. She was a headstrong 13-year-old, still a bit of an ugly duckling, but beginning to mature. Her friendship with Espe continued and they shared many a laugh at the happenings around them and they were able to keep up their Spanish when they were alone. Espe always insisted that they continue in English if anyone was near them and so the lilt of the valleys began to enter their voices and they knew that their "foreignness" could only be detected with difficulty.

At 14 Maria left school, her English teacher pleased by her progress. Not only was she top of her class, but also the school. It seemed amazing that in four short years she had learned so much.

About a year later, when Maria was nursing at Caerphilly Miner's Hospital, Bill and Mary received a letter from the Basque Children's Committee in London suggesting that Maria go for a holiday to one of the remaining colonies. She was met at Paddington by Mary's youngest sister and taken to The Culvers, a large mansion in its own grounds near Carshalton. From that moment, she once again became Mari Carmen and was introduced to all the other young Basques who lived there. Because they were from the same part of northern Spain, they all got on well together and Mari Carmen was very happy to be part of this communal life. They talked and sang in Spanish and one or two could actually speak Basque, but they all knew the Basque songs and dances.

Because of the bombings in London, it was decided that the girls and some of the younger boys should be evacuated to Norfolk for safety. Once on the train, they treated this like another adventure. When they arrived they found a reception committee waiting for them and they were put into groups of girls and boys. Mari Carmen was paired with her friend Feliciana and they were taken by a Miss Lambert to her house. They were given a room to share and when it was time for bed they fell asleep in seconds after such an extraordinary day. Miss Lambert seemed rather severe. The only thing was that the girls didn't really understand much of what was being said! Autumn passed and they heard from London that the second of Hitler's secret weapons was a rocket filled with explosives that made no noise at all until it hit the ground and blew up. They were glad that they weren't in London for this latest atrocity.

Bill Jones, meanwhile, had been in contact with Maria each week by telephone and letter. Maria knew that Mary was due to go into hospital for a serious operation and as this got nearer she was determined to return to Barry Town. Whilst Mary was in hospital, Maria looked after the household, cooking and cleaning and generally making sure that the boys got off to school and that Dad Jones had breakfast before work. When Mary (now called "Mam" by Maria) arrived back from hospital, Maria looked after her until she had properly recovered from her operation.

Soon it was May 1945 and peace with Germany was declared. Mari Carmen's parents finally traced her in 1946. She started work locally and settled down to life in Barry. After all the years of thinking herself abandoned, the post-war years were a happy time for her.

Mari Carmen is proud of being born a Spanish Basque and having been brought up and loved by the Welsh family who took her in. She also feels proud of being a British citizen, and was even sworn in as a British subject late in 1949, in London. This was partly so that when she eventually managed to get to see her parents again, Franco could not whisk her away whilst she had a British passport. The telephone keeps her in touch with her family in Bilbao, but her husband says the sense of loss is quite often with her still.

(Transcribed by Peter Wood, husband)

Mauri Antolín Cordovilla

Mauri was born in Ortuella, where her father worked for the railways. The family was poor. There were five children and the parents were keen to send them to England, not only to escape the bombings, but also to eat properly, as it was difficult for her mother to feed them all. In fact, only three children went to England – Mauri, her sister Victoria and Teo, who were both younger than she was. Another sister, Juanita, stayed with her mother, and the oldest of the children, a 17-year-old brother, escaped to France but was interned in a concentration camp. Her father tried to escape over the Pyrenees but was shot. He managed to hide but her mother was in a terrible state not knowing where he was.

In England, Mauri was sent to the colony at Aston, where she was one of the older girls. The house-mother there was a young woman called Pili Merodio, and she was a wonderfully kind person.

A Spanish teacher had been sent with the children to the colony. She was prone to hit the children when they misbehaved. She was universally disliked. One of Mauri's tasks was to clean her room, an unenviable task as she was very dirty. Once, when a child disobeyed her, she hit him with an umbrella and broke his arm. Eventually, they managed to have this teacher removed from the colony. The teaching was taken over by Pili and Ketty Maíz, one of the older girls, later helped by Cora Portillo, who would come over from Oxford at the weekends.

They had an English cook, an elderly woman, and she too had to leave as she was caught stealing food. So Mauri and another girl had to take over the cooking, having to cater for large numbers, a job they were not at all used to. She remembers trying to cook rice for the first time in a huge cauldron and how it overflowed all over the kitchen when the rice swelled as it soaked up the water.

When the colony closed in 1939, Mauri went with the older girls to a council house in Witney that the Basque Children's Committee had found for them, before going to Barnet to look after a child whose mother worked.

She didn't have news of her parents for years. However, she remembers that Ronald Thackrah of the BCC went to France and managed to get her brother out of the concentration camp and sent to Chile. In 1953 Mauri finally met up with her parents on the Franco-Spanish border at Irún.

In spite of the uncertainty regarding the whereabouts of her family, Mauri remembers the years spent at Aston as happy ones. She feels that the children were well looked after and treated very kindly by the English volunteers.

(Transcribed by Natalia Benjamin)

Josefina and María del Carmen Antolín Pintado
Josefina: Our story begins in a small town in northern Spain called Berango, in the heart of the Basque Country. Carmen, Ángel and I enjoyed an idyllic childhood. But, when the Spanish Civil War broke out, it changed our lives forever. After the slaughter at Guernica by Franco, it became apparent to our parents that we were not safe and it was decided that we had to be evacuated. We travelled to Portugalete on 20 May 1937. We were all crying and it was awful to be torn away from our parents. I didn't want to let go of Mamá's hand. I was going to be ten years old the next day and I was disconsolate to be leaving her and all that I held dear. We left on 21 May – little did I know it was to be the last birthday I would have in Spain. So our journey to England began, a journey we will never forget. Since then I have never crossed the Bay of Biscay again.
Carmen: On Sunday 23 May the *Habana* docked at Southampton quay, where there were many people waiting to greet us. The Salvation Army was playing music. We were given sweets and ice cream. Seeing the strange hats the ladies were wearing and the double-decker buses made us laugh and realise how different life was in this land! We were taken to the camp at Eastleigh, and when we saw the fields full of tents, we said: "Indians!" We had never seen a tent in our lives, let alone thought of sleeping in one.
Josefina: We weren't there for very long, since the Salvation Army agreed to accept responsibility for 450 children in a hostel in east

London called Congress Hall. When we arrived we were taken up great iron staircases, through long corridors. It was all so big and dark, it seemed like a prison. We were shown our dormitories, four girls to each room. There was an awful smell of what I discovered later to be strong carbolic soap, and the smell has stuck with me ever since. I wasn't happy at Congress Hall. It was cold and overcrowded. The children said there was a ghost of a young girl who had killed herself and I was very scared.

Eventually, some of us were sent to another of the Salvation Army's orphanages in Brixton. It was a little better, but the food was not. I just couldn't eat. My sister Carmen would eat her food and then mine so that we could get two helpings of fruit that she would give me to eat. It was the only thing I liked and it reminded me of home. Sadly, at Brixton I lost my teddy bear. One of the girls took him and threw him over the wall outside. My sister tried to get him back, but the English people on the other side of the big wall couldn't understand us. I was devastated. As time went on, with so little food and nourishment, I became quite weak. The London fog and cold conditions didn't suit me.

One night, we all had to go down to the large courtyard to watch a big bonfire. It was 5 November. We didn't understand its significance until many years later. The smoke and fog were making me feel ill and I couldn't breathe very well. That night I went to the teacher's bedroom door. The next thing I knew was that I saw my sister Carmen at the side of my bed. I can't say how long I was there. All I know was that I almost died and it was decided that I should leave London and go to another colony.

We believed that we would be reunited with our brother Ángel at the next colony. Late in November 1937, we left Brixton and boarded a train to Southampton. We were told that a Miss Vessey would meet us. She was there waiting for us and spoke to us in Spanish – how lovely! She told us that we were going to a place called Moorhill House, near Southampton. We asked anxiously whether Ángel was there. She replied that no other Antolín was registered.

We arrived at Moorhill House and Miss Vessey introduced us to Miss Lewis, the cook, Srtas Carmen and Rita, and Sra Eulalia. The children all seemed so friendly and happy. I felt much better there than at Brixton and, as time went on, I started taking an interest in things and eating the now not so strange food. Life was coming back to us.

Carmen: We were much happier at Moorhill House. It became home to us. Miss Vessey was very strict but very kind and we all loved her. She was a typical Victorian lady, starched but truly lovely. In the mornings we had lessons with one of the señoritas. We both enjoyed this since we hadn't had any schooling since we'd left Spain. There was a big garden at the back of the house, trees to climb and fields to run in. There was so much to do! On Sundays we would go to church with Miss Vessey, then back to the house for Sunday lunch. In the afternoon, a little man would come and take about five of us to Southampton docks to see the ships. Sometimes there would be Spanish ships in port, which was great fun because we could speak to the sailors in Spanish!

At Christmas 1937 all the children were invited to a party in Southampton. It was held in a grand hall and we saw the biggest Christmas tree ever, laden with presents.

Josefina: We played musical chairs and the game where you mustn't be on the mat when the music stops. How different from our games back home! Then they put us all in a line and we had to join in singing *The Lambeth Walk*. We could only say the "Oh!" part of the song! We all laughed so much and had a wonderful time. We sat down for a lovely tea and opened up presents.

On one occasion, a Mr and Mrs Keys (Robert and Sybil) asked Miss Vessey if they could take me on holiday. She said they could, but only if they took my sister too as we wouldn't be separated. We were taken on a second holiday to a big house in Bournemouth to see a gentleman who wanted to give us each a pair of shoes. We went into this room full of shoeboxes where a nice man was seated in a big armchair. His name was Mr Clark – he was the big shoe manufacturer. We were both excited by our new shoes and thanked him very much.

The day came when Miss Vessey told us that some of the children would be going back to Spain and that those left would have to go to another colony. We were all very sad at having to say goodbye to our friends. Our brother Ángel wrote and told us to be ready to go home. We met this news with mixed emotions. We were waiting to hear from Miss Picken, who was the Secretary of the Basque Children's Committee. We heard from Ángel that the Committee was going to send him home. When he did get home, he sent back word to Carmen and to Miss Picken that we were not to go back. Mamá was in hospital and Papá was in prison and we had no home. Food was scarce and the Basque Country was in a sorry state after the Civil War.

Carmen: When it seemed certain that England too would be at war, everything changed. We lived with Sybil and Robert Keys at Southbourne until Dunkirk. After this, Sybil's parents felt that it would be safer for her and Robert to join them in the country in Staffordshire. Reluctantly, she contacted Miss Vessey, who found us a home with Mr and Mrs Miall in Brighton. They too showed us much kindness.

Josefina: They would take us on lovely walks in Brighton, or to the Pavilion, and to museums and other interesting places. One day, Mr Miall took me to London for the day to see some of the historical places. We finished at 33 Victoria Street, the BCC headquarters, and we saw Miss Picken. I met Pepe Estruch there. He was a friend of Ángel's.

The war continued to escalate and every day and night German planes would pass over Brighton to London and other places. We had to sleep in the cellar every night. During the day we would see some of the battles going on. We think that we witnessed some of the Battle of Britain.

Mr Miall had to go to Portsmouth to work for the Admiralty. He felt it was too much of a responsibility for his wife to care for their three children and us. So he wrote to Miss Picken and asked if she could find another home for us. Miss Picken wrote to Sybil Keys to ask if she knew anyone who could have us. Sybil wrote back and said that her parents, Mr and Mrs Fawcett, would give us a home and take us as their own girls. On 28 February 1941 we travelled to North Staffordshire.

The Fawcetts were good and kind people and we learned to love them very much. We were known in the village as "The Fawcett Girls". We called them Mother and Dad and grew up with Sybil as our big sister. It was an idyllic part of the country and far away from the noise and strife of London and the south. Although we still heard and saw planes and were aware of the bombing raids, we felt fairly safe out in the country with our new family.

Carmen: By the time the war finished, we were both young ladies, having left Spain as two little girls aged ten and 12. Now in 1945, we were 18 and 20 years old. Life had changed forever.

Josefina: I met my husband in 1946 and we were married in 1949 at the Old Church in Leek. For a wedding present, my "English parents" paid for a trip for us to go back to Spain. My "dad" came with us, and so after 13 years in England I was able to go back and see my parents. The whole village came out to meet and greet us. People were dancing, the band was playing, Papá and Mamá were crying to see me and meet my husband and the man we called "Dad". They could not thank him enough for all he had done for us. We stayed for a month. It was hard to leave them again, but they knew in their hearts that my life was in England. We went to see them every year, and they came over and stayed with me and with Carmen for long periods.

We have now been in England for 70 years and we would like to say a great thank you to everyone for the care and devotion they showed us at a very sad time in our young lives. But in my heart the little town of Berango will be with me always.

Carmen: As Josefina says, we had settled down to the English way of life. I too met my husband here and we married in 1953. We eventually both came down to the Bournemouth area where we settled down and where we both still live.

On that day in 1937 when we boarded the *Habana*, little did we know how our young lives would be affected. For so many of the children, return to Spain was almost impossible. For some of us, repatriation was possible, but not until after the Second World War. Life as we knew it had changed, we had changed. Happily our brother Ángel did return to our motherland. He married and had five children for the *abuelos* to dote on!

José María Armolea Bustamante

To look back over events that turned a child into an adult is not easy. They began as a nightmare, saying goodbye to parents and family and the long journey that awaited us. Yet there is an element of adventure that grips you as you move on. Our parents made a sacrifice by wanting to save us from air raids and war, but of course it was "only for three months".

My brother Martín and I started our journey in Portugalete where we lived, which is within walking distance from Santurce. My father, who was home on leave from fighting Franco and the rebels, led the way towards the *Habana,* which we had seen dock a few days earlier. On our way we stopped to say goodbye to our mother for the last time, as she was working as a cook in a military hospital next to the beach in Portugalete. In those days it was very difficult to take time off, as everyone was busy in the war. On arrival in Santurce we said goodbye to our father and family and boarded the ship. The journey was horrendous, and it has been well documented by others.

We arrived at Southampton after another medical examination. Our journey to the camp was very strange, with bunting and photographs of the royal family everywhere. But our adventure really started on seeing the entrance to the camp, a picture that has been imprinted on my memory ever since, and a day to remember as our 70th anniversary in England approaches.

Having been sorted into groups, life took shape as we were given responsibilities to become good Spanish boy scouts. For example, there were competitions for the best-kept tent, elections for tent leader, for those to fetch and carry meals from the main kitchen. Life was hard at times, as the rain never stopped and several times the inside of the tent was flooded, until we learned to dig trenches outside the perimeter of the tent. As we had little schooling at the time, it was a good pastime to raid the mountain of second-hand clothes and shoes. We must have been in the camp for nearly three months, as we saw a lot of friends going away without knowing where they were being taken.

We didn't get a lot of news from Spain and our family. I suppose it was difficult for them, but the blackest day of all was the news of the fall of Bilbao to Franco and the rebels. The news came over the loudspeaker system without prior warning. We all went berserk with anxiety as our world fell apart. The older boys left the camp and went towards the docks to try and board a ship to find our parents and to fight the rebels. Many volunteers and police had to search the area to find them and bring them back.

Soon after, it became more urgent to disperse the children since the camp had to close down. When our turn came we didn't know where they intended taking us. The journey was a long one to a little place called Brechfa, outside Carmarthen in Wales. It was beautiful countryside with a river running by the side of the camp, perfect for the rest of the summer.

As we left the coach we realised we were on our own, with only one man in charge of about 50 boys and nobody to greet us. The camp had been for sick and unemployed miners. There was an urn in the middle of the camp full of cocoa and lots of corned beef sandwiches that we ate for days afterwards. First we had to fill our mattresses and pillowcases with straw, which we then put over wooden platforms to sleep on. In the morning there was the same cocoa and sandwiches and so it was for some time. There was no school, no supervision and some boys misbehaved and were eventually caught in the village shop helping themselves to sweets. The owner gave two of our lads a clip around the ears, but they told a different story to the older boys who then marched to the village to show them not to ill-treat their friends. Unknown to us, especially to the group of boys marching towards the village, the police had been informed by the villagers and a coachload of police had been dispatched from Carmarthen, arriving in time to disperse the boys and stop them from entering the village. We saw the boys coming back having been badly treated by the police, some having had to cross the river fully clothed. The police also chased us into our huts, where we hid under our beds and then they drummed their truncheons on the metal roof to frighten us.

Changes soon came about as these events were recounted in the national press: questions were asked in Parliament about the "red" boys and many MPs wanted to send us back to Spain. People from Carmarthen had heard about us and several coachloads of people came to see us to help in whatever way they could. They came with presents and were very helpful in organising our football team and concerts all over South Wales. This continued until it was time to depart as winter was approaching and it was only a summer camp. I remember the last project that made us unhappy to leave. We had damned the river near the camp to make it easier and deeper to swim in, not realising why fishermen were complaining further down river about the lack of fish. It was another reminder of our stay in Wales.

We went on our way again, not knowing where we were going, and after a long journey we arrived at Laleham School in Margate. We found a well organised colony with a girls' section, supervised by señoritas and other personnel. Unfortunately we had had little schooling and eventually we attended the local schools, but our knowledge of English was very poor and we were provided with picture books to keep us occupied. This continued for some time and what we most enjoyed were the sports – swimming, athletics and even cricket, in which some of us excelled. It was very difficult to do the cross-country runs in hobnail boots, so we were very happy when Spanish teachers came and proper lessons were established.

There was a long period of normality in the colony, contrary to what others might think. Basque dancing was organised, a good choir was formed and concerts arranged in many towns in Kent, which were very successful and well attended, as were the garden fêtes, which brought in much needed money. The colony in Margate was quite large, so it was difficult to organise responsibilities apart from looking after our own bedrooms. We had a large vegetable garden and orchard with all types of fruit trees. The older boys were always in charge, so they had all the spoils. The younger ones enjoyed themselves by going scrumping, so we had our share. Football was always a good pastime as we had a good field and lots of boys to pick 22 players from.

My brother and I had very bad news from our sister, who was a refugee in France, telling us that our mother had died. A journey that had started as a nightmare had become reality. My father, who had crossed from France into Catalonia to continue the fight against the monster that had destroyed our family, was unaware of the sad news. Bad news continued to follow, as my brother became ill and was sent to hospital in Margate.

Soon after and at the beginning of the Second World War, life in the colony started to deteriorate, maybe through lack of funds. Sr Landa was in charge and he did his best to keep us under control, as we were a rowdy lot. I remember returning from seeing my brother in hospital. Approaching the colony we could hear the noise and he would tell me of the complaints he had had of our behaviour in general. Soon after, the boys and girls were moved to other homes. My brother went to a hospital in the Reading area and I went to a lovely place in Barnet, Rowley Lodge, a very well run home with a good bunch of children.

Money was the reason for moving there and after a while we started work and made some contribution to our upkeep. It wasn't much. My first week's wage was 12 shillings and threepence. This continued over the hard winter of 1939–1940. We walked to save our bus fare to Boreham Wood. I was doing war work in a stocking factory. The young man I was working with invited me to stay for a week with his parents. We got on so well that later he persuaded them to foster me and I stayed very happily with them throughout the war.

Carlos Asensio Montenegro

On 5 September 2006, 70 years after the event, the Basque government rendered public homage in the Ajuría Enea Palace to the "children of the war" who were evacuated to different countries in Europe. We were each greeted by the Lehendakari, Juan José Ibarretxe, who shook our hands and I felt very moved. Amongst other things, he said: "You and I will see peace established in the Basque Country".

I remember that I was sent to the United Kingdom with other children like me. For a start, I didn't know where England was. The circumstances created by the Spanish Civil War took us far from our families and changed our lives completely. The Salvation Army looked after 50 of us boys in the Hadleigh colony. This was in open countryside with sea views, and I used to look at the boats coming and going along the Thames estuary. I remember one day as I watched them going by, I wondered: "When will I return?", but I didn't talk about it with anyone. I remembered the times spent with my family and how far away I found myself then. I don't remember having any complaints that would have justified my wanting to leave. We were well looked after, the food was all right. I remember that on Sundays they would give us a banana and an apple so as not to have to work on that day. If I ate the apple, I couldn't finish the banana; if I started with the banana, I couldn't eat the apple. The distribution of letters brought cheerfulness and sadness. Those who received letters were happy and said: "Look at what my mother says"; others were sad as they hadn't had any news, but they would receive some another day, and all replied telling them at home what it was like in Hadleigh.

My brother and I also received mail, but not from our mother. An aunt, who was in the Franco zone, wrote to us. We didn't know where my father was because of the circumstances of the cruel war. My mother was a victim of Franco's bombers in Erandio, trying to save a child from the bombing. That was why we were evacuated to Britain. We were the last ones to be registered for the expedition, our numbers being 4121, 4122, 4123, 4124 and 4125.

That's how the new situation arose with us, being far from our loved ones whose presence was so necessary to us, being the age we were. We were also at that stage in the war when we felt hatred for everything. When we left the *Habana* and were taken to the camp at Stoneham, I didn't know what to do in the tent to which I had been assigned. We were organised into long queues to collect food, and there were a lot of children everywhere, children like myself who were totally confused by all the comings and goings. My brother guided me and together we got on better. That was on the first day. Later we followed the instructions given out on the loudspeakers. On the second day, we went all round the camp trying to find our sisters, who like us were also frightened and muddled. One of my sisters was seven years old, she couldn't be left alone. We'd lost her on the boat and when we found her, she was very frightened.

English people invited us to tea in their homes, and I really liked the sandwiches that we were given. The families were very kind and would take photos of us and give us copies to keep as a memento. I have to say that one family treated me as if I were their son. I spent Christmas with them and we went into the town to sing the carols that they had taught us.

From the Hadleigh colony, we were taken to Kingston Hill, near London, and we were reunited with our three sisters. The colony was in a splendid house, with a lovely garden, a vegetable garden, a schoolhouse and a gymnasium. It was run with great dedication by Miss Winifred Newby, and I have happy memories of her and of the helpers who were always so willing. Here, it wasn't like in Hadleigh, where there had only been 50 boys. In Kingston, I don't think there were as many as that, but girls as well as boys. Everything was very different there. We all got on well together and played a lot in the garden. One day a dead bird appeared in the garden and one of the helpers who looked after us got us all together to bury the little bird. We prepared a grave for it covered with grass. It reminded me of my village where we would kill birds with our catapults. This was a lesson to me and made me think.

In the colony, the señoritas who had accompanied us had a lot of work. Srta Pili Masa was the teacher, María Teresa González was in charge of the clothes, Mertxe and Rosario Bilbao and Auxilio taught us the Basque dances, Ezma was another teacher and Isabel, our cook. Sr Ceballos with his apron and white hat made us clean the kitchen on Saturdays. We read out aloud in the dining room from the letters we received. I remember in particular one from a mother to her two sons whose surname was Anchía. I felt it was my mother writing to me because she said that she remembered me. It was as if I was reliving the experience. Some girls told me that in that colony we were like a family, and they were right. We were all brought there by the cruel war. When the Second World War broke out, the colony changed. We were often visited by Poles or Germans who had left their countries to escape the war. I was very confused, they greeted us with a clenched fist salute. It wasn't aggressive, but I felt I was reliving what I had left in Euskadi. I remembered what I had seen in Bilbao, because living in England we weren't living through the same circumstances as in our own country.

We soon returned to Euskadi once the war started. When I crossed the border at Irún, a soldier, his gun slung over his shoulder, said to me: "Oh laddie, you're going to have a bloody awful time here." And he was right. We had a terrible time, remembering what it had been like living in England, especially since we had lacked a mother's presence at an age when we most needed her. *

Bittor Azkunaga Goikolea

At the camp in Stoneham the boy scouts, who were in charge of keeping order and the smooth running of the site, were very helpful, as were the people in charge. We had visits from English volunteers eager to lend a hand. We were woken every day by loudspeakers with a tune that I can still recall perfectly, after 70 years, and they read out announcements and any news. One of the items that most affected us was the news of the fall of Bilbao to Franco's troops, which caused us great agitation and tears.

From Stoneham we were dispersed in groups to different colonies. We were a group of 13, all with one or more brothers, and we were sent to a boarding school run by a teaching order of Dominican nuns for children who lived in London. It was called St Dominic's Priory and was situated in Ponsbourne Park near Hertford. It was a fine estate with parkland and fields, to the north of London. This is where we stayed for a large part of our time in England. We have fond memories of the school for its warm welcome, even though no one spoke our language. One nun looked after us on our arrival and tried to console us, seeing our general tearfulness. Later on we got to know the English pupils. These were calmer times. One of the nuns, Sister Josephine, was appointed to care for and give special attention to the little group of "Spanish boys". Some Spanish priests, who were attached to a church in Potters Bar, were often asked to come over to minister to us spiritually.

Towards the end of October 1937 we were moved (I believe it was a misunderstanding) to Wales, to a place near Carmarthen. It was a large house and I rather think, from the Latin inscriptions over some of the door-frames, that it had formerly been some ancient abbey. But before the week was out, they brought us back to London, this time to a fairly large house, to the south of the city. It was next to a racecourse. Everyone in the house was Spanish and our home was run by teachers. There were about 30 boys there. We remained until after Christmas and then the boys were repatriated. This centre, which I suppose will by now have been totally absorbed by the city, was called The Grange and was at Kingston Hill, Surrey.

My recollection of the reception we were given was that we were treated very well and that everywhere people showed us friendship and a desire to help, being conscious of our situation with our memories and our sense of fear, especially among the older ones.

When those times were past and we were back in Bilbao, we continued writing to the nuns in Ponsbourne Park and to some of our English classmates at the school, always with the greatest affection.*

María Dolores Barajuán Fernández

In July 1936 my brother and I were enjoying our summer holiday with no inkling of what the future held in store for us. Just a few days later there burst upon us the hell that would turn not just Spain but the whole world into a huge cauldron of fire.

My brother Ricardo and I were among those who went on the journey to England. Heading for the port, the train went under a bridge as it left Portugalete station, and it seemed as if the whole population of Bilbao had gathered there, crowding against the railings, waving handkerchiefs and calling out words of love and farewell. This was perhaps the most vivid of the pictures that has remained etched forever in my memory.

Getting on board the boat was absolute chaos – hundreds of children arriving, all frightened and bewildered, carrying their parcels of clothes, and with no one to tell them where to go or what to do. My brother and I, with my cousin Isabel and two refugee brothers from San Sebastián, found an empty cabin and settled down there. But not everyone was as lucky. Emerging that night from our cabin to find the WC, I was met with a vision of Dante's inferno. Every gangway was filled with children of all ages sleeping stretched out on the floor, one on top of the other.

It must have been about four in the morning when suddenly the ship seemed to come to life. It started a peculiar shuddering and there were heavy thuds as anchor was weighed and the vessel, a small town tossing on the water, with its odd cargo of suffering and hope, set sail. With only one thought in mind, we all dashed up towards the deck. We wanted to bid a last farewell to our beloved country that we were leaving behind with everything we loved.

Two days later, after a really rough voyage, we arrived at daybreak at Southampton on a typically English rainy morning. We were taken by bus to Stoneham, an enormous camp outside the city. Several hundred tents had been put up in which we were accommodated in groups of ten. We were put in quarantine, given medical examinations and a whole series of prophylactic vaccinations before being dispersed in little groups over the whole country. We were treated extremely well and given a great deal of love and attention.

On 19 June 1937, the camp loudspeakers requested our attention for the following announcement: "Bilbao has just fallen to the rebels". The general despair was heartbreaking. For us Spain *was* Bilbao, the world *was* Bilbao. Our neighbourhood, our school, our family, our whole life *was* Bilbao. That's where our parents were. Why leave anything standing when for us the world was in ruins? Various groups began to destroy everything they could see, seized by the rage of young children driven to despair. The teachers and all the English staff immediately started to gather little groups together and with a lot of patience and care succeeded in calming things down and resolving the situation.

A few days later, Ricardo and I, as part of a group of 100 children, set off for the Ipswich colony. We were quite happy; we had lessons with our three teachers and the two English teachers who came to give us English lessons. On Thursdays we had no classes and used to go for walks round the interesting places in the area. The beaches at Felixstowe were one of our favourites. We still had no news of our parents, and after the Stoneham scandal were given no more news of what was happening in Spain. I tried to distract myself by studying and worked very hard at learning the language. But at night when no one was watching I gave vent to my despair and cried quietly for hours until overcome by sleep.

Five months later, in October, I was told that Miss Vulliamy wanted me in the office. She handed me a letter and, smiling, said: "Do you know who it's from?" I immediately recognised my mother's handwriting, and Miss Vulliamy explained that an English couple who were passing through France had visited a refuge where they met my mother, and she had asked them to pass on this letter to the organisation that had brought us to England. I left the office and, together with Ricardo, read the letter. Our mother told us that as the rebels were approaching Bilbao she had managed to get to Santander and from there, with a group of refugees, to set sail for France. Our father had stayed on and she had no news of him.

Miss Vulliamy used to organise parties on Thursday evenings to which she invited pupils from a nearby school. The older girls went early in the morning to help the cook prepare the cakes and drinks for when our guests arrived. For us the party started there. We had fun learning to bake cakes, at the same time planning how we could get on with the good-looking boys, knowing as we did hardly anything of the language. Miss Vulliamy, who was a first-class pianist, sat at the piano and made us dance till midnight when the party ended.

Christmas was approaching and we wanted to do something to please our new friends, so we started to rehearse our regional songs and dances. Miss Vulliamy found out about it and wanted to know what the typical costumes were. Then next day a pile of fabrics in the right colours arrived at the colony to make the costumes. With the help of the teachers and an old sewing machine, we set to, and a few days before Christmas we put on our performance.

The next day, 22 December, a husband and wife arrived wanting to take a couple of siblings home with them to spend the festive period in London. Miss Vulliamy asked if Ricardo and I would like to go. I had longed to go to London for ages! We spent two months with them and then, when classes began again at the end of February, we went back to the colony.

On our return to Ipswich we found a few changes. Firstly, our performance had been such a great success that we were presenting it in various schools and halls. Then, Miss Vulliamy explained that as it was the fruit picking season, we could do a bit of work on the fruit farms in the area and contribute some of the money we earned towards the campaign to help our country. Everyone was delighted and we started work at once. The buses would arrive early in the morning to take us out into the fields and then back again in the evening. When we got our first wage we all thought we were donating the whole of it to the campaign funds, but Miss Vulliamy made us keep half for our own personal expenses. I kept that money without spending a penny of it – I had a strange presentiment that one day I might need it for something important.

In June 1938, as the house in Ipswich had been lent for only 12 months, we had to move to Wickham Market. The change was terrible, leaving the lovely house in Ipswich and arriving at an old mental hospital. The feeling of neglect was overwhelming. We all set to and in a very short time cleaned and tidied up the chaos as best we could.

Doña Margarita Lanvin, who taught the older ones, asked me to help her decorate the communal areas and off we went covering the walls with paintings to try and liven up our gloomy surroundings.

In September my mother discovered my father's whereabouts and went to meet him in Barcelona. Coincidentally Miss Poppy, Miss Chloë Vulliamy's sister, was asked to take an ambulance and spare parts to Barcelona for the campaign and she came to the colony to ask if anyone had relatives there. I gave her a letter and in it put the two pounds I had saved. Subsequently my father confirmed he had received not just the two I sent but four pounds. Thank you Miss Poppy. God bless you! A few months later, when they had to flee to France, it was the only money they could use as Spanish currency was worth nothing.

In England feverish preparations were being made for the start of the war. The house in Wickham Market was converted into a depot for gas masks and ration books. So we were dispersed in small groups to other colonies.

Ricardo and I went as part of a group of 25 to Margate. When the war broke out on 3 September, the Basque Children's Committee in London foresaw difficulties in continuing to maintain us, so they suggested that the older children could work and help with the upkeep of the younger ones.

At the beginning of December I received a call from the London Committee asking me to go up there the next day. No explanation was given. I arrived at nearly midday, and was made to wait in a side room next to the office. Hours went by and I was dying of cold and hunger. It was seven o'clock in the evening when a smartly dressed gentleman arrived and, after speaking to the secretary, asked me to accompany him. We went on the Underground and walked through the dark streets of the city in the snow, which was falling heavily, finally arriving at a house. There I was told I would be working as a nanny. The lady of the house had been one of the helpers who came with us to England and had married soon afterwards. She had asked the Committee for a nanny for her child and they appointed me.

I won't say too much about my time in North Finchley. The treatment I got was similar to that of the slaves of antiquity. Total control over everything: the amount of water allowed for washing up and for my personal cleanliness, the portions of food on my plate. The bed was made of canvas with no mattress, not even a bit of blanket to cover me, just a cotton bedspread. The winter of 1939–1940 in

London was terrible, cold enough to freeze the Thames. My friends had invited me to spend Christmas Eve with them, but Doña Carmen only allowed me to go out on Christmas Day in the evening after clearing up the kitchen, and with the requirement that I be back before dinner.

My parents were now in France. The Second World War had just started and with all the propaganda from the French Government about how secure the Maginot Line was, my father thought that the war wouldn't go beyond Paris. So he asked for us back, and on 3 February 1940 Ricardo and I boarded the cross Channel ferry for Dieppe. Our group of children and an English gentleman accompanying us were the only civilians on board – all the other occupants of the boat were Forces' personnel. It was possibly one of the last boats to transport civilians across the Channel for many years.

After crossing the whole of France by train, we arrived in Bayonne at two in the afternoon. Bayonne is very similar to the towns of the Basque country since all are on one side or the other of the Pyrenees, and this made us feel a little bit closer to home. We could see the mountains in the distance. There beyond them was my country – everything I had lost and would never find again. They were the barrier separating me from my happy childhood, from a world of peace and love lost for ever.

The next day we were in Toulouse and in our parents' arms. After three years of anguish, that could have been the end of a sorry tale. We had simply no idea then what the next five years would bring. But that is another story. *

Rafael de Barrutia Calera

The Director of the colony at Faringdon was a relatively young man about 25 to 30 years old. I think he was an Austrian Jew and he spoke Spanish well. We called him Leon. We also had an Englishman who gave us language classes, another multi-talented Englishman who went by the name of "Skipper", and our cook, the good "Camuñas". Apart from the staff, we used to receive frequent visits from lecturers or students of Spanish from Oxford University, who would sometimes give us talks on various cultural themes. There was also another group of people who came to see us regularly, amongst whom were Dr Russell and Dr Ellis, who were the two English doctors who had given us all medical examinations in Bilbao before the evacuation.

Likewise there was the organiser of the group, Miss Poppy Vulliamy. I remember her as being typically British, young, blonde, energetic. She was lame in one leg and had to wear a special boot. I have some very good memories of my time in Faringdon, but also some sad ones. I think that period in my life greatly influenced my future character.

On one of her visits to the colony, Dr Russell invited me to spend a few days in her house in London. On the first day we went to the theatre. From what I gathered, the show had been put on in aid of the Republican cause in Spain, and there were world famous artists performing. What I liked best of all was the black bass singer, Paul Robeson. I can still hear his voice singing: "Oh by and by, I'm going to lay down my heavy load." The theatre was full of people. We were in the stalls, near the middle, and we could see well. There was a lot of applause for the Andalusian dancers, as there was for the black singer, whom they said was the best in the world.

The following morning, Dr. Russell took me to the London Zoo. Then we went to Hyde Park and listened to one of those orators declaiming on his soapbox. We also went to Harrods, the huge and famous department store. Later, she took me all over London. These were unforgettable days for me. They are etched on my mind forever. The welcome that we were given by the British people was not limited to taking us away from the cruel Spanish Civil War and finding us a safe place to live peacefully, to clothing and feeding us, even to educating us. What Dr Russell did for me is palpable evidence of human kindness, of human warmth, which is what is most appreciated at such a time.

One day one of the little boys in the colony knocked on the door where we were having an English lesson and said that the Director wanted to see me in his office. When I knocked on his door, Leon, with his usual kindness, bade me come in and took me by the shoulder up to a chair and I sat down. He sat down near me at the desk and without more ado said: "I have some bad news. The Committee in London has just rung me to tell you that they have received news that Franco's troops have shot your father and brother." I was stunned, incapable of saying a word. For a few moments it was as if I was dead, then I burst out crying disconsolately.

I remember Leon stroking my head and trying to console me, to calm me. All I could say was: "Mamá, why? Why?" Oh my goodness, what dreadful moments I was going through! Whenever I remember that moment, I am overcome with such anguish that I can't help my eyes welling up with tears. The Director didn't prepare me for that news. I don't know why he didn't break it to me in a more gentle, more humane fashion. Perhaps in his culture it's normal to give out news without any preparation as he did to me, but the fact is he left me chilled. Leon tried to ring Bilbao to contact my family and get more information. I wanted to be alone and took my leave of Leon. I went downstairs and crossed the hall towards the outer door. My friends murmured something and asked me: "Rafa, what's the matter? What's the matter?" I didn't answer because I couldn't. I went outside to the garden. I felt a great relief come over me and noticed that the anguish that had overtaken me was abating. After a while, I heard voices calling me as it was lunchtime. All my friends knew what had happened, I could tell by their sad looks. They all wanted to help me, to share my sorrow, my pain, but...oh, how alone I felt! I felt very uncomfortable, and got up and went to my room. There I fell into my bed, my thoughts churning. That night I slept like a log. I was exhausted by all the emotions I had been through. The next day I got up as usual and went on with normal life.

A few days after having given me that horrible news, Leon called me urgently again and told me that he had just spoken to the Committee and they had notified him that the news they had given him of the shooting of my father and brother had been a mistake. I was happy at the news, but at the same time I found it difficult to come to terms with these diametrically opposed stories. The new news filled me with happiness, but at the same time there was a lingering doubt. A short while later, I received a letter from my parents. Having that, I became calmer and could play normally with my friends.

One of the things that surprised me when I first came to England was that Sundays were days of complete rest. There were no football matches or shows. There was nothing at all. Everyone stayed at home or went for walks, just the opposite of what we were accustomed to in our country. For us, Sundays meant a day of amusement, entertainment, for the English it was a religious day, a day of rest.

They moved us to Shipton-under-Wychwood. At that time someone from Madrid called Luis Portillo came to our colony. He was a very serious and kind man. In the classes he gave us, he'd talk about everything and would teach us songs. I remember that he liked the one that went like this: "Every morning dawn comes and takes away the sad and betraying night."

What I most remember about my time at Shipton was the interest that the English boys had in football and how they wanted to compete with us in matches. As far as we were concerned, we asked for nothing better than to play against them, as we were getting bored of playing each other. We played the first game on a Saturday afternoon and beat them easily to put them to shame. The score was 6 or 8-11. The next game was against a school with boys of our age and we crushed them. At the end of the match, we went into the centre of the pitch to take our leave of the spectators. With what gusto we said: "Hip, hip, hurray!" We were the talk of the town!

(from Barrutia de, Rafael (no date), *Desde Santurce a Southampton*, published by the author.) *

Fausto Benito Gómez

Against this very dangerous background of the war, my parents, along with all the others, had no other choice and, sad as it was, they decided to put us down for one of the expeditions to a foreign country, which was the advice of the Basque government to all parents. There were six children in my family, three girls and three boys, and it was decided that the three boys should be sent away.

When my father found out where he had to register us, he didn't know where they were going to send us. As it happened, the authorities had just opened registration for the expedition to England and my father arrived at a most opportune moment, as we were the first on the list. The hexagonal identification disc we wore round our necks stated "Expedition to England" and a number: my brother Juan, who was 12, was number one, my brother Ángel, who was 11, was number two and I, who was nine, was number three.

Saying goodbye in those circumstances was something unforgettable. The docks and the port were full of families, with handkerchiefs out, shouting, crying, hugging endlessly, giving final words of advice and recommendations: "Be good! Look after yourselves! Write!" My mother and my sisters were very upset at saying goodbye but my father was stronger, he scarcely showed his distress and remained in control of his emotions, although he felt it inside. It gave us confidence and stopped us becoming more worried.

The ship was very large, more like a gigantic hotel than a boat, full of rooms, passageways and tiny windows. It was a real labyrinth. Once the ship set sail and was on the open sea, you began to notice the boys and girls on the ship's deck beginning to be seasick. On deck there was a row of large wicker chairs with cushions and my brother Juan said we should stay a while on the chairs to see if the breeze on deck would help the seasickness pass, and this is what we did. But I must have fallen asleep and when I opened my eyes, my brother wasn't sitting next to me and I was alone and didn't know what to do.

I didn't find my brother for the two or three days that the voyage lasted. Luckily, a señorita saw me. She knew me because she was from Basauri and her aunt Encarna was a friend of my mother. On seeing me alone, lost and frightened, she decided that I should stay with her until she could find my brothers and she fixed a bunk for me in the girls' quarters. She tried to find my brothers but without success. On arrival at the port, she left me with a group of children and told me to stay with them until I found my brothers.

Once in Southampton they took us to a very big campsite. As I had lost my brothers and was alone, I was put in a tent with boys aged 14 and 15 whom I didn't know. I still couldn't find my brothers, but one day, when I was walking through the campsite I heard someone calling me: "Fausti!" I turned round and saw that it was Manuel Landazuri, a boy who lived in our neighbourhood. "What are you doing lost round here?" he said. "Your brothers have been looking for you every day. Come with me, we're all in the same tent". It was such a relief and I went along with him. There they all were from our neighbourhood: the two brothers Bautista and Ángel Lopez, Manuel, who found me, my two brothers Juan and Ángel and another two or three I didn't know, one of whose name was Rodolfo.

Bautista was the oldest of us. Being 14 or 15 years old he was in charge of the tent, organising and telling us what to do about cleaning it and keeping it in good order. There were prizes for the cleanest and tidiest tent and I think that we once won a prize because Bautista, besides being neat and conscientious, was a very clever and a good person, always treating us very well, and we respected and obeyed him.

The major upset we had in this camp was the day that they told us over the loudspeakers that Bilbao had fallen into the hands of Franco's troops. Collective panic broke out with hysterical cries and confusion. Everyone was agitated and some ran around in all directions without knowing where to go or what to do. Many ran off towards the airfield close by. The biggest problem was not knowing anything about our parents and family, whether they were alive, wounded or dead. There was total anguish. The tears and shouting were contagious to the little ones and soon we were all crying.

Those moments were the saddest and most anxious times we went through during our stay in England and can never be forgotten. Although at that age there are many things you can't remember, nevertheless these tragedies stay with you forever. In spite of my young age and the fact that I couldn't understand the future implications of what had happened, I do remember that event as being momentous, very sad, causing great anguish, and having the feeling that something very bad was happening. After a few days we started to get some news and things began to calm down. Being so young we had the capacity to overcome these problems and soon things got back to normal.

A couple of weeks later, news went round that we were going to be sent in small groups all over England. The six of us from Basauri, with 50 other boys, were sent to a small campsite, also in the country, in a place called Diss. We only spent a short time there.

Soon they took us to another colony on the outskirts of Great Yarmouth on the east coast. It was a large house with a football pitch and was surrounded by beautiful trees and fields. I estimate that we were at this colony for about five months and it was the one where we had the best time. We even had quite a good football team made up of the older boys and English teams came to play against us. Some of their young supporters came by bicycle to watch the game.

The rest of our stay in England, until we went back to Spain, was in Tythrop House. The colony was also a large house on two floors with very wide staircases going up to the first floor. When we arrived it was already occupied by another group of boys and girls. Up to that point we had always been in a group of 50 boys. This colony was better organised than our previous ones had been and I believe there were lessons, but I don't remember going to them regularly.

We returned to Spain in January 1938. As soon as we crossed the border between France and Spain they told us to sing *Cara al Sol* and, as we didn't know it, they told us to sing something we knew. We began to sing the *Internationale* and they promptly ordered us to be quiet. We went to Bilbao in two buses that took us to the Colegio del Amor Misericordioso in Iralabarri where our families were coming to fetch us.

The happiest and most emotional moment that I remember was meeting my mother again. I was leaning out of the window of one bus, my brothers were on the other one, looking at the people to try and find my parents or one of my sisters. Soon I heard: "Fausti, Faustito". It was the unmistakable voice of my mother. She had seen me before I saw her. I got off the bus and we fell to hugging each other. Even now I tremble with emotion remembering this episode in my youth. That moment was undoubtedly one of the happiest in my life.

Looking back, one of the most important things was getting to know an extraordinary and excellent person called Henry Jeffery, who was 26 or 27 years old, and who, we found out later, was a Protestant priest. I met him at the first campsite at Stoneham. This young man came to the main gate and offered me sweets. He asked me my name and was very interested in knowing if I had older brothers. I told him that I did. Then he said that I should go and look for them. I only found my brother Ángel, who was with Manuel Landazuri, and they came back with me and the man was still waiting for us. He said that at the weekend he would come and fetch them. After that for many weekends he would take the two boys, but sometimes he would also take Juan and me.

Every time we went to a new colony, Henry would also come to take us out at the weekends. Sometimes he would take us by bus or taxi and other times collect us in a motorbike with a sidecar. When we went in the sidecar in the thick London fog, we were scared because we couldn't see anything. He would take us to the cinema and once we went on a trip along the Thames on a pleasure boat.

Some weekends he took us to church. Henry celebrated mass dressed in everyday clothes which seemed odd to us as he didn't put on vestments like the Spanish priests. As we couldn't understand a thing, we put up with it ungraciously, and Manuel, who was pretty badly spoken, protested and even swore. Henry would say to him: "Oh Manuel! Don't say that. It's an ugly word."

We were always very grateful for the way he treated us and for his kind attention and we understood that we in turn had to treat him with respect. At Christmas time, he took the four of us to his house in London to spend two days. He lived with his parents in a very nice area which I believe was Kensington.

Word began to circulate that we would be returning to Spain. Even though the Spanish Civil War had still not come to an end, Franco's propaganda machine said that we were not being looked after and that were wandering around, totally out of control. They encouraged parents to write reclaiming their children. The first return journeys began in November. We returned on 4 January 1938.

When our friend, Henry Jeffery, found out that they were sending us back to Spain, he was very upset. He stayed with us until the last moments before embarkation to Spain, bringing along some sweets and toys. When it came to say the final goodbyes, he couldn't contain himself and he began to cry and we did too, we couldn't stop hugging each other. He was very sensitive and humane, and even now after more than 60 years I remember him with great affection for what he did for us, parentless children, in those difficult times. He tried to fill, in some way, that irreplaceable gap and made us believe that we had, at the very least, an older brother there to look after us. How we looked forward to the weekends to see if the loudspeakers were going to call out: "Your attention, please. Would the brothers Juan, Ángel and Fausto Benito come to Reception where Mr Henry Jeffery is waiting for them to spend the weekend with him."

When he came to Spain to visit us in July 1940 (the war had ended on 1 April 1939), he stayed at our house for about eight days. One day we took him to the bullring to see a bullfight with young bulls. At the beginning of any event you had to stand with your right arm extended whilst they played the national anthem. It was the Franco salute and you weren't allowed to sit down until the anthem was finished. Our friend Enrique (Henry) refused to stand, let alone put out his arm, saying: "I am English and am not pro-Franco", and he remained seated. We spent a bad time fearing the worst, but fortunately nothing happened, as luck would have it no police saw him. We held him in great affection and he always told us that he remembered us in his prayers.

In conclusion, I must say that my stay in England was a good experience. Another thing is what would have happened if there hadn't been a civil war. Without doubt that would have been the best thing for the majority of evacuees. We lost three terms, we weren't able to study and we started work before the age of 14. There was hunger and tuberculosis from 1940 to 1960, the loss of freedom, 40 years of dictatorship.

Let us preserve historic memory. *

Teodora Bueno Fernández

I don't really remember much about my stay at the colony in Langham (Colchester) as I was only seven years old. What I remember is that on Saturdays we had sausage and mash for lunch. I also remember playing endless games of cat's cradle. The only one of the grown ups that has stayed in my mind is Srta Peque, who was very good to the little ones and always cheerful.

The Langham colony was supported by the Peace Pledge Union (PPU), and when it had to close down in 1939, there was an appeal in *Peace News*, the PPU newspaper, for homes to be found for the two youngest little girls, Espe and myself.

I was nine years old then and I was taken in first by a lady in Dagenham. I wasn't at all happy there as I was treated like a servant, and I remember one day in particular. Her adolescent son had told me to do something. I replied that I wasn't his maid and he pushed me down the stairs. Soon after that, his mother was sent to hospital and I learned that she was suffering from some nervous illness, so they had to find me another family.

Mrs Emily Ranson, who also lived in Dagenham, had heard in her church that homes were being sought for Basque refugee children and her oldest daughter Irene said that she'd pay her mother the necessary amount for my keep from her wages if she'd have me. Mrs Ranson came to fetch me from the first house and I walked back with her, holding my suitcase, which had a large hole in it, and, as we walked, various things fell out, but I didn't dare say anything.

The Ransons lived at 257 Hedgeman's Road. The husband was called Ernest and he worked in the British Museum. They had two girls: Irene was 20 and Vera was two years younger. They both had some sort of office job. All the family was very kind to me and I was really happy with them. I was always with Mrs Ranson and loved hugging and kissing her. When I had been at the colony in Langham, all the girls, regardless of age, had been encouraged to help in the cleaning of the house, so I was used to housework and would go around the house with Mrs Ranson, dusting and generally being useful.

They were Baptists, a truly God-fearing family. They never went to the cinema. They regarded it as a sin and said that if God came and saw you with the sinners, he wouldn't take you to Heaven. But I loved Sundays. When I was ten years old, I was baptised in their church by total immersion. I wore a white dress and remember the pastor pushing me quickly under the water. I felt I belonged to Jesus and that all my sins had been forgiven. I recited this poem in front of all the congregation:

> I'm a little sunbeam
> I'm only ten years old
> I love to shine for Jesus
> And love Him all the day
> I'll be His little sunbeam
> The Bible says I may.

The whole family went to church every Sunday. Mr Ranson would leave the morning service a quarter of an hour before the end to make sure the lunch was ready when we got home. On Sunday afternoons, I'd go back to church to lead a Sunday School group, when I would tell the little ones stories from the Bible. All the family went to church again in the evening, this time everyone brought some food to share.

I went to the local school until the age of 14. I don't remember much about it except that I got into a fight with someone who called me a "Spanish onion"! After that I worked in the nursery school as a helper, with a lovely teacher called Mrs Hugues. She was very kind to me and sometimes took me to see the ballet in London. The little ones were made to have a sleep after their lunch in little beds, and they each had a blanket with a different animal on it. There was one little girl who was especially fond of me, called Mavis, and she was forever jumping into my arms, but Mrs Hugues was quick to point out that I shouldn't have favourites.

When I came back home from working with the children, Mrs Ranson would prepare Marmite and peanut butter sandwiches for me. That was all there was for the evening meal, except for a large glass of hot chocolate before going to bed.

I had a friend who lived next door called Lily, and I'd always call on her when I came home. She came from a very poor family and when I knocked on the door, I was never allowed in. We used to juggle with three balls against the church wall, or else see how many times we could jump with the skipping rope. There was another neighbour whose husband was very ill with lung problems: she asked me to walk the dog for her, and sometimes I even bathed it. I remember it was called Spot.

My favourite day was Saturday: Mrs Ranson took me to London every Saturday. She'd take me round the shops, or perhaps to Hyde

Park and we'd listen to the speakers on their soap boxes at Speakers' Corner. We'd have lunch in a snack bar and sometimes go to the British Museum where her husband worked. I remember especially seeing the mummies there.

All through the winter evenings we'd sit by the fire and Mr Ranson would read a page from the Bible. Irene would perhaps be doing some embroidery, and Vera would play the piano and I'd sing. They had family photos on the piano and these included a lot they had taken of me. I called the Ransons "Mummy" and "Daddy" and they wanted to adopt me, but it wasn't possible as my real parents were still alive somewhere.

Because of the awful bombings, Mr Ranson had prepared an air raid shelter in the garden which had little beds in it, so when bombs fell and the siren went off, we all rushed off to it. We all had gas masks and we'd been told to throw ourselves down on the ground if we heard enemy planes. As Mrs Ranson was frightened that something might happen to me, she sent me with a whole lot of other British evacuees to Bristol. So I became an evacuee for a second time. The two ladies who took me in also took in other children, but they treated me as a maid and I was made to serve at table. I wasn't at all happy there. The only positive thing to come out of it was that I was sent to learn how to type, and I was able to type my first letter to my parents.

Mrs Ranson, having found out that I was being treated badly, came to Bristol to fetch me and had some sort of a row with the ladies. When we got back to Dagenham, they wrote her a horrible letter, telling her all sorts of lies about me, claiming amongst other things that I'd said that she hit me. I saw Mrs Ranson when she received the letter and she was crying. But she knew I wouldn't have said such things.

In December 1945 my family, whom the Red Cross had found in France at Famel in the Lot et Garonne department, claimed me back, together with my three brothers and a sister who had also been sent to England. Cesário was an apprentice carpenter, Carlos was in Shrewsbury working with a chicken farmer who'd taken him in and Herminia had been helping her teacher, Srta Peque, by then married to an Englishman, with her two babies, Sonia and Natalia.

That first meeting with my family after so many years went well, and we met our other brothers and sisters. We ate a huge meal, in spite of the fact that rationing was in place, and only learned later that our parents, who were poor, had been obliged to borrow money to be able to provide for us so copiously. But everyone was speaking Spanish and I didn't understand a word any more.

Obviously money was needed to care for such a large family, and I was sent out to work in a porcelain factory in the Lot. I gave all I earned to my mother and worked very hard, most days doing overtime to help make ends meet. Mrs Ranson wrote regularly to me and I'd read the letters out to my mother. My mother would say: "She's not your mother, I'm your mother". Nevertheless, I still wrote back to her.

We continued this correspondence over many years. In 1956 I married a Spanish refugee, and two years later had a son, Tubal. I sent a letter and photo of him to Mrs Ranson, but the letter was returned to me with the words "address unknown". I never knew what happened to her. Later I had a disabled child who required my constant attention, and so I didn't have the time to find out what had happened to the Ranson family. This is the greatest regret of my life.

(Transcribed by Natalia Benjamin)

José Vicente Cañada García

I'd just had my seventh birthday when I arrived at the camp in Stoneham. I wore on my jacket a card with the number 1702, a number which I've never forgotten and which I use as the number of my mobile phone as it's easy to remember.

I remember how, when we were in the camp, we would have escapades into the town. These were organised by the chief of our group, a certain Armando Santos. His second surname was Blanco, and his number was 2584. I remember that he wore glasses, which at the time was unusual for children of our age; he was thin and was good at playing pranks. He was then ten years old. I remember very clearly the messages on the loudspeakers, like this one: "Your attention please. Listen everyone! Letters received this morning!" followed by the names of those who had received them, or "Listen everyone, listen everyone! Will Armando Santos, Vicente Cañada please go to the medical tent".

Then I went to Dymchurch and all I remember about it is the beach, from where we imagined we could see France. We made all sorts of plans to repair a ramshackle boat that was lying around, in which we dreamed of returning home to our families. I also remember a miniature train on which we had short rides. Much later, in Spain, I read in some newspaper that the same train, in spite of being so small, had been of great use during the war, carrying troops and weapons for the coastal defences.

After this I went to Scarborough with my two cousins who had been with me all this time. We made friends with Elsie Robinson who looked after us, and we all had fond memories of her when we went back to Spain. Elsie was a young girl, a very good person, like all those we met there. And I know that not all the English are first-rate (as is the case for all nationalities), but I was lucky enough to find myself amongst the best.

Our new destination was Bradford, 245 Manningham Lane. Bradford is the place I remember with the greatest affection. There it was that I spent my happiest times, although all my stay in Britain was positive. It was a good change because, just as in Scarborough there were a lot of us, on the contrary in Bradford there were only about a dozen of us. That's where I met Harry Seed. This man was the best person I met in England, a kind, affectionate man, a really good person. I loved him as much as my father (and I even think I loved him more). He'd take us out in his car in the holidays and would be as attentive as could be to all our wants. We stayed at his house for Christmas and waited for our presents. His wife was also a sweet person. They didn't have any children. After I returned to Spain, I learned that his wife had died and he subsequently married her sister and they had two children. I saw him for the last time when I went to visit for a week. It was the first time that I had gone back to England since our exile. Our meeting was very emotional and tears streamed down my dear Harry's face when we said goodbye. Many times in my life I've thought of this man, and I still do. *

Ángeles Cubas Piñera

My sister Susana and I arrived at the Brampton Colony. There must have been at least 100 Basque children and we were welcomed by Lady Cecilia Roberts. She was a wealthy lady who took us to what seemed to us to be a palace for tea and showed us some traditional dancing – we had a wonderful time. Lady Robert's daughter was a painter who taught us twice a week. I remember her name – Mrs Nicholson; she was very nice and a wonderful painter. The people of the village took us home for tea and we made friends. But after a while everything changed because of the war and we had to start working. We formed a dance troupe so that we could survive in the colony. We travelled around different villages and it was during one of these tours that I met Mr Livingstone. Something made him like me – I think I just appealed to him because he adopted me and paid all my expenses. He lived in Scotland and we used to write to one another. I let him know I had a sister and he took charge of her as well.

Whenever I had a holiday, he took us to his house in Scotland; we went on lots of excursions, visiting Ambleside in the Lake District. It was an unforgettable time. We also used to go camping, something I loved because it was outdoors. When we got back to the colony, we would tell everyone about the wonderful time we'd had and he sent boxes of sweets for us to share around.

When we went back to the Basque Country it was a sad homecoming. The people had suffered a lot. We continued writing to Mr Livingstone and it was he who suggested we return to England. It was a hard decision, but that was what my sister decided. When she'd learned the language, she started work and stayed on in the country that we love so much and which helped us so much in difficult times.

When we celebrated the 60th anniversary of the evacuation, we went back to our colony in Brampton and put up a commemorative plaque. We were welcomed by the Mayor and other dignitaries – it was an emotional moment. There was a short report about it on television and I have a photo of the event. I will never forget it. *

Alfonso Delgado Álava

One day, a chubby red-haired man told us that a group of about 15 boys would be sent to Bath. Once everything was ready and we got together in the dining room, I was relieved to see my sister. Saying goodbye to our friends, we headed for the coach. We were consoled in those moments of farewell with promises that we'd see each other again, promises that evaporate and have no substance. We were at that indefinable age, the tender age near puberty, when a child's brain works with no objective but is searching for one. I don't know why, but the journey was interminable. Where was the Bath colony?

At about eight o'clock at night, that handful of Spanish refugee children left the coach. We were on the pavement in front of a block of houses waiting for instructions from our teacher. He took us towards a house where one could read in big letters and in English: "Basque Children's Home". It was a Victorian building with bay windows. As we crossed the threshold, we were greatly surprised to see Spanish girls as we went through a wide passageway. They too were surprised and curious and looked at us as we passed by. They were neatly dressed and had many different coloured bows in their hair. I remember that green, blue and red predominated. We were embarrassed about our disastrous clothes, some of us in winter clothes, others in shirtsleeves. According to the lady who was in charge, the big girls would see to it that our clothes were clean and that we went to school in the colony. Having been told the house rules, the lady went on to tell us that in a few months we would be able to go to English schools. When one of us asked a question, she'd pay great attention, treating it with all the seriousness that her position conferred. She was a tall, stout woman with a pale complexion and curly hair which made me think she was a serious and haughty woman, but later, after I had had dealings with her, I could see what she was really like and found that she was a kind and confident woman. With the passage of time, I realise what a mistake it is to rely on first impressions.

In the morning they would wake us up early, that is to say, using methods employed in boarding schools to get us used to a healthy and disciplined life. Getting-up time would be marked by the ringing of a bell, three times only, no more, no less.

I remember finding a little boy in the dormitory who was packing his case. When we asked him why, he replied: "I'm going to ask the Director for permission to go back to Spain." Some of us tried to comfort him, telling him that things weren't so bad and that we were sure that the Director wouldn't allow him to leave.

It was breakfast time. At each table in the dining room there was a Spanish girl in charge of serving. They greeted us in the sweet tones of Basque women. What happy memories and days! The Director of the colony appeared at the door. As she checked the tables, she lingered tenderly over the youngest ones and asked them questions about their health, their feelings: she was the most maternal woman I've ever met in my life. To me, she represented something sublime as a woman. Once breakfast was over, we had to rest for 15 minutes – that was the rule. *

(Alfonso Delgado died in 2003. This extract comes from an unpublished manuscript found by his daughter María in his loft.)

Flori Díaz Jiménez

I was one of the girls who was evacuated to England in 1937 during the Spanish Civil War. I was ten years old. I have fond memories of the time I stayed at Eastleigh camp. We were very well looked after as regards cleanliness, medical check-ups and food. In those days I felt only gladness not seeing planes coming over to bomb us and not having to run to the air-raid shelters.

One thing I remember is that I was always asking my mother to buy me some Wellington boots for when it rained, but the moment never came. While we were in the camp there was a tremendous storm. They handed out wet weather footwear and great was my joy when they gave me the boots that I had so craved.

I don't remember when I was taken to Mrs Manning's colony at Theydon Bois, but that was just like a fairy story. In my own home we used to have our baths in a large pail, but when I arrived at this colony I was shown to a bathroom with towels and sponge bags for each of us, containing soap, toothbrush, toothpaste and eau de cologne. And then there was the bedroom: four beds for the little girls, with eiderdowns and curtains. I've often wondered how could we have been so lucky, after the hard times we had had the misfortune to live through in Spain during the war.

Life in that colony was splendid. We 21 children seemed like brothers and sisters, the older ones caring affectionately for the four smallest girls. Mrs Manning was marvellous, she was full of kindness and attention. English people used to come and visit and would take us to London to the cinema or to tea. Two married couples also came, I think they were from Valencia. I always say that they were the happiest days of my life.

Now comes the worst part. My brother was three years older than me, and for me he was not only my brother but like a father and mother too, so the day I was told I had to go home to Spain, but that my brother would be remaining, I can't begin to tell how I felt. They said it was only to visit my parents and that afterwards I could return to England. Like a silly girl, I believed them.

When we arrived back in Spain, at the frontier in Irún, people were waiting for us to ensure we reached our respective destinations. Their attitude was hostile and their behaviour despicable. They appeared unaware that we were simply boys and girls who had been sent away because of the bombing and famine. They had no regard for the suffering of our parents who had been forced to part from us for these reasons and for our benefit. My parents didn't know that I was coming home. Moreover, my brother's name was on the list, not mine.

Once I was back in Bilbao life was totally different. It was the post-war period and we lacked many things. I found that relatives had died, others had been forced out of their homes and left in the street with nothing. My grandmother on my father's side had to be put in an asylum after she went mad when she learned of the death of one of her sons. As a result of this she died a short time afterwards.

For me, it was all so traumatic that my whole life became tinged with sadness. Events made it impossible for me to go back to England, but my recollections of the period I spent there are so good that I have never been able to forget it. That's something only a person who had been there can understand.

As for my brother, he returned to Spain a year and a half after I did, without my parents having requested it. It was just as had happened to me, and in neither case were they told that we had arrived in Bilbao. They learned of it quite by chance.

My brother was 16 but he was very unfortunate, since to obtain work he had to join the *Frente de Juventudes,* which was the Francoist youth movement. As he was unwilling to belong to that sort of organisation, he was not allowed to work. The years passed and he was called up for national service in the Spanish Navy. He was released before serving the whole of his term, owing to a foot deformity. In his mind he still cherished the desire to return to England. So he tried to leave, but had the misfortune to be arrested at the frontier with France and accused of being a member of the *maquis.* The torture and ill treatment he was subjected to in police stations and prisons brought about his death at the age of 24. In spite of the years that have gone by, I cannot forget what they did to my brother and what he suffered. *

María Victoria Domínguez Elias
Now that I remember, it seems to me like a dream that on 20 May 1937 we went aboard a large ship in the port of Santurce called the *Habana.* I won't forget the white bread that they gave us to eat, and the sponge cake for breakfast. During the crossing, as there were so many of us children, there weren't enough cabins for everyone. My sisters and I (there were three of us), were very lucky to have one.

We arrived at the port of Southampton early in the morning. Before going ashore we were given a check-up by some doctors and then we were taken to Stoneham, a camp site with tents just like those used by Indians in films. Our stay in the camp lasted two months, after which we were moved to a colony.

They sent us to Birkenhead, where we really enjoyed the year we spent there until we returned to Spain. To be frank, we had a most pleasant time at the colony. There were 30 boys and 30 girls in a large-sized summer mansion set in the countryside. We were looked after by an English couple and three Spanish ladies, a teacher and two helpers. We had general lessons with the teacher, and one day each week an English master taught us language. The girl guides used to take us to the swimming pool. They also entertained us with occasional parties that they held for us. On Sundays the English master's pupils used to come to practise their Spanish with us, since he was teaching it to them.

The boys in the colony started a football team. They played on Saturdays against English teams. Although when I returned to Spain I was sent after a few months to a boarding school where I stayed for seven years, my stay in England 70 years ago hasn't faded from the memory of my childhood. *

María de los Ángeles Dueñas Montes

Although my mother's parents went to France, they decided to send the girls to Britain, because of my grandfather's professional association with the engineering company Brown Boveri.

The Sutton-on-Hull colony was called Elm Trees and was a large red brick Victorian house on a corner site in the village of Sutton. The house had a large garden where the children could play. It was owned by Mr Herbert Sewell, a local builder, who was an active Methodist and philanthropist.

Amongst the people who came into contact with the children was a Mr Hudson, a young businessman who was deemed special because he had a car and would take the children out for rides. There was also Mr Priestman, who owned a large engineering factory and who also took some of the boys on as apprentices there. Mr Priestman and his wife were Quakers and they took a special interest in my mother and her sister. They were among the lucky ones who were invited to their home for afternoon tea sometimes. They were served by a maid called

Ivy, whom they found difficult to understand because she had a cleft palate.

The children weren't given formal English lessons, although they went to the local school, Chapman Street School. Indeed, when my mother first arrived, she found that she could communicate with the others in schoolgirl French. My mother often said how amazed she had been when she arrived in Sutton because there were still gaslights. (Her father had been head of the hydroelectric plant at Burceña that served the north of Spain, so gaslights appeared primitive.)

My mother spoke little of her adolescent years in Sutton-on-Hull. She and her sister Lola went to live with Mr and Mrs Sewell and their adopted son, Douglas, in Chestnut House. It was a farmhouse and also contained the joinery workshop and the builder's yard. It also had greenhouses, chickens, fruit trees, and vegetable gardens and so was largely self-sufficient.

Prior to her marriage, Mrs Sewell had been a teacher and she was a great believer in the value of education. My mother was lucky in that Mrs Sewell recognised her potential, and the Sewells paid for her to be privately educated at Hull College of Commerce. They also paid for the education of the children of several of their employees.

One day, when my mother and Douglas were carrying a heavy bench together, he dropped his end and my mother's end flew up, hitting her in the face and knocking out her teeth, so she had to have them crowned. I don't think either my mother or my aunt regarded the Sewells as parents, since their own parents were in France and they were in contact with them. However, for me, they definitely fulfilled the role of grandparents.

When my mother left school, she went to work for a few months at the Citizens' Advice Bureau. Most of her duties there seemed to have involved the typing of letters to soldiers in France from their relatives in Hull. She then trained as a nurse from 1942 to 1945 at Hull Royal Infirmary. As soon as she became a student nurse, she left the Sewells and lived in the nurses' home. (Her sister Lola stayed with them for another six years until her parents returned from exile in France. She then joined them in Seville.) My mother worked for six years as a night sister, followed by six years as an outpatients' sister at Western General Hospital, Hull. After this, she worked for many years as a district nurse and finally worked as a schools' nurse before she retired.

In the 1950s and 1960s she would sometimes be asked to act as interpreter in court cases or, more informally, in the hospital. As Hull is a port, Spanish sailors were sometimes involved in legal cases or admitted to hospital. My mother was able to visit her uncles in Paris in 1947. She then got married and visited her sister in Seville with her husband and me in 1955. She didn't go again until 1975 and thereafter went annually to see her father and sister until she was too unfit to travel. She spent all her life in Hull, except when she asked to be admitted to a residential home in Edinburgh to be near me.

My impression of my mother's and Lola's attitude to their stay in Sutton is based on their eternal gratitude that kind-hearted people had seen fit to shelter defenceless foreign children, who had spent much of their last few weeks in Bilbao fleeing from air raids.

(María de los Ángeles Dueñas Montes died in 2004. Her daughter, María del Carmen Coupland, wrote this.)

Celia Elduque Jaime

My mother, Celia Elduque, was born in 1923, in the city of San Sebastián, where her parents, originally from Aragón, had moved at the beginning of the 1920s and they remained there until the start of the war. Her father, like many others, had gone to enlist in the fight to defend the Republic, but they told him: "We don't even have enough weapons for the young ones." Thinking then that their side would win the war, they decided to leave San Sebastián and head for Bilbao.

When they arrived there around 24 April 1937, they were given accommodation in a flat near the entrance to the Gran Vía, close to the Commercial Bank, whose cellars were used for shelter when the alarm was given. From then until my mother's evacuation to England, the memories that stayed with her, she told us, centred always on the same thing: the hunger and the air raids. One day, it would have been the beginning of May 1937, they found out that an evacuation of children to other countries was being organised. When they heard that there would be one going to England her parents didn't think twice and rushed to put down her name and that of her brother Eduardo, who was 11 at the time. My grandmother remembered how parents queued up to register their children. This contrasts with the idea later circulated by Franco's propaganda that "the children had been torn from the arms of their parents and taken away". Following their return to Spain after the war, several people asked them if they had indeed been taken by force or, on the contrary, with their parents' consent, in reply to which they would always mention the long queues of people waiting to enrol.

When the day of departure came they packed their "suitcases" (in reality, cardboard boxes tied with bits of string) and went to Lanaja station to take the train to Santurce. She and her brother said goodbye to their parents, whom they didn't see again until January 1940.

Once the *Habana* had left port, my mother started to feel very unwell and seasick. Her brother told her that the boat was protected by the warship *José Luis Díez* until on the high seas she continued her journey escorted by two English ships. When the *José Luis Díez* was pulling away to allow the English ships to take over, her crew stepped up on deck to salute the *Habana*, fists raised high, and just at that precise moment a wave knocked them all down.

When they docked at Southampton they were taken to the camp at Stoneham. Having always lived in a city environment, my mother had never before slept in a tent. One of the first changes that she noticed after a few days at the camp was that her hair turned blonde.

It must have been the end of the summer 1937 when a group of about 20 children were sent to a colony known as The Oaks, which was situated on the outskirts of Carshalton in Surrey. Once in the colony, they were given English classes, in addition to the lessons that they received from the señoritas. It was a pleasant period, living near the countryside and the parks, with outings to London every now and then, and other less frequent trips they made, such as one to the Isle of Wight. They also organised shows that included Basque folk dances (her brother Eduardo learnt how to dance the *espatadantza* at that time) and various songs. At the end of each performance they used to sing "John Brown's body lies a-mouldering in the grave ... Glory, glory, alleluia" etc., which would always bring forth hearty applause from the audience.

They used to be taken to a cinema – The Plaza – for morning showings every other Saturday, in such a way that one group would go one Saturday and the other would go the following one. Many films were comedies, featuring actors such as Chaplin and Laurel and Hardy. Since the actors were British and they had already acquired some knowledge of English through their classes and because of the length of time they had been living in England, they were able to understand the gist of the dialogue, except when they showed a film with the Marx Brothers. The children couldn't understand the American accent at all.

My mother recalled her impressions of British life, for example, visits to people's houses and invitations to meals. Though they would sometimes feel shy, thinking that perhaps they would not know how to behave appropriately in a country where customs were different, they would nonetheless react differently when they were shown inventions that the British people believed were unheard of in Spain. For instance, on one occasion, the children were told that they would be shown what was called an "automatic telephone", that is, a telephone on which you didn't need to ring through to the operator. Instead, you could make a call by directly dialling the number. "Imagine their surprise when we told them that this was already a well-known invention in Spain," she said. On another occasion, whilst on a trip to London, the person escorting them wanted to take them to Tower Bridge and, in particular, show them the bridge elevation system that enabled both road and river traffic, something of a novelty, at least for the children. They replied with genuine pride saying that in Bilbao there were no less than three the same. The children had felt the urge to counter "British pride" with "Spanish pride".

On other occasions the children would go to playgrounds with swings and slides, which they would take over to the extent that there would be no longer any space for English children to play. When recalling this, my mother would say: "At the time we believed we had every right, but now when I think of it I realise how patient and generous the English were towards us."

Toward the summer of 1939 my mother and her brother were moved from Carshalton colony to a private house in Lymington where a Mrs Williams lived. On one occasion, Mrs Williams asked them if they were familiar with kitchens of the type that they had in the house, as she had been to Spain and had seen people cooking on the ground. This observation greatly surprised my mother, who could barely believe what she was being told, until the lady explained that she had seen this in a village in Galicia.

For the duration of the Spanish Civil War my mother and her brother had not been claimed back by their parents. Following the fall of Santander they had returned to San Sebastián, where her father spent a while in prison until, not without difficulties, he was released. After that, and once the war was over, they were able to reclaim the children. Just before Christmas 1939 they embarked for the Channel crossing to France at the port of Newhaven. It was night time and the boat was small, with the lights turned out due to the threat of German submarines. The sea was rough and Mamá became so seasick that, as she had begun to vomit, they took her up on deck and, holding on to her, a sailor held her head over the railing, over the blackness of the sea. So vividly did these bad memories stay with her, just as did those of her sickness during the crossing three years before, that never again did she board a boat.

When they got to France, they took the train to Paris, where she remembered being helped by nuns who gave them food while they were changing trains. From Paris they took another train to Irún. She recalled that when they arrived at the border, what she first noticed upon re-entering Spain was the presence of the *Guardia Civil*, and her initial feeling was one of sadness at the thought that they were coming home having lost the war. Once there, they stayed in a shelter managed by *Auxilio Social* in Irún or Fuenterrabía, in which they lived for about two weeks until their parents learned of their return.

Her parents, who had by then moved to Madrid, didn't know that my mother and her brother had returned. But one day, an Englishman, whose name, as we learned many years later, was Ronald Thackrah, and who was a member of the Spanish Aid Committee, found them in Madrid, as the Committee was overseeing the return of the children to Spain. When he asked them about the children, they replied that they were surprised that they hadn't yet come back from England. The Englishman informed them that their children had been at the border for no less than a fortnight. At once an uncle, who lived in Madrid, went to fetch them and thus they were finally reunited at the beginning of January 1940. One of the first things that the parents noticed during the first weeks, apart from the changes that one would expect to have taken place during their separation, was the children's new habit of saying "please" whenever they asked for anything, which often annoyed their parents. It turned out that the children returned just in time, since only three months after their reunion, their father died.

All that remains now is to mention some of the people that my mother met, who, on the children's side, include the García Aldasoro siblings (Helvecia, Delia and Elvio), José Sorozábal, the Sancho siblings, Teresa David and all the others. Among the British, there were people like Mr Croft and Mr Lawrie, as well as Mr Alan Hunter who, according to what she told us, looked after them and fussed over them. She would also regularly mention, and write to, Charles West and Ken Dow, who was always so careful to remind them that he was not an Englishman but a Scot, and who would some time later marry Pili, one of the señoritas who, just like the two others, Ana María González and Carmen Díaz, continued to live in the UK.

All her life my mother kept her memory of those years alive, telling us time and time again how and why she had gone there, the journey, the anecdotes, everything. Despite the fact that these events related to a war, we never stopped noticing the joy with which she would tell us about her stay in England, to the extent that her memories have now come to form part of our own.

(Celia Elduque died in 2004. Her son, Miguel Ángel Cubero Elduque, wrote this.) *

Angelita, Paula and Rosita Felipe Gómez

Angelita, Paulita and Rosita Gómez were three sisters who went to England on the *Habana* in 1937. They lived in Calle de las Semanas in Portugalete/Sestao. Both parents were dead; the girls were cared for by their aunt Marcelina and their older sister Paquita. Most of their time was spent in air raid shelters and they had to endure terrible food shortages as Franco began preventing food supplies from entering northern Spain. Soon they had to resort to eating family pets and sparrows. The three sisters escaped from Spain on the *Habana* in 1937, leaving behind Paquita, who eventually fled to France, only returning home after the war had finished.

From the camp at North Stoneham, the three sisters were moved to a centre in Bristol and, due to a shortage of carers, from there to Cambria House in Caerleon. There they were put in the care of a Spanish lady, Mrs Fernández, from Dowlais, whose descendants had come from the Bilbao area to Merthyr Tydfil to work in the iron industry at the beginning of the century.

While most of the children returned to Spain at the end of the Spanish Civil War, the sisters remained, as they had no home to return to. They were split up and sent to different homes in South Wales. The three still remember how the authorities treated them like foreigners. They weren't allowed to become British citizens until they married. Angelita remembers having to have official permission to work in the Metal Box Steel Works in Neath. She also had to inform the police if she was going to Swansea.

Angelita returned to Spain 15 years later and was reunited with her sister Paquita. Paula had to wait 25 years before returning to Spain, and her visit was an emotional one. Besides counting themselves Welsh, the ties between the sisters and the country of their birth are still strong.

Paulita's daughter asked her mother and Angelita some questions.

What do you remember about living in Spain during the war?
Paulita: I remember spending all day down in the shelter while my older sister Paquita went to look for food. I remember the noise of the planes overhead. I remember being hungry. When my father was alive, he would go out to shoot birds and rabbits for us to eat, but after he died, and with our mother also dead, we went to live with an aunt who had children of her own, so food was scarce. I remember having no toys or dolls to play with. When I had children of my own I enjoyed making clothes for their dolls or furniture for dolls' houses out of matchboxes. When you have had so little in your early life, it makes you very resourceful and you never want to waste anything.
Angelita: I remember feeling very much the older sister, having to look after the younger ones when I was really only a child myself.

What do you remember about the boat crossing?
Paulita: We were all very sick, but I'm not sure if that was because we all ate so much food all at once when we had been used to eating so little. We were lucky. as one of the stokers on board, who we knew, managed to get us a sort of cabin. When we docked at Southampton, the quayside was lined with Salvation Army people, playing music to greet us. We thought that all English people wore those uniforms and that they were very strange! There were also lots of flags and bunting everywhere and we thought it was to welcome us. Later we realised that it had been left over from the King's coronation ten days previously. I remember being scared about leaving Spain, as Paquita our older sister had said it would just be a short holiday and we would soon be back home. In some ways it was a bit of an adventure. As it turned out, I didn't go back to Spain until my mid thirties when I had two children of my own.

What did you like best about living in the Caerleon colony?
Paulita: I liked the weekends, because we all went swimming and,

more importantly, sometimes had "glass pudding" which was a special treat. That was what we called jelly! It was nice in Caerleon. There were so many children, there was always someone to play with. We'd give concerts to help raise money and would dance the *jota*. It was fun and people were very kind. The miners would come every Sunday and bring us all sweets.

Angelita: I liked it when we all told ghost stories together. I suppose it gave us a sense of security all snuggled up. Once we went and pinched some apples from a local garden, but when we got back, we couldn't decide where to hide them, so we tried to put them out of the window onto the guttering, but suddenly they started rolling along and eventually went out of reach so we never got to eat them. Served us right!

(Transcribed by Sian Massey and Sandra Shaw, daughters. Angelita died in 2008)

Isabel Fernández Barrientos

When the Spanish Civil War broke out, my mother, who was a widow, kept a boarding house. She had previously been a cook. The two of us lived very well because I was an only child, but we were afraid of the bombs. Then an uncle and aunt convinced her to send me to England with two cousins, who were rather older than me, as I was only seven.

We sailed on the *Habana* and when we arrived all of us were medically examined and they fastened coloured ribbons on our wrists. They were red, white, and blue. They tied a white one on me, though I liked the coloured ones better. Later I learned that the coloured ones were for children who had lice or other conditions.

We were taken to a camp with tents and there we spent some months until we were dispersed to colonies. I had toothache badly, and as it was so painful they took me to a dentist for an extraction, but while I was at the dentist's my two cousins were taken to the north of England and I was very lonely. I knew no one, except a teacher from my school in Bilbao, who was called Doña María de Dios.

After a few days I was taken to South Wales. The colony was called Cambria House and was in Caerleon. It was a huge house. The rooms were vast because all of us girls fitted into one and all the boys into another. There was an enormous courtyard where we played and we also had all sorts of games: ping-pong, jigsaws, books and many other things. I got to know many children from Vizcaya and Guipúzcoa. At weekends, married couples used to come and take us out.

In the colony the older girls looked after the smaller ones. They used to do our hair and help us to get dressed. The most enjoyable thing was when Christmas came and they hid our presents so as to give us a surprise. Those were very happy years. The only part I didn't enjoy were mealtimes, because I hardly ate anything and always left food on my plate, and the older children used to pile onto my plate what they had left over. As the poorest eater I was given a spoonful of cod liver oil, it was always my lot to swallow it. At tea time they gave us a big slice of bread thickly spread with butter and, when fires were lit, we used to scrape off the butter and toast the bread, which we liked very much.

A few months before my mother asked for me to go back, a married couple who had no children came to the *colonia* wanting to adopt a girl and they chose me. They were called Trevor and Iris Berry. They loved me as if I'd been their daughter. The time that I lived with them was my happiest period in England. They humoured all my whims and as I didn't care for tea, Iris brought my breakfast up to me in bed: orange juice and cocoa with biscuits. They sent me to an English school and I learned a great deal. Who'd think so now? I've forgotten everything!

When the war ended my mother asked for me to be sent back to Spain to live with her. But Mr and Mrs Berry didn't want to be separated from me and they conceived the idea of sending for my mother to come to England. The Second World War had begun and she wasn't allowed to come over. We said goodbye with great sorrow, thinking we should never see each other again. The day I got back to Spain was my 11th birthday. My arrival was very sad. There was nothing but wretched poverty. You could see dogs abandoned in the streets, dying of hunger. I thought that was dreadful, being accustomed in England to seeing pets very well cared for by their owners. The Spanish Civil War had not been over long and there was no work.

The flat where we lived had been taken away from us, so we had to go to live with an uncle and aunt in Logroño until such time as my mother found employment. Mr and Mrs Berry wrote many letters to me, sending me lots of kisses. They remembered me constantly. I too used to reply, but I don't remember how we stopped writing to each other. They were very difficult times. But I never forgot them and I continue to remember them with great affection. I still keep some photographs of them and of the *colonia*.

I've always been careful not to lose those photographs in spite of moving house time and again. I was married for over 50 years, but my husband died six years ago. I now live in Bilbao with my daughter, her husband and their two girls. *

Carmen Fernández Learra

I was born on 24 November 1927 and I remember that I started school at the age of six. The war started in 1936 and there was no more school. I was nine when I went to England on the *Habana*, I went with my three sisters (Manola, the oldest, Asun, the little one, myself and Carmen, the middle one), and a brother Loren. My parents sent us away to escape the bombings and the horrors of war. At first, I cried when I was on the boat, but then I stopped. One gets used to it. A little girl gets used to it.

I remember that, on the boat, we were examined by English doctors, and what I always remember also is that we were given hard boiled eggs decorated with bright colours and that cheered us up no end.

We arrived at Southampton and went to a camp full of white tents. It was the first time in my life that I'd seen tents. In fact, it was really rather pretty because there were many tents. They gave us boots there because it rained a lot. We didn't stay there very long. After two or three days I believe, a very nice man called Sr Urra, took us by bus to Clapton, the Salvation Army colony. We didn't stay there long either, about a month or so. Then we were taken to Brixton. I don't think there were any boys in Brixton, they were sent to other colonies. My brother went to Scarborough.

We stayed for about three months. The food was so different from what we'd been used to that it became a big problem, especially for my little sister Asun, who didn't like it. We didn't eat meat, so, of course, they gave us some sort of minced meat which we didn't like. They gave Asun the same meal for a whole week. As she wouldn't eat, they'd put the meat in the fridge, then they'd bring it out again, she wouldn't eat it, back it would go in the fridge. My oldest sister and I did eat it, but the little one didn't want to.

From Brixton we were sent to Laleham School in Margate, Kent.

It had been a school and it was given over to the children who'd been evacuated from the Spanish Civil War. There were also boys in this colony. We were really happy there. We were getting used to life in England. We were lucky because as well as feeling good there, we were adopted. I was adopted by a family of two sisters, my little sister by a family with one daughter and my oldest sister by another family. In fact, they didn't really "adopt" us, but they paid for our clothes, for school etc. We slept in the colony, but I used to go and stay with the sisters, sometimes staying for a month, but I didn't live with them all the time.

They looked after us all very well in the colony, with much love. We were gradually getting used to living there, at least, we all were except for Asun, who still found it difficult to get used to. We liked to drink a lot of milk and there they gave it to us in large quantities. We had a gym teacher who was a Hindu, and we had a piano teacher called Srta Bonasera. I liked everything, especially gym. There was a gymnasium which later I came back to see with my husband, when I was married, during a holiday we spent in England. In the bedroom, there were 12 beds, two rows of six. And in the evenings I used to read to the girls. We also had parties, with sack races etc. My English was improving. As I went to school it was bound to, since everything was in English, but with the other children in the colony I spoke in Spanish. I think the other children in the colony didn't go to school, and they used to have classes in the colony.

We still managed to keep in contact with our brother in Scarborough. He'd call us and we'd speak a little. I remember that his voice was changing to a man's voice. He looked English, since he was fair-haired and had blue eyes. He told us he was playing a lot of football and that he was happy, although he wasn't in such a nice place as we were. Where we were was better, we were very lucky. Of the few people that I have seen since who were at the colony, no one has spoken badly of it.

We also acted and danced our typical Basque dances and we would get dressed up as sailors. We always went to London. I remember that at the start of any concert, there would be a hush and people would sing the national anthem, *God Save the King*.

Some English people, not those who had adopted us, would from time to time take a child from the colony on holiday. Once someone came to the colony to invite a child to the Isle of Wight and Sr Palomba, who was one of our teachers from Madrid, told them to take me. We crossed at one of the ports. It was a place where there were slot machines. The people who invited me had a house on the island and had a daughter who was studying voice production. The girl was a year older than me and was an only child. I stayed for three days with them. They gave me a lot of money and on the way back I took presents for my friends in the colony.

I think that I spent two or three years in England. I remember that before we left, they tried out the gas masks on us in the colony. The Second World War was just about to begin. My parents had escaped to France, and after passing through various different places, ended up in Paris, because one of my father's brothers had been living there from before the start of the Spanish Civil War.

We were still in England, but my parents discovered where we were and the names of the ladies helping us. My parents, above all, my mother, wanted us to be sent to Paris, but the English ladies wanted us to stay, they even offered my parents work in England. I preferred to stay, as did my sisters. I wanted to see my parents, but I wanted my parents to come to England instead of us going to France. In the end, we were sent to our parents, I think through the mediation of the Red Cross. We took with us two basketfuls of presents from the ladies and presents I'd been given at school. There was money, things for my father (a telescope), photos and heaps of other presents for everyone, but just as we were about to cross the frontier, one of the baskets was stolen.

At Customs there were many queues of people returning, and a soldier asked my mother if we were coming in with Lenin. My mother, who was good at repartee, replied: "No, we are coming to our homeland, which is Euskadi, perhaps you are not from here?" Then as I was frightened, I said "Mamá!" and plaf! my mother slapped me and said: "Must we bow down to these men? Am I going to bow down? Don't you dare!" And that is how the postwar era began.

We got to Irún. There they put us in a large shed where there weren't even any toilets. From there, we went home by train to Erandio. After that the horrors of hunger, which happens after wars. How many times did I hear my father say: "María, what have we done with these children? Why didn't we leave them in England, they were so well cared for there."

One day, when we'd been home for a little while, a neighbour said to my father: "Balbino, these girls have changed a lot, because when they came back from England, how they used to like saying

'Sorry' and 'Thank you'." Then my mother answered: "Well, it can't be because we've brought them up badly!" What was happening was that, as with English, we were losing what we had learned. Then after a little while, seeing what was happening in Spain, we started to say to our parents: "Why did we come back? Why didn't you come to England?" What happens too is that one tends to idealise everything. When you go somewhere as a child, you see everything in a favourable light. We didn't see the bad things, only how well we were being treated, how kind and educated our English families were. Then when we returned, as we forgot our English, because nobody spoke it, we only remembered the songs and even those we started forgetting. Just as we learn things as children, we start forgetting through lack of practice. *

Rafael Flores Siosalido

My days are spent practically all the time in queues, trying to get bacon, or a bit of soap and things like that, and also running to the nearest tunnel when the German or Italian planes bomb us.

The Salcedo family live at 5 Calle Zabala in Bilbao. The father speaks to my father and says he'd like to send his only child, Irene, to England, if my father sends Rafa, his middle son, and he thinks it won't be for very long. Andresi, José Luis and Lorenzo Bilbao from the sixth floor are already going. So it's organised that we shall all go like a family of brothers and sisters.

My father, at his cutting table, for he was a tailor making uniforms for the Basque militia, tells me that I'll soon be home. I never saw him again. I learned of his death in 1940. I took leave of my grandparents at their house and my grandfather gave me a silver *duro* from the last century. I never saw my grandparents again either. My oldest sister had just married Agrupino, who tells me that I must never forget the Spanish Republic whilst I am in the fair Albion. This man was imprisoned as soon as Franco's troops entered Bilbao, and he was in jail for three years for what was described as the crime of "speaking". I had a new-born sister called Maite who I saw again 22 years later. I saw my mother again 10 years afterwards, crossing the bridge over the river Bidasoa on the border at Hendaye, shouting: "Rafa! Rafa!" and running like a mad woman.

The journey on the *Habana* and our arrival at the camp at Eastleigh have no doubt been described by others. We were a bit disappointed because we couldn't understand why we were going to be allocated to tents. Indeed this is where our world and our lives changed completely.

White bread was our obsession. We hadn't seen any for a year. One morning a young lad carrying a large tray full of sliced bread was pushed, and he tripped. All the bread fell to the ground and we gathered as much as we could under our shirts, taking it back to our tents. We believed that we'd be able to take it back to Bilbao very soon! Food was basically barley soup, onion soup and corned beef, prepared very simply. It nourished us and gradually got us fit. There was a constant queue in order to get a drink of Horlicks, for as soon as we drank one cup, we went back to the end of the queue in order to get another one.

The climate that summer in England was marvellous and life in the camp was more and more bearable as time went on. You could see in the middle of the camp girls washing their brothers' and sisters' clothes and hanging them out to dry in the sun.

Soon the day came when we had to leave the camp, about two months after our arrival. Two Walsall Corporation double-decker buses came up to the camp and out stepped a man in a bowler hat who was Labour Councillor John Whiston of Walsall, later Alderman Whiston and much later, Mayor of Walsall.

There were 50 of us children, three adult women, two teachers, Lucita and María Luisa, a helper and social worker Paquita. Our destination was Aldridge Lodge, near Walsall. It would be our home for the next two or three years. We went up a road between two grass fields belonging to Mr and Mrs Adams' dairy farm at the back of the lodge and finally we reached the house. I am sure that when we saw it, we breathed a sigh of relief and had a feeling of security, for it was a beautiful place. It was surrounded by green fields with cows, and facing the house was a civil aerodrome which was mainly used for training.

There are two events worth mentioning about this aerodrome. Amy Johnson, the famous flier, was in a gliding contest one Sunday afternoon. Her glider wing touched our fence as she was landing so low. The machine turned over and she was left hanging from the safety belts she was wearing, but she was unhurt. The excitement was tremendous: I think the 50 children and all the adults were looking at her until the people from the aerodrome came up with the means to get her out.

The second incident was in 1939. The Second World War had already started and a Lancaster bomber had to make an emergency landing at the aerodrome, which was too small for it. The plane ended up on the Walsall Road!

Mr Whiston himself was a real public man, president or chairman or member of anything you can think of, all to do with social issues. Mr and Mrs Whiston, together with their four Staffordshire bull terriers came to live with us. I think his hobby was putting his dogs in for shows. Their two sons, Tom and Ron, and their girlfriends Ivy and Winnie, spent a lot of their spare time with us at weekends, and some of their holiday time. Mr Whiston never learned a word of Spanish except *cura* which he thought meant First Aid. Last thing before going to bed a queue of children would line up in front of his office and he and his wife would dab iodine on anything that was presented to them: cuts and bruises, scratches. Mr Whiston was a natural actor and with his miming and the odd English word, we understood what he wanted us to know.

Tom taught us handicrafts, and took us by car to evening classes in art, woodwork and cabinet making. He transformed a room in the back yard of the lodge into a workshop for us and we sold what we made to visitors for funds. He made us see the importance of being busy and occupied all the time. Many years later I realised why he was a very progressive man and learned that the Spanish Civil War had affected him very much politically.

One of the first visitors was a wonderful lady called Peggy Gibbins from Birmingham. She used to invite me and some others for tea and she presented us with a real feast. She had a Morris 10 but one day it got stuck in muddy ground at the entrance to Bosty Lane. She walked up to the house and said: "Can you get the car out for me please? Here are the keys." So we went down, got in the car, switched the engine on and somehow the car shot out of the muddy ground. When she saw us, she grinned and said: "I'm going to give you your first driving lessons." And so she did. Once or twice a week she would take us to the swimming pool in Walsall. A man there gave us a book with drawings of the movements and instructions of how to learn to swim. We took part in a swimming gala against an English school and I won one of the events. I still have the little medal that was given to me.

Thomas W. Wooley of Tipton was a great friend of the colony. He and his sister took José Luis Bilbao and me to London for a long weekend, and they showed us all the sights. Thomas also used to take us to Walsall Gaumont Cinema. We'd see a film and have tea in the restaurant: egg and chips, tomato ketchup and tea, with bread and butter and jam. Another treat! He was a wonderful person, and later became a clergyman.

Mrs Whiston and two of the oldest girls managed the kitchen, but Mr Whiston had two tasks. One was last thing at night to prepare the porridge for the following day. It became solid overnight and in the morning it was cut, actually cut, put into bowls, then milk and sugar was added. The other time was the Sunday roast. He would enter the kitchen wearing an apron and carrying a large carving knife and fork and deal with the joint, slicing the meat and serving it out to each plate while Mrs Whiston and the girls would serve the vegetables.

We were encouraged to make a bird house and put it on a stump of wood. They taught us how to love birds and not hurt them in any way. But what we did hurt were field mice. There were hundreds of them. As soon as night came on, we used to sit in the kitchen with the lights out and wait for five minutes with shovels in our hands and then put the lights on. Every time we did that, we caught 14 or 15 of them. But you didn't see them during the day at all.

Life in the lodge began to change when a man called Manuel Lazareno, a musician and composer, arrived from France as a refugee. He formed a choir and using the book *Songs of the Basque Children*, taught us to appreciate Spanish folk music. I personally enjoyed it very much. With the help of a boy who played the *txistu*, we learned to dance Basque dances like the *espatadanza* and *jota vasca* and dances from other parts of Spain.

Cadburys, the chocolate firm, supplied Aldridge Lodge with chocolate and every afternoon Mr Whiston would dish out a tablet of milk chocolate for *merienda*. We were all invited to Bourneville during Christmas 1937 or 1938 and we had a tremendous time. We performed our songs and dances in front of the Cadbury family. They showed us round the whole factory and loaded us with different types of chocolate. Everything that was made was offered to us. We came out with boxes full of chocolate. That's another visit I shall never forget!

Learning English was difficult. Tom Whiston attempted to teach us English in the colony, and wrote the word: "enough" on the board, pronouncing it "inuff". We wanted to say an "eno". How could it be "inuff"? I remember thinking I'd never learn the language. Of course, I did gradually pick it up.

The Whistons taught us to sing *Song of a Rover* in English. It went something like this:

> This is a song of a rover
> A rover who stays in your room
> I am the rover and this is my song
> A song for home sweet home
> I'm singing a song to the old folks
> Wherever they might be
> I'm singing to your mother and my mother
> Although they're far apart
> I'm singing to the old folks at home
> Wherever they may be.

When we sang this in public, tears streamed down people's faces!

The workshop had a small window through which we had a view of part of Mr Adams' farmyard. One day, we four oldest boys had a natural anatomy lesson. Mr Adams and his son were bringing cows to the bull and we saw the whole performance for the first time in our lives. We couldn't get over it for days! I think it was a very good nature lesson and that all children of a certain age should see it.

From the beginning of 1938, names of children supposedly reclaimed by their parents were read out at breakfast time by Mr Whiston. Whenever I heard my name mentioned, I would say to him: "I'm not going back." Eventually, one day, Mr Whiston said that if Raf (he used to call me that) didn't want to go back, then Raf could stay with them. And that's what happened, I stayed with the Whistons until the colony was closed and then I went to live with them in Walsall.

I lived with the family for another two years until only four of us were left in the Midlands. We didn't stay much longer, because every time we went to London we felt the need to live near the Spanish refugee population that was settling in London. There I met Valeriana. She was another of the *Habana* children. We married, had two children and now we have five grandchildren all living in London.

We now live in Denia, Alicante and teach English voluntarily to *Las Aulas de la Tercera Edad*. These are classes for retired people organised by the local authority. People like to hear our story and we sometimes compare our lives in England with the same generation of children who had to live under the dictatorship. Comparing the two situations makes for a very interesting part of Spanish history.

Helvecia García Aldasoro

My father died when he was 56 in 1933, leaving my mother with five girls and two boys. My oldest brother, Oscar, who had been the head of the family, had left for the front. We lived in a mining village very near Bilbao, called La Arboleda. Ten months after the beginning of the war, when we had gone very hungry and had been very frightened by the bombings, my mother told us that she had put my name down, (I was 14), and those of my youngest siblings, Elvio, who was nine, and Delia eight, to go to England where there were no bombings and where food wasn't scarce.

When we arrived at Southampton, they took us by bus to an enormous camp. After a few days, groups of children left for colonies in different parts of the United Kingdom. In August, one of the helpers who I didn't know, came up to me and asked if I wanted to go to a small colony, as they needed three more who were brothers and sisters. I said I did and we went off on the train to Carshalton in Surrey. The colony was called The Oaks and there were only 20 children (12 boys and eight girls), one teacher and two helpers. There was a resident cook, a housekeeper and another person who came in daily to help. We older sisters had to look after the little ones, wash and iron their clothes etc. As well as that, we took it in turns to help in the kitchen.

It was a superb mansion with crenellated towers, but we only occupied part of it. In the other part lived an English couple with two children; the father was the Warden and he looked after the place. It was surrounded by gardens and trees. There was a large courtyard for us to play and run in, and also a field where the children played football. We were very happy there and got on like a family. But in winter, it was very cold, as in those days there wasn't any central heating and there was a long and cold passage to get to the toilets. At night we used to put our coats on the beds.

A local committee was in charge of the administration of voluntary donations from local organisations and individuals who had answered the advertisement placed in some left-wing papers, which said that for ten shillings a week, they could adopt and maintain a child. One of those who replied to the advertisement was Mr Cadbury, whose family was in the chocolate business, and he was assigned to my sister.

After some time, the Cadburys found out that there were three of us and they would take us out from time to time, either into central London or to their home. They had two lovely little girls, one was a baby of a few months and the other about two years old. In January

1939, they arranged with the committee that I should go to their house in north-east London for a month, in order to improve the little English that I knew. They had a live-in cook and nursemaid, so Mrs Cadbury had time to talk to me and help me with the language.

Every night, we would listen to the news from Spain and one night the news was so bad that I started to cry, and I told them as best I could that our family didn't want us to return for the time being. (Franco had been trying to repatriate the children since he had taken Bilbao.) They comforted me and promised that they would look after us until my mother sent for us, and they began proceedings to adopt us. They thought that it would be best to go to a co-educational boarding school, so we shouldn't be separated. I thought that was a good idea, as long as we spent holidays in the colony with the other children.

We visited three Quaker schools and chose the one nearest to London, The Friends' School, Saffron Walden in Essex, and by April 1939 we were settled there. I was put in a class of children of my age (16 years) so as not to be humiliated. They were about to take what was called in those days the "matric". The teaching methods were very different from those I was used to, and I understood very little. They told me to follow as best I could and that the important thing for learning the language was to listen hard. The maths teacher found my method of doing long division very strange, and the geography teacher was pleased because it just so happened that they were studying Spain that term, and he would ask me how to pronounce the names of the towns and the rivers, and then try to imitate me. At the beginning, we missed our friends from the colony very much. As my brother and sister were so young, the change didn't affect them so much and they easily adapted to their new life.

The school was on the outskirts of the town, surrounded by fields, and we used to play hockey, cricket and tennis. One afternoon, as I was watching the older boys play hockey, the ball, which is very hard, hit me in the right eye and I had a huge bruise for two weeks. The boy who had caused the accident came running up to apologise, and from then on he was always very nice to me. The odd thing is that two or three years later, when I was playing hockey with the team of the firm I worked for, the ball came up and got me in the left eye, this time much harder. I was frightened that I might have lost my eye: I covered it with my hand, and didn't dare take it away – I shall never forget it – until they took me away from the field and forced me to take my hand off. What a relief it was to see that I'd been mistaken and still had my eye!

Every Sunday morning we'd be taken to the town in a crocodile to share the Assembly with the Quakers of Saffron Walden. They sat in a room with a table in the middle, the Bible on the table, with no decoration, and they remained silent until the spirit moved them, when they got up and gave out the message. They sat down again, and the silence continued: all that lasted at least half an hour. It was a very spiritual experience. After dinner on Sundays there would always be a visitor, perhaps someone who had been teaching in Africa or a missionary. The one I remember the most is Mahatma Gandhi, with his extraordinary clothes.

One day, talking of the future, I told Mr Cadbury that I wanted to become a shorthand typist to be ready to work and to help my mother when we went back. At the end of the academic year he arranged for me to go to Birmingham to study in a commercial college and to stay with a widowed friend of theirs and her brother, a bachelor who had been wounded in the First World War. They were good people and were very fond of me.

Before I went to Birmingham, Mr Cadbury contacted the Basque Children's Committee in London, and he found out that in Birmingham and its suburbs, there were quite a lot of Basque children working in the factories and that there was an adult who was in charge of their wellbeing. Mr Cadbury made an appointment with him for the three of us. His name was Walter Leonard, but he was called Leon. He was born in Germany and had lived in Spain. He spoke very good Spanish and furthermore, he'd been in charge of a colony of Basque children. He told me that five Basque boys, a Catalan couple and their child, and two of the helpers that had come with us, lived in Birmingham, and that on the outskirts, and scattered around various towns, there were about 15 others. He added that his future mother-in-law held open house and provided tea on the first Sunday of each month for any Spaniard who wanted to go. I promised to go, and I did.

When I went for the first time, Leon was there, with his girlfriend Peggy and her mother, Mrs Gibbins, together with some of those who lived in Birmingham. As it was a lovely day, we spent the afternoon in the garden, but we could use a room with a gramophone, a ping-pong table, books and magazines. The next time I visited, more boys came, and gradually I got to know them all. I don't know where the idea came from, but we formed a club which we called The Midlands Boys' Club, of which I was secretary. Later, thanks to Mr Cadbury, we were allowed to use the sports field and pavilion that belonged to Cadburys. As I lived nearby in Bourneville, it was easy for me to open and close it. We decided that people should meet there every Sunday. If there were enough boys, they played football and afterwards we had a good tea in the pavilion. We were in contact with the Basque children in London, and all the Spaniards who came through Birmingham would come and see us.

Little by little, the boys left for London, including the Catalan family, since the husband, whose name was Domingo Ricart, had been offered the post of Secretary to the Juan Luis Vives Trust. Soon after, I received a letter from Sr Ricart asking me if I wanted to be his secretary. He mentioned that I would use both languages, as up to then I had only used English. I liked the idea of using Spanish as well as English, and as I was now alone in the Midlands, I told him I was interested in the job. One Sunday afternoon I was interviewed by Don Pablo de Azcárate. He told me that they had set up the Spanish Institute in the same building, and that since both organisations had only just been set up, there wasn't much work and he wanted me to work for both of them: for Sr Ricart in the morning and for Sr Salazar Chapela, who was the Secretary of the Institute, in the afternoons. I decided to accept.

The Institute offered a range of Spanish language classes every week, and in the afternoons there were literature classes. Each week there was a lecture: these were given by famous hispanicists, such as J B Trend, diplomats from South America and other personalities. We also put on various concerts: one of these was given by the great cellist Pablo Casals, who accepted the invitation as it was a private concert. Every three months we'd publish a magazine with the texts of the lectures.

When I arrived in London, I went to meet my friends in the *Hogar Español* in Bayswater, at 22 Inverness Terrace. It was a centre where the exiled Spanish Republicans used to meet and where there was a lot going on. There was a choir and a drama group: I put myself down for acting and we used to rehearse twice a week. The director of the group was Pepe Estruch, from Valencia. One year we put on *La Zapatera Prodigiosa* in a little theatre in Notting Hill Gate and it was a great success.

In 1945, when the Second World War finished, many Spaniards

who'd been fighting in the British army came to London. Amongst them was José Hidalgo, whom I married.

My mother came for a visit in July 1948 when my daughter was three months old. Elvio, Delia and I went to meet her at Northolt Airport. It was a field surrounded by barbed wire, and we waited there. When she got off the plane and saw us, she started to run towards us, but a policeman followed her. We had to explain to her that she had to follow the other passengers. Then they called me to translate. It was an incredibly emotional moment. We hadn't seen her for 11 years and we were no longer the children she had seen off at the port of Santurce. We found it strange that she was much smaller than we remembered. She enjoyed being with her granddaughter during her stay, bathing her and taking her out in her pram. She stayed with us until we moved house and she helped me to make the curtains. After a little while she said she'd like to go home and so she went. She came back again in the summer of 1958 when I had another child, a boy this time, who had been born in March 1952 and who was six.*

María Dolores Gómez Sobrino

My first memory is of saying goodbye to my father Timoteo Gómez. He was there at Santurce to see us off. "Don't worry," he said. "It will only be three months – you'll be back for Christmas." I never saw him again. It was May 1937 and I was just 12 years old.

Together with my mother, Ramona Sobrino, plus my elder brother Ignacio and my younger sister Tere, I boarded the *Habana* to Southampton. (My elder sister, Luchi, was deemed too old at 20 to be one of the Basque children.) We had made our way there from the requisitioned house in Bilbao that had been our home since the Civil War broke out in Spain. It was all very exciting for a young girl. There was quite a commotion at the dockside with everyone saying their tearful goodbyes.

The journey took two days, and it was very rough. We were chased by one of Franco's ships, and I can still hear the "boom boom" of its guns firing on us as we left Spanish waters. Accommodation on the ship was very basic. We slept on mattresses on the floor. There were 4,000 of us, mainly children, but also priests and teachers like my mother looking after us all. Some children were crying, either because they were all alone or because they had got lost on the big ship. I remember a big old Basque priest playing his *txistu* and *tambor* to keep our spirits up.

As we approached England, a Royal Navy ship came to escort us. And then, on 23 May, we were in Southampton, disembarking to be taken to North Stoneham camp in nearby Eastleigh, where my mother, my sister and I were housed in a big tent with other girls. All 4,000 of us waited to be allocated to somewhere more long-term. Early each morning loudspeakers blasting out military marches woke us up for our daily exercises. But it was all a lot of fun.

After a couple of weeks, 25 of us children under my mother's charge were transferred to Baydon Hole Farm near Newbury, with a further 75 following a few days later. One of the boys was Marcelo Segurola, also from my home town Azpeitia, in Guipúzcoa, later to be my husband. In Baydon we lived in Nissen huts. Major and Mrs Tomkins were in charge, and a huge youth called Tom cooked for us – the food wasn't bad, actually. The most dramatic moment for me came one day in the washroom, when my shrill screams brought everyone running. Mamá was sure I had caught my arm in the mangle. She found me cowering in the corner, terrified by a daddy-long-legs. They still scare me, 70 years later.

We stayed in Baydon till October 1937. It was a wonderful summer but, with winter coming, somewhere warmer was needed. So it was that my first Christmas in England was spent in Bray in Berkshire. We had moved to a massive mansion called Bray Court where I remember an enormous Christmas tree. Largely thanks to the mayor of Reading, Mr McIlroy, the place now served as a home for Basque children. Bray Court had a rose garden, a football pitch, tennis courts and its own stable with horses. We would ride bikes around the grounds. Previously a hotel, it had closed down because of some scandal or other. The director was a tall, thin Irishwoman called Miss Burke. With her long, pointed nose she reminded me of a parrot. Silence at all times was her golden rule, and every time we ran down the big staircase she would tell us in her bad Spanish to be quiet.

Bray Court was to be our home for nearly two years, and it was my favourite of all the colonies I stayed in. We used to hold open days to raise money and I remember I did a parasol dance. Classes were held in Spanish by Mr Sánchez – he was young and very goodlooking. The village shop was nearby and some of the boys used to squeeze through the hedge and go there. Once, the shopkeeper came round to complain that someone had been pinching his sweets: eventually three boys owned up. You have to realise that it was a long time since any of us had seen any sweets.

In the summer of 1939, the Bray Court colony was dismantled: no doubt with a world war coming, funds were short (years later we heard it had been reopened to shelter refugees from Czechoslovakia). Our family was split up: with other boys, my brother Ignacio went to the Midlands to work, in his case picking mushrooms (he later joined the RAF), while my sister Tere, too young to work, was found a foster family in Newbury and started to attend the local school.

As for Mamá and me, we were transferred to a colony not far from Bray, in Camberley, Surrey. Again, our accommodation was a nice country house, but not as beautiful as Bray Court. Another Irishwoman, Miss Britton, ran the place, together with a lady whose name now escapes me. The colony was already established and had its own rules. Perhaps for this reason, we found her to be a bit snooty.

Now I was 14, I had to go out to work. My first job was in a Camberley hotel, as a scullery maid. This meant washing pots, some of which were bigger than I was (I'm still only small). Miss Britton could see it was hard for me, so in 1940 I was found a place as a live-in housemaid with a family at 71 Kenton Road, Harrow. Alone in the world for the first time, I cried at first. Mr and Mrs Axton had two sons – one in the Army and one in the Navy – and a daughter. She used to take me ice skating. I missed my mother and the others: by this time, Camberley had closed down and she was working in a hotel in Frimley. They needed more staff and Mamá asked if I could have a job. So I began work as a hotel chambermaid.

In 1942 we went to Oxford to work in domestic service: Mamá to be housekeeper and me to be nanny to a little girl called Patricia. The family had a hairdressing salon and Mrs Peggy Underwood asked if I would like to learn the trade. So it was that I became a hairdresser, working in Bond Street when the Second World War was over. By now we were living in Kensington, where I met up again with Marcelo and his family (they had escaped to France during the Civil War and later managed to join him in England). We married in 1951.

Marcelo died in 1978 when he was 53. My mother, Ramona Sobrino, died in 1992 and my brother Ignacio in 2006. My elder sister, Luchi, remained in Spain and died in Madrid in January 2007. My younger sister, Tere, lives in Hampshire. I now live with my daughter in Wokingham, very near to Bray.

As for my father, he was arrested and imprisoned in 1937 and released when he was very ill. He died in San Sebastián in 1942. *

(On 12 February 2007, a few weeks after she dictated these words, Loli died at home in Wokingham in her daughter Tere's arms. Her ashes will be transported back to Azpeitia to be laid next to the remains of her beloved husband Marcelo.)

Benedicta González García

The bombing of Guernica galvanised my mother to remove us from the danger of the bombs and she went to the Town Hall to register our names to go abroad. We were five children: they then informed her that initially only two of us could go, and on 5 May the youngest left for France. Three of us remained on the waiting list and within a few days she was told we would be going to England on 20 May 1937.

That day dawned grey with the threat of rain, no blossomy spring day, even less a happy birthday for me as in previous years. As she wished me many happy returns, my mother gave me lots of advice and guidance for our journey and stressed that it would only be for a short time, a month at most. Mid-afternoon we left the house and set out for Portugalete station in Bilbao. When we arrived, some group leaders put us on the train. We said goodbye to our mother and I saw such sadness in her face that I felt all alone, but I had to be strong as I was in charge of two younger sisters.

It was almost dark when we got on board. It was raining slightly, drizzling, what we call *sirimiri*. As night came on, lots of children started crying and calling for their mothers. I remember next to me a little boy of six or seven, calling for his mother. I said: "Shush, she'll be here soon", and he looked up at me and said: "Do you know my mother?" I think I said "Yes", whereupon he stayed next to me all night. I think he felt protected. What a shame, I never saw him again.

At daybreak the boat started to move and sailed out of port, heading for England. In the morning I began to suffer from the seasickness which would affect me for the rest of the voyage. Two days later, we arrived at Southampton. At the port lots of buses were waiting to transfer us to the camp where I stayed for three months before being sent to Montrose in Scotland. I won't describe the camp, as other children will do so. I do want to say, however (as it was a very important part of my evacuation), that I found the three months I spent there a very difficult and negative experience. But I mustn't forget to mention, in the middle of all this, the first English woman I ever met. She was called Miss Mary and with another girl at the camp I was invited to tea at her house. She was an elderly lady, very gentle and very considerate to us, given our sad situation. She taught me my first words of English, like bread, milk, coffee, thank you, please, and a few other things. She was like a soothing balm counteracting the effects of life in the camp. When they told us we were leaving, we went to let her know and say goodbye. She told us that she wanted to take a photo of herself with us as a souvenir, and when she said goodbye I saw tears in her eyes. I've never forgotten her.

After a long night on the train, we arrived at Montrose station. It was a pleasant September morning and lots of townspeople were crowding around, perhaps out of curiosity, but there was a lady standing at the bottom of the steps holding up a box of chocolates, saying sweets could speak every language.

The group consisted of 35 children, Miss Wilson, a Spanish teacher Doña Adelina Larraga, and a helper, Maria Blanco. We walked to the house as it was very near the station. We came to a park and had to walk on a few metres: Mall Park House came into sight. I thought it was really lovely. In the hallway we were met by some people who, I discovered later, were members of the committee of the colony. Among them was the Spanish Consul, Sr Izaguirre, who translated for the others.

It was a grand looking manor house: from the main door through the great hall, the floor was of lustrous marble. The girls' and the teachers' dormitories were on the first floor; the boys were on the lower floor near the kitchen. The house was set in large grounds, so we had a great deal of space to play in.

For me it was the beginning of a new, more peaceful, life, because we had hardly arrived at the colony, when I received news from my mother, and although it was only a short letter she told me we would soon be home. We started going into town, but always accompanied by Miss Wilson or the Spanish teacher. On Sunday mornings, Miss Wilson took us to an Anglican church where we were all given a Bible. Once a week they took us to the cinema, and as soon as he set eyes on us, the usher called out: "*Silencio*", and that is how we children greeted him every time, so he got stuck with the name. Two things struck me in particular when I first arrived in Scotland: seeing women wearing trousers and smoking, and then seeing men wearing the kilt.

There was a committee in charge of the colony: there were four members and they visited us once a month. When they visited they would stay for lunch and I remember they always wanted to have potato omelette that the cook made so well. Miss Wilson, the Director, was in charge. She was 50, very tall, with red hair and freckles. She had a strong character and commanded respect, but she was also loved. She was sweet and affectionate with all the children and we liked her very much. For me she provided some of the support I needed in the absence of my mother. The Spanish teacher only looked after her two daughters who had come with her, one of 12 and one of eight. She never taught even one lesson. The helper's job was cooking. She made the sort of meals we had at home and was a very good cook. She was very kind and demonstrative to everybody.

Winter came and with it the first snowfall before Christmas – it was a great event as the park was covered in a thick layer of snow, much deeper than we were used to in our country, but we enjoyed ourselves playing and having snowball fights as a way of passing the time. Then we had our first Christmas away from home and I was worried; it was seven months since our arrival and there seemed no sign of our going back. The war continued in our country and the news wasn't good.

Days before Christmas a lot of parcels started arriving from the townspeople, even from some of the shopkeepers. I had never seen so many presents in the Director's office. On Christmas Eve the little ones were sent to bed early and only we four older ones stayed up. Some people from the town arrived with a huge tree. They set it up in the dining room and we started helping putting out the boxes, which Miss Wilson had labelled individually, one for everyone. In the morning when everyone came into the dining room, it looked very pretty and you could see the pleasure on everyone's face. The little girls got beautiful dolls, the boys nice cars and everyone a happy memory. By 1938 our stay in the colony was extended and the people running it needed financial assistance, so we became involved in putting on performances to raise funds. We organised shows and made Basque costumes specially for the weavers' dance and we performed in various theatres, mainly in Dundee, Glasgow and Edinburgh.

In the summer of 1938, we had to vacate the premises for a fortnight for the use of some students. I was sent to a family in Edinburgh. They had two children, a boy of ten called John, and a girl of seven called Elisabeth. It was a very enjoyable time and they were very kind to me. One of the things I will never forget is that the family would get together after dinner to read a book for an hour. When I arrived, the father, to keep the custom going, bought me a book in Spanish; it was a play – a comedy. One evening as I was reading, I burst out laughing and he said: "I'm glad it's like that, mine is very sad."

On our return to the colony, it was back to the normal routine. It was my job to get one of the youngest washed – she was six years old – and comb her hair. In the morning after breakfast, I would wait for the postman. We had grown used to living as brothers and sisters. Life in the colony was quite boring and we had a lot of spare time. I missed having lessons. None of us had any, although we had a Spanish teacher with us for this purpose. I don't blame anybody, perhaps everyone thought we would be returning home any day, but they were two lost years in this respect. We managed to speak English through our contacts with the people, but couldn't write it – what a wasted opportunity!

The year went by and the second Christmas was similar to the first. In Spring 1939 came the news that the war was almost over, and with that the first lists of children going home. It was time for the first return journey, but I wasn't included. One day the Consul came to the colony. He told me that within a few days another group would be leaving and I was on the list, but that at my age (I was nearly 17), I could stay in Scotland. Spain was in a bad way and the post-war period would be very difficult. I had two days of mental conflict. On the one hand I did like the country. In the time I'd been there I had noticed the differences from my own: it had a higher level of education and was more advanced in everything. On the other hand, I remembered my home and parents and that my mother had asked me to stay with my two sisters. So finally I decided to return, and ten of us left in that second party.

When I left and arrived in Irún we were given lunch in the centre of the *Sección Femenina*; they treated us rather badly, calling us children of "reds". Our homecoming and the following few days were a time of great joy and happiness, but once this passed, we faced reality. Bilbao was in a bad state. The war was over but the aftermath was awful. Food was rationed and to supplement it you had to buy on the black market. I thought for a while that I had done the wrong thing in coming back, but this only lasted till I heard about the outbreak of the Second World War, which reconciled me to my return.

I started evening classes to catch up some of what I had missed, but I had to break off and start work at a dressmaker's as there were a lot of us at home and the older children had to contribute. They were difficult years up to 1943 and then things began to improve.

I have to say in conclusion that I very much appreciated the people of Scotland, their courtesy, warmth and humanity, which I have never forgotten and which have left their mark on me – for the good. The only negative thing, and I blame this on the war, was the three years education that I missed and never caught up with. *

Ernesto Grijalba Grijalba
After a few weeks at the camp in North Stoneham, I was sent to a colony in the north for boys only. It was called Harwood Dale and was near Scarborough; I stayed there until the beginning of the winter. Another colony was set up in Scarborough itself, but I was sent to Riddlesden Sanatorium in Keighley (Yorkshire). Our first job there was to prepare the centre for the maximum number of children, as it was one of the largest colonies. From there, together with four friends, we managed to get sent to another colony, Hutton Hall near Guisborough. I was there until January 1939 when I left for London, where I got a job working for a fortnightly communist periodical called *Russia Today*. My salary was one shilling a week, I think they paid for my keep. The office was in Holborn.

Apart from the fact that I was separated from my family, the memories I have of my stay are good ones. I played football, I did some acting, I made English friends, especially with Harry from Carlisle, whom I kept up with until his death four years ago.

I have several stories, the first being the impression I got when we first arrived at Southampton and saw the quayside all decorated. I thought that the flags were to greet us, and how distressed I was when I found out that they had been put up for the coronation of the new king! Another thing I shall never forget is the day Franco's troops entered Bilbao. I was having tea with some people in Eastleigh and when I returned to the camp, I was met by the murmur of voices and the sound of sobbing. It was the children, who, when they heard the news, packed their small suitcases, jumped over the fence and started walking towards Bilbao: there was no way of stopping them. That is unforgettable.

Another thing I remember was being at Hutton Hall with five other boys. As we were the oldest, and to keep us busy, we were sent to a nearby wood to cut logs, but we found something else to do there. The wood was full of rabbits, so we decided to catch them. Luckily, we found some traps in a hut which, because of their size, must have been for foxes. Several weeks went by in this way, until a gamekeeper saw us and told the police, who came to the colony. We weren't punished, although we were hunting in a reserve and in the close season. They considered it to be a childish prank, but we didn't eat any more rabbits. Oh, how tasty they were! *

María Teresa Grijalba Subirón

We sailed from the port of Santurce, in Bilbao, at the end of May 1937. There were around 4,000 of us children, with various helpers, teachers and a cook. I recall that one of the helpers was Srta Cayetana Lozano. We arrived at Southampton, all of us very seasick and escorted by British warships. We were quarantined in tents in Red Indian style, and very pretty they looked. We stayed there for a month until I was sent with 30 girls and four little boys to the town of Worthing on the Sussex coast. There we lived in a beautiful house, called Beach House. We spent several months there until we were accommodated definitively at Penstone House in Lancing, a neighbouring town.

I feel grateful to England for the warm and considerate welcome that her people extended to us. We girls were quite happy, far from the war. We were not provided for directly by the British government but by popular subscription and voluntary gifts from English friends. Nor was the Basque government involved. We didn't go to English schools because they didn't allow it. Once a week we had a German refugee, called Mrs Truman, who came, in theory, to teach us English, but she didn't speak it well herself and we couldn't understand her. For my part, I had already reached higher baccalaureate level in San Sebastián.

I decided to learn English and I read whatever magazines or books came to hand. I tried translating them into Spanish. I set myself the task of learning ten words each day. Eventually I became able to write, read and speak English well.

The Director in charge of our colony was Sra Rosa Omegna and when her husband – a specialist in the cultivation of oranges – returned from Israel, he too helped run the colony. I kept up my friendship with them over the years by letter and telephone and later, in 1984, we also visited them.

The house we lived in was beautiful, three storeys high, with a cellar and an enormous common room with a grand piano. This was where we held meetings and all sorts of activities. We started a small choir and our Spanish teacher, Felicia Velasco, who was a good pianist, conducted us. We divided up the housework and carried it out in groups. I was the bell ringer. At 6.30 every morning I rang a brass bell to wake up the girls. The cook was Spanish too, and everything she made tasted good. English people gave us clothes and we altered them to fit. It was there that I saw my first gas-fuelled washing machine. I liked the milk particularly. They gave us china mugs with pictures of the King and Queen on them. The bread was very white and spongy. I remember sending my father food parcels with chocolate and white bread, but they never arrived. He sent me books.

On Saturday mornings we walked in single file down the street to the local cinema. The beach was close by and when the weather was fine we often swam or paddled in the sea. However, we always had to carry our gas masks slung over our backs and our ration books in our pockets.

We formed a Basque dance group and made our own regional costumes. During one of the performances given to raise funds for our upkeep, I met the Duchess of Atholl, a cousin of Queen Mary. I made a speech in English, which was printed in the newspapers and presented her with a scroll which said: "In the name of all my compatriots, I ask the people of Lancing, the Mayoress of Worthing, our beloved Chairman, Mrs Barber, and all here present, to go and tell others that we, the future generation of Spain, will not forget what England has done for us."

When the colony was shut down, because Franco made many of my companions return home, I went to live with the Mayoress of Worthing until I was 18 years old. While there I was allowed to work in the hospital at Shoreham-by-the-Sea where I began to train as a nurse. I spent two months there until my parents, who were in Toulouse in France, requested my return, as they were going to leave for Mexico. I travelled to London, and from there to Dover, where I crossed to France on 17 May 1940.

It was very difficult to meet up finally with my parents and siblings. My family had been scattered for a long time. My brothers, who were four and ten years old, had sailed in September 1936 from San Sebastián to France in a fishing boat. Another brother who was eight went alone to France. Then I went to England. My mother and two elder brothers went to Belgium. Papá turned up in Barcelona.

With the help of the Red Cross, Papá located us and brought us together. However we were unable to go to America and we spent the Second World War in Toulouse. We suffered hunger, bombing and cold, all this in an unfamiliar country. At least we survived to tell the tale.

In 1949 I married a young Spanish exile and we left for Venezuela. That was 57 years ago, and now I see myself as a citizen of the world.*

Eric Hawkins

The Cambridge committee was a strong combination of "gown" and "town". It was supported by societies and clubs in the university (including the crew of one of the college boats) and in the town, who "adopted" individual children and became responsible for weekly payments for their lodging. The problem of accommodation for the children was solved at a stroke when the Rev. Austin Lee, vicar of Pampisford, some five miles south of Cambridge, offered to vacate his rectory for use as a hostel.

The Pampisford Rectory was a spacious building, set in a large garden, with useful outbuildings, but it was not in good repair. A posse of volunteers started to prepare the building in April. Most of the rooms were derelict, not having been lived in for some time. Floorboards had to be replaced, dry rot removed, windows and doors repaired. Professional help was brought in to remedy the drainage and install electric light in the top floor. Floors were stained, curtains hung, crockery and kitchen utensils laid in.

At an early stage in the planning, I was asked to be ready to move in to the hostel when the children came, as volunteer resident tutor and house-father for the children. With 30 children eating and sleeping, working and playing in the vicarage, I had to look for a classroom. I found one to dream of, in the loft over the stables, reached by an outside wooden stairway. Under the low rafters, two rows of desks ran from end to end of the loft.

Eight older boys and girls stood out clearly as more experienced than the rest, and they became the top class. Some eight or ten of the others grouped themselves as "infants", leaving a middle class of varying attainments, but workable as a class. The infants were soon shepherded away by our matron, Srta Carmen, and they set about building words with blocks and enquiring into numbers.

Our timetable began at nine o'clock, when the two junior classes began lessons, leaving the seniors to an hour's housework before joining in the morning's work in the loft. In the middle of the morning there was a half-hour break for exercises. The committee had agreed from the outset that physical training should have an important place and provided shorts and vests for the boys and sleeveless Grecian tunics for the girls. They often did their rhythmic exercises in bare feet on the lawn, and here the children, naturally graceful, made rapid progress. Then followed two more lessons before lunch at one o'clock. After lunch and an hour's "quiet time", the afternoon was usually given up to painting, music or handicrafts, with the help of a patient, devoted band of outside workers.

In the formal lessons in the morning, reading and writing were our chief care at first. Reciting verses helped to improve speaking, and when the sun was very hot, we sat under a tree with Tornor's *El Folklore en la Escuela*. Intensive study of English was postponed in the days at Pampisford because we thought that some knowledge, even if rudimentary, of the structure of Spanish ought to be acquired first (the children had been told, after all, that their stay in England was "only for three months"). With the older children a beginning was made with discussions of history and geography, though we were handicapped continuously by lack of books in Spanish which they could investigate for themselves. We had to remind ourselves continually that the pupils were acutely shell-shocked. Their minds, as Professor Ryle (chairman of our committee) said, seemed to be vibrating still from their bombing experiences, so that one could only touch their attention momentarily, as on a pendulum swing. Rest and quiet had to do their work before formal study could, as it later did, succeed. Meanwhile, we concentrated more on "interests", that part of the curriculum which occupied our afternoons.

Here the children responded at once and with great enthusiasm to the sympathy and carefully planned methods of Mrs Youngman, who inspired them to paint in a sweeping, free style with free choice of bright colours, and of Dr Hertz who gave them another outlet for their feelings in clay modelling, coloured cut-out pictures and plasticine. Expression at first was all of one kind. Bombing aeroplanes and fighters, warships and guns were painted and modelled week after week, until the war-shock began to respond to the quiet of the new surroundings. Then slowly trees and flowers began to creep in and bombs lost their interest. They began to paint their ideal homes, and to model their castles in Spain.

Music too played an important role in Pampisford. We were fortunate to have from the start the support of a fervent Republican, Rosita Bal, a young concert pianist who had the distinction of being one of the very few pupils to have studied under Manuel de Falla. She opened the lesson by playing the Republican hymn. Then followed nearly an hour and a half's concentrated work on Spanish folk songs. They learned entirely by ear. Three lessons brought the tune and words to perfection.

As soon as the curriculum and other interests were established, the obvious need for a school magazine suggested itself. A meeting of the older boys and girls carried the motion with alacrity and lost no time in inventing their own title, *Ayuda* (Help). With Mrs Youngman's encouragement a linocut was produced for the cover, showing the "help-ship" cutting through the waves.

(from Hawkins, E (1999) *Listening to Lorca*, CILT)

Eulalia Ibáñez Gómez

All the time I was in England, I was with my older sister, María Teresa. She wasn't yet ten years old and I was eight. We stayed in two colonies, Lancing and Upton, but I can't remember which one came first.

I remember the journey on the *Habana*, but not the moment we reached England. But what I'll never forget is arriving at the colony. There was a pile of dolls, and there was one for each little girl. But I wasn't allowed to get one, which made me sad. But when there were no more dolls left, they brought out a lovely one, the most beautiful of all, and to my surprise, they gave her to me, as I was one of the youngest of the children.

There was an older couple in the colony called Mr and Mrs Owen. They had two dogs, Tim and Mark. Tim was white and very friendly, Mark on the other hand, was black and had fleas. The house was very big. It had a lot of land and fruit trees, especially apple trees, whose fruit never really got ripe as we would eat the apples when they were still green.

On Fridays we would have an inspection and they would give us some coins to buy sweets with. At weekends, we would go out with local families who came for us – this happened frequently. Once, a couple took me and my sister to a department store, where we spent all day. However, when we came out, we couldn't find the car, since the husband didn't remember where he had left it! They bought my sister a lovely doll in that shop, and me a yellow teddy bear. I liked it so much that I kept it for years.

They took us to many places. I remember going to London, which I didn't like very much as it seemed very big and especially, very dirty in comparison with what I had seen of the rest of England. I also remember going to Liverpool, where we drove through a tunnel which went under the river.

I enjoyed going to the school at South Lancing. There was a teacher called Miss Peskett who was very nice to us. As I was good at drawing, I often got a red or blue star as a distinction, depending on how I'd done.

I'm not sure in which colony it was, but I remember that on Tuesdays a boy with a projector would come, and he would put on episodes of films, which we really loved. Just when the young woman was tied to the rails and the train was about to crush her, the film would stop and we'd have to wait for the following week. But the best time was when we were all taken to the cinema to see "Snow White and the Seven Dwarfs". How exciting it was to see it, with full sound and in colour!

Every Tuesday we went to the girl guides' swimming pool, and the water was freezing. Perhaps that's why we were given a biscuit as a treat when we got out of the water; my sister loved these. Until she died in 1990, she would always remember that biscuit which was waiting for her after having had a really great, but also rather cold, time.

When the Second World War began, we had to take a gas mask with us everywhere. It went into a cardboard box, which had a strap round it and which we had to wear over our clothes. If the police caught you without it, you were made to go back and fetch it. I still remember planes passing overhead, and the fire alarm practices that we had to have.

In the first colony there was a boy, one of those who looked after us, who was very fond of me. Sadly, I don't remember his name. But I do remember his coming to see me and the presents he used to give me. The day that they told us we had to go to the other colony and I realised that I wasn't going to be able to take my leave of him, I decided to look for him to say goodbye. My sister and two other girls came with me. In fact, we had no idea of where he lived, but in our naïveté we thought that we'd find him in the town. But it wasn't so easy. We left the colony without telling anyone and we started off on our way, until two policemen found us, and when they realised who we were and where we came from, they escorted us back. That was the end of the adventure, but to my chagrin I had to leave without saying goodbye to the boy who was so fond of me. *

Fidela de Juan Quintana

My brother and I, and some other children, went to the colony at Camberley where we were very well cared for. It was there that I found out what democracy was, I shall never tire of saying so. The colony was in very large country house – how I would like to see it now! It had a kitchen garden and other lovely gardens with fruit and flowers. I remember it as something magical. The house was surrounded by a huge field where we played to our hearts' content. The building was big, with fine bedrooms, the girls sleeping on one side and the boys on the other. The food was appropriate for our ages. We had a cook and a helper, and two teachers for Spanish lessons. They were Spanish. There was also an Englishwoman and an Irishwoman, who taught us English and an Irishman, who taught us chemistry. Once a team of nurses came to teach us first aid and there was also a priest for those who wanted to go to mass. Apart from them, there was a lady Director who dealt with everything else.

I have happy memories of life there because everyone got on so well. From time to time, English families would take us out on trips. For example, I was taken on holiday with a family and stayed with them for at least a fortnight. They treated me like one of the family. I kept in touch with them when I went back to Spain, and went to see them several times in London with my husband and children, until they died. My brother, who is five years younger than me, also has good memories. He was operated on for appendicitis and, according to him, he was treated with great kindness in the hospital. He returned to the colony transformed into a veritable English boy, speaking the language just like a native, although he too eventually forgot it through lack of practice. As I learned English studying grammar in formal lessons (we had good teachers), I can still get by, although I have forgotten a lot.

All my life I've remembered the experience of being exiled as a positive experience. If there is one thing I regret, it's having been separated from my family. I always think that I lost my mother when I set sail for England, because she died soon after I returned to Spain.*

Luis Lavilla San Vicente
We left Bilbao on 21 May 1937. The journey wasn't at all pleasant as I was sea-sick and had to sleep wherever I could find room. I only got better when I arrived at Southampton, because I found the kitchen and they gave me as much as I wanted to eat since I hadn't eaten at all the previous days. When we got off the boat, I was separated from my brother and was sent off with some others to shower, have a hair cut and change my clothes. From there we went to the camp.

After only a few days, I believe it was six, they announced that there was an expedition to London, so I put my name down for it. It was to Congress Hall in Clapton, which was run by the Salvation Army. A lot of us went and our behaviour wasn't anything to write home about. A few days later, a group of us were moved to Hadleigh, at the mouth of the Thames. I found my brother there and he convinced me to go with him to Diss. Whenever we went on trips, we would sing and these two songs were made up in Diss:

> In the camp at Diss
> There's a fine kitchen
> Where Lucerito cooks
> For El Chato and co
> Over there in Diss
> We've left
> Poor Lucero
> Half in love.

and

I am an elegant young man
Intrepid and gallant
My urge is to chase
After a woman
Although people call me a rogue
From Spain I came to England
After a fine Englishwoman
Fine and graceful
Like an April rose
Which perfumes the lovely day.

It was summer and the weather was fine, but when it started to change they moved us to Rollesby, near Great Yarmouth. The following change was to Tythrop House, where there was a larger group than ours already. There were girls too, and we hadn't had any with us until then. We didn't stay there very long and again we moved, this time to Faringdon. None of the Diss boys went there, on the contrary, new ones came.

At this point my life in the colonies finished and I was found a job in London in a hospital, in the path lab. The hospital was called Guy's Hospital and was near London Bridge. At the beginning, they found English families for me to stay with, first in the New Kent Road and later in Balham, but as there were then more boys like myself, we went to live in West Kensington. That is where my life in England finished. That was my last home until 12 December 1939 when I returned to Spain.

The memories I have kept of that time are very pleasant. I remember great kindnesses that I can't forget. I haven't lost any opportunity to go to England and keep hoping that I will get the chance to go again, if only for a few days. *

Colin Leakey

My mother, Frida, by 1936 abandoned by her husband Louis and living with two small children, had a circle of close academic friends. These included Jessie and Hugh Stewart at Girton Gate, Francis and Frances Cornford and my godfather Hugh Heywood, then Dean of Gonville and Caius College. Just up the road in Pepys Way lived Anna Hertz who, with her mother, had left Germany during the time of Nazism and come to England for refuge and to practise as a specialist children's doctor.

Professor Cornford's son, John, was the first British casualty of the Spanish Civil War, and by 1937 Cambridge was a place well attuned to the needs of refugees from the Basque Country and my mother and her circle of friends were a part of this awareness. Many were of a somewhat left-wing political persuasion. My mother was not, describing herself as a "mini capitalist" who had bought the house in which we lived by selling her dress allowance. It was by no means only the political left who were worried about the rise of Fascism in Germany and its spreading to Spain.

Hugh Heywood became secretary of the local Basque Children's Committee. Anna Hertz became the doctor who helped to look after any medical and care problems of the *niños*. Mrs Youngman, who was another of this circle of friends, taught them art. Most particularly perhaps, Dr and Mrs Stewart, from their large and ever-welcoming home, Girton Gate, in Huntingdon Road, Cambridge, turned their house into a sort of continuous International Centre. Jessie Stewart in particular, and her daughters Jean, Frida, Katherine and Margaret, were all active and supportive.

When it became appropriate for some of the Basque children to be repatriated and the colony closed, some of the Basques who were orphaned stayed on as members of families in the area. By now they spoke good English and were used as much to English as to Basque ways. Carmen Moreno joined our family as an additional sister and family member. My mother had by this time decided that home education was in many respects a good idea and hired governesses, both to be home helps and companions, and to teach not only my elder sister Priscilla and myself, but also quite a number of children of other friends who were away, busy doing war work, and who would share with my mother the costs of professional tuition to make home schooling possible. Carmen fitted very well into this system and lived with us until she was 16, when she went on to The Friends' School in Saffron Walden. We in turn went off to boarding schools and subsequently scattered.

Carmen never lost touch with my mother. After school she took up training in professional photography from the well-known Cambridge photographer, Lettice Ramsay, who ran the Ramsay and Muspratt Studio near St Andrew's Church. When she was older, she met and married José Mari Villegas and went back to Spain. She and other Basque friends continued to keep in touch with my mother and my sister, though less with me. She and her husband visited Cambridge several times, the last visit being, I think, when she was widowed and with her daughter Sonia.

Manuel Leceta Ortiz

A few days after arriving at Southampton, we were taken to Langham in a double-decker bus, which was the first I had ever seen of its kind. We arrived at Langham in the late afternoon and were allotted rooms according to our ages. Seeing the gardens, we were very happy, especially as there were fruit trees. Daily life for us consisted in getting up at eight and, after washing, going to breakfast. Afterwards we had lessons in Spanish and a few in English. In the afternoons, after class, we would play games.

Some days after our arrival at Langham, Franco's troops took Bilbao. They gave us the news in the dining room: there was much crying, and we left our food. That afternoon, Mr Stirling took us for a walk in the fields near the house.

Mr Stirling formed a choir and a theatre group which would put on shows in various towns. There was also a football team which would play against local English teams. In the evenings, we would have music and dancing until it was time to go to bed. On Sundays, we were given pocket money according to our age, which gave us great pleasure. At the beginning we would mix with the English boys through the fence, until we got bolder.

My sister and I spent the Christmas and summer holidays for the two years we were in England in Watford, at the home of Mr and Mrs Russell and Eva Hartley. For Christmas 1938, they surprised us by inviting two more siblings from a colony in Oxford, because it just happened that we all used to go to school together. Their names were Mª Angeles and Santiago Elorza.

In 1939 my sister and I were returning to Colchester on the train from the Christmas holiday, in the care of the train inspector. We discovered when we arrived at Colchester that there was no bus to Langham that day. A couple who were nearby offered to take us, as they had to go near the colony on their way home.

Later, in 1989, my sister and I went to visit Langham, and as we were waiting to go there, a lady approached us and signalled us to get in her car and she drove us there. She explained why. She showed us a photograph of both of us sitting on a horse and one of us which had been taken one day when we had been invited to tea at her house.

It was also very emotional for me when I met Srta Celia again. I didn't know that she had returned to Bilbao. I recognised her on a bus. We now celebrate the Langham *niños* at an annual meal. I kept up with Leonard Read until his death.

I would like to put on record that the English behaved magnificently towards us. *

Valeriana Llorente Guerrero

1936, what a significant date for the Spanish people, and for thousands of Spanish children, to save them from the bombings and poor nutrition.

I was separated from my parents, my brothers and young friends, and I was only ten years old. My town, Portugalete, stayed behind, with its hanging bridge which has just been declared a national heritage site. Portugalete, with its splendid square and bandstand where the band played every Saturday and people danced. On Fridays, the country people would come to sell their produce, fresh fruit and vegetables, eggs and also chickens.

Going to England implied a very great change for all of us children – a very different country, different people and a strange language. Today I sometimes stop and think: "How did we so readily accept such a deep change to our young lives?" Some of us were luckier than others, many others had a very bad time. I didn't stay long in Stoneham. Together with the ten girls in my tent I was taken to the colony at Langham near Colchester, to a large house with some fine gardens, and with some very kind adults who would look after the 50 to 60 children who lived there.

In Langham I made some very good friends. Tere, Mariluz, Luisa and Berta were sisters, Asunción, Begoña and Aurora too. Some of these friendships lasted a long time. (We separated in 1939 and in 1946 I met up with some of them again.) How loving our dear teachers, Celia and Berta Echevarría, were to us! I remember Otto, who used to repair our shoes, and Leonard Read, the Director, with his red beard, such a good man, always kind to the children.

In the summer of 1938 I got to know the people who had been taking care of my education, the Streatham group of the Peace Pledge Union. These groups declared themselves against war and against participation in war. That same summer, I went on holiday to the lady I called Auntie Bee's house. She also belonged to the Streatham branch of the PPU. She had two older children who both went out to work. Mary, her daughter, was unmarried. I don't know what sort of work Phillip did. They lived in a lovely house in a part of London called Norbury. Auntie Bee treated me very kindly. She had beehives in her garden and used to harvest her own honey. As I write, I can see her wearing her hat with its special net to protect her from the bees. How did we understand one another? Well, I'm not sure, as my knowledge of English was very limited. The main thing is that I feel very grateful to all the good people of the Streatham PPU. They generously paid for me to go to a private school for six months. There I learned to speak better English, and also to play the piano. In a concert for the parents, I played a piece called *The Wind in the Trees*. Music is the same as cycling, one never forgets it.

I returned to Langham, I'm not sure for how long, but before the beginning of the Second World War, I went to live with another family from the same PPU group, Mr and Mrs King. They had two girls, Barbara, who was younger than me, and Eileen who was older. There was also a son called John. I went to Streatham Secondary School, an all-girls' school, with Barbara and Eileen. I was getting to know much more English, or so I thought. Mrs King was like a mother to me. She was also a very fine cook and used to make delicious desserts. I was very happy with this family. They were good sorts.

The Second World War brought about more changes. I was 13 and in 1940 they evacuated our school to Chichester in Sussex, because of the bombings in London. We were all given a gas mask and taught how to use it. I don't recall my feelings then, but I must have been confused. In Chichester, I was put with a young couple, Mr and Mrs Sweet, who were kind to me. They had a little girl, and I went to school and got on with my studies.

When the school went back to London, I went to live with my third family, Mrs Dignassa, her son David and daughter Muriel, both over 40 and neither of them married. Muriel, or "Minky" as I called her, had lost her boyfriend during the war and I think that I was like a daughter for her. What is sure is that she wanted to adopt me, but my parents didn't give their consent.

With this family's backing, and I shall always be grateful to them, I was able to enrol in the same school that I had been attending since 1939. I soon took secretarial and accounting courses, which enabled me to get good jobs.

I had lost contact with the people from my colony and I no longer spoke Spanish, so much so that my letters to my parents were in English and they had to get them translated. My sister saw to this problem by sending me the address of a Basque boy, Antonio Tudela. I went to see Miss Picken and I finally met up with many of the Basque children of 1937, among them friends from my colony at Langham.

More important for me, I met Rafael, my husband, and we had two children, Rubén and Raimundo. Rafael and I both came over on the *Habana* and London brought us together. We managed to make a go of it, without our parents' support; we had our problems, but then also many happy times.

We are part of a large family – the Basque children of '37. *

Eduardo López Sanz

Parting from one's family was sad that day in May 1937, so was the weather, as I remember that it was raining. I was going on the expedition to England, together with my brother Alberto, who was two years older than me. I had just had my tenth birthday and he was going to be 13 in August. I even remember our expedition numbers: his was 2500 and mine 2501. Also going on this trip was a neighbour of ours called Delfino del Olmo. All of us lived in Urioste, a town within the municipality of Ortuella, in Vizcaya.

While we were waiting on the quayside and until we got on the boat, we were with our mothers. They were hugging us, crying and sobbing, as is natural in such circumstances, because nobody knew what lay in store for us. These moments of waiting and embarkation can be clearly seen in a documentary film made at the time and in which the three of us appear with our mothers.

Once we were on the boat, we found another boy on the deck who was alone and crying. My brother Alberto comforted him and persuaded him to stay with us, and so we were together for the whole trip and for all of our stay in England. His name was Gumersindo González and he lived in Uribarri-Bilbao.

I don't remember anything about the crossing, possibly because I was seasick all the time. I only remember that it took two and a half days to go from the port of Santurce to the English port of

Southampton. When we disembarked, they took us to a camp not far from there, all 4,000 of us, plus teachers and some priests. We stayed in this camp for approximately three months, until they sent us to different parts of the country. We were very lucky, as 40 of us boys and girls were sent to Guildford, in Surrey.

We would get up at eight every morning. If it was fine, the first thing we did was to go for a walk on the outskirts of the town. If it was rainy, we'd do some gym in the colony. Afterwards it was breakfast and then a few hours of lessons. After lunch we had to have a siesta. In the afternoon we'd go for a walk in the town or stay playing in the garden, football, or cycling and many other games. On Fridays we were invited to a gym and on Saturdays, we went to the Odeon cinema in Guildford to see the film that was showing that week.

On Sunday mornings we were taken to mass in a crocodile, and we went for walks in the afternoon. In the summer, they used to take us to a swimming pool in the suburbs of Guildford, which was called the Lido and which was very fine. We were also lucky enough to spend a week on holiday at the seaside.

As well as all this, we were taught to sing and dance our own traditional dances and we would put on shows for the British public. One of these shows took place in a theatre in Kent and during the interval they gave out a magazine about the war in Spain. We learned all about this, as there were two ladies who told us all about it. One of these was a helper whose job it was to look after all our things: her name was Purificación Vela. The other one was a teacher called Juanita Aizpuru. She married an Englishman who looked after all of us and whose name was Mr Jenkins.

We stayed in Guilford for approximately two years. Then we were moved to another colony in Camberley, Aldershot. There were rather a lot of children at that colony and it wasn't as good as the previous one. But my brother Alberto and three other friends, as they were then 14 years old, were found jobs and they didn't have to be moved because they earned a salary that they could live off. The four of them were quite involved in the boy scout movement, but my brother, not wanting me to go back to Spain alone, decided to go back with me.

We went back on 15 December. We crossed the English Channel and followed the coast of France until we got to Hendaye, where we got off. Then we crossed the international bridge at Irún. I thought the sky had fallen in when I saw how much destruction and filth there was. Poverty everywhere. We spent that night in a school in Fuenterrabía, and the next day we caught a train which took us to Bilbao where our family was waiting.

To end this short account of my memories of such an exceptional and important time for us, I would like to say that words can't express the gratitude and admiration that I feel for the British people, for all their effort and work looking after us, and for the love they gave us.*

Pilar Magdalena Iglesias

I arrived at Southampton when I was 11, together with my sister Julia, who was 15 and brothers Fermín, 14, and Federico, seven. After a short while, Julia, Federico and I were transferred to Hutton Hall in Guisborough. A brother and sister, Maurice and Carmen Short, who were of Spanish descent, came with us from Southampton. Maurice was in charge of the boys and Carmen was to look after the girls.

As the committee at Hutton Hall had decided to keep families together, Fermín joined us, together with my cousin Pepe. As Federico was so young, he was fostered with a family almost immediately, so just the three of us and Pepe stayed at Hutton Hall until the beginning of the Second World War.

About 30 girls and boys, all from Bilbao, lived at Hutton Hall. It was a huge place, very grand, and I was put into a room with five other girls. I was quite excited about living in such a grand place, especially after having lived in a tent in Southampton. All children under the age of 12 went to school. This was in the dining room, which every morning was turned into a schoolroom. As I had just turned 12, I had to help with the chores. I helped in the kitchen and stayed there all the time I was in Hutton Hall. Cook took a shine to me and I enjoyed helping her, although the hours were long and the work heavy. Other girls worked in the laundry, washing, ironing and mending clothes. The boys did the heavy work of keeping fires going, chopping wood and gardening.

In order to help pay for our upkeep we would hold sales. The girls would embroider and knit and the boys would make wicker baskets. We also held concerts. Ruth Pennyman, who was on the committee, lived at Ormesby Hall, and she used to arrange them. We made flamenco dresses for the concerts and would dance and sing traditional songs. We were very imaginative and would make bullfighter outfits and even stage mock bullfights. We would also pick daffodils or snowdrops and sell them to the audience to make extra money.

At the weekends, people would come to help and take some of us children out for the day. They also gave us clothes which we were able to alter and wear. Doris and Frances Oates were two sisters in their early twenties who used to come and visit us. They would leave sixpence for me and a few other children, so we could get the train to Middlesbrough and back. Once there we would have tea with them and their parents. Sometimes Doris used to take us to the seaside or to the cinema. It was a lovely treat, and these sisters also collected funds for us. They were so kind, nothing was too much trouble for them. I have had a lifelong friendship with both the Oates sisters. Frances' daughter was my bridesmaid, together with Doris. Sadly Frances died, but Doris and I are still in contact with each other, although her health is not very good now.

At the beginning of the Second World War, Hutton Hall was commandeered by the army and, sadly, we were all split up. Those who were able to went back to Bilbao, including my cousin Pepe. Our little family was unable to go back as our parents were in France in a refugee camp. My sister Julia eventually married Maurice Short, who had looked after the boys, and they had a happy long life together. My sister Julia and brother Fermín have since died. I remain in contact with Federico and we are the only two still alive, living in the North East who went to Hutton Hall.

(Transcribed by Maria Jusis, daughter. Pilar died in 2007)

Enriqueta Maíz Esteban

I was 15 years old and lived in Bilbao la Vieja with my parents and my two younger sisters, Carmen and Felisa. When the Spanish Civil War began in 1936, I had already left school. My father was a lorry driver. The authorities (the elected Republican government) had requisitioned the lorry and as a *miliciano* he was posted to Aloeta, a tiny village, where he lodged at the priest's house, with four others. Franco's troops had already advanced to Vitoria and my father's mission was to keep the *milicianos* at the front supplied with food and ammunition.

One day, my father came home for a short visit. I found it very odd the way he kept sniffing his hands all the time and I asked him the reason. What he then told my mother and me was horrendous. On the previous day, a Sunday, he had finished his deliveries at the front and returned to Ochandiano. It was a beautiful sunny afternoon and the population had been enjoying the *paseo* – an evening stroll. An aeroplane approached which they thought was "one of ours" dropping goodies. Great excitement quickly turned to horror as bombs exploded in the middle of the square. The destruction of houses, the sight of bodies everywhere, was frightening. The wounded were assisted by the luckier ones who had escaped the onslaught. My father and other helpers began to load the lorry with dead bodies and dismembered limbs. The smell of blood, he said, wouldn't go away from his hands, however much he washed them – hence the constant sniffing.

Felisa, my youngest sister, was so petrified that she became unwell. She'd heard that children were being evacuated to France and wouldn't give my mother any peace until she consented to let her go. The bombing became more frequent and destructive and casualties were great. I heard that children were now being evacuated to England and it didn't take much persuasion for our parents to give their consent to our evacuation. For me, it was not so much the danger that propelled me as the thought of three months' holiday and the chance to visit another country. What a thrill! A chance not to be missed! To my shame and regret, I didn't give much thought to my very dear mother's sentiments and sorrow. The thought that I might never see her again never crossed my mind.

Boarding the *Habana*, Carmen and I lost each other and with so many children it was impossible to find her again. When we arrived at Southampton, we were put into groups and filed in one by one for a medical examination. There I was reunited with Carmen, but it was a very traumatic meeting. At the medical she was found to have a head full of lice and her lovely long hair had been shaved off. At the sight of me she burst into uncontrollable tears and all she could ask was what would Mamá say if she were to see her now, when her last words to us had been to look after our hair and keep it clean.

Coaches arrived and we were driven away and eventually arrived at a huge encampment full of large tents. I remember that one night, after a beautiful sunny, hot day, we were woken up by an almighty thunderstorm and strong wind. Suddenly, the tent collapsed on top of us. Reassuring the children, I gathered them up and, just as we were, we ran like mad to one of the marquees. The storm didn't last too long, but at dawn we could see the chaos the storm had left behind. Not many tents remained standing.

Carmen and I wrote letters to our parents but received no reply. We'd been at the camp for a month when we were instructed to gather our belongings. Forty one children and two helpers boarded the bus to Aston in Oxfordshire. We couldn't believe our eyes at the sight of the beautiful big house that was to be our home. We alighted from the coach and entered the large hall, from which an imposing wide staircase led to the floor above.

Two members of the Basque Children's Committee were there to bid us welcome. Pili Merodio introduced herself. We hadn't seen each other before, but the name Merodio was well-known in Bilbao and her sister lived almost next door to us. We didn't know the teacher. The committee took us on a tour of inspection of the house, which was very spacious. On the ground floor were two large rooms, a dining room and a living room. The kitchen, scullery and a small retiring room led from the hall. Upstairs, there was a passage the length of the house from which two equally sized rooms, matching those downstairs, formed two dormitories. These were furnished with mattresses on the floors, covered with red blankets, provided by the Witney blanket factory (bedsteads arrived later). There were also three single bedrooms and a large bathroom. Outside was a large garden with fruit trees. For us children, used to living in high flats with small rooms, it was luxury indeed.

From that day onwards it was a case of getting used to the place, getting to know each other and learning to live together. Someone from the village had been engaged to come every day to cook meals, but she didn't last long. We didn't like her cooking, and even less the cigarette dangling from her lips as she worked. So Pili became our cook. There was no piped water to the house, but a hand pump installed in the scullery was used to raise water to fill a tank in the attic. Two young lads from the village came in handy for this task, and also to cut the grass. My job was to look after the young ones, help them dress and wash. The older ones were in charge of making the beds and keeping the bedrooms clean.

We hadn't been at Aston long when Pili and I realised that the teacher was a liability rather than a help. So Pili had a word with Mrs Dalgleish from the committee and the teacher left. I started taking morning school lessons for the younger ones. Only one thought marred our existence – no letter or news from our parents. It was always tomorrow, tomorrow.

We had great attention from the outside world. Organisations such as the Womens' Institute, Toc H and the Rotary Club organised tea parties where our children entertained the local children with Basque songs and dances. Children from Witney began to visit on their bicycles.

Days and weeks passed and finally one morning a letter arrived from my mother. It was a very short letter. She said she had obtained our address by calling at the Spanish Embassy in Barcelona. She gave no news of Papá. We wrote back by return. Two, three weeks went by and we received a second letter, which I opened with a sense of dread. Her heart and soul were contained in that letter. When Franco had entered Bilbao, my parents had already left – first to Santander and on to Gijón in Asturias. Franco's troops advanced, destroying by air, bombing everything on their way. My mother had been staying in a flat and my father arrived to pick her up in the lorry. As she was running down the stairs she heard an explosion and when she arrived at the doorway she was confronted by my father's bleeding dead body. She related how she had cradled his head and prayed to God to send another bomb to take her as well. Tears are running down my face as I write this 69 years later. We idolised our father and to him we were all four his "harem". Reading that letter nearly destroyed me. I couldn't eat, I couldn't sleep, and I understand that for a month I was a cause of great concern to all around me. But I was young, and gradually began to recover.

In September, the children started going to school, the under 11s to the village school and those over 11 to school in Witney. My sister Carmen was very artistic and she was placed at the Oxford School of Art. The remaining three older ones were of great help in the running of the colony.

I must pay tribute to our fantastic committee: Mrs Lee, wife of the Witney ironmonger, Mrs List, the butcher's wife, Mrs Dalgleish, the doctor's wife and last but not least Rosemary and Patrick Early of the Witney blanket-making family. Mrs Dalgleish used to arrive in a beautiful green Riley; Patrick was a young man in his early thirties and he owned a large black saloon car.

One of our most memorable outings was to the Morris Motors factory, where we had all been invited to a tea party. We were warmly welcomed by William Morris – later Lord Nuffield – who took us on a tour of inspection. First call was the paint shop, where car bonnets, doors and wings were being dipped in vats of paint and lifted up to drip dry. On then to a very large conveyor belt where the wheels and other parts were being fitted to the chassis. Next to the sewing machine shop, where the seat covers were made and fitted. As the conveyor continued on its journey the engine, steering wheel, brakes and seats were added and by the time it reached its final destination a driver was waiting to take the car out for its test run. As for us, after such a wonderful experience, we were herded into the canteen for a lovely English tea.

Months went by, and one day a young woman called Cora Blyth arrived at Aston. She was an enchanting young Scottish lady from Kircaldy, and we took to her like ducks to water. Older than I was, she became my English tutor. To Pili, who was about the same age as Cora, she became a great friend and helper. Cora remained at Aston and later at Witney with the Basque children until they were finally repatriated or found other homes. It was at Aston that Cora met Luis Portillo, a Spanish university lecturer who was also a political target of Franco. They later married and one of their children is the former Conservative minister, Michael Portillo.

One of the Aston girls, Mauri, and my sister Carmen went to live in London. Carmen met and later married another of the Basque evacuees, Jesús Alcón. Teodoro, Mauri's brother, and I remained in Witney. The Second World War broke out and, like every other young single woman, I had to do my share of war work. My job was at the Witney uniform factory of Compton and Webb, where we produced all kinds of caps and headgear for British, and even Russian, troops. In 1941 I married a Witney lad and my daughter Carmen was born in 1943. I now have three grandchildren and ten great-grandchildren aged from three months to 15 years. My youngest granddaughter now lives in southern Spain with her husband and three children!

As for my much-loved mother, we never heard from her again, and we have no idea what happened to her after she reached Barcelona. We know that ships carrying refugees from Spain to France were bombed, and we can only surmise that this may have been her fate. Sadly, my sister Carmen died in 1947, six months after giving birth to her son Marcos, and I looked after the baby until his father remarried three years later. My youngest sister, Feli, had a rather unhappy time in France, being treated as a servant by the people she stayed with, but when the Second World War broke out, she was repatriated to Bilbao, eventually marrying and having two daughters. Her husband died last year, but she has a large family to comfort her.

So that is my story. It has its happiness and its tragedy but, along with all those who either returned to Spain or remained in England, I will never forget our happy Aston colony.

Leonor Marcos Prieto

I was born on 1 February 1925, in Erandio, Vizcaya, the eldest of four children. When the war broke out, we moved to Bilbao. The advancing battle lines and the dreadful Fascist bombings compelled my parents to send their two oldest children, Mari Carmen, who was ten, and me to England. Papá, Mamá and the two younger children stayed behind in Bilbao, suffering the war, the bombings and the threats on my father owing to his intellectual inclinations and socialist leanings.

Our parting took place on a beautiful and clear morning, one of the best that spring. Nevertheless, it was very sad because all the families had to bid farewell to their children. We travelled by train from Bilbao to Santurce. I can remember the harrowing cries and tears at the train station. What a terrible parting! Would we ever see our beloved families again? At first, Mari Carmen and I, innocent as we were, thought it was fun, although, when the time came to leave our parents and brothers and sisters, everything became terrible. This is something I will never forget, no matter how many years go by.

We finally boarded the *Habana*, and when we arrived at Southampton we were taken from the port to a camp in Stoneham. We spent 22 days there, and I must say we had quite a good time. Then we were sent to different colonies all over England. We went first to Thame, in Oxfordshire, together with 50 girls. We certainly had a wonderful time there. We were very well looked after. Our every wish was immediately fulfilled, the volunteers tried to cheer us up to forget the sadness of the past. There I became familiar with the noble heart of the English people. I will never forget the townspeople, especially, Mrs Michaelis, our Director and protector. During the summer, after our *siesta*, we would go to the surrounding fields and gardens, where English children welcomed us to join in their games as if we were part of their families.

I remember a naughty thing I did there. There were machines in the local shop where you got sweets when you put in money. I had a Spanish coin which I put in, in the full knowledge that I wouldn't get either sweets or my money back. Then I went into the shop and told the lady who was serving that I had put my money in and had got nothing in return. She asked if I had put Spanish money in, and I answered "No." So the poor lady had to give me back something that wasn't mine.

The first journey I ever made to London was while I was in Thame. I travelled there for the first time. I was very impressed with that magnificent city, the greatest in the world, enormously populated, with tall buildings and large stores with several levels. This was a city with a lot of traffic, especially double-decker buses which, as I had never seen them before, greatly impressed me. What surprised me most, nevertheless, was that, around three o'clock in the afternoon, the fog was so intense that it was impossible to tell one person from another, however close they might be. The traffic had to stop, because it was impossible to continue driving.

We lived in Thame for seven months until, after the first Christmas there, on the Feast of the Holy Innocents, we were told the sad news: the colony was closing and we were to be sent to other colonies. We were transferred to a really beautiful place – Langham, near Colchester. We were certainly very comfortable there. It was a beautiful house, with a large garden and fruit trees, especially apple trees, whose fruit we used to eat directly from the tree. We were treated very well, and the food was delicious and abundant. My sister and I were assigned to foster parents who visited regularly. We were very lucky because they were wonderful people, treating us as their real daughters. The little news we had from home and the war, unfortunately, was usually bad and troubling.

My foster parents, the Purlings, were a young couple, recently married, living in Norwich, and they came to see me periodically. My sister's foster parents, the Clarks, were a childless couple, about 50 years old, who loved her very much. We kept in touch with our foster parents well after the war in Europe was over, corresponding many years later, when we were in Mexico, until one day the letters stopped coming. I remember the Purlings specially fondly, and I would love to know what became of them.

Later we were transferred to Margate, a fine and pleasant city, as well as one of the most elegant in England, with the largest beach I had ever seen. I cannot say we had a bad time at this colony but, for the first time since we arrived, we were living with people who were a bit distant and cold compared to our previous experience. Where were our beloved señoritas Peque, Gloria, Elena and Virginia?

The lack of warmth we encountered in comparison with our experiences at Thame and Langham, as well as the scarcity of food, made it difficult for us to enjoy our stay there. Moreover, since the Anglican Church supported us, we had to go to mass every Sunday.

After the war in Spain was over and England entered the European conflict, we went back to Bilbao. During those years my father had been imprisoned when he returned to Bilbao from Barcelona, denounced by someone he thought was a good friend. He was accused of being a "red" and for owning many books. He was freed almost a year later, helped ironically by a captain in the Civil Guard who had known him years ago and who spoke up on his behalf before his situation became even more difficult.

Shortly after our return, we went to live in San Sebastián for nearly two years. We returned to Bilbao, but we were frightened by the persecution of my father and the pressures he was under, so we decided to seek exile in Mexico, leaving Spain on 10 June 1947. We disembarked in New York and travelled on a Greyhound bus to Mexico City, where we arrived on 3 July.

In Mexico we were welcomed by one of my mother's brothers and began a new life. We made new friends and I met and married José Ángel Gutiérrez Sánchez, who was a surgeon and with whom I had a wonderful marriage. Together we raised eight children, three girls and five boys until 1977, when suddenly and painfully, my beloved husband died of severe leukaemia. Today I have a large and wonderful family, with 19 grandchildren and one great-grandson.

Now, after so many years, I realise that my roots are planted in three places. The Basque Country of my birth; England that took care of me during the Spanish Civil War and, of course, Mexico, the wonderful place that welcomed me with open arms and that has given me so much.

Unfortunately, on the other hand, I am sad and disappointed to see how the same mistakes of those years are being made all over again in the world and how injustice still prevails. I keep hoping that one day we will learn to live in peace and strive for the well-being of all.

I would like to send greetings to all the girls and boys who left as refugees to go to England. Also, my deep appreciation to Natalia Benjamin for making this effort to record some of our stories but, most of all, for her wonderful mother, whom I remember very fondly.
*

Javier Martínez Castillo

I arrived in England with my two brothers, José Mari and Tirso. We came from a very poor family in Bilbao, from the Barrio Ochurdinaga, near Santuchu. We came to England on a ship, the *Habana*, with 4,000 other Spanish boys and girls. I don't remember the trip very well, as I was only ten at the time and very frightened, but it was a rough voyage and when we reached England, we were taken to a massive camp full of tents. I don't remember much of the camp either, but I do recall that one day, when I was inside the tent resting my head on the canvas, somebody hit me with a mallet and I was taken to the "hospital" in the camp!

From Southampton, my brothers and I went to a colony called Bray Court in Maidenhead. From there, in 1938, we moved to another colony in Brighton. A year later, my brothers and I were separated. I was fostered out to a family in Coventry (with Mr and Mrs Keeley), along with another Spanish boy named Pepito. On the day we left, we were put on the train to Victoria Station in London, where we were met by Miss Picken, who was the secretary of the Basque Children's Committee. She was a very kind lady and she put us on the right train to Coventry. When we arrived in Coventry, Mr and Mrs Keeley were waiting for us at the station and took us to their nice semi-detached house. I have fond memories of my time with them. I went to an English school for the first time. I didn't know how to speak English, so it was hard for me to communicate with everyone.

When the Spanish Civil War ended, Pepito was claimed by his parents. I had to stay on my own with the Keeleys as my parents had escaped to France with my young brother Valentín. My parents had a bad time under the German occupation of France, which lasted five years. They never returned to Spain and both died in France.

In the meantime, I was still in Coventry. Mr Keeley was a very keen rambler and used to take me on walks with the club, which I enjoyed enormously. In 1940, when the Germans bombed Coventry, the Keeleys decided it wasn't safe for me to stay with them, so they took me to the Barnet colony in Hertfordshire. I stayed in Rowley Lodge for about two years and joined in many activities with the Spanish children. In Barnet we were bombed out again and had to go to a temporary home called Cambrian Lodge while Rowley Lodge was being repaired.

When Rowley Lodge closed I was transferred to The Culvers in

Carshalton, the last colony to stay open in England. There I was reunited with my older brother, José Mari, whom I had not seen for years. My younger brother, Tirso, was fostered by Mr Polling in Brighton and he was there for many years.

I was happy at The Culvers. By now I was 14 and had started work in a garage in Cheam, Surrey, but I was evacuated to Perth in Scotland with our cook, Mrs Somerset, who came from there. She was a nice lady and she took care of us. I was there for two months and worked for Pullens of Perth, a dry cleaning company. From Perth, we moved back to Carshalton, and then I went with my friend, Herminio Martínez, to work on a farm in Colchester for a year. After Colchester, in 1945, I went to live in Reigate, Surrey. Mr West, who was involved with the Basque children at The Culvers, found me work and lodgings. I was very happy and worked for five years alongside my friends, Miguel Larraz and Tomás Martínez, making Multico saws. It was a good period in my life.

From Reigate I moved to London, which I didn't like so much, as I have always enjoyed the countryside environment. Here I met up with many Basque friends. At a *verbena vasca* held in the Firs School, Notting Hill Gate, I met my lovely wife, Josefa, and this changed my life. She was from Jerez in Andalusia. We married in 1954 and after a year in London, we moved to Luton, where we have been for 45 years. We have three children, two boys and a girl, and four grandchildren.

Thanks to Mr and Mrs Keeley, I joined the local group of the Ramblers' Association, the South Beds Ramblers. This was the best period in my life, as with them I visited many countries, including Spain.

All I all, I have had a good life in England and have no regrets. England has been good to us and now we are a couple of old codgers, we have more time for arguments!

José María Martínez Castillo

1937 – North Stoneham Camp, Eastleigh

Concentration of 4,000 Basque children plus medics and boy scouts in an encampment forest of tents we three brothers José María Javier and Tirso sheltered protected by a mesh wire barrier enclosing this vast open field camp which during the best part of our stay was pelting with rain consequently forming floodwater inundating our tents habitation with mattresses becoming rafts under our bodies reminding me of the Atlantic Ocean crossing from Santurce to Southampton in that overcrowded *Habana* liner epic voyage rough passage sea sickness and tears through the Bay of Biscay on hungry stomachs lamenting the departure from the bomb stricken homeland

Not far away from North Stoneham an airfield which flying aircraft made noises murmurous like those German bombers that scattered firebombs from the sky on Guernica – Bilbao bringing flashback memories of insecurity to this green lonely landscape and yet the camp was swarming with children but then I was a loner and had witnessed the devastation starvation of the siege in Bilbao for one year...the worst was when they announced the surrender to the Fascist troops our hearts were downtrodden and there was a silent gloom at North Stoneham camp the black clouds of doom soon manifested in each child's face "what about our parents?" this soul rendering agony was contagious throughout the camp whilst thinking of our families left behind in despair and wondering what had become of their children in such a remote island far away from the motherland Euskadi

1937 – Baydon Hole Farm and Army Barracks

This farmyard was our next move from Eastleigh Southampton chickens ducks geese pigs cows dogs they cut our hair no more irritating fleabites our bodies dipped in a tub to be sterilized then scrubbed in case of measles which was a repetition experience at Stoneham camp medical examination and they decided to set fire to all our luggage with sentimental contents from Spain...I can still smell the smelly cow dung heaps of this long ago farmyard recurring periodically in my lifespan specially at night that odour through the barracks dormitory was overpowering to my nostrils ever since some stinking perfume

1937 – Bray Court Maidenhead

The most luxurious hotel home that we three brothers encountered meanwhile and possibly the biggest most populated Basque children's colony ever in the UK realm this Victorian mansion built in the 1800s by the John Haig Whisky Family took four years to build it has 365 windows one for each day of the year fabulous skirting gardens with tennis courts encircled by a fringe of trees an idyllic bliss for the multitude of Basque children inhabiting its spectacular splendour and facilities for learning dancing in the open grounds eating traditional English succulent dish-ups at dinner time marvelling lifestyle after the Civil War traumatic experiences in Bilbao – Euskadi 1936-1937 annihilation bombardment

Sometimes Anglo-Spanish benefactors would come to Bray Court and pick up children for day outings in their cars and often coach loads which was most enjoyable high tea trips and walks around Windsor close by this impression gave me a taste for the leisure and pleasurable tranquillity of English living standards in the late 1930s akin to pastoral infant pastimes in my mountain pueblo of Navarra somehow the future was non-existent in those formative years in Albion for there was a calmness of spirit within this luscious panorama which is England and tolerant society host to us Basque children with serene feelings forthcoming from the people

1938 – Girton House Brighton

Down from Maidenhead to Sussex seaside once again linking ocean waters to memories floating from Spanish soil relativity that knowledge is not absolute but conditional subconsciously by the umbilical cord remote memoranda which connects the cerebral wavelength to memories past-present-future…at this home by the sea ozone pungent invigorating air we went swimming often or laid on the pebbles sunbathing and sometimes Padre Don Cirilo would treat us to tea at Lyons Corner House across the main seafront thoroughfare

Eventually the home closed down and we three brothers separated Tirso went to live with Dick Polling active organizer of Girton House altogether he fostered five Basque children and my foster father Charles Gildersleve took me to live with his family at Hove Poplar Avenue Javier sent north to Coventry…my gratitude abounds for the generosity of Mr Gildersleve (inventor engineer) his wife and daughter for it was while living with them that I attended Hove Grammar School my first tuition in English began with parental care that followed and intimate family life tenderness that was absent previously unfortunately it was reaching the Second World War climax and towards the snow winter of 1939 they decided to transfer me to the safety of The Culvers Carshalton

1940 – 1946 The Culvers, Surrey

With the Second World War in full swing I landed in this Victorian home The Culvers Surrey amongst many Basque children inmates and strange encounter after being secluded sociable at Hove colony Sussex though the staff were welcoming Mrs Somerset Miss Vulliamy Mrs Temple Mari Cruz and Pepe great community administrators idealists all inspiring cooperation from the household's Basque children and beloved for their attentive attitudes towards our loyal behaviour and respecting their wisdom

In this Carshalton domicile stayed six adolescent years and was the most diffused cultural dynamic aesthetic awakening apart from the constant incendiary bombings by the Nazis and the ferocious Battle of Britain above the sky beneath the homes cellar shelter tremor each time the anti-aircraft batteries fired and the same tortured agony as the Guernica – Bilbao sleepless nights of bombs thunder then buzz-bombs plus A1 A2 rockets five years of it from Hitler and three years of it from Franco eight abominable years of wars by the time I was 19 – 1945 crazy world of man's massacre and self destruction evermore hostile world warfares

The only consolation was some frequent correspondence with my new USA foster mother and daughters through the Foster Parents' Plan (Women's International League for Peace and Freedom) 1940-1947 the Rose Comora family then a scholarship from the Juan Luis Vives Trust to study art at the Croydon Art School 1942-1945 this helped to alleviate tormenting blitz psycho traumatic war years cycling to school four times a day passing by Croydon Airport with dogfights above and bullets whizzing by like arrows while riding on bike and returning home along Beddington Park ... rationing of food another problem and coupons for clothes besides incendiary bombs we used to put out with dustbin lids when they rainfell on the front lawn of the Culvers house by the river Wandle mind you the tutorial supervision of Pepe and Chloë made this last residential Basque colony the most talented tuitional progressive enterprise that I have experienced in my six years domicile also a creative resourceful period in my formative years erudition holding my first exhibition at The Spanish Institute 58 Princess Gate London SWI in 1944 followed by other shows at the Archer Gallery Westbourne Grove London W11 1946-1951 and many one man exhibitions in the West End to 1993 Sculpture Paintings Drawings which had been my constant driving force since I was born April 1926 and believe it's the only remains of civilization's final achievement from history-prehistoric times since origin of species ... all this and poetry too running parallel with 69 years exile I came I saw I stayed ad interim and in 2007 our 70th Anniversary Expatriated in UK survival's last refuge-aftermath-1936-1946-2006–2007

(José María died in 2009)

Álvaro Martínez Olaizola

Álvaro came to England with his older sister María Luisa. The oldest sister escaped to France with his mother after his father was killed fighting against Franco. After being at the camp for a little while, they were taken to Pampisford, to a vicarage just outside Cambridge. There were 29 children altogether. The younger children were taught in the vicarage by professors and students from the university. After a few months, the children had to leave and went to Salisbury Villas, in Station Road, Cambridge, which was leased to the Basque Children's Committee by Jesus College. They learned to sing and dance and gave concerts to earn money for their keep.

All the children thought that the Spanish Civil War would soon be over and that they would be returning to Spain. When the Second World War broke out, the children were on holiday in Hunstanton and they had to return to Cambridge. Álvaro was very lucky as he was taken in by a family, Mr and Mrs Stearn, who had two boys of their own and treated him like a son. Dad Stearn was head gardener for a titled family in Cambridge and he used to take Álvaro to the gardens, where he learnt about being a gardener. Álvaro also went to school in Cambridge, but found it difficult to learn the language. However, he managed to get by.

His greatest wish was to see London, so he left Cambridge and went there, where he got to know many of the Basque *niños* from other groups, and from his own group, as they often shared the same rented accommodation. After a while he found work in an engineering firm called Light Alloys, and trained as a toolmaker. He lived in Ealing and was befriended by an Argentinian couple who moved into the flat above him. They had a son, Ñato, and a daughter, Lale, and the father worked in the Argentinian Embassy in London. He told Álvaro that there was a job going at the Embassy if he was interested, so Álvaro applied and was taken on. The job was decoding messages and transmitting them to Argentinians living in England. Álvaro was taken on as part of the family. He was invited to all their meals and even to this day Álvaro and I have kept in touch with Ñato and his family. Ñato was captain of a container ship and he always invited us to stay on board whenever he docked in London. We lived in Spain for ten years in the 1990s and whenever he visited Spain, we would stay on his ship. We were waited on hand and foot – a great life we thought! Of course, after the Falklands War, he couldn't dock in London, so we used to go over to Le Havre in France to see him.

Álvaro and I were married in 1958, and for our honeymoon, we camped in the Pyrenees, getting there by Lambretta. Álvaro couldn't get across to San Sebastián to see his mother, as Franco was still in power, so I made the journey alone to meet his family.

We had three sons, and in 1965 we moved to Somerset, where Álvaro was employed by Westlands Helicopters as a skilled engineer. In 1988 we took early retirement and moved to Torrevieja, near Alicante, where we had a lovely house with a swimming pool. We used to have an annual anniversary lunch with the *niños* who lived near Alicante. We returned to England ten years later to be nearer our grandchildren.

Looking back on it, I think Álvaro's life has been very eventful and he is among those of the *niños* who have done well for themselves, after such humble beginnings in a new country!

(Transcribed by Joan Martínez, wife)

María Luisa Martínez Olaizola

My father was killed and my brother and I were sent to an orphanage in Bilbao. We were separated from our mother and older sister who had to go to Santander, from where they walked over the Pyrenees to France.

It was very different coming over to Britain. We were in a boat like sardines in a tin. A group of us already knew each other from the orphanage in Bilbao. On arrival at Southampton, we were put in a big camp where they sorted out who was going where. We were lucky, all the ones from Bilbao were sent to Cambridge.

By all accounts it was the best colony. At first, we were sent to the rectory at Pampisford, outside Cambridge. We were all quite happy and were well looked after. The house was large and had tennis courts and a big garden, and the stables were used as our classrooms. Eric Hawkins was an undergraduate at the time and he used to come and teach us. It was lovely to see him again two years ago when we unveiled the plaque. It brought back a lot of memories.[1]

I also remember a merchant seaman whose father was a professor at the university. He used to come and do the garden and I got on really well with him. He would write to me from the Antarctic and

---

1. In May 2005, Professor Eric Hawkins unveiled a blue plaque at the Station Road colony in Cambridge on behalf of the Basque Children of '37 Association UK.

tell me about his experiences, which were always really interesting. I remained good friends with him and his wife but, unfortunately, he died last year.

During our time at Pampisford, we used to have to do keep fit exercises in the grounds. When my children were little, they used to find the photos of us exercising very funny. Álvaro, my brother, and I taught the others how to dance the *jota* and we would give concerts of Basque songs and dances to raise money for our keep, travelling to London and Lincolnshire.

Álvaro and I were amongst the first ones to receive letters. Our sister, Titi, used to write a lot. She was really good at doing the impossible and always managed to find a way to get her letters to us. It was a good thing really that Titi stayed with our mother as she would have been lost without her.

When we had to move from Pampisford, Jesus College very kindly provided a house for us on Station Road in Cambridge. There we were all quite happy and well looked after by people from the university and volunteers. When the Second World War started it had to close, and the older children had to go to work. The younger ones, however, did get to go to school. As I was almost 14, which was the school leaving age at that time, I was sent to live with one of the Basque community members. I went there with Amparo Moreno. She was six months younger than me, so she was sent to school. But, for two shillings and sixpence, I had to do all the cleaning in the house, which for me was hard. From there I moved to a titled lady's house where I earned seven shillings and sixpence and was made to wear a morning uniform and an afternoon uniform. I was really unhappy there, but then luck struck as my friend Carmen Belón, who had a job looking after children with a very good family, was moving to Australia and I was told about the job. So I went to work for the family and I was really happy there for a few years. I started as a nanny and ended up like the older daughter. I was really happy there and got married from the house.

I met my husband, Brian, in Cambridge. He was an undergraduate at Gonville and Caius College. So, I ended up making my life there, getting married, having children and now I have grandchildren. Although I'm British on paper, in my heart I'm still Spanish, still Basque. I go to Spain every year and it still feels like home there. It's true what people say, one is always pulled back to one's roots. But, after so many years here, it would take a lot longer to get used to living there again.

Herminio Martínez Verguizas

The years following the end of World War two had been very unsettling. Many of us young exiles had been living in a sort of limbo. We were neither British nor Spanish. We could not reconcile ourselves to accepting the Franco regime and returning to what we still considered "home".

By 1960 I had settled down considerably. I had been teaching for a year and I had married Verena, who was Swiss, and a teacher specialising in the teaching of the partially deaf. I had also by this time sorted out my nationality problems. I had been refused British citizenship but now had a Spanish passport instead of the "stateless" UN travel document with which I had travelled up to then. At about that time, the Spanish government offered exiles like me an *indulto* This allowed us to return to Spain for a period of not more than four weeks and permitted us to get out again. In this way we would not be subject to the three years of military service in Franco's army.

So, for the first time since 1937, I went to Spain for two weeks with Verena. We arrived by train at the frontier in Irún. I handed in my newly issued Spanish passport. The official took it and went inside. I was apprehensive. My friend Manolo Andrés, like me, had also returned to Spain and had spent a good part of his two weeks stay in jail. The official came back after some time and said in a quiet voice: *"¿Pero qué hace Ud. aquí?"* (What on earth are you doing here?) He had a card with my details which he showed me. Herminio Martínez Verguizas. It went on to say I was a political exile and so on. I said I had left Spain at the age of seven and that of course, I had no political views at the time. Now, certainly I had them. He must have been a nice fellow. He said: *"Pase buenas vacaciones, pero tenga mucho cuidado."* (Have a good holiday, but be very careful.) We were through!

We had to change trains at San Sebastián. A burly Civil Guard took us aside for no apparent reason and went through our luggage with great thoroughness, taking everything out. I asked him mockingly what he was looking for and that if we had it, I would tell him. He merely scowled. We arrived in Bilbao. My mother and a young woman were waiting for us on the platform. I took her to be my sister Mari, who was born shortly after we left for England, and greeted her as such. But she was in fact my sister-in-law Ester, my eldest brother's wife.

My parents now lived in the *huerta*. Some years before my brother Victor and I left Spain, my father had found a hillside, tucked away in a *barranco*, a ravine overgrown with brambles and scrub that seemed to belong to no one, though subsequently we found it belonged to the local authority. That was the time of the depression when father, who had worked in the iron ore mines and in Altos Hornos, the steel works, like so many, had been sacked and was out of work. Those were the years when there was hunger. We were destitute. Father would go to Baracaldo, knocking on doors, begging for bread. He would often take my eldest brother Santi or Victor with him to show he had children to feed. We lived in El Regato which had become a mining village for the iron ore mines further up the hillside in Arnabal. We had the first floor of a rented house with a *cuadra,* a large shed at the side of the house. There was no water or sanitation. We had hens, a donkey and a cow which grazed on the hillside.

My father worked hard, gradually clearing the brambles and terracing the hillside. He created a paradise. He planted fig trees, apricots, cherry trees. Eventually we grew all our vegetables. This saved us and saved them after Victor and I left, during those dreadful hungry years, when father was put in prison, after Bilbao fell to the *Nacionales.*

Verena and I stayed at the *huerta* with my parents and young sister Mari. She was 23, but we had never seen each other. Born just after Victor and I arrived in England, she had a terribly hungry, deprived childhood and her education hadn't been up to much. She was very bitter. She seemed to hold it against me that I had had it so good *"en Inglaterra"*. Little did she know. My other three brothers and Begoña, my elder sister, were by now married. Before being put in prison, my father had quarried the stone from the hillside by hand and my brothers had gradually put up the house while father was in prison. It was very basic and very rough. There was electric light in the rooms but no water in the house. Everything was very basic and rudimentary.

We met my brothers, Santi, Manuel, and Felix, and my sister Begoña, and wives and children. I found myself amongst strangers and out of my depth with the ways of my family. The 23-year separation had made us strangers. This was specially so with my sisters. Verena took things as they came. For her, accustomed to the secure, ordered way of life of the Swiss, it must have been even more of a shock than for me. She had no problem with the food or the way we ate: when we had *caracoles* (snails), each dipping his spoon into the *cazuela* and *untando el pan* (dipping the bread in the sauce). My father was most impressed by Verena. He took to her. She had a good appetite and big feet, requisites for hard work.

My father I remembered as being very affectionate to me. He was a physically powerful man, always working and rushing about. I now found a broken man, a cripple, who had difficulty walking but who nevertheless worked on the *huerta* from dawn to dusk. The dreadful hardship and misery of the life he and the others had had to endure had taken their toll on all the family, but more so on him. His imprisonment for things of which he was not guilty, and which perhaps he could not understand, and his ill treatment in prison had made him withdraw from others. He seemed to have been cast aside. I liked to sit with him and get him to talk. There are so many aspects of his life and of him I would have loved to know, but it was not easy to talk, my brothers and sisters simply did not wish to dwell on the past and on such *miserias,* and Mother certainly didn't like it when I talked with Father about his experiences after he was imprisoned

Father was denounced as being an activist of some sort and arrested. Father was not an activist in any way. Mother, yes. She organised women in the village to knit and make clothes for the *milicianos* at the front. We didn't know who denounced Father. Denunciations were often done in secret. Though he had not taken part in the actual fighting, he was put in the prison boat on the Nervion, where he was badly beaten. He was sentenced to death, which seemed to be the norm at the time, but the death sentence was commuted to 30 years in prison with hard labour. While in prison in Leon, the prisoners were fed food prepared with industrial oil. Some 60 of them became partially paralysed. They were no longer able to work, so they were released.

My family were certain it had been my school teacher who denounced Father, to avenge herself on my mother. I need to explain. I started school when I was four in one of the schools opened by the Republic in El Regato. I learned to read and write quickly, but my parents were more or less illiterate. Father had had no schooling of course, but he was just able to string words together, but without a break. A teacher who had shared the same lodgings when father came to work in Vizcaya had taught him. Mother was outspoken in her views. She was, she said, a *"Socialista"*. She didn't go to church, she said she didn't need priests to help her talk with God. My teacher on the contrary, was quite an ardent church goer. She used to take it out on me, blaming me for whatever mischief took place. To get her own back on my mother, my punishment was to be sent across the plaza to kneel in the church. I felt the unfairness of it all. The feud between Mother and my teacher went on and on. I would get my own back quietly. My teacher had to pass by our house on the hillside to go home. I would hide among the trees and pelt her with stones. This inflamed things all the more.

Verena and I encountered a state of fear in my family. I was told not to get tangled up with the Civil Guard. If they should fine me, pay up and don't argue. Don't dare sing the songs of the past. Don't trust anyone and don't get involved with anyone outside the family. They feared that with some indiscretion I might bring troubles down on the family and on myself. It took me some time to understand that they still felt very threatened and, as I realised, with good cause. My mother was a small person, but with a strong, determined character, above all very practical and hardworking and with a mischievous sense of humour. She had kept the family together throughout those difficult years when father was in prison, each having to pull their weight. Santi was 15 at that time. He was bright and able and was the mainstay of the family. There was no work to be had so it was a matter of working the *huerta* so as to survive. Manuel, 14, got a job as a shepherd living out, which paid for his keep. Begoña was ten when father was imprisoned and mother gave birth. She had to take over from mother and bring up Mari, our baby sister, during those years of hunger. Felix was five, but when father was released from prison some years later, he would accompany him to report to the Civil Guard, as father was required to do periodically. Felix lived in fear of those occasions, never knowing the sort of reception father would receive. They all survived, but at what cost to each of them and to the family? What a disaster it would have been if Victor and I had been repatriated in December 1939 as had been the intention. Mother had refused to sign the form claiming us, even though she had been visited by a priest and an official, who had threatened to imprison her and take her other children away. She said that if we returned, we would all starve, but her signature was forged, so that we were being repatriated. It was the intervention of the Red Cross, who contacted our mother and reported to the Basque Children's Committee in London that we shouldn't go back, that prevented our return at the very last moment.

My brothers and sisters worked incredibly long hours. A transition in the way of life was taking place, from rural to industrial life. My brothers were all involved in this process. Many families had the husband working in factories in Baracaldo, Burcena or Zorroza, whilst still tending the *huerta* and keeping a few hens, pigs, a cow and so on. Altos Hornos, the steel makers, employed a lot of the men, and though the mines at Arnabal were not working, it was clear there was plenty of work and that life was improving after years of hunger and stagnation. Industry was booming. It was like an industrial Wild West with all controls and safety ignored. Later, all this was to have disastrous consequences for our family. At a time when things were improving for them, my two elder brothers, Santi and Manuel, were killed in industrial accidents within one year of each other. It devastated us all, leaving two widows and their children in the family.

Everyone spoke of *los años de hambre* (the years of hunger). My brother Felix described those times to me. He said that some elderly people in the village had died of hunger. They had survived on vegetables, particularly on cabbage, hence the obsession now with eating well and eating meat.

We felt that people were very conformist, very concerned about their dress and appearance. There was, I remember, some nonsense that men could not walk about without a jacket in short sleeves unless their shirt had a pocket. Women had to have their arms covered and wear stockings and of course, bathing costumes were like those in Victorian times. Apart from the role the church played in all this, I understood that the Mayor of Baracaldo enforced these stupidities. I also felt that people, and certainly my family, tended to think that the written word in newspapers was the gospel truth. The strict censorship was clearly having an effect and the ideas I brought from the wider world clashed with what they had been fed. This caused problems between us. They couldn't accept that their thoughts, like their lives, had been restricted.

We were with my family for San Roque. This was the fiesta of the *pueblo* and we were invited to my brother's for the day. Families started to arrive from early morning, walking from Baracaldo, Retuerto and other places around. There were few if any cars on the roads. They all settled with their food and children at Las Arraguas, a *campa* immediately across the river from our old house. There were plenty of trees and people sought the shade. Soon fires were lit and the women started their cooking. The *botas* of wine came out and the men settled down to their cards. The children went into the river to paddle and catch tiddlers amongst the rocks.

I went down hoping to meet some of the people I had known as a boy. I met Felisa. She was one of the *Socialistas*. One of her sons was a *miliciano* and I remembered he was killed at the front. She still had her fiery zeal and was soon questioning me about life outside Spain. I got her to fill me in on some of the things that had happened under *el franquismo*. I also asked her about some of my old friends. She was bitter that some families had welcomed the *Nacionales*, hanging flags from their balconies. She told me that the family of the brothers Ricardo and Jaime had run into trouble with the church. The parents had never married through the church and the two boys had never been christened. When the *Nacionales* took over, they were paid a visit by the priest. He told the parents that the *huerta* they worked now belonged to the church. If they didn't marry and christen their sons, they wouldn't be able to cultivate their *huerta*. In those days of hunger, this would have been a disaster for them. Early one day, the parents were married in the church and Ricardo and Jaime were baptized! Felisa also told me that the daughter of La Sorda (the deaf one), who was now a nun, was on a visit to her younger sister, La Morena. This was a family I remembered well. They lived across the river to us in a hovel over a *cuadra*, (stable), in what had been the hay loft. I had always wanted to know what had become of these poor people, and of the two boys who had been my friends.

I remembered that the father worked in the mines further up the hillside. I remembered seeing the father brought down to the village on a plank by some of the miners. He had been killed in an accident. This was a disaster for the family. It was impossible for La Sorda, the mother, to cope. The little sister, La Morena, was taken in by one of the neighbouring families, and the elder sister and the two young boys disappeared. Their return to the village for what must have been a brief stay with their mother had always played on my mind. They joined, as usual, in our games. There were the usual squabbles and, of course, the usual language interspersed with a good measure of swearing. The reaction of the two brothers was incredible to all of us. They told us not to use such bad words, it was a sin. We listened as they described Hell, with Satan and the devils with their forks, and the cauldron of fire which was attended to by the devils, where sinners were boiled. It was a picture that I think impressed me when they told us, as much as they had been impressed when the nuns threatened them with the fires of hell. When they were taken from their mother, they had gone to some sort of religious institution. The nuns had done a wonderful job of education on them!

I found the elder sister at La Morena's house, still the same house as she had been taken into by the neighbours. She came out to meet me in her simple light grey nun's attire. She remembered me well. She was lovely. We had no problem looking back on those terrible years they had suffered. She told me about her brothers, who were now living in Vitoria. She was at a convent in Belgium, and as her order was quite a liberal one, she was able to keep in touch with her sister and brothers. She spoke French and had received an education. Yes, she was happy, but I sensed a touch of sadness. What would she have done if life had not been so hard on her? It was clear she was at peace with herself. She liked to visit her sister La Morena, who had two young children, but I wondered if perhaps the family at the convent didn't fulfil her natural instincts. This encounter was for me a joy, that out of such misery as had befallen her family, some happiness had resulted.

San Roque was of course a day for feasting. We sat down much too much for our liking, simply eating. I could quite easily have become a vegetarian as a result of the general lust for flesh. The women were sweating over the greasy frying pans on the *chapas* (rings), trying to keep everyone going with food. The men were only concerned with making sure they were well provided for. They would call out: *"¡Pan!"* and more bread would come: *"¡Agua!"* and the jug would be filled.

People were not accustomed to dealing with foreigners. When we went to the plaza in Baracaldo, Verena would find people shouted at her because, if she couldn't understand, clearly she was deaf! If they shouted, she would understand. We walked a lot because there was very little public transport. However, we would take a bus from Baracaldo to Retuerto and then walk the rest of the way to the *huerta* in Gorostiza. Verena found this a martyrdom. The bus would be crowded, fleas were everywhere. She could feel the beasts crawling over her but was unable even to move. Her flea bites became large, painful lumps. I, like most of my family, was immune to them.

We had been warned to be careful what we said and not to get involved with people outside the family. We became aware there was something strange in the attitude of the locals in Gorostiza towards us. It was August. As we walked through Gorostiza, they would be sitting outside their houses on wooden stools or small rough chairs of woven bark. The dogs also would be enjoying the late afternoon fresco. As we walked past, the eyes of the locals and the dogs would turn and follow us as we passed. There was no greeting or recognition of our presence, no response to our: *"¡Buenas!"* This we found strange. We became aware that my family also received the same treatment from most of them. Gradually we realised that the resentment of these people towards my parents in particular went back to the time when my father had found the piece of hillside and started to work it nearly 30 years before. They felt resentment that an outsider should encroach upon their domain. We were considered "immigrants". This dreadful behaviour towards my parents was contemptible.

As we walked past those seated outside their houses, I would stop, confront them with my eyes, and say: *"Hola, buenas tardes."* Grudgingly the answer would come: *"Buenas."* After a few times, the response came without the need for the confrontation. Some years later, Herminio was very useful. I lived in London. There was incredible interest to learn English in those days. We had some of the youngsters from Gorostiza with us in London, or we placed the girls with families as au pairs after first staying with us. I was taken into the confidence of some of the parents and asked to intervene and to advise on one youngster in particular.

Those first two weeks we spent in Spain, we were on the move all the time. We even managed to hire a little Fiat 500 and make a trip to Santander, and then onto the *meseta* in Burgos.

How our return journey to England didn't end up in disaster, I still find it difficult to explain. The two weeks flew past. We caught the train in Bilbao for San Sebastian. The farewell hadn't been too difficult. We knew we'd be back. We changed trains at San Sebastian and took the train they called *el topo* (the mole), because it went in and out of tunnels, stopping at all the stations on the way to the French frontier.

The train was made up of open carriages. We were at the very entrance of a carriage in the first seats. People got on at the various stations, some with the produce they had bought, presumably in the *plazas*. Others carried bundles and baggage tied up with string and rope. Our luggage on the luggage rack was brand new. Some of it was Verena's Swiss luggage. It contrasted sharply with everyone else's bundles. We also contrasted quite sharply with the other passengers. Our dress was different. It was also quite obvious that Verena, with her fair hair and Swiss complexion, was a foreigner. The carriage became quite full with many standing. At one of the stations a fellow got on, a small man. I noticed that, as he entered the carriage, he just lifted the lapel of his gabardine. He was insignificant in his looks except for his gabardine and a thin, sharp moustache – the moustache of the Falange. He said nothing, but immediately there was silence. The women started fumbling in their bags and the men got out their wallets. I realised the fellow was a plain clothes policeman. People started to get out the permits they had to have in those days to travel from one province to the other, even though it was 21 years after the end of the Civil War. We had crossed from Vizcaya to Guipúzcoa.

I still wonder what came over me. One of the things that had shocked Verena and me during our brief stay had been the fear people had of the Civil Guard and all forms of police. Armed to the teeth and always in pairs, so that they were referred to as *la pareja* (the couple), they were intimidating and seemed to relish their repressive role and the fear they invoked. They seemed to be everywhere. I was annoyed by the manner in which the fellow, a little chap, just assumed people would respond to his position of authority and, as I saw it, to his impertinent approach. I said to Verena: "Play dumb". I was on the outside seat and the first in the carriage. As I didn't respond in any way, he said to me: "*¡Documentación!*" I simply looked at him, shrugged my shoulders and smiled. There was silence. He realised we were foreigners. He then said: "*Yo, ustedes, documentación*". I simply didn't understand a word. The other passengers crowded round and tried to be helpful. They started saying in loud voices :"*El, quiere, su, documentación*" ("He wants to see your papers"). If I didn't understand, clearly I was deaf. The fellow tried again, this time with gestures, pointing to himself and saying: *"Yo"*, then pointing at me: "*Usted, pasaporte*". At last I understood! I said in English, also with gestures: "You, want, my, passport". Everyone shouted: "*Sí!*" and I said to Verena: "Let me have your passport." Verena got out her passport; it was red, with a white cross. They all shouted: "*Suizos*". I handed the passport to the fellow. He looked through it and handed it back to me respectfully. I returned it to Verena. Then it was my turn. I tried clumsily to extract my passport from my rear trouser's pocket. I did so slowly and with great difficulty and at last, sheepishly offered him my passport, my Spanish passport. There was a burst of laughter, an explosion from all around as though a dam had burst. The fellow didn't even attempt to look at it. He simply fled through the carriage. There was no inspection of travel permits.

I have often wondered why I got away with such stupidity, how I didn't get the hiding of my life at a police station. I can only explain it by the fact that in those days Spaniards, except the privileged of the regime, found it difficult to travel abroad. Here was this fellow with a Spanish passport, clearly going abroad, and above all, he was married to a Swiss woman. He must be *un jefazo, un pez gordo* (someone with influence), someone who could permit himself such pranks. He wouldn't want problems with such a person. Apart from the general fear of the Civil Guard that we had experienced in people, we'd also realised the corrupt way in which one got things done and the power and influence of privilege. Perhaps I had my Guardian Angels by my side!

Tomás Núñez Toledo

Before I was evacuated to Great Britain I lived in constant fear, because I was completely terrorised by the dictator's bombing raids, and would spend hours, indeed sometimes whole nights, sheltering in a railway tunnel that had been converted into an air raid shelter. That was why my mother, a widow with two sons, the oldest of whom at 17 was fighting at the front, decided that in view of my fear of the bombing, she would send me, aged 11, away from the Basque Country, even though it meant she would be on her own. So she requested my evacuation to a friendly country.

After a few days, we were asked to go for a medical exam. Imagine my mother's surprise when she was told that they were sending me to the USSR, when we had expected France or England. So she decided not to send me. I don't know how she managed it, but she managed to get me on the list of those going to Great Britain, a few days before the so-called expedition left.

We left Bilbao on 20 May 1937 for Santurce, the port from which we boarded the liner, the *Habana*. I remember the scenes as the relatives of those who were leaving said farewell amid sobbing, wailing and last minute advice from our parents, who were probably wondering whether they would ever see us again.

Before embarkation, we had two labels fixed to our lapels, as if we were parcels to be sent, although I appreciate that as there were 4,000 girls and boys travelling, we had to wear some sort of identification. The ship put out to sea and for the first time we felt no fear. Because of our age, we didn't know what dangers the journey could bring. The truth is that I had a good crossing, because I was hardly seasick at all and ate with a hearty appetite, then I ran around the boat everywhere they allowed us to.

The journey lasted for three days and I think that it was on the second day that a warship came up to us. We were really frightened as we knew it wasn't a friendly boat. Signals in Morse code were exchanged between our boat and a British destroyer that was escorting us. Soon the enemy boat veered to port away from the *Habana* and didn't bother us any more. It had been a moment of suspense but we soon forgot it.

Our arrival at the port of Southampton was spectacular because the port was lined with people eagerly welcoming us and we disembarked full of anticipation. They took us to some buses that caught my attention and interest as they were double-deckers and I'd never seen such big ones before. We were taken directly to a camp where tents had been erected, for eight or ten people per tent.

The fact is that I had a very good time. The camp was surrounded by barbed wire and English people from outside would come and see us and would give us sweets and were very friendly towards us. When I had been in the camp for three months, I got appendicitis and they took me to a centre for immigrants outside the camp. They did tests and immediately took me to hospital in Winchester by car, where they operated on arrival. I stayed for a month in that hospital, as I had complications, some sort of an infection had set in. The care I received from the doctors, nurses, patients and patients' relatives was second to none and I have pleasant memories of my stay in hospital. When I was discharged and sent back to the camp, I was moved to another section in the camp, as the boys I had been with before had been moved to a colony.

I remember one day having an argument with another boy which ended in a fight – he gave me such a hard blow on my chest that they had to take me to the infirmary because I couldn't breathe. (Moreover, it's obvious that the boy who hit me already had talent as a pugilist, since he later became a boxer of some renown in Bilbao – his name was Zulaga.) As a result of this, I got to know the doctor or nurse who looked after me. She was Mrs Winifred Russell and she lived in Southampton. Every weekend she would invite me and another boy called Juan José Anda, whom I knew because we had been in the same class at school in Bilbao, to her house. She would take us to the pictures and to playgrounds in parks so that we wouldn't get bored. In the garden, her husband, who was called Dennis, would place a penny coin on the back of a chair and we would try and dislodge it with an air rifle. If we did, the coin was ours. As at that age one covets money and as we had none, we aimed carefully and were so eager that we nearly always hit the target.

One day, in the camp, Srta Celia Echevarría, who had been my teacher before I'd gone to hospital, came up to me and said: "You're Tomás, aren't you? Look, as an end-of-term prize for those who have done well in their studies this term, we've come here on a trip. Do you want to come back with us to the colony?" I accepted, either for the sake of a change or to get to know other places, and I went to Langham, near Colchester, where I was so happy that I didn't want to return to the Basque Country, as I will explain later.

The best months of my stay in Britain were spent at the Langham colony. The Directors were Mr Stirling and Srta Celia Echevarría. The teachers were Mr Theo Wills and Srta Amada. The monitors were Mr Leonard, Otto and others whose names I don't remember. They became second parents to us in our second homeland. Every weekday we had lessons in English and Spanish. For recreation we played tennis, hockey and football. We'd go swimming in a nearby stream. There were trips to the seaside and football tournaments with other colonies. We acted in plays, which we put on with other colonies and societies to help with our living expenses. We made dolls with typical Andalusian costumes. We'd paint large jam jars so they could be used as flower vases. All this was to help with our upkeep. We would dance in the sitting room. There was a choir which had a repertoire of Spanish regional songs and some English ones. We were immensely happy, so much so that, perhaps because of my age and lack of experience of life, I neither missed my country nor my family, although I would write periodically to my mother and my brother, who had been taken prisoner by Franco's troops.

When I heard with only a few days' notice that I had to go back to Bilbao, my friend Rivera and I took two bikes and ran away. I was so happy in England. When the teachers noticed that we had gone, they got on to the police, who soon found us and took us back to the colony. Incidentally, they didn't punish us.

I could write about many things, but my memory fails me. I remember one curious incident: there were four of us in our dormitory, Recaredo, Félix, Eloy and me. Eloy was a sleepwalker, and we had a real laugh when he used to get up, fast asleep, and go walking along the corridors and outbuildings.

The return was a sadder affair. We crossed the Channel to Calais and were put on a train to Hendaye. When we arrived there, and as the group of us crossed the international bridge, a man in a uniform and a red beret got up on the pillar which held up the barrier and started shouting: "Long live Spain! Long live Franco!" and truth to tell, we were rather frightened. We were stopped and searched at Customs and asked if we had any English money. Then we were given two lovely sandwiches and two bananas. They put us on the train and we were taken to the Amor Misericordioso school in Bilbao, where our parents came to collect us. And I, even though I was with my mother, felt shy and ill at ease with so many people around, and of course, having been used to hearing English, it felt strange to hear Spanish being spoken. *

Esperanza Ortiz de Zárate

When the Spanish Civil War broke out I was nine years old. I was living with my family (three sisters and two brothers, with me in the middle) in Zaldívar, a village in Vizcaya. My father was the local teacher. Our very peaceful life ended abruptly with the outbreak of war in July 1936. After the bombing of Guernica, my parents left our house and were evacuated to Bilbao. When the Basque Government announced they had organised an evacuation of children to England, I suppose my parents saw it as our salvation and signed me up with my sister. The day they told us that we were going to England, we were taken to a park in Bilbao where Dr Ellis, an English doctor, examined us. My sister Pili, who was two and a half years older than me, didn't want to go. For me, though, it was a big adventure and so I was quite happy about it.

The night before we were to leave, we realised my sister was missing. We looked for her everywhere, even in the street, and finally found her hidden in the clothes cupboard. She cried inconsolably and my parents spent hours talking her round, saying we were only going for three months and we would come back speaking English.

20 May 1937 dawned grey and overcast, like every other day since we had arrived in Bilbao. My mother said that our father would take us to Santurce, because she couldn't go with the two little ones. Saying goodbye was terrible. When we arrived at the station to go to Santurce, the platform was thronging with parents and children. The moment came to take our leave: my father hugged us and said he

would write often. I could see his glasses steaming up – it was the first time I'd ever seen my father cry.

My only memory of the journey is that the ship was almost bursting with people.

Coming into Southampton was like a fairy tale. The individual little houses in the distance made me think of Wonderland, they were so different from the apartment blocks in Bilbao.

We were taken to a huge camp with tents at Eastleigh. My first impression of Englishmen, from the camp volunteers in their shorts, was that they were thin and lanky, a very different type from the men of the Basque country. We had to queue for everything except the latrines – trenches dug in the ground with wooden planks across them. They were very precarious, particularly for the little ones.

Some weeks after we arrived at the camp, they transferred us to the Catholic convent school of the Sisters of Charity in Manchester. There were 15 to 20 of us girls and I was one of the youngest. I was fascinated by the Sisters' habits – with their highly starched snow-white wimples they looked as if they could take flight at any moment. We attended classes and, although we didn't speak the language, in those subjects which didn't require English, for example geography, we got good marks. I remember too that the nuns were amazed at our way of doing division. Sometimes we'd get a star for excellence, which we'd very proudly stick in our exercise book.

One day one of the Sisters told us to go out to the convent entrance where a group of journalists and photographers were waiting for us. They took a lot of photos and asked us to raise our fists, doubtless to continue the propaganda spread by some of the papers that we were daughters of "reds". This infuriated the older girls.

We were then sent to the colony at Bray Court, a somewhat neglected house between Maidenhead and Windsor, where there were already about 100 Basque boys and girls. English people used to come to the colony wanting to invite the children out for the day. That is how we got to know Mr and Mrs Rickards, a couple who took my sister and me out every Wednesday. I'll never forget my first impressions as we arrived at their house. It struck me as enormous and it was surrounded by wonderful gardens. When we sat down to eat, the table was so elegantly laid with beautiful crockery and there were so many sets of silver cutlery, that my sister and I didn't know which ones to use first. They had three children, somewhat younger than we were, and their good behaviour at table surprised us very much. It seemed as if English children didn't speak at table as we were used to doing.

At the Bray Court colony we felt happier, although the food was very poor and in winter it was very cold as there was no heating. We did have classes, but not regularly, as other tasks called, such as doing household chores and rehearsing for the shows of Basque traditional dancing that we put on in and around London, to raise funds for our upkeep.

When this colony closed, they transferred us to The Oaks in Carshalton, Surrey, approximately an hour from London. It was a deserted mansion where about 20 boys and girls were accommodated in a wing which had been made habitable. After Bray Court, The Oaks was like the Ritz. The food was excellent, the cook wore a chef's hat and he made desserts that took your breath away, with the result that I immediately put on several kilos in weight.

When the Second World War broke out on 3 September 1939, a very hot day, we were on holiday, camping on Hayling Island in the south of England. In charge of us was Mr Edgar Philips, a member of the committee, who immediately made arrangements for our return to the colony. Mr Philips was very sympathetic to the Republican cause, and he gave up all his free time to the Basque children and to improving our lives.

A few days later he informed us that the British Government was not prepared to let us stay on in England. Straightaway the committee started to draw up a list of those children who could go back, but they opposed the return of any whose parents had died or been imprisoned. My sister and I were the only ones in the colony who couldn't go back. Our father was a prisoner and our mother had been exiled from her home town and was living in Eibar with a sister who had taken her in with our two young brothers.

As we were now on our own, they transferred us to another colony nearby, The Culvers, also in Carshalton, where a small group of children was already living. We had lessons, but not regularly as again we had to help clean the house. I was in charge of washing and ironing the boys' clothes.

A catastrophe that I'll never forget was my first attempt at cooking. My sister and I were preparing the spaghetti bolognese. We were in the small kitchen. My sister had put an enormous pan of water on to heat and added the spaghetti. Seconds before it came to the boil, she had gone to the toilet, leaving me to watch the pan. When the contents started boiling up, there was no way of stopping it. I was paralysed with fear and in a trice the stove and kitchen floor were carpeted with spaghetti. I rushed screaming out of the kitchen and someone heard me and came to the rescue. They turned off the gas and managed to stop the "volcano". The floor was so slippery that we took hours to clean it up. Never again was I delegated any kitchen duties, but I had to put up with a lot of teasing for a long time afterwards!

There was a happy atmosphere in this colony. I particularly remember the lady in charge of us, Miss Chloë Vulliamy, a plump lady whose accent immediately marked her out as being of the upper middle class, and Pepe Estruch, a very cultured exile from Spain with progressive ideas. He introduced us to Spanish literature, the plays of Unamuno and Lorca and in general awoke in us a curiosity and thirst for knowledge which for years had been dormant. The years went past and it was decided to send me to Pitman's Secretarial College in London, probably with a view to prepare me for the job market. I followed a year's course. I would get up early to catch the London train, taking my books and sandwiches for lunch. I will always fondly remember Mrs Somerset, the Scottish cook at the colony, who lovingly used to prepare those sandwiches with a cigarette hanging from her lip while I had breakfast. Nearly every day classes were interrupted by bombing raids.

Later, the Republican Government in Exile, headed by Dr Juan Negrín, set up the Juan Luis Vives Trust for the education of Basque children and other refugees, and a number of us girls and boys received grants. We were given £3 per week board and lodging, not a very generous sum seeing as we were living independently in London, where we shared a flat with three other Basque friends. We studied at the Polytechnic in Regent Street, again with a lot of interruption as London continued to be the target of German bombs. Fortunately we did not suffer any damage, although a flying bomb landed on Earl's Court near our house. One night we went down into the Underground to sleep to avoid the bombs, like many Londoners, but it was such an unpleasant experience that we preferred to stay in the house when the siren sounded.

During the war years the *Hogar Español* was formed in London. It was a Spanish Centre, subsidised by the Republican Government in Exile, which became a meeting place for many refugees from the Civil War. For us Basque children, now adolescent, this became a real home from home where we spent all our free time. The atmosphere was very political, as is only to be expected. Lectures and concerts were held there and demonstrations were organised against the Franco regime. It was here that we formed our organisation *Amistad* (Friendship). Bautista López, who later became my husband, was for some time the Chairman. On Sundays there was dancing where we met other friends from outside. That's how I met Bautista. He had lived in London, but at the beginning of the war he had moved to Stafford in central England where, with a group of young Basque people, he was working for English Electric, who were making armaments.

In the the *Hogar Español*, under Pepe Estruch, we formed an arts group and put on plays and concerts. Manuel Lazareno, another exile, conducted an excellent choir and a lot of us young Basque people took part. We sang in concerts at the Albert Hall and for the BBC. The year after the war ended we went on tour to France and Czechoslovakia, to raise funds for prisoners in Spain. In Prague we met Dolores Ibárruri, the Pasionaria.

My father wrote us lots of letters and poems during the seven years he was a prisoner, always giving us advice about being honest and grateful to the people who were looking after us and not to forget Spain – better times were round the corner. I'm sure these letters helped us maintain a positive image of Spain.

During our childhood we came across some very kind people who treated us extremely well and to whom I shall always be grateful. However, I have to say that our education was much neglected, probably due to lack of resources and because our stay in England was supposed to be a short one. The war in London was hard, but I personally suffered far more because of the Spanish Civil War and its aftermath. Being separated from my parents at such a tender age and feeling abandoned affected me greatly. I know it was all done to keep us safe, but if something similar should occur again today, my advice to my daughter would be not to become separated from her children. *
(Espe Ortiz died on 28 March 2007)

Agustina Pérez San José

I left Bilbao when I was seven in May 1937, accompanied by my eldest sister Asun, who was 13 at the time, and a younger brother Antonio (Tony), who was five. We left our parents, two other sisters and our two youngest brothers behind.

As soon as we boarded the crowded boat, I lost my brother and sister and I didn't see either of them again until we arrived at the camp in Eastleigh on 23 May. I can still vaguely see the lady who gave me a white ribbon and told me to put it around my wrist. Another girl, who I had become friendly with, was given a red one. Red has always been one of my favourite colours, so we exchanged ribbons. Little did I know the significance of the coloured ribbons. However, it didn't take me long to find out. As we disembarked, those with red ribbons were separated from the whites. The bus I was ushered into finished up outside the Public Baths. I recall feeling shocked and scared when they showed us the swimming pool. I had never seen one before. I remember being taken to a cubicle and having my hair cut, after which they gave me a bath. I was taken to the camp and discovered that the small case I had brought with me from Bilbao, carrying the one change of clothes we were allowed to bring and a small book, had gone. I never saw it again!

Our stay in Eastleigh was brief, as we were one of the first groups to move out of the camp. We were transferred to Brampton, a small town in Cumbria. The journey was long, lasting the whole day. We arrived in the evening and were taken into a large house or mansion. I slept in a large dormitory with six other girls of my age. It had a large fireplace at one end, and a door leading to a toilet near by. I felt happy and safe in Brampton. It was wonderful not to hear the air raid sirens, the bombing and sometimes the sound of shooting which at that time was the norm in Bilbao.

In the colony, we had a few Spanish teachers and helpers who had come with us. Now and again we would have a visit from a Spanish priest. Also there was Mr Froelich, a Jewish Austrian refugee, who had managed to escape his homeland. Of all the teachers and adults there, Mr Froelich was my favourite. He was a talented physicist and fluent in Spanish and English. He would often read to us and tell us stories. Now and then he would take us to Carlisle.

My brother and I were often hungry in Brampton, which reminded us of the Civil War. Luckily for us one of my sister's duties was to prepare food and serve in the adult's dining room. When it was her turn to serve, Tony and I would rush to the garden and hide below the dining room window before the teachers arrived to have their meal. Asun would pass us a sausage, a potato, a piece of bread. At tea time it would be a biscuit or a piece of cake.

The home we stayed in belonged to Sir Wilfrid Roberts, who at that time was a Liberal MP. I remember his mother, Lady Cecilia, who to us was someone very special. Sometimes she would come to see us and spend time with us, or we would be invited to her beautiful country house, which seemed like a palace. I remember her showing us some beautiful trinkets. On other visits she would show us round her wonderful garden. We were always taken there and brought back by her chauffeur. Her daughter was an artist and used to come to the colony and teach the older children how to paint.

Gradually, some of the children went back to Spain. We couldn't go back, as my mother and two young brothers were in a French refugee camp. My two sisters who had remained in Bilbao were being housed by nuns near Bilbao and my father, who had fought for the Republicans in the defence of Bilbao, had been captured in Santander in the summer of 1937 and was now a prisoner of war in Spain.

Years later he told me that when he was captured, he, along with thousands of other Republican soldiers, was marched into the bullring by Franco's soldiers. Here they expected to be shot, just as other Republicans had been killed by Franco's soldiers in the bullring in Badajoz at the start of the war. However, they were saved by a contingent of Italian soldiers who, under orders of their officer, placed themselves between the Republican prisoners and Franco's troops and refused to move until they were given guarantees that the prisoners would not be shot.

We stayed in Brampton for two years until the middle of 1939, when my brother and I went sent to live with Mr and Mrs Nichol in the Knightswood area of Glasgow. This meant being separated from our sister Asun, as the authorities could not find a family that would look after the three of us. She went to live with Mr and Mrs Phillips and their three children in Clydebank, also near Glasgow.

My brother and I enjoyed living with the Nichols family. Their son Billy was studying to be a teacher. They sent us to the local school in Knightswood, where we quickly learned English with a Scottish accent. This had a big impact on me, but even more on my brother Tony, who would have been six or seven at the time. Even to this day Tony speaks English with a very broad Scottish accent.

On Saturday mornings we would go to the cinema in Annisland with our new "cousins", Archie and Nicol McLean. "Auntie Mary", their mother, was Mr Nichol's sister. On Sundays we would go to their home for tea. We played Monopoly and other board games. They also taught us how to play games with English playing cards. Grandad

Nichol, who lived with them, often joined us in our games. He was a loveable character and a great, kind man. He had been an engineer and had worked in the USA. He fascinated us with stories about his life there. He was a strong anti-Fascist and he hated Franco, Hitler, Mussolini and their cronies with a passion.

Mr Nichol worked in Glasgow Town Hall. Once or twice he took us there to have a look round. Unfortunately, our stay with them didn't last long. In 1940-1941 the German Luftwaffe bombed Glasgow and Clydebank with great ferocity. Our school, along with other schools, was evacuated to the south-west of Scotland. Most of the children from our school were, like us, taken to Gatehouse of Fleet, which is in Kircudbrightshire a small county in south-west Scotland.

Gatehouse is a delightful little village on the Solway Firth. Tony and I lived with Mr and Mrs Halliday and their daughter, Betty, who was a hairdresser. Most of the young people were called up and some never came back. A few were left to work on the land. Food was rationed and so was petrol. I can still remember being allowed 8oz of sweets per person per month. Rationing lasted until 1952-1953. Milk and bread weren't rationed, neither were chicken or fish. Mrs Halliday always seemed to have food in the larder. We were never hungry. I must add that there was no shortage of rabbits or hares or, for that matter, poachers.

We went to the village school and quickly made friends. As we were learning English, we were losing our Spanish, so much so that by the time I left Gatehouse for London in 1946, I had completely forgotten it, as had my brother Tony who joined Asun and me a year or two later.

In the village my brother was called the "wee Scottish laddie" because occasionally he wore a kilt. One Sunday he came home from playing cricket in the park. When Mr Halliday realised what he had been up to he called him a "wee heathen"! He had very strong Presbyterian principles. One never saw him reading a newspaper on a Sunday.

In Gatehouse we attended church on Sundays. We also joined the Scout movement, Tony became a boy scout and I a girl guide. Once a month we had church parade. For us youngsters, it was the highlight of the month taking part in the parade. After the service we would walk out from the church and get into our places. There would be the Home Guard, which was mainly made up of farmers and farm workers, men who worked in the Forestry Commission and the

Voluntary Social Workers, and then us – scouts, cubs, guides and brownies. The man in charge was the local butcher, who had been a captain in the 1914-1918 war. Most of the men in the Home Guard had been in that war too.

All of us looked bright and smart in our uniforms. The captain, or should I say, the butcher, would have all his regalia on and would walk up and down inspecting us. Then it would be time to march up and down the main street. There he would give orders: "At ease. Attention. Eyes right. Eyes left", and he used to say a lot more too.

In January and February I would go after church with a few ladies and some girls to pick snowdrops. We picked and packed them and sent them by train mainly to the Red Cross in Glasgow, where they would be sold to raise money for various war funds. In the spring, as soon as the daffodils and primroses appeared, we would do the same. In the summer we picked sphagnum moss. There was a demand for this moss to make bandages.

Now and again when I feel a bit melancholy I realise how higgledy-piggledy our lives have been. I married a fellow Basque refugee. Both of us have worked very hard. We have a wonderful family and two grandchildren, who are the apples of our eyes.

Although I have been happy in the UK, I have often wondered what our lives would have been like if we hadn't left our families at such an early age. We missed them, and couldn't help but worry about them. For the first year or so after our arrival we had no news of them. Later on a British lady wrote to my sister in Brampton telling her that she had been visiting refugee camps in France and had spoken to our mother and brothers and that the three of them were well.

If I had my life over again and knowing what I know now, I think I would have taken my chances with the rest of them. Most of us were too young to be separated from our families at such an early age, because it marks you for the rest of your life. But on the other hand, because of our shared experiences, I have made many lifelong friends amongst my fellow Basque children. Some, like me, were in Brampton, but most I met when we all seemed to end up living in London after the war.

I have met some wonderful people in this country. But in particular I will always have very special fondness for the Scots. To us they were always pleasant, jolly, warm and kind-hearted and I will never forget their kindness and generosity to us.

Cora Portillo

As a student of Spanish at Oxford University, I wasn't able to go on my year abroad, as Spain was closed after 1936. So my tutor found an elderly Valencian lady to take me for conversation. One day, I met a young woman from Bilbao who was staying with this lady. She was one of the volunteers who, with a teacher, had accompanied a group of children evacuated to England in May 1937. Her name was Pili Merodio and she was the house-mother at the colony in Aston, five miles from Witney, in Oxfordshire. We struck up a warm friendship and she suggested that I visit the children. So the next Saturday I took a bus there. This was the beginning of a whole new era in my life.

The colony was a happy place. It was fairly small, and run by an excellent local Basque Children's Committee, headed by the Early family, who owned the blanket factory in Witney and who gave each child a red woollen blanket on arrival. Other local people who were involved included the doctor's wife, Mrs Dalgleish, and the owner of a bike shop in Witney, Mr Tidy, who supplied bikes for the children. The colony was internally run by Pili, helped by Ketty, the oldest of the teenage girls there. The atmosphere in the house was one of sharing: of sorrows, joys and material possessions.

The house had a lovely garden, which the children from war-torn Bilbao loved playing in, but inside, conditions were stark. There was no running water and just a coal range for cooking and heating water. The only room that was heated was the kitchen. Upstairs, it was icy.

The children loved having visitors, and would clatter down the uncarpeted stairs with squeals of joy at the weekends. Besides myself, regular visitors included Geoffrey Turner, the Convenor of Oxford University, who, although he walked with crutches as a result of polio, carried a gramophone under one arm and a box of records of Spanish songs and dances under the other. These were most valuable, as the children had to give concerts to raise money for their upkeep. Another visitor was a 19-year-old man, Edwin Edwards, who worked in the Oxford Library. He taught himself Spanish and was one of the most endearing characters I have ever met. The children called him "Eduardísimo", and he was like a big brother to them. He used to pump up water for hours to fill the tank for bath night!

When the Second World War was looming, and Franco began demanding the return of "his" children, the colonies were closed as soon as return journeys could be arranged. Aston was one of the last to be closed, and one Saturday I arrived to be told that a Spanish professor had been sent to us. (Adult refugees, of course, stayed in exile, and in Oxford and Cambridge many Spanish professors and intellectuals were offered provisional shelter in the homes of college staff.) Our visitor, Luis Portillo, had been *profesor auxiliar* of Civil Law at Salamanca University before joining the Republican Army. He was invalided out. He then served in the legal department of the War Ministry under the Basque Minister, Manuel de Irujo. Pili and I noticed that, although he was wearing a wedding ring, it transpired he wasn't married but had a fiancée in Vitoria. I had been immediately attracted to this romantic figure and when the few remaining girls, with Pili and another house-mother, were moved to a council house in Witney, Luis and I visited them there. He found a basic room to rent in Oxford round the corner from St Hilda's for five shillings a week, and earned money peeling potatoes in a café 11 hours a day!

We became engaged. My sister "vetted" Luis for my parents, and Luis faced the ordeal of visiting my parents with me, to be looked over. In his favour, he was a professor with beautiful manners, but penniless, a Catholic, a foreigner!

However, very soon Luis acquired enough English (mostly by reading *The Times*) to get a good job with Reuters, translating Churchill's speeches – such a responsibility! We were married in March 1941, in the crypt of Westminster Cathedral (as I am a Protestant) and the Basque priest Onaindía was allowed to assist the resident priest. The reception was at the Basque Embassy, by invitation of Don Manuel de Irujo, and my sisters took over the refreshments, while I had to go with Luis to be registered as an alien in order to have a travel document to go on our honeymoon! We arrived back and had just enough time for one toast, and then had to catch a train to Oxford. Once there, we crossed fields on foot, Luis carrying a heavy case, to a modest farmhouse recommended by Spanish friends! Few people can have had such an austere wedding! No veil or white dress.

We had five sons and although 19 years passed before Luis was able to visit his family in Spain, I was able to take the boys to see their Spanish relations. His parents came to stay with us once, daringly by plane! Luis died aged 86.

María Jesús Robles Hernándo

My first impression of England wasn't strange – it could have been anywhere. Spanish was being spoken all the time and by now familiar faces were all about me.

It was in Wickham Market that the English language came to my consciousness, or perhaps I should say that the native idiom hit me with extraordinary force, which was to be remembered for years afterwards. To me the language seemed toneless and monosyllabic. The people spoke too quietly and without any expression on their faces. Looking back and my memories of it, I would say that the English language to me, then, was insipid, colourless and lacked animation. Of course, I couldn't explain it in those terms. One has to understand that the Latin races speak as much with their hands, face and the tone of voice as they do with their tongues. Three short years later, I could have told a very different story. I grew to love the richness of the English language, even with its crazy grammar, and to really appreciate the diversity of dialects.

My memories of the various colonies where I stayed are fragmented and some scenes are often somewhat nebulous. There are cameos, which have a subject in relief cut upon the layers, colourful and demanding to be noticed. Such is my memory of Chloë Vulliamy. She is stamped clearly on my mind, and although she must have been with us in other colonies, she is the most prominent, and belongs in my memory exclusively to our first colony, Wherstead Park, near Ipswich.

Miss Vulliamy, as we called her, was to me at that time a very daring lady. She and her friends would gather downstairs in one of the rooms off the entrance hall. Painted like dolls, wearing "flapper" dresses, they would dance to the music of the Charleston and other dances that were popular then. Chloë Vulliamy had dark hair, which she wore parted in the middle, severely pulled back behind her ears and twisted into a bun at the nape of her neck. Her dark hair and bright red lips accentuated the whiteness of her skin. Arms bare, low cut dresses and smoking through a long cigarette holder, she inspired awe in me and I stared at her. She had a pleasant, smiling face. Her voice was cultured (I realised that years later) and her laugh came from deep down, what we would now call a "throaty" or "belly" laugh, which was infectious. It never failed to make me laugh with her.

I think, probably, that it was in Wickham Market when we started receiving letters from our mother. My father, at that time, was a prisoner of war. How my mother learned where we were I don't know, but we soon started having regular correspondence.

The colony at Wickham Market was somewhat Dickensian, an ugly looking red brick building, spread over perhaps several acres of ground. My memories of that colony are always of hot summer days, when we would walk to the river and spend the whole afternoon swimming. The colony had a number of outhouses and often some of the bigger girls would be in one of these outbuildings curling each others' hair with hot curling tongs. I would look on fascinated at the transformation taking place.

I also remember the cook, who was a big, untidy woman, who had a daughter about 18 years old and her young brother, who was about eight. One day, we all went to a park with swings and roundabouts. This young boy was hit on the head by a swing and had to be carried back to the colony by one of the teachers who was with us. I don't remember seeing him again and I think he died.

My first introduction to Spanish literature was at Wickham Market, when a young man read to us from *El Cantar del mío Cid*. The Spanish was strange but the beauty and flow of the language enthralled me and, although I understood little of what was being said, it held my attention. I had seen this young storyteller about on a motorcycle, dressed in a long brown coat with a cloth cap on his head, but I have the impression that he was not a member of staff.

From time to time the children were fostered out to private homes. Usually I went alone, that is my brother did not go with me. The first time I went to a family of five boys and a girl. The girl, Patty, was the youngest of the family and about my age. I was greeted with the Communist salute, the clenched fist that I had never seen before. What was interesting was that Patty's father had been in the International Brigade. I had never heard of the International Brigade or what it stood for. This man, Mr Sines, spoke some Spanish and I spoke some words of English. Soon I was hearing how Mr Sines had lost his finger and how some of his comrades had been wounded or killed.

My brother and I were fostered out together to a family in Birmingham. This couple had a daughter in her early twenties and her young brother had died a year or so earlier. The idea was that my brother should work with Mr Thomas in their small market garden, and I should work in the house, thus freeing Mrs Thomas and her daughter to run the grocery store. Here, for the first time in my life, I knew hunger. This family had a dog, and it was my job to give this animal his food – scraps from the plates and leftovers from cooking. This dog had more food on his plate than I had on mine and, on the way to his kennel, I helped myself to his food until I was caught. We left soon after that and went to Margate.

It was very cold and a few weeks later I was sent to two elderly sisters. They loved children and already had 12 London evacuees. Their very impressive mansion lay at the end of a long tree-lined drive. It belonged to Miss Isabel Fry of the Quaker Fry family and it was to be my home for 18 very happy years. It was February when I arrived. I have a vivid memory of being taken by the housekeeper into a big room with a huge log fire.

For a short while I went to the village school, but then Miss Fry decided to teach me herself. She had been a grammarian and had had a book on grammar published. In Wales she had her own school where she taught children from poor families, particularly those from mining communities. After two years under her tutelage, she told me that she thought I was ready for boarding school. I loved it there and, of course, I spent holidays at home. Both at home and at school I was given every encouragement to think and express myself.

The Fry sisters had many friends to stay. Some I have learned since were famous people, including the Bonham-Carters and Professor CM Joad. I was always encouraged to sit in on their conversations, much of which went over my head. Often Miss Fry would bring me in saying: "Now María, my dear, what do you think?" No one laughed at my opinions or made me feel inferior. Every evening after tea the gong sounded; everyone, including the servants, would congregate. One sister would read from the Bible or a book, or an interesting item from the newspaper and comment. After a few minutes' thought, a short discussion followed. Before we left the room, it was suggested that we children should put right the wrongs of the day before going to bed. Our disputes were usually settled amicably, but sometimes a grown up would be asked to act as arbiter.

Then there was what we called the "quiet room". Any child needing to be alone, for whatever reason, could go there and not be disturbed. There were 13 of us children, ranging in age from eight to ten or 11. We were all away from our families and from time to time the longing for our mothers was too much for us. In later years, when I was doing children's nursing, I realised how wise that provision for our needs had been. In that room we not only gave vent to our grief, but also to temper, frustration and the like. Outdoor games were kept there, including boxing gloves. No one saw what one did, and one emerged from there refreshed. Had we not had the use of a secluded place, imagine what 13 crying children would be like, or a pack of screaming and fighting youngsters!

I can't remember when the other evacuees began returning to their homes, but eventually I was the only one left. I think Miss Fry perhaps protected me more than the others, because I was foreign and because of the language difficulty. I often found myself in her company as she read aloud and I knitted or sewed, or I walked with her as she spoke about the wonders of nature or answered my endless questions, which she always encouraged.

In a quiet way, unknown to me, I was being taught principles to live by and which I in turn would pass on to my children. I was also taught to question what I read and what "truths" I was being told, when in fact they may be men's ideas only. I was to remember this later when I read philosophy.

I left school at seventeen and a half and began nursing children in Hackney, East London. At the same time Miss Fry had arranged for me to do a postal course studying philosophy (now called linguistics) and English literature, under the supervision of one of her friends who taught at a ladies' college attached to Cambridge University. At that time I had the idea that I would like to return to Spain and teach English, but after a year I realised that it was nursing that I wanted to do. From children's nursing I went on to general nursing, midwifery, tuberculosis and finally to oncology. After a 12-year break, when my children were old enough to be left unsupervised, I returned to nursing cancer patients, and I have done this for most of my working life.

Miss Fry had wisely encouraged me to return to the colony for short or long periods. She thought it important that I should maintain contacts with my Spanish roots. Hence, I stayed at The Culvers in Carshalton, Rowley Lodge in Barnet and a place in Finchley, North London. But gradually I visited the colony less and less often as school and the pressure of study and then work became more demanding. My brother and I of course corresponded and sometimes visited one another, but I lost sight of all those children I had grown up with.

It was not an easy time for any of us. We lost and at the same time gained a great deal. I lost my identity. I am neither Spanish nor English.

When next I saw my mother, I was grown up. The mother-daughter relationship was lost, but we became good friends. I gained a foster mother who understood me a great deal better than I understood myself, and saw to it that I grew up a useful citizen, fulfilling my potential. I am grateful to both my mothers and thankful that I was looked after by two excellent women who wanted the very best for me. I salute them both.

Paco Robles Hernándo

We spent three very bad nights on the *Habana* vomiting and unable to sleep because we hadn't found berths. Finally, on the morning of 23 May, we saw that we had arrived at Southampton, England, and on deck there were several doctors in white coats giving all of us injections before we went ashore. All the way from the port to Eastleigh, which was where they were taking us, the road was decked with flags and bunting. I thought it must be in our honour, but later on I learned that the British had put up the flags to celebrate the coronation of King George VI.

At the camp in Eastleigh they allocated almost all of us to tents, eight of us to each one. We didn't undress and soon many picked up fleas and lice, and the worst thing was that almost everyone caught scabies, which we took with us when we went on to the colonies. The English came out on bicycles to see us, and brought us sweets, pastries and lots of sponge cakes. Naturally, many of us got diarrhoea because we hadn't eaten that sort of thing for a year. We'd only eaten black bread and horsemeat, and in one or two cases I had seen neighbours skinning their cats to eat them. At Eastleigh every morning they broadcast music over the tannoy. They used to play *Land of Hope and Glory* and that wake-up call became fixed in my memory for ever afterwards. It is one of my favourite songs.

I was allotted to Wherstead Park, Ipswich, and in that colony we were very happy. There were large gardens and a small wood and in autumn the owners of the property came down to shoot. We lads used to retrieve the game birds for them, as if we were gundogs, and the owners used to pay us sixpence for every bird we found. After some months at Wherstead Park they took us to Wickham Market. The colony was in a former hospital that was truly ancient and it had been shut down years before but was opened up for us. I disliked that colony because we suffered from scabies, which had been brought in by some children who came from a different colony, and moreover it was infested with rats.

Shortly after we arrived there they sent us teachers so we would learn English. I didn't want to learn because I found the pronunciation very difficult and, in any case, since we were told that we would be going back to Spain in a few months, what use would it be for me to learn the language? In the end I decided to take an interest in English, because it had a phrase that appealed to me, which was "I think so". Whatever the reason, I became very keen on learning the language, with a friend called Pedro Encinas. I ended up top in English and he was second, and as our prize we were taken to London for a week's holiday.

After living in several colonies, such as Margate, I was adopted by a family in Birmingham and spent two years with them. I didn't enjoy my stay with them at all, because they only wanted me so I could work on a smallholding they owned. I had to get up at six in the morning to feed the goats and the pigs, and then muck out the stables, before setting off for school, which was five miles away. I was one of the best pupils in the school because I had already learned what they were teaching when I was with the Salesian Brothers in Baracaldo, so these teachers took a liking to me.

Two years later I returned to Margate and from there they moved us to Carshalton. Finally, my sister and I ended up in Rowley Lodge in Barnet. I started work in an armaments factory in Boreham Wood and from there I moved on to work in a bakery on Barnet High Street.

As our colony was in a direct line with the factories in Boreham Wood and, moreover, we had a barracks for neighbours, bombs used to fall nearby, and one night at around 1.00 am a 1,000-kilo bomb fell in the garden of our house and killed all the animals we had. Fortunately, none of us was killed or injured. Within an hour of the bomb falling, the police arranged buses to take us to an old people's home run by nuns where we were given two large rooms, one for the girls and one for the boys. That was in High Barnet.

We continued going to work and a fortnight later we were told they had another house ready for us three or four miles away. That was on Friday at about 6.00 pm and they told us they would send two buses round in the morning to take us to the house in New Barnet, but that if we preferred they would give us the address and we could walk there that evening. We all decided to go that Friday, and thank goodness we did! Around 3.00 am on Saturday morning our centre was hit by a parachute mine of enormous explosive force, which devastated the whole area where we had been living for almost a quarter of a square mile, killing the nuns and the old people who were still there. Later on, after New Barnet, we went to another colony in Woodside Park and from there to Landsdown Walk, Holland Park. Shortly afterwards they allotted us to private houses. A friend, Imanol Iriondo, and I were taken to Kensington Gardens Square in Bayswater until the war ended. *

Vicente Rodríguez Elorza

Some memories last and remain with us for all time, and they are there to be unearthed by those who are sensitive to them. I shall try and describe a small part of those unforgettable memories.

I was 13 years old and one of the children evacuated to Great Britain. Our exile began on 20 May 1937, when we embarked on the steamer, the *Habana*. When it left the port and reached the open sea, the ship began to lurch and we started being sea sick. There was wailing and crying, it was a terrible sight. At that moment I was overcome by a great loneliness, a great sadness. I remembered my family and wondered whether it would have been better if I had stayed with them.

Finally the ship docked in the port of Southampton on 23 May. We arrived exhausted and disorientated, but on the other hand, happy to have finished the sea voyage. We were taken by bus to the camp at North Stoneham in Eastleigh. At the camp, many tents had been put up and we occupied them in order. Each one could hold eight children. I had been in the camp for three or four days and was in the tent when I heard shouting. I went outside and I saw a group of children surrounding some English people who were distributing bread. Some in the group of children came closer and I could see that a little girl had moved away from the group and was coming towards me, gesticulating and shouting something I couldn't hear. Soon I understood everything: she was hugging the piece of white bread to her chest and was shouting out: "This is for my mother, I'll keep it for my mother." At that moment, all she could think about was giving her mother the best thing that she had, a piece of white bread. As she passed by me, I could see her better. She was a little girl of about eight years old and with dark hair. A deep tenderness and happiness was written over her face, yet at the same time, tears were falling down her cheeks. She went off, still hugging the piece of bread against her heart and she kept on shouting: "This is for my mother, I'll keep it for my mother."

I never saw her again. Sometimes I wonder what became of her, if she remembered that day and whether she was able to tell her mother about it. All that affected me deeply, so much so that when I remember it, I am filled with emotion and I can't help my eyes watering, because, like the little girl, at that moment, I also remembered my mother.

I read somewhere that history is made up of instants. Perhaps that is right, I don't know, but I suppose that my stories allow us to remember all the consequences of war, especially for the weakest, and to reaffirm that there is no just war.

After two weeks in the camp I heard that, together with 28 boys and 29 girls, we were to be taken to a colony. The buses came to fetch us at the beginning of June. We got in, the coaches started to leave the camp behind, and we left behind too some of our worries, our sadness, our fears, our joys.

Once the coaches joined the main road, we started singing, and we sang for a long time. We were happy but the journey was becoming long and boring. We sat down, our eyes tired by looking through the windows for so long. I think we had been travelling for five hours when we reached Colchester. Then the road took us to the lovely house at Langham. Before our eyes was a great stone building, The Oaks, which at that moment looked to us like a palace.

We went in, marvelling at what we saw. We were longing to see all the land round the colony. It was marvellous to see green fields, separated by narrow paths with leafy trees – it all exuded a feeling of tranquillity. We were lucky: Basque House, as The Oaks came to be called, was renowned as one of the best colonies of the Basque children.

Very soon, the person in charge of the colony organised our participation in the running of the house, and we were put into groups for cleaning, helping in the kitchen and for the other jobs that needed doing.

We started having lessons, the teachers trying to teach us subjects at the right level. At the beginning, I don't think we paid much attention, but soon, the lessons seemed more interesting. I remember how Mr Stirling would insist on our reciting poems. He really loved poetry and was especially fond of the poems of Federico García Lorca. In the sitting room there was a piano, I think Caridad played, and with the help of this piano we were taught our songs and regional dances, so that whenever a visitor came from the PPU, we would put on a show for them.

We also got a football team going. The gardener, who was very hardworking and who took great pride in his garden, used to complain about the state of the lawn after the games, so we started playing in another field where the grass was hardier. We played against the team from the Ipswich colony with fairly good results, and that boosted our confidence and encouraged training. After the matches, we would have a party.

I was really happy when I was told that an English family wanted to invite me to spend a few days with them. Some of the boys had already enjoyed spending time with English families. When they returned to the colony, they were very cheerful and never tired of telling us the minutest details of all they had done, and we would listen to them with great attention. And sometimes I had wondered whether I would ever have the same opportunities that they had had.

So, one morning towards the end of July, I got up feeling rather anxious, and hurried through everything until it was time to go. I bade an effusive farewell to my companions, as if I were going away for a long time. I was taken to Colchester station and the London train drew in. The ticket inspector was to look after me, and when I got on the train, he very kindly took me to a seat by the window. The train went off and I felt a surge of excitement because at last I was going to do what I had so wanted to. I went to the window. It was a sunny morning, a slight breeze lessening the heat that was coming in through the window. I stayed there a long time seeing lovely countryside, vast green fields, some farms and cattle sheds here and there. Soon the inspector came up again and told me that we were just about to arrive in Stafford, where the family was waiting to pick me up. The train stopped, we got down and he introduced me to a couple with a daughter, who greeted me warmly.

They took me by car to their house, a fine building. We went into a large hall from where a wooden staircase led to the first floor. It was elegant and I liked it very much. It was lunchtime and we all sat down at table. They were looking at me expectantly, perhaps they were worried that I might not like the food. That wasn't the case although I wasn't used to English cooking.

In the house I'd seen a typewriter and it reminded me of the one I had left behind at home. The next day they took me by car to look round the town. Another day we went to have tea with a family who asked me a lot of things about Langham, and about how I'd lived during the Civil War. They had to be patient with me and speak slowly so that I'd understand them. The following day they took me to the zoo. I really liked seeing all the animals. In between times, I started practising on the typewriter.

Then the day came for me to go back to Langham. I was sad. I had spent a marvellous few days. We said our farewells, they with their usual kindness and I, surely, with a mixture of both sadness and happiness. I hoped that that family would invite me again. After two weeks, I wrote a letter which they translated into English for me and sent it to the family. I didn't have any news from them. I have always wondered why. What did I do wrong? Didn't I know how to adapt? I have always had this disappointment and doubt in my mind.

It was the first time we were being taken to a beach. When we heard the news, we were very excited. It was a summer's morning. There were a few clouds in the sky, like cotton wool, which sometimes allowed the sun's rays to filter through and which made one think that it was going to be a hot day. Full of expectation, we got into the coach, and what with looking through the windows and later, when the coach hit the main road, singing lustily, we hardly realised we'd arrived. The bus was parked near the beach. We got out and looked at the sea. The beach looked like a toasted carpet. With cries of joy we ran towards the water, the waves weren't very big and the water wasn't too cold.

Later, we went up and down the beach, running along the shore and leaving our footprints on the wet sand. I was tired. I spread out my towel on the sand and sat down. I began looking at the horizon, beyond the blue sea and my memories came flooding back, memories of my family, my town, swimming at Las Arenas, but I soon realised that this was neither the time nor the place for nostalgia and solitude, but rather for hope, joy and optimism. I went back and played with the others until it was time to go.

One afternoon, we started out towards the river. It was a pleasure to go walking along the path with trees on either side, whose leaves allowed a little sun to filter through. Sometimes our young voices, raised in song, would resound along the way. We got there and went in slowly, very slowly, because the water was cold. There were puddles at the sides of the river and we splashed about in them, having a lovely time, our voices breaking the silence of the place. We were certainly tired when we got back, but very happy, and were longing to return..

Our life in Basque House continued happily, with our lessons, our dancing and the football matches against teams from Colchester schools and the colony at Ipswich. The dance troupe, made up of six girls and two or three boys, gave a series of performances outside the colony, and so helping in the upkeep of the house became a reality.

We already had new costumes (made by the girls) for each of the dances we would perform. The day came for us to go to Northampton. The first show was a success, the public clapped a lot and this gave us more confidence. And by the next performances in Bradford, Rushden, Didsbury and three or four other places, we no longer had stage fright. So we were thrilled to dance, and the audience didn't tire of clapping and congratulating us.

I am very grateful to the staff: Srta Celia Echevarría, (whom I think was the soul of the colony), Mr Stirling and Mr Darling, Srta Cecilia Gurich (la Peque, as we so fondly used to call her), Srtas Berta, Amada and Deme, as well as Theo Wills and Leonard Read from Cornwall, with whom I maintained correspondence until a few days before he died.

If I have one criticism, it is that I think we were too isolated from the inhabitants of Langham. We didn't know the young people, which would have allowed us to have English friends, and we would have chatted with them and improved our English. In any case, I wish to express my gratitude to all the inhabitants of Langham for their hospitality in those times, and to all the members of the Peace Pledge Union, who did all they could so that our stay at Basque House should be as agreeable as possible. Also my thanks to all those English people who gave such badly needed donations, which were so helpful to us.*

Pilar Rodríguez Izaguirre

On 2 June 1937 we arrived at Rowley Lodge, Barnet, 20 boys and 20 girls. It was a lovely place and very well run: Lady Tewson was the secretary and would invite us to her house in turns for tea. She was very kind and loving. We were lucky in Barnet, as some of the homes were not very good. When some of the children left for Spain, others would come from different homes and that is why we knew so many of them. We were all like brothers and sisters.

144

We were happy in the Barnet home until 1942, when we were bombed. We were sent to Oddfellows Hall for two days until the committee found a large enough house in New Barnet. We moved the same day and that night a land mine fell in the hall. It was horrible. Everyone in Barnet thought we had all been killed. When some of the boys went to work the next day, the other men couldn't believe it. How lucky we'd been!

Earlier, I had met three brothers who had come from another home. Their surname was Murga. That day, unknown to me, changed my life. I married the older one in 1948 and lived in Barnet. His name was Antonio Murga, known as Tony. The brothers were Julián and Jesús, better known as Chechi.

Barnet was considered one of the best colonies, as the homes were called, and it was one of the last to close, in 1942. I lived there until the end. Then the committee found me lodgings and a job. I started in a store as a junior in the underwear department and I finished as a buyer. I was in charge of five departments and 18 staff. I was very happy and loved my job.

In 2002 my Tony died and my sister Mila and I bought a house in Wales to be near my other sister and her family, but I miss the friends who used to come and get together in London.

Alfonso Ruiz López
At dawn on the third day we reached the port of Southampton. In the docks the huge liner *Queen Mary* was moored, and by its side the *Habana* looked like a cockleshell. We were taken by bus, in many double-decker buses, to an immense camp made up of over 500 bell tents, which accommodated, eight to a tent, the 4,000 boys and girls who had travelled on the *Habana*.

There were also very large rectangular tents, which were to serve as hospital, kitchens and stores: everything was very well organised, like the country itself. Each tent had a table with benches on either side, to serve as our dining room. The camp had been set up and organised by the boy scouts. The food was a little strange: noodles, cakes and sandwiches, and synthetic milk that tasted like chalk. Our tent was number 126.

When we had been there a month, children began to leave and I was afraid they would separate us, but fortunately we left together, sponsored by Lady Cecilia Roberts, who adopted 40 girls and 40 boys, a great piece of luck. We all set off together in two buses and arrived late at night. The house was huge and spacious with large gardens and a small field which we turned into a football pitch. It was divided into two identical wings, one of them for the girls and the other for the boys.

Everything was well organised. There was a Director, Don José María, two teachers, Srta Lolita and Srta Kiny, and Spanish cleaning and cooking staff, who had come with us on the *Habana*. In addition, there was an English teacher, Mr Froelich, and a maths teacher, Sr Calzada. For me the most marvellous person was the artist Mrs Nicholson, Lady Cecilia's daughter-in-law, who began giving us water-colour classes and, as we progressed, introduced us to oils. I enjoyed those classes as I was very keen and loved painting. Finally, there was Harry Herrington, who came on his motorcycle in the afternoon to give us singing classes. He taught us English songs and at the same time he learned from us popular Spanish songs, arranging them for piano.

Mrs Nicholson showed us the potential of colour, how to mix colours and especially how colours depended on light. One day I painted a storm at night, with lights in the distance to indicate a village and lightning flashing over the dark sky of the canvas. She congratulated me! From that day on Alfonso Clemente and I were her favourite pupils, and on Thursdays she would take us in her splendid car to her studio. We'd paint all day, having cups of tea every hour. Afterwards, she took us home, invariably saying as she left us: "Be good boys".

We soon became well known in the area. Watching our rehearsals of English and Spanish songs, Srta Lolita – a person of considerable culture – had the idea we might give concerts in the neighbourhood, without charge, as an expression of gratitude for the generous hospitality of Lady Cecilia Roberts. We began rehearsals full of enthusiasm and the results were excellent.

We formed a choir, "The Brampton Chorus", and gave small concerts in the area. People welcomed us with great affection, and fêted and applauded us. Srta Lola gave me the embarrassing task of making the speech of thanks to the audience at the end of the evening. I was shy at that age, but summoning up my courage, I stood at the front of the stage with a face as red as a tomato and said: "Thank you very much for all that you have done for the Basque children. Thank you!"

These short trips were not only pleasant, but also had a spiritual and sentimental value, since though we were saddened by the constant remembrance of parents and siblings whom we had left behind in the war, the trips nonetheless inspired in us a feeling of unity and reflected back to us the joy we inspired in our audience.

As time went by there was snow, football, lessons, painting. Our orderly life and the good-natured companionship existing among us allowed us to bear our existence with something akin to nostalgic cheerfulness. We were young and happy by nature, albeit somewhat embittered by our fate. Inevitably, Christmas came round, precisely what we least needed. The house at Brampton, which was in effect one large family, was sad and all of us, both young and old, were pensive.

In the great dining room, which occupied the centre of the building, we were all present – or rather absent – at the Christmas dinner, because here nobody would even have recognised a Spanish carol. We were all far, far away, thinking of our mothers and fathers, our brothers and sisters. The Director and Srta Lolita tried to cheer us up. We had all the support we might wish for, but we were so far from our loved ones. We were all in the lowest of spirits. How cruel it is when spirits are so low at so tender an age!

We withdrew to our rooms to open the envelopes where we kept our family photographs, turning them over time and again. Then, peering through the windows, we fixed our gaze on that snow-filled sky as if trying to see in it the persons who were present in our thoughts. I would never have imagined that Christmas could inspire such sadness.

There came a pleasant piece of news. The Basque Children's Committee announced that it was mounting an exhibition of paintings by Basque children and asked us to take part. Mrs Nicholson was enthusiastic and set us to work tirelessly. Eighteen of my pictures went, and they were all sold in London, ending up in English homes as reminders of us. I received £38 from their sale, which was a small fortune for me, and I had already decided how to spend it. We weren't short of anything ourselves, so I would buy clothes for my siblings in Spain who didn't have any.

Srta Lolita sent for me. She told me they'd had a request from Barcelona for 18 young English language translators, so that children sponsored there by American Quakers might read the letters sent to them by their sponsors, while similarly we would translate back into

English the letters they wrote in Spanish. I decided to go. I knew Alfredo would look after his brother Luisito. I thought it was the right thing to do.

Brampton left me with an enchanted, life-changing memory and, for the rest of my days, I would remember my years there with great fondness, as I found it then, and many times I did so in my mind.

When I left my brothers and was on my way back to Spain, I had a premonition of some dark fate and, inevitably, I turned to familiar thoughts, lapsing into a state of moral depression and feeling truly more alone than Faust.

Those 29 months in England brought about a great change: I ceased to be an adolescent. They acted as a catalyst which made me mature prematurely and leave behind my adolescence. *

(from Ruiz López, Alfonso, 1989, *Cuando la sangre llama*, published by the author. Alfonso died in 2008)

Alfredo Ruiz López

I was the last but one of six sons born to Pedro and Felisa Ruiz López. I was born in 1923 in the beautiful city of San Sebastián in northern Spain. My childhood was spent playing and going to school, getting into scrapes as children do, such as having my foot run over by my uncle's cart. Not only that, my friends and I would make fun of the local policeman, who was bow-legged. We called out to him: "You can't catch me, Ha! Ha!" having forgotten that, as we walked to school, the same policeman always stood on the corner and as we passed him, he grabbed us and gave us a slap, saying, "Can't catch you, eh?" Happy days!

As a child I was not aware that those times were the beginning of the Spanish Civil War. When I was about 11 years old, the whole family had to move to Bilbao, as my three eldest brothers were fighting for the legitimate government.

In May 1937, two of my brothers and I boarded the liner *Habana* for England. On arrival at Southampton, we were put in a camp that had been erected by the boy scouts. After a while, about 100 children, including myself and my two brothers, Alfonso and Luis, teachers and a helper, were sent to Brampton. Here we were placed in a hostel and saw snow for the first time, which we thought was magical. The people were friendly and invited the children into their homes for meals. This is how we first started to learn English.

After two years of living in Brampton, finances were short and our colony, along with many of the other colonies housing Basque children around the country, had to close. Some of the children were repatriated to Spain. My older brother, Alfonso, went to France to work for an organisation that supported refugees from the Spanish Civil War. This left Luis and me, who were then separated. A doctor and his wife in Glasgow fostered Luis and I was sent to Coventry. We were sad to leave our colony and the care of Srta Lolita (Mrs Southern), whom we all loved. Over the years I kept in touch with her, and when she died in the late 1990s, Ricardo Martinez, Luis Porras and I attended the funeral and had a wreath made in the colours of the Spanish flag.

When I was 16, I went to Coventry, where I was found employment in an engineering firm, and shared lodgings with Antonio Tudela and Juan and Victor Cantalapiedra. Little did I realise I was about to be involved in another war. I decided to volunteer on 14 May 1943 and was called up on 7 June 1943.

I joined the Fleet Air Arm full of enthusiasm. I was good at practical work, but my command of the English language was not so good. I was transferred to *HMS Victory* in Portsmouth. In order to qualify as an able seaman, I had to learn about the various knots and all about the ships' guns and equipment. Just before going to commission a boat, I did a short course on radar, which later proved to be very important.

My next journey was to Fort William in Scotland, to become familiar with small boats. The training lasted about two weeks. Whilst we were there, we were called out in the night to put out a fire in the commandos' training centre. We had to go on the roof to put the fire out, but what we didn't know was that there was some ammunition in the building and soon we were having to dodge the bullets. Returning to our quarters in daylight we had a hair-raising ride. We had raced up there in the dark and not seen the sheer drops and winding road.

After Fort William, it was off to Lowestoft to commission *ML 147*. We tested everything to make sure it was seaworthy, then had orders to return to main base in *HMS Hornet*. We had to escort ships carrying supplies across the English Channel. Then we were sent to the Atlantic. This was because the U-boats used to lie in wait for the convoys from America. Whilst there, using ASDICs [now known as sonar], we dropped two depth charges. This resulted in items floating to the surface and meant we had scored a hit. But the Germans were crafty, as they used to put items through their torpedo tubes in order to mislead us.

After escorting the convoys, we were called back to base and realised that something was imminent, due to the amount of shipping and accumulation of troops. This was proved when we were ordered to sail to Normandy in order to lay submerged buoys with sonar, to mark the channel for mine sweepers to clear the area ready for the landings. Ten days after D-Day, King George VI arrived aboard *HMS Arethusa*. We had orders to transfer him and his high-ranking officers via our own craft to an amphibious vehicle, which was ready to take them on to the beach, where General Montgomery was waiting for them.

On the Normandy coast, the only protection we had were a few merchant ships that had been sunk close to the beach in order to provide shelter for the small boats until Mulberry harbour was brought in and erected. When we were attacked by air, we had to protect the bigger ships by setting up a smokescreen to camouflage them. Although the landings were going as planned, the port of Le Havre was still under German control, therefore the Canadians surrounded the city by land. We blocked the entrance and exit by sea, making sure that even the U-boats did not have access to the port.

Having spent five months on the French coast we were recalled to our home base. In November 1944, we were looking forward to some home leave, if only for a short time. But this was not to be, we had orders to escort a convoy of landing craft to Walcheren Island (Holland) for the invasion. It was my turn to relieve the coxswain and take over the wheel, as the second in command from the captain. Soon after I had taken over, I was given orders to alter course. Apparently the order was given too soon. The night was pitch black and we collided with the lead landing craft. We thought we had lost a gunner, but he had been catapulted on to the landing craft and, thankfully, was unharmed. These events put us out of action. We were towed back to base and so we were out of the invasion. After our return to base, we did finally get home leave.

In November 1944 we commissioned our new boat, *ML 913*. We were detailed to go to a base at Stornoway. It was our job to gather the U-boats, and we brought nine back into dock at Stranraer. As there were no facilities to accommodate the German personnel, we stripped the U-boats of their armaments. We were forced to accommodate them then in their own boats temporarily, although they were taken for showers and medical attention as necessary. In his frustration, one of the German officers, who spoke fluent English, said: "You won the First World War and you won the second one, but let's see who wins the third!" Once they had been repatriated and the submarines sent to Ireland to be destroyed, we returned to *HMS Hornet*.

We brought our boat back to Poole harbour and I was made boatswain. All of the German craft were collected into the harbour and my job was to take two sailors with me on a boat to pump out bilges, which were filling with water. Once this was done, we were sent back to Peterhead for demobilisation.

With the liberation of Paris, I requested compassionate leave to visit my three older brothers, who had fought alongside the Republicans. I travelled to the Gare du Nord and showed a local man the address I needed to find (as I didn't speak French in those days). He was kind enough to take me right to the door. I thanked him by giving him a packet of English cigarettes. He was thrilled to receive them. You can imagine my brothers were anxious and pleased to see this young sailor who stood there instead of their 12-year-old brother, whose nickname had been "Chato".

When we were demobbed we were given a suit, hat, waistcoat and some money, so that we were equipped for "civvy street". I returned to Coventry, to lodgings I had occupied before the war and was lucky enough to return to the same job.

In 1947, the whole family got together in Paris. My parents had been given permission to cross the Spanish border to join my four brothers. This was because my mother had terminal cancer. My brother Luis and I lived and worked in Paris for a year, and all of us looked after our parents. My father died shortly after my mother and they were both buried in Paris. Luis and I then returned to England.

After the war it was back to engineering and, like most people, I married. I was to become the father of five lovely children. Twenty seven years later I married for a second time and became stepfather to three, grandfather to 14 and great grandfather to two. My final achievement was to be able to recover my Spanish nationality.

Looking back, I feel that the people of Britain, who organised the evacuation of so many Spanish children to this country in 1937, proved to be our salvation. I felt it was my duty to contribute something in return by volunteering to fight for this country against Fascism, by joining the Royal Navy. I happen to have had a choice and have had the privilege to love two countries, the one in which I was born, which is always in my heart, and my adopted one. I keep strong links with my home town and visit whenever possible.

I feel strongly that I must mention my present marriage. From the day I met my wife, we have been there for each other. In fact I feel I could not live my life without her and she without me, although as Christians we know that life must go on.   (Alfredo died in 2008)

Valentín Sagasti Torrano

1936 – and the bombs fell. We sheltered in the church of Santa María on the Calle 31 Agosto in San Sebastián. There was an understanding with the enemy that religious buildings were sacrosanct and so churches were large assembly places available to seek refuge.

As the fighting moved north, the family evacuated San Sebastián and we all went to Baracaldo, a small town near Bilbao. My sister Carmen was nearly five and we played in the streets and the sirens went. Everybody ran for shelter and we followed. The tunnel ran into the hillside and we all crowded in. Carmen and I held hands and stood to one side of the track. I had always assumed that there were two tracks and that we had chosen to stand on the lucky one. It was not until many years later that I learnt that there was only one and my recollection of the incident confirmed this.

Planes inhabited the sky and bombs sought targets. Along the track, a train, as if out of control, sped toward the tunnel seeking shelter. The driver had obviously panicked and in abject fear headed for safety. Brave people stood on the track, waving their arms and extolling the train to stop. To no avail, it thundered into the tunnel and straight into innocent victims seeking shelter. Somewhere it stopped, leaving a trail of carnage. I remember nothing of the graphic details, only seeing some of the soldiers giving aid.

My parents decided to send me to England. Did they want to protect me from the travails of war? Perhaps they thought that a boy would be more vulnerable in time of war. The truth was just their desire for my safety. It was a departure that would last a lifetime.

My family dispersed, my mother and two sisters took refuge in France and my father, who was a municipal policeman, lost his job, like many Basques who supported the Republic. He was imprisoned, first in Santoña prison near Santander and then in San Pedro de Cardeña, Burgos. All his life he had to endure the indignity of having to eke out a living in an industry he had not been prepared for and seeking jobs wherever they presented themselves. For a number of years I lost all contact with my family.

The *Habana* set sail from the port of Santurce on 21 May 1937. Child evacuees, their elder siblings and adult helpers crammed on to the ship. I was seven years old, which was the lower age limit, unless accompanied by older siblings, but Carmen was not yet five and must have been too young to accompany me, as I could hardly have been considered old enough to look after myself.

On the *Habana* there was no one close to me. I was one of a multitude being shepherded within the shelter of the ship, recognising no one. We were all of the same flock. I never felt fear. I was never alone, but I knew loneliness. Someone would take my hand and guide me to the company of others: "Here take care of him."

We arrived safely at Southampton and from the camp at North Stoneham were sent to a variety of different homes. My first home was the colony at Brampton. When we arrived at Citadel Station in Carlisle we were met by Lady Cecilia Roberts and Charles Roberts and were taken to the colony by bus. We were 100 children in all, 33 girls and 67 boys.

The colony was a very large house in its own grounds, bounded by a stone wall and mounted with cast iron railings. Being of an active nature, I recall jumping from this wall onto the lower branch of an adjoining tree, with a rope harness tied to my upper arms. Though it had become entangled in the railing, it did not impede my flight, but my grip on the slippery branch failed and I fell heavily to the ground, dislocating my left arm.

Occasionally we used to raid a local field and steal potatoes, which we roasted on an open fire. At other times we toasted whatever bread we managed to procure. How we always enjoyed the bounty! Some boys chased chickens in an adjoining garden and we were similarly chased ourselves.

By this time I was a member of the entertainment group, which comprised 14 girls and one boy. Dressed in typical Basque costume, we toured local communities and displayed our talents, singing and dancing. Rewards from these performances took the form of money, which went to help the funds. We were also given presents which we took back and distributed amongst ourselves. One such prized gift, which I selected, was a small melodeon. This item, along with a pair of trousers and some socks with adequate holes, became the subject of amusement for my Scottish "father", as they were the only possessions in my case on my arrival at his house.

The call came to go to Glasgow, although I knew nothing of my destination. It must have been hurriedly arranged. Someone brought me a case and placed my worldly goods in it and I was taken to the station at Carlisle. The train appeared to be leaving on my arrival, and I was dispatched with a hastily conveyed: "Look after this child" as I was placed in a compartment. I had no means of identification, and I didn't know what my destination was in Glasgow. The final indignity must have been due to haste on the part of the person who took me to the station, as he forgot to give me a ticket for the journey.

This was August 1939 and my predicament, on arrival at St Enoch Station unaccompanied, surfaced as I stepped down on the platform and was confronted by a ticket collector. I said to him in Spanish: "A man has it". No one was there to meet me. The problem was quickly dealt with and I found myself being taken to the residence of the Spanish Consul in Park Circus, where I spent the night. My only recollection of this affair was being shown a portrait of General Franco decorating a wall of one of the reception rooms. The following morning, Mr Blackwood, my Scottish "father", arrived and took me to 392 Edinburgh Road, Carntyne, Glasgow. It was a family sympathetic to the cause of Socialism and to the plight of the Spanish refugees.

My education at Brampton had been nil and my knowledge of English matched it. My introduction to the language began when I was about ten years old. School beckoned and I started at Carntyne Primary School. Spelling exercises took the form of the teacher calling out ten words we had to write down. Usually I wrote down about three or four, which were totally wrong, spelling what I heard phonetically. In the space of one year I was proficient in English, but had forgotten all my Spanish.

My arrival in Glasgow had been in August 1939 and war broke out in September. In 1941 the Luftwaffe penetrated the shipyards of Glasgow on the river Clyde and devastated the area in what became known as the Clydebank blitz. This generated mass evacuations, and Mrs Blackwood and I settled in a holiday camp three miles south of the town of Irving, where I continued my education. I settled in quickly and recall showing my enjoyment and ability by willingly raising my hand to answer teacher's questions. At the end of my education I returned to Glasgow.

During my stay at Brampton and early days in Glasgow, I had no contact with my parents except by correspondence, for me in English, for them in Spanish, which made communication difficult. So, 13 years after leaving Spain, I decided to visit my family. As I was still a Spanish citizen and due for military service, I decided to go to the border between France and Spain.

The year was 1950 and I left Glasgow with a total fund of £12, which I obtained from Mr Blackwood. With a friend I hitched to London. We bought tickets to Paris for £7. My friend stayed in Paris. I bought a single ticket to Nantes, hoping to hitch to the border. After various adventures I arrived in Bordeaux and bought a one-way ticket to Hendaye, on the French side of the border.

I had written previously to my father telling him I was coming. I didn't know when I would arrive, so I did not appear to have planned it very well. However, when I reached Hendaye, I expected a welcome party, which did not materialise. I walked towards the river, which was the international boundary. At the riverside I encountered two men working on a boat. The older of them was Pedro Carasatorre, whose parents had come over from Spain and settled in France. Pedro worked in the factory and we became acquainted. Every day, I did the same thing: walk to the station expecting my parents, back to the riverside, sleeping under a hedge, and consuming the little food I had brought with me which only lasted the first five days or so. The only thing I got free was the water I was able to drink at the station.

By the fifth day I was desperate. I wrote a letter to my parents telling them of my plight. Local trade was common between France and Spain with many people coming over daily, mainly to purchase bread, as dual nationality was common. I asked Pedro to post a letter for me and he offered to post it in Spain, as it would arrive quicker. But that evening he went to my parents' house and delivered the awful news. Late in the evening on his return, he woke me up and gave me my father's identity card and money to buy food. Early the next day, at a local café, I ate the most wonderful meal ever, a breakfast of coffee, bacon, eggs and bread.

Later on, I maintained a vigil on the bridge awaiting my parents. They had experienced difficulty in obtaining authorisation to cross into France. Over the parapet, necks strained to get a glimpse of each other until we made contact, then came the final moment.

They came over. My mother, father and, I think, two of my sisters, but I don't remember which. The joy of our reunion was palpable, embraces, smiles and an undying love contained within us. They had brought food and drink with them and we sat on the roadside on the French side of the policeman's outpost, as they weren't allowed to come any further. This first meeting lasted two hours.

Miguel San Sebastián Pérez

We were taken from the camp at Eastleigh to Dorking, (19 boys and girls and two ladies, a teacher and a helper). There we met wonderful people like Mr Charles Duffield and his mother, who frequently took us to their house for tea and to spend odd weekends with them.

When the colony at Dorking closed they moved us on to Redhill, also in Surrey, where we lived until the time of our repatriation. Ascension House, as the colony was called, had been bought by Mr Richard West, a member of the Basque Children's Committee, to house 20 boys and girls.

A few days after our arrival in Redhill we were enrolled at the state school in Cromwell Road. José Ramón Valentín and I played in the school football team, he as inside left and I as goalkeeper. Many of the spectators at the matches knew that two Basque lads were playing for the school side and somehow we were one of the attractions at every match.

One particular incident, which was absolutely typical of the attitude of the British general public toward us, took place in London. Mr Fred Lilley, who owned a greengrocery and a fishmonger's in Merstham, Surrey, took me one day to the London market. We left early in the morning and after buying the produce we went to have breakfast at a pub near the market. When he went to pay for the breakfasts, the person who served us told Mr Lilley he would only take payment for his breakfast and refused all attempts to pay for mine. We constantly came across similar attitudes.

The day we were repatriated, the farewells between those of us who were returning and those who were remaining were intensely emotional. I have always been puzzled as to why my brother and I were repatriated, since nobody had requested our return. The goodbyes at the port of Newhaven were very emotional. Hugs and kisses were exchanged between those leaving for Spain and English friends who had accompanied us to the port. Ronald Thackrah, another excellent person who was a member of the committee, was in charge of the expedition.

During the journey we thought unceasingly about the people we were leaving behind in England, and about how we would find our parents and other relatives, but what we could not conceive of was the absolutely radical difference we encountered no sooner had we crossed the frontier from Hendaye to Irún. It is hard to explain: it was as if we were stepping from one world into another that was completely different in a negative sense, and was made even worse by the unjust treatment we received from some people at the Spanish frontier. In Irún once more tears sprang to our eyes as we bade farewell to those who had shared with us in England our joys and sorrows and the love and affection of so many good friends.

We realised at once how difficult it would be for us to adapt, not only to living again with our parents, but also to life in the repressive atmosphere that was everywhere. It was not the atmosphere of freedom we had been used to. It was a strange mixture of fear, uncertainty and unease. We were constantly being told not go near such and such place, that we shouldn't speak in English in front of people or pronounce a single word in Basque (this, our own language, was banned) because of the risk involved, given the delicate situation in which our father found himself. There was a shortage of so many of the things that we had in plenty in England. There was a lack of food and of the basic necessities of life.

The trauma we underwent after our return from England, and the subsequent times of difficulty and anxiety which both our parents and my sister and I were to live through, left an indelible mark on us.

Except for the reasons why my sister and I were evacuated and the fact that we were separated from our parents, we can say sincerely that our time in England constituted one of the happiest periods in our life. *

Marguerite Scott

I had trained as a children's nurse and was working with a family in High Wycombe when I first heard of the Spanish refugee children at Baydon Hole Farm near Newbury. A friend of mine had spent a fortnight there, so when my annual holiday came up, I went too for two weeks.

I enjoyed the work helping the children shelter from their war-torn homeland so much, that I gave in my notice in High Wycombe and returned to the children at Baydon Hole as soon as possible. There were many things to do, but I remember helping the children to learn English by taking them for walks up the hill behind the camp and pointing out things in English and they would tell me the Spanish name. That way we each learnt a little of each other's language.

A little later a benefactor, Mr McIlroy, who owned a big department store in Reading, together with a local committee, organised the colony for the *niños* at Bray Court near Maidenhead in Berkshire. I wasn't there to help with the move, because I had a very bad sore throat that the doctor thought might be diphtheria, a dangerous disease in those days, so I went home for a few days. Luckily it was not diphtheria, so I was able to join the children at Bray Court. Not long after my arrival at Bray, the lady who I had worked for in High Wycombe visited Bray to ask me to go to work for a friend of hers, but I knew the children at Bray needed me more, so I stayed with them.

There were three Spanish people, Doña María, Doña Rosario and Eduardo Sánchez. Eduardo was from south-east Spain. Doña María gave me the recipe for *leche frita*, which I still have. María, Rosario and Eduardo looked after the older children and I looked after the younger children up to ten years old, and any of the older children who were unwell. As well as myself, there was another English volunteer, Kathleen Hawes, who had grown up in Spain and who spoke fluent Spanish.

Soon after arriving at Bray there was an outbreak of scabies amongst the children. They hated the treatment! One night, one of the *niñas*, Teresa, was screaming and doubled over with severe stomach pain for a long time. Kathleen and I thought that she had appendicitis, but Matron thought that there was nothing wrong with her and she was just doing it to get attention and refused to call a doctor. In the end Teresa was in so much pain that I slipped downstairs to go to phone for a local doctor, who had said that he would come to the colony at any time of day or night. I was worried that if it wasn't appendicitis, I would get into trouble with Matron, but luckily I met Eduardo in the hall, who asked what was happening and he went to phone instead to save me from getting into trouble. The doctor came,

Teresa was rushed to hospital for an operation and afterwards spent a week in convalescence with my mother in Twyford. Matron left soon after, Kathleen Hawes became Matron and I became deputy Matron.

Of the *niños*, I remember in particular José Alberdi. He stayed in England after the Spanish Civil War ended and became a famous sculptor. He made the bull for the Bullring Shopping Centre in Birmingham.

A local benefactor (perhaps Mr McIlroy) paid for the children to have a smoked fish dish, *bacalao*, once a week, so Doña María and Doña Rosario taught the kitchen staff how to cook it. He also provided a box of oranges for the *niños* to have afterwards. Another benefactor provided a coach to take the *niños* to church on Sundays.

My brother, Cyril Scott, used to come at weekends and took many photographs, some of them colour slides. Towards the end, Ronald Bates came to help with the older boys, after he came back from the International Brigade, and he stayed until the colony closed down. We were married in 1940.

When the Spanish Civil War ended many of the children went home in dribs and drabs. Kathleen escorted two groups and I was due to take the next group, but the colony was closed down and the remaining children were sent to other colonies. I never did get to Spain until my husband took me for the commemoration of the 65th anniversary of the Spanish Civil War, organised by the International Brigade Memorial Trust.

(Transcribed by Robert Bates, son)

Miren Solaberrieta Mendiola

On 20 September 1936, our father left Zarauz alone, with just a small case and a few friends, bound for Bilbao. Soon after our mother, and a group of women whose husbands had also escaped, were sent to prison, leaving my sister and me alone: we were just nine and 12 years old.

My mother was exchanged with prisoners from the opposition jailed in the same city, and so on 4 December 1936, she took me and my sister Begoña to Bilbao to join my father. While we were in Bilbao, we suffered several bombings, including the one in Guernica. At this time our parents decided to send us to Great Britain, having first asked us whether we wanted to go.

On 21 May 1937, we left the port of Santurce on the *Habana*, arriving at Southampton two days later. I can't forget as long as I live, and I guess none of the children who were with us in the camp at that time will either, waking up on the morning of 19 June, when we heard that Bilbao had fallen to Franco's troops. None of us had had any news of our parents' whereabouts. Everyone was crying. My parents had to escape from Bilbao in separate ships and from different ports. They both arrived in France, where they stayed for several months not knowing where each one was. When they finally met, they worked very hard, trying to better themselves until such time as they could have us back with them.

We had been in Southampton for a couple of weeks when we were told they were taking us to a house called Shornell's, together with our friends from Zarauz, Elisabete, Lore and Pirmin Trecu, and another 16 children. Shornell's was an old and marvellous mansion, like those described in English novels, with large woods all around. It belonged to the Royal Arsenal Co-operative Society, in Abbey Wood, South-east London, close to Woolwich and 20 minutes by train to London. We couldn't believe our luck. It was idyllic! We received a great welcome from the Head and the staff of the centre. For the first few days they made a great effort not to let us go hungry.

We went to St. Joseph's Convent Secondary School, in Abbey Wood itself, a five minute walk from the house. The first classes we followed were language classes, and later we were able to join in the classes with English pupils and follow two more courses. I remember at the beginning of September that year, how our ears were glued to the radio, listening to Mr Chamberlain announcing the outbreak of the war between Germany and Great Britain. They were very sad moments, not knowing what was to become of us and still without news from our parents.

The Head of the school considered that where we were living was dangerous in case of bombing, as we lived very few miles away from the Woolwich Arsenal. Therefore all the girls, English and Basque, were moved to Canterbury, where they continued to teach us. (The boys didn't come with us as there were so few.) We stayed in private houses, where the families took us in and treated us like their daughters. The time we spent at Canterbury was very interesting and fruitful. We had lessons every morning and in the afternoons the teachers would take us to visit historic places in the area, of which there were many. I can remember those times perfectly, as I made some very good friends. I'm still in touch with one of them; we still write to each other. We're both 82 years old. Throughout these years we've met several times, either in Bilbao or Canterbury. We returned to Shornell's in mid December 1939. Paradoxically, at that time, Woolwich suffered less from the bombing than Canterbury.

On 2 December 1940, when the Second World War was in full swing, we met up with our parents again in Biarritz. As Hitler's troops were approaching Biarritz, our mother and we two sisters had to go back to Bilbao to start life afresh there, but our father couldn't join us for political reasons, so he remained in exile for another ten years. Our contacts with him were infrequent as the border was closed. We couldn't write, but we managed to maintain some sort of contact through friends who crossed the frontier clandestinely.

This then is my story from the start of the Spanish Civil War on that unforgettable day – 18 July 1936. My experience in England all those years ago has been one of the most interesting and pleasant events in my life. It really had a big influence on my way of understanding life, as well as teaching me about democracy. Thanks to the English people I was educated and got a good job as a bilingual secretary in a large company in Vizcaya.

Some years later in Bilbao, I met the man who became my husband, Juan José Mancísidor. He was also a passenger on the *Habana*, No 1054, and he admired England as much as I did. In our long life together we've always remembered how happy we were living in England, and have returned to the country at fairly frequent intervals.

My husband was sent to Gainford, a small town in the north of the country, in Durham. I understand that it was a coal mining area, near Darlington. He was taken, with a group of boys, to a home for Catholic orphans. Many years later with some friends, he returned to that place, rendered inhospitable and forlorn by the climate. They brought a statue of the Virgin Begoña, as a token of their thanks for the welcome they had received during those difficult times. He also spent some time in Scarborough, in a large colony called The Old Hospital.

The Trecus went to Biarritz when they returned from England. The oldest sister married another Basque *niño* and she still lives in England. Lore went back to Zarauz, married and raised a family, and she's a grandmother now. Pirmin, having founded his own ballet school in Oporto where he taught until he retired, went back to Zarauz and lived with his brothers. He was the youngest of the group and we all looked after him. They were marvellous times. *

Fernando de la Torre Fé

My parents and I arrived in England on 26 March 1939. We arrived having followed the "via dolorosa" from Barcelona to Figueras, La Junquera, Le Perthus and Vernet-les-Bains, where we stayed a few weeks until we had our first contact with the *niños*. We received a letter, dated 2 March 1939, from Mrs Jessie Stewart of Girton Gate, Cambridge, inviting us, unseen and pretty much unknown, to come and live with them.

Carmen Martínez Lorite, a friend of my mother and heavily involved with the Cambridge colony at Station Road, had mentioned to Mrs Stewart my father's wish to come to England – hence the letter, the start of that never to be forgotten gesture: "We are great friends of Srta Martinez and all the Basque children and shall welcome you and Sra de la Torre very warmly. Believe me, Jessie G Stewart." Such is the ending of that marvellous letter and our introduction to the existence of that corner of Euskadi that was established in England's green and pleasant land.

My father's family from the town of Balmaseda, Vizcaya (where I still vote), go back centuries. My maternal grandmother was born in San Sebastián, so the whole Basque ethos has always been very close to us. It is therefore not surprising that my parents would find a significant echo with *los niños vascos de Cambridge*, particularly within the context of the tragedy that was our Civil War.

I was 13 years old when I arrived in England and my main need and activity was to go to school and learn English. I started straight away at Girton Village School, then Impington Village College and finally completed my education at the Perse School. At all stages, it was made very easy by the total acceptance and kindness of the teachers and children, supposedly cold and standoffish Britons.

My reminiscences of the *niños* are limited, as by necessity our lives followed different paths. However, we did meet early on at Girton Gate, Mrs Stewart's home, for I have a selection of photos, mostly taken by my father. I did join the *niños* for a football match, which we played on Jesus Green and I recall that we wore large blue and dark red checked shirts. I don't remember who we played, but I have a terrible feeling that the score was 11-11, but it could have been something totally different. This was the first soccer match I ever played in and I think also the last!

The main occasion when both my parents and I did meet up with the whole group was for a holiday at a windmill in Burnham Overy on the Norfolk coast. It was in August 1939, just before the start of the Second World War. The biggest thrill I remember from that holiday was having to try the fire escape, descending from quite a height on the outside of the mill tower. I also remember a choral concert given at the bandstand on Christ's Piece by the bus station and my father taking some of the practices for it at the house in Station Road. I joined the choir more to make up numbers than anything else.

A very early and unlikely connection occurred whilst I was at the Perse School, when the arts master, Cecil Crouch, who had taken parties to the ballet at Covent Garden, and to whom I had mentioned the Basque children, told me that one of them, but not from Cambridge, had become a dancer with the Royal Ballet. His name was Pirmin Aldabaldetrecu. Later he rather wisely changed his surname to Trecu.

Snippets of news about the Basque children came to my notice second-hand, from my parents, Carmen Lorite or Mrs Stewart. We learned that Domingo Arana, who was working at Cambridge Instruments, had had a very bad accident, possibly to do with traffic, which required him to have a metal plate inserted in his head, but he came out of it well. I know that Enrique Murgui boxed, for I saw him fight at a fair in Cambridge. Sadly, I believe he died in a fire at his workplace. I recall Carmen Lorite telling me that Benito Tomé had become a commando in the British army.

My mother, Caridad, became a good friend of Luisa Gallego, the mother of the Gallego clan, who after an extremely traumatic life travelling Europe as a refugee, managed to join her five surviving children in Cambridge in 1947. I remember visiting their house at 34 Trafalgar Road in Cambridge. José was also there with his young son, playing ball and saying to him: "Use your left foot as well". Both Antonio and José, who played goalkeeper and outside left, became professional footballers.

I next saw Carmen Lorite during my first visit to Spain in 1953, at her house in Madrid, in Calle Juan Bravo 12. She talked a lot about her *niños* still in Cambridge and I do hope that some kept in touch with her. Later I met up with Salomé Moreno and her husband Juan, also Ascensión Belón, by then married to Miguel Ramira, who had not only fought in Spain but also in Norway with the French army. She told me how my mother had always encouraged her and the other girls to strive for the best possible education and social goals.

I am glad that the Basque Children of '37 Association UK has taken the decision to maintain the memory of those dark, though glorious, days when the kindness of the British people gave some respite from the horrors of a brutal civil war.

Carmen Uribarri Bilbao

My brother Juanito and I were amongst the thousands of children evacuated from the Spanish Civil War in 1937 and embarked on the *Habana* on 21 May, bound for Southampton. I was only seven years old and the number on my card was 2879. I was very young and only have a vague memory of the journey. Once we arrived in England, they put us in a camp at Stoneham, where the boys and girls were separated, so I wasn't with my brother. After a little while in the camp, I went with some other girls to a colony at Weston Manor on the Isle of Wight until September 1938, when my uncle José Antonio Bilbao took me to Belgium. My brother Juanito went to the colony at Cardiff.

One of the things I remember best is life in the camp. There was a great storm one day and we spent a long time holding up the tent poles so that it wouldn't blow away. Another thing I remember about Weston Manor is that we went to mass in the chapel every day. All the girls took communion, and I did too. The strange thing was that I hadn't been able to take my first communion in my country: before being evacuated, my brother and I had been preparing for it, but we hadn't had time for the ceremony. So my first communion was organised in England. I still have a photo of myself at the ceremony, wearing a white dress and a veil, and holding a rosary.

I also have fond memories of my uncle. He was a sailor and was in England when the war broke out. He used to take great interest in us and came several times with my brother to visit me. On one of these visits he bought me a dress and shoes - I still have the photo of me wearing my new clothes for the first time. Another time, he bought a doll for each of the girls in the colony, and there we are in one of the photos, each child with her doll and with our *andereño* (teacher) in the middle.

As little girls do, we sometimes got up to mischief; next to the house there was a vegetable garden with fruit trees. I don't remember how we got in, but we used to steal fruit like apples and figs. The gardener was a short, stocky man, and we used to call him "Fatty". When he saw us in the garden, he shouted out to us in English, things that we couldn't understand and we ran away as quickly as possible, with the advantage that we could run faster than him. Some days English couples would come to Weston Manor and invite us to their houses for tea. In spite of the fact that 70 years have passed since the experience of being in England, I'd love to go back there some day.

During my stay in Belgium, my sister and I were taken in by M Pierre Jansen, who was involved in the care of the Basque children. We went to school there, and Flemish was spoken. In three months I learned the language and nearly forgot my Spanish. In the summer of 1939 I went to stay in the country with the Jansen family and spent a happy summer with the five nephews who were there.

I never felt unhappy about being away from my home and parents. Perhaps this is because I am of a very tranquil nature. I was so happy that when they told me I had to go back home, I was very sad, so sad that I threatened to hide on top of a kitchen cupboard so that they wouldn't find me and send me home. On 10 October 1939 we went back to Bilbao shortly after the Second World War broke out. *

Pablo Valtierra Martínez

The actual crossing was dreadful. When we reached Southampton, we didn't want to get off the boat and were running all over the decks. Finally we were taken to a sort of huge campsite where they had erected lots of tents, army style.

We didn't stay in North Stoneham for long as we were taken to the colony at Langham near Colchester. I was lucky, because I remember that I wasn't very popular because I used to fight with everyone, and thanks to a boy called Vicente, I went with them. Also quite a lot of those of us who went to that colony were from my home town of Sestao, so we knew each other already.

When we arrived at the very comfortable Basque House in Langham, all the children were taken into this big room filled with as many toys as you can imagine. This made us think that we weren't going to see our parents, brothers and sisters for a while. The 20 of us fought for the toys.

With us there was also a group of young girls from Bilbao and they played a very important role during our stay there. There was Rafaela, the cook, Marina, a wonderful teacher, footballer and pianist, and others that I don't remember. And how could I forget our teacher and philologist, who tirelessly organised many events, Mr. Leonard Read, son of an Oxford professor. He was always there when we needed him.

They checked our clothes and according to what each person needed, we went to the top part of the house where there was a small room and inside there were people distributing clothes. The whole town had donated all sorts of things, toys, new and used clothes. They looked to see what we needed, sometimes shoes, sometimes trousers. It was a bit of a mix-up – for some, the trousers were too long, for others, the shoes were too big. It was a real laugh seeing what we were given.

After that we went out to look at the garden. I remember the gardeners, and amongst them one in particular whose name was Otto and he was German. He was a shoe-repairer and he used to mend all our shoes. But we also discovered that he was a great ping-pong player and he taught all of us in the colony to play this game. Mr Leonard showed us round the area beyond the gardens. There was a wood nearby where we would go on our own later to hunt rabbits. We would place string to catch them when they came out from the burrows, we also surrounded them when they were running out in the open, penning them in.

At first we had to get used to the teachers that had come from Bilbao - with all the books being in English, it was quite difficult. We studied literature and mathematics, among other things, and they also used to take us outside to draw, and I ended up drawing quite well. Afterwards we started going to the local state school, where we were mixed with English boys and girls. We did handicrafts, for example, I made some ties that I took back with me to Spain. Everyone enjoyed these activities, as we had never done this before. So when I went back to Spain I noticed the difference. One must realise that Spain was 30 years behind England.

The days went by and the families were still coming to visit us. They would always bring us things, sweets and clothes for example. I think they felt sorry for us being separated from our parents. In addition, there was a change of government in Spain, some fathers in jail, mine in particular had been sentenced to death, although he was released in the end. I didn't know much about what was happening. When visitors used to take him food, they would hide my letters in it and so when he went to eat his sandwich and found them inside, he was very pleased.

There used to be heavy snowfalls in England in winter and it was very pretty. The children in the colony used to make a giant Father Christmas snowman in the garden at the front of the house, first making a very big snowball at the bottom for the body, then a smaller one on top for the head and then came the red hat and the red scarf of Father Christmas. The weather was so cold that the snowman never melted. We also threw snowballs and the ones who got hit the most were the girls.

I still remember how we used to get to school and used to see sledges pulled by horses with children being taken to school, as the cars couldn't use the roads. You could also see mothers taking their children on small wooden sledges.

Some children, like me, used to take eggs from thrushes' nests and we also used to see blackbirds frozen to death on the ground. I remember that in Spain we used to eat little birds, but I noticed that in England they respected them.

In the summer they used to take us to the river and we had a very good time. We learnt to swim and sometimes we would stay for lunch and spend the whole day there. We even went there when it rained, as we used to in Bilbao, where it rained almost all the time. The stretch from the house to the river was very beautiful. We went across fields where there were pheasants with their young. The landscape reminded me of the Basque Country – it was always beautifully green.

We also had artistic activities in the colony. We formed a concert party with boys and girls and when English people came to see us we used to perform our shows. We would do flamenco dances and we would sing. I remember singing *Asturias, patria querida* and the famous *Los cuatro muleros* by García Lorca, and people liked it very much, as they did listening to the Basque songs. The girl from Bilbao, Marina, who was also our teacher, used to accompany us on the piano and she directed our shows. We used to perform our shows in other parts of the country and to other colonies.

I remember we also organised a football team, captained by Vicente. He was a very good captain and great companion. Marina trained us and used to play football very well. The famous Otto used to organise treasure hunts in the woods. They would hide things and we had to find them. It was fun because they gave us a sort of sketch and clues how to find them.

At one time, some of the children developed scabies and they had to bath us in yellow sulphur. We were isolated from the rest of the group until we were completely cured, so that we wouldn't pass it on to the others. Mr Leonard used to prepare the sulphur bath.

I remember that every week they gave us pocket-money, a few pence or farthings, and we would go to Dedham village to spend it. We were quite mischievous. We would go into the sweet shop and while some of us were paying, the others would steal some sweets. When we returned the following week, they would keep an eye on us and ensure that we didn't leave without having paid. They were good people and as we were children and they knew we were separated from our parents, they let us get up to all sorts of things.

After a while, some of the children in the colony, whose parents had asked for their return, went back home. Mine didn't, and one day a man came to the camp to adopt me and a girl named Petra Martínez. This man worked as an engineer at a paper factory in Kent. We lived there in a beautiful house. He made a shelter in case we were bombed. He also took us to the Town Hall to try on different gas masks, in case the Germans used gas. We weren't allowed to go out without the family and we always had to walk holding their arms.

Living in a family was very different, especially at the weekends when we were taken for drives in the car as we'd never done that before. With his wife and daughter, we'd go to the country and we'd eat by the river Thames. It was very nice and sometimes we'd hire a boat. I liked this a lot because it reminded me of Bilbao, which is on the estuary. At other times we'd go to the zoo, where the parents and their daughter laughed a lot because they would give us peanuts to feed the monkeys, and instead of feeding them to the monkeys, I'd eat them! We had everything we wanted, although we had a hard time because of the language barrier, since up until then we had only lived with Spanish children in the colony.

The family tried hard to make us happy. In the evenings, before going to bed, all the family would play card games like poker, and in the winter we'd play fun games, sitting next to the fireplace. They were wonderful people. I can't remember how long I stayed there, but it is a shame that I lost contact with them.

My parents asked for me to return and, although I was pleased to go back to Spain, it was also sad to say goodbye to the family who had looked after me like parents. I always regret that through laziness I never knew what became of them. We were taken in a small boat to Calais. We crossed the channel with the lights switched off, because it was still wartime and they thought there might be German submarines. We couldn't make any noise, so we were quite frightened and imagined the worst. We finally got to France and from there went by train to Irún and Bilbao. Then there was the reunion in Sestao. It was an unforgettable experience: we were all so happy to be together again.

But it was hard to adapt to this new situation, since all the family had been separated in some way: my father in prison, my mother and brother in France, and my sister in Switzerland. It was especially hard for my father who had been fighting against Franco's army, as he couldn't find work anywhere. His friends were too frightened to help him. One day when my father knocked on the door of some firm, it was opened by the Director himself. He had been a commander in Franco's army, and my father had known him when he was a prisoner. When he saw him, he nearly ran away. But the man called after him and, in the end, it was the enemy who gave him work and later helped us a great deal too.

I also remember those who stayed behind in the United Kingdom. And I have to conclude saying that the English people that we met were very good to us. *

Álvaro Velasco Luengo

Although life in the camp at Eastleigh was fairly regimental, at times it could also be tedious. One day, to relieve the boredom of everyday existence, my friend Pedro Sáenz and I toyed with the idea of stealing a rather fashionable pair of trousers that we had spotted on the communal clothes line. The main attraction of these trousers was the *gudary* or *mil rayas*, which highlighted their quality. The plan was successfully carried out with military precision, and I then concealed the booty at the bottom of my kit bag, never to be worn at Eastleigh for fear of recognition.

A few months later I was transported, together with 80 other children, to the colony at Brechfa in west Wales. At last I would have the opportunity to wear the new trousers! I pressed them meticulously between two straw mattresses, then I put them on and strode out like a Hollywood film star, confident of receiving admiring comments.

True to form, a compatriot from San Sebastián named Tomás paid much attention to my new trousers. He looked closely at the nametag on the waistband to reveal that, in fact, the trousers were his! What a small world!

Another story concerns the football matches. Rivalry between the boys of Donostia and Vizcaya was as fanatical at Laleham School, Margate, as it had been in Spain. A weekly match between the two factions was promptly organised. It was mutually agreed that there would be a grand prize of afternoon tea cakes, which was a daily treat for the boys.

Unfortunately for me, our team from Donostia lacked the individual technique and team cohesion to beat the Bilbao boys. Consequently, each week my team mates and I went hungry at teatime, missing out on a greatly relished delight. Frustrated by this situation, we hatched a plan to relieve the bread delivery man, who came at seven o'clock every morning, of his tastiest delicacies.

The scheme involved three reliable brothers-in-arms. Pedro Sáenz from the Barrio Aguea was the look-out, telling his fellow conspirators when the bread man was out of sight. Juan Cantalapiedra, meanwhile, was in charge of opening and closing the doors of the bread van to allow me, the third link, to secrete a selection of cakes and a loaf of bread, before making a quick getaway to conceal the ill-gotten goods. Much to the surprise of the Bilbao boys, the Donostiarras, in defeat, somehow managed to give the impression that they were in fact victorious!

(Transcribed by Andrew Velasco, son. Álvaro died in 2009)

The camp at North Stoneham in Eastleigh

Breakfast

Comrades

Washing-up

Exercise

['The War Cry' June 5, 1937]

The **WAR** ✠ **CRY**

WILLIAM BOOTH
FOUNDER

Official Organ of The Salvation Army

[Registered at the General Post Office as a Newspaper]

EVANGELINE BOOTH
GENERAL

No. 3,176—58TH YEAR   INTERNATIONAL HEADQUARTERS]   SATURDAY, JUNE 5, 1937   [LONDON, E.C. 4   PRICE ONE PENNY

'NUESTROS CORAZÓNES SE LLENAN DE GRATITUD A INGLATERRA Y A LOS INGLESES'

('Our hearts are full of gratitude to England and the English'—words constantly on the lips of the Basque children now in our midst)

['The War Cry' photo]   [The General welcomes the Spanish children in the Clapton Avenue]

The Army's new family of Spanish refugee children, shortly to be increased to fourteen hundred, asks for your practical sympathy and prayers   [SEE PAGE 12]

Front page of Salvation Army paper

The Oaks, Carshalton

Bradford

Cambridge

Margate Football Team

Dining room at Langham

Marguerite Scott, nurse, with children at Bray Court

Boys at Faringdon

The Gallego family at Cambridge:
José, Antonio, Victorina, Genoveva and María Luisa

School room at Bray Court

Staff at Langham

*Group from
Margate going
back to Spain*

Bray Court

Shipton-under-Wychwood

Children from Cambridge on holiday at Hunstanton

Miss Chloë Vulliamy

Fundraising leaflet

Oakley Park, Diss

Cyril Arapoff

Aston

Langham

Christmas card from Guildford colony

Dancers from Bray Court

The Medical tent, North Stoneham, 1937

The Culvers, Carshalton, 1945 – the last remaining colony

RECUERDOS

RECUERDOS

Niños Vascos Refugiados en Gran Bretaña

editado por

Natalia Benjamin

Agradecimientos

Deseo agradecer a todas aquellas personas que han ayudado a producir este libro, tanto transcribiendo como traduciendo, corrigiendo pruebas o repasando la primera impresión. Sin su colaboración desinteresada no se podría haber publicado.

Ellas son:
Isabel Anjarwalla-Jones, Germán Ferrer, Jen Gardner, Tere Gautrey, Penny Harper, Anne Harrap, Gerald Hoare, Norman Jones, Shirley Jordan, Pilar McGillycuddy, Monique Moreton, Irina Nelson, Jesús Nieto, Patrick O'Kane, Alicia Pozo-Gutierrez, Ana Reynoso, Laura Román, Helen Sawyer.

Por supuesto, un agradecimiento especial a los propios niños, quienes contribuyeron con sus historias.

Obligada mención también al Ministerio de la Presidencia español por su subvención, que ha cubierto parte de los costes de publicación.

En particular, querría reconocer la labor de Adrian Bell, quien ha sido enormemente generoso con su asistencia en todas las etapas de esta empresa y ha hecho físicamente posible que el proyecto llegara a buen puerto.

Y por último, y no por ello menos importante, quiero expresar mi gratitud a mi hija, Victoria, quien me ha apoyado en todo momento, animándome, ayudándome a sistematizar todos los textos y, en general, organizándome.

Prólogo

El 21 de mayo de 1937 unos 4.000 niños junto con sus maestros y auxiliares salieron de un País Vasco destrozado por la guerra y pusieron rumbo hacia Southampton a bordo del buque *SS Habana*. A su llegada, la responsabilidad de su cuidado recayó sobre un comité formado exclusivamente a tal efecto, primero en un campamento en Eastleigh y después en los varios hogares temporales que se establecieron por toda Gran Bretaña. La llegada de estos niños, su dispersión, a menudo a lugares remotos del Reino Unido, y su participación en actos culturales para recaudar fondos contribuyeron a un mayor entendimiento del coste humano de la Guerra Civil Española entre los británicos. Muchos de los niños retornaron finalmente a sus hogares tras la caída del País Vasco, pero otros tantos, incluyendo aquellos cuyas familias estaban en el exilio, permanecieron y se establecieron permanentemente en este país.

La primera vez que tuve conocimiento de la historia de los refugiados vascos fue cuando trabajaba con mi investigación doctoral en los años ochenta. En aquella época, mi aproximación al tema – realizada principalmente a través de los documentos oficiales del gobierno británico y del *Trades Union Congress* – me resultó bastante distante. Cierto es que por aquel entonces algunos académicos, como Jim Fyrth y Dorothy Legarreta, comenzaban a publicar estudios detallados sobre las experiencias de los niños y sobre las redes de voluntarios que se habían hecho cargo de su cuidado en Gran Bretaña. Sin embargo, con la excepción del mundo académico, los niños parecían haber sido olvidados. Sus historias personales no habían side todavía recogidas y tampoco existían oportunidades de conmemoración pública de su estancia en Inglaterra.

Hoy la situación es muy diferente y esto se debe en gran medida al extraordinario trabajo que Natalia Benjamin y sus colegas de la *Basque Children of '37 Association UK* han llevado a cabo. Natalia, hija de una de las maestras, formó la asociación en noviembre de 2002 con el fin de reunir a los niños supervivientes y de preservar y divulgar su historia. Desde entonces la asociación ha erigido numerosas placas conmemorativas y ha organizado una serie de exposiciones y conferencias, a la vez que actúa como punto central para la coordinación del material histórico que se está recopilando y que próximamente será depositado en la Universidad de Southampton para beneficio de investigadores en el futuro. Como resultado de estas iniciativas, la extraordinaria historia de estos niños finalmente ha comenzado a recibir la atención pública que merecía en Gran Bretaña. Con motivo del 70 aniversario de la llegada de los niños la asociación ha iniciado un ambicioso proyecto de recopilación de memorias escritas (Recuerdos) de los niños sobrevivientes y de otras personas que jugaron un papel importante en estos eventos. La respuesta ha sido casi abrumadora y este volumen es en si un claro testimonio del deseo que sentían tantos niños de contar su historia. También hay que constatar que para que el proyecto alcanzara sus objetivos, muchas personas se han ofrecido de forma voluntaria a traducir estas memorias.

Esta colección editada de memorias constituye un magnífico monumento al extraordinario viaje de los niños y a la cálida recepción que les brindaron muchos ciudadanos británicos. El leer las memorias aquí recogidas no solo me resulta fascinante como historiador, sino tremendamente conmovedor, pues en ellas uno puede ver – a través de los ojos de los "niños", muchos de los cuales ahora rondan los ochenta años – las experiencias más dolorosas de separación, dislocación y ansiedad. Afortunadamente, el lector también se puede encontrar con actos de tremenda lealtad (especialmente entre hermanos), y de increíble resistencia frente a la incertidumbre, así como de amistades inesperadas y duraderas que se establecieron entre los niños y los británicos que les apoyaron. A pesar del sufrimiento y de la constante inseguridad que los niños debieron de sentir, resulta emotivo leer cómo a través de estas memorias tantos recuerdan de forma positiva y con cariño su estancia en este país. No cabe duda de que esto se debe en gran parte al tremendo apoyo que recibieron de los muchos voluntarios británicos que se prestaron a ayudarles. Pero también es reflejo de la emoción que sintieron al llegar a una sociedad tan nueva y diferente. Indudablemente, esta colección constituye en parte una historia social de la Gran Bretaña de finales de los años treinta: un mundo ya desaparecido marcado por las lámparas de gas, los autobuses de dos plantas y la coronación de Jorge VI. En particular, ese mundo nos revela las convenciones sociales y la vida asociativa de las pequeñas ciudades así como la vida de las clases medias suburbanas de la sociedad británica, quienes gozaban de las condiciones adecuadas para acoger a los niños vascos en sus hogares y quienes disponían del tiempo de ocio necesario para llevarles de vacaciones. Pero sobre todo, a través de estas historias aprendemos cómo los niños se adaptaron al cambio de circunstancias tan abrupto que experimentaron – a menudo enviados a viejas mansiones de la campiña inglesa situadas en grandes extensiones de tierra – y como mantuvieron vivo el recuerdo de sus familias y la esperanza del reencuentro.

Tom Buchanan
Kellogg College, Oxford.

Introducción

Todos estamos familiarizados con los actos de conmemoración publica y colectiva que se suelen celebran después de una guerra – por ejemplo, las ceremonias que tienen como objeto recordar a los soldados que combatieron, programas documentales, diversas formas de expresión narrativa en prosa y en verso, o la consagración de la memoria que se realiza a través de monumentos públicos. Pero ¿qué sucede con los que fueron arrancados de su país a una edad temprana sin poder decidir por si mismos su futuro? En 1937 unos 33.000 niños fueron evacuados durante la Guerra Civil Española. Muchos de ellos nunca volvieron. La guerra destrozó su mundo familiar. Salieron de su país para escapar de los bombardeos, del hambre y del miedo. Desprovistos de una infancia normal junto a sus padres y hermanos y desarraigados a una edad muy joven, estos niños fueron enviados a países cuyas lenguas no hablaban y cuyas culturas intentaron asimilar. Estos exiliados olvidados son también víctimas de la Guerra Civil.

Mayo de 2007 marca el 70 aniversario de la llegada de los niños vascos a Gran Bretaña. A pesar de la negativa del gobierno británico a admitir a 4.000 niños, la ciudadanía del país respondió de forma admirable y numerosas familias y voluntarios se movilizaron para acogerlos y cuidarlos. "Es imposible no quererles" rezaba el titular de un folleto informativo distribuido por el Basque Children's Committee que animaba a los ciudadanos a que "adoptaran" a un niño vasco y a que se comprometieran a donar los diez chelines semanales que eran necesarios para asegurar su manutención: "Puede enviarle regalos, sacarle de paseo por el día o tenerlo durante el fin de semana," indicaba a continuación el folleto. "Son pequeñas personitas morenas, con pelo largo y oscuro y ojos alegres y vivarachos". Estas personitas de tez oscura, que son ahora abuelos, son conscientes de su pertenencia a un grupo histórico específico: el de "los niños de la guerra".

Cuando empezamos a estudiar los diversos proyectos a través de los cuales podríamos conmemorar este aniversario se nos ocurrió enseguida que debíamos producir un libro de testimonios que brindara a los niños de la guerra la oportunidad de recopilar sus memorias y así evitar que éstas cayeran en el olvido. Desde el principio tuve la certeza de que este proyecto merecía la pena, sobre todo a raíz del creciente interés por la recuperación de la memoria histórica que España viene experimentando en los últimos años. Parece existir en estos momentos una verdadera fascinación por el pasado, que se hace patente a juzgar por los numerosos libros sobre diversos aspectos de la Guerra Civil que se exhiben en las librerías. Los españoles quieren finalmente leer lo que pasó en los años más oscuros de su Historia. Este contexto nos ha proporcionado una oportunidad única y pertinente para pedirles a los niños que nos contaran su historia.

En mayo de 2006 envié una primera carta a los niños todavía residentes en Gran Bretaña que pensé que estarían interesados en participar. También quise incluir a los niños que habían retornado a España. Por suerte, durante una visita a Vitoria en septiembre de 2006 con motivo del homenaje a los niños de la guerra organizado por el Gobierno Vasco, pude distribuir copias de la carta original. Esta iniciativa tuvo mucho éxito pues en las semanas que se sucedieron empezaron a llegar testimonios de España. En la carta yo especificaba que probablemente tendría que editar los relatos, pero que no obstante incluiría todos aquellos que me fueran enviados. Pedí a los niños que contaran sus primeras impresiones al llegar a Inglaterra y sus experiencias en las distintas colonias a las que fueron enviados. También decidí intentar localizar a los pocos ingleses todavía vivos que habían convivido o trabajado con los niños y tuve la suerte de encontrar a una enfermera, una maestra y un antiguo estudiante universitario. De los testimonios, tres fueron extraídos de libros, dos de los cuales no estaban publicados. Muchos de los niños estaban ya un poco cansados de contar su historia a estudiantes de investigación o documentalistas y yo pensaba que éste sería un proyecto de pequeña escala y que, a lo sumo, obtendría unos veinte relatos. Por eso me sorprendió el número de narraciones que recibí, nada menos que 28 escritos en inglés y 34 en castellano. El deseo y entusiasmo con que estos escritores se unieron a la aventura me impresionaron muchísimo y la manera en que los niños recuerdan su estancia en Inglaterra sirve para constatar el impacto personal y significado de sus experiencias.

Desde el principio decidí que como muchos de los niños ya sólo entienden una lengua, el inglés o el castellano, habría que hacer traducciones de los recuerdos para que todos pudiesen leerlos y comprenderlos. Esto duplicó la cantidad de trabajo y estoy muy agradecida a todos esos amigos que se ofrecieron a traducir con tanto empeño. (El símbolo * marca una traducción.)

Por lo que respecta a la temática general de los testimonios, se constatan en estos recuerdos varios aspectos comunes y temas recurrentes, como son el viaje desde Bilbao a Southampton, la vida diaria en el campamento de acogida inicial, la reacción de los niños al conocer la noticia de la caída de Bilbao o la dedicación de los voluntarios. Por ello, y para evitar que hubiera demasiadas recolecciones de los mismos eventos, decidí editar los textos.

Sin embargo, lo que se pone de manifiesto en estas historias es la diversidad. Para empezar, la presentación varía enormemente. Como era de esperar, muchos de los recuerdos que recibí estaban escritos a mano, lo que conllevó a menudo el tener que descifrar la escritura. Otros estaban en formato de cassette o en CD y tuvieron que ser transcritos. Otros estaban mecanografiados. Otra dificultad a tener en cuenta es que a las personas mayores no siempre les resulta fácil delinear sus historias, lo que en este caso significó que algunos niños no escribiesen ellos mismos sus memorias. En algunos casos me fueron relatadas a mí y en otros a sus hijos o esposos, y nosotros transcribimos lo que escuchamos. También se dio el caso de algunos hijos de niños que escribieron las historias de sus padres ya fallecidos. El tamaño de los testimonios también varió considerablemente. Habiendo ingeniosamente dado como orientación una longitud de "entre una y diez páginas", recibí escritos que oscilaban entre 350 y 6.000 palabras. A la luz de la enorme respuesta recibida, que superó todas mis expectativas, me vi obligada a resumir los textos más largos para evitar que el libro acabara siendo demasiado voluminoso. Por lo que respecta al contenido, es evidente que mis indicaciones iniciales fueron interpretadas en un sentido muy amplio, lo cual enriquece considerablemente la lectura, en la que se constata una enorme diversidad de experiencias: desde descripciones del terrible viaje en barco a Inglaterra y de la vida cotidiana en las diferentes colonias, pasando por anécdotas variadas y memorias de la vida en Gran Bretaña durante la Segunda Guerra Mundial, así como recuerdos de la repatriación, de lo que supuso retornar a España después de un periodo de 15 años o de la experiencia de haberse alistado a la Royal Navy.

En cuanto a la duración de la estancia de los niños en Inglaterra, las experiencias fueron muy diferentes. Algunos niños se marcharon después de menos de un año, otros después de la Segunda Guerra Mundial, y un grupo reducido de ellos permanecieron y construyeron sus vidas en este país. Algunos tuvieron la suerte de vivir en la misma colonia durante toda su estancia. Otros, sin embargo, sufrieron un estado de provisionalidad constante al ser enviados de una colonia a otra a medida que éstas iban siendo cerradas al iniciarse el proceso de repatriación. También hay que tener en cuenta que la palabra "niños" tuvo diferentes significados según la edad de cada uno. Los más jóvenes tenían unos cinco años y nunca habían ido a la escuela en España, con lo cual crecieron en Gran Bretaña, país cuyos valores culturales adoptaron como propios. Por su parte, a los que llegaron en edad adolescente y a los que acababan de terminar la escuela en España les resultó más difícil adaptarse a las costumbres inglesas. Muchos de los niños mayores sobrepasaban la edad máxima fijada para la evacuación. Habían mentido al rellenar las fichas, pues sus padres querían que vinieran a Inglaterra para estar más seguros. Muchos de ellos estaban muy politizados y habían actuado como cabezas de sus familias al hallarse sus padres ausentes por la guerra, escondidos, en prisión o muertos. En tales casos, no estaban acostumbrados a ser tratados como niños. Sus memorias de Bilbao y de la guerra hablaban de hambre, de miedo, de la explosión de las bombas, del cierre de las escuelas, y del tiempo interminable que pasaban en los refugios, además de haber visto personas morir, cadáveres y escenas espantosas que los jóvenes no estaban acostumbrados a presenciar. La mayoría de los niños fueron finalmente repatriados pero algunos se quedaron, por decisión propia (si tenían más de 17 años) o en aquellos casos en que no se podía localizar a sus familias.

Los años pasados en Inglaterra aparecen en sus vidas como un periodo de estabilidad y paz lejos de los peligros de la guerra. Rodeados la mayor parte del tiempo de cariño, volvieron a ser niños de nuevo y a jugar, fueron a la escuela o recibieron clases en las colonias, mientras que los más mayores se incorporaron al mundo del trabajo. Los que volvieron a España en el periodo de posguerra se encontraron con un país destrozado y todavía convulsionado por los efectos de la guerra. Su retorno constituyó una vuelta al hambre y a la miseria, en muchos casos habían perdido al padre o la madre, o a los dos.

En cierta medida, las historias no son del todo representativas de las experiencias de los niños, pues la mayoría de los que contribuyeron a este libro vivieron su estancia en Gran Bretaña de forma positiva. De hecho, muchos incluso consideran que el tiempo que pasaron en este país fue el más feliz de sus vidas. Hay algunos testimonios en los que se pone de manifiesto la tristeza y la tragedia de las familias fragmentadas por el exilio. Sin embargo, la manera más frecuente de recordar los años pasados en Inglaterra con independencia de la edad de los niños es como un cúmulo de experiencias positivas. En el caso de los niños que pasaron menos de un año en este país, esa época de sus vidas la recuerdan de forma muy vívida y esos años han acabado ocupando un lugar desproporcionadamente significativo en su memoria. Es normal que los que tuvieron vivencias positivas quieran escribir sobre ellas. Lo que se pone también de manifiesto en las memorias de los niños es que la experiencia global de la evacuación fue un gran logro – para muchos el más importante que hayan alcanzado – y que los recuerdos de la misma revisten un carácter muy especial. Existen varias explicaciones para este fenómeno: la salida de su país supuso algo extraordinario en sus vidas. Vieron por primera vez el mundo que existía más allá de sus hogares en España y vivieron la evacuación como si fuera una gran aventura. Esto les proporcionó nuevos conocimientos sobre el mundo y nuevas formas de concebirse a si mismos. Desde esta perspectiva, podemos interpretar sus historias como la narración de una fase de transición crucial en sus trayectorias vitales, que para algunos marca incluso la entrada en la edad adulta y una etapa de auto-descubrimiento; el momento en que el chico se convierte en hombre y la chica en mujer. Efectivamente, el desarrollo personal a través de la aventura delimita ineludiblemente las memorias que se tienen de la evacuación y consecuentemente, la estancia en Inglaterra ocupa un lugar central en la identidad de los niños.

No obstante, sabemos que algunas colonias fueron mejor que otras y que la vida no fue siempre tan idílica como ha sido descrita: en los conventos, por ejemplo, se trató a los niños con innecesaria severidad. El reencuentro con los padres al cabo de los años fue una experiencia traumática para algunos pues los niños ya no eran los pequeños que habían marchado; se habían hecho adultos y en muchos casos no reconocían a sus padres, habiendo incluso olvidado la lengua materna. Pero es evidente que el hecho de ponerse a recordar y a escribir sus memorias ha sido para muchos un proceso catártico que ha contribuido a que se vayan cerrando heridas y a que se acepte finalmente su infancia fragmentada. A través de estos testimonios, recuerdos importantes que habían sido reprimidos han sido recuperados por los niños y reafirmados como significativos, no sólo por lo que respecta a sus vidas personales, sino también en el contexto de su pertinencia histórica. La constatación de que 4.000 niños llegaran a Gran Bretaña en un momento histórico determinado es un hecho característico sobre el que se sabía muy poco. Para Gran Bretaña fue indudablemente un evento importante. Para algunos niños, reflexionar sobre estos hechos que han marcado sus vidas y su identidad ha sido algo claramente liberador.

Mi tarea fue decidir cómo presentar los recuerdos y cómo poner en orden el material que los niños me enviaron. Podría haber adoptado un enfoque narrativo, es decir, extraer de cada contribución ciertas partes de la historia de los niños, como la salida de Bilbao, el viaje a Inglaterra, el campamento de North Stoneham, la vida en las diferentes colonias, etc. Sin embargo, en vista de los imperativos de la publicación, que debía estar lista para el mes de mayo, esto no fue posible, así que opté simplemente por presentar los testimonios de cada autor en orden alfabético. Este método tiene la ventaja de desplegar un mosaico de experiencia colectiva que una narración estructurada de forma más artificial no hubiera logrado. Como recopiladora de estos recuerdos no quise imponer un plan predeterminado, sino dejar que el lector navegase por la diversidad narrativa de las historias presentadas.

A continuación tuve que pensar en el tipo de lector al que interesaría un libro como este. Claramente, los hijos de los niños figurarían entre los lectores privilegiados, para que pudiesen aprender más sobre este periodo de la vida de sus padres. No solemos escuchar lo suficiente a nuestros padres cuando nos hablan de su infancia. Yo ciertamente no lo hice. En este sentido, el libro proporciona una oportunidad para rellenar lagunas existentes en la historia de las familias. También creo que este libro interesará además a historiadores sociales, antropólogos y a cualquiera que esté comprometido con la recuperación de la memoria histórica. Considero vital que estas historias sean publicadas para que al menos podamos aprender de ellas y situar las experiencias de los niños de Inglaterra en su preciso contexto histórico. Algunos de los testimonios concluyen afirmando que si los eventos narrados tuviesen lugar hoy en día, ellos nunca se separarían de sus hijos. En 1937 las familias vascas querían proteger a sus hijos de los peligros de la guerra y alimentarlos debidamente; al evacuarlos, pensaron que la separación sólo duraría tres meses.

Mi interés y el afecto que siento por los niños vascos se derivan del hecho de que mi madre, originaria de Madrid, partiera para Inglaterra en julio de 1937 a la edad de 21 años. Su ficha de identificación la calificaba como "refugiada independiente". La enviaron a la colonia de Langham, cerca de Colchester, donde enseñó inglés a los niños. Hace aproximadamente cinco años me embarqué en una odisea por averiguar más sobre ese periodo de su vida y sobre los tres años que pasó en la colonia. Enseguida me di cuenta de que la historia de los niños vascos era prácticamente desconocida en Inglaterra y de que existía una cantidad importante de valioso material de archivo que podía perderse para la posteridad. Esto me animó a hacer algo y así fue como se constituyó la Basque Children of '37 Association UK. Desde entonces he llegado a conocer personalmente a muchos de los niños, tanto los que continúan viviendo en este país, como los que se encuentran en España.

Recuerdos como los que aquí se presentan constituyen una fuente de conocimientos extraordinaria sobre experiencias históricas individuales que no suelen aparecer en las fuentes documentales tradicionales. Estos relatos también tienen el gran valor de ayudarnos a recuperar una parte importante de la historia reciente de Gran Bretaña y de España. Nos ayudan a comprender el pasado desde una perspectiva más personal y añaden otra dimensión a la historia de la Guerra Civil Española, contribuyendo a que los exiliados no se conviertan en "los olvidados."

.

Natalia Benjamin
Marzo 2007

Josefina Álvarez Álvarez

Era el mes de julio del 36, había acabado cuarto de bachiller en el instituto; estaba contenta, pues había aprobado, no tenía que examinarme en septiembre. Eso fue justo antes del 18 de julio. Nos preparábamos para ir de vacaciones y visitar a nuestra abuela cuando nos dijeron que los trenes no funcionaban. No deshicimos nuestro equipaje hasta que mis padres se dieron cuenta de que no haríamos tal visita y que el alzamiento de Franco era peor de lo que pensábamos.

Echando la vista atrás es difícil pensar que un gobierno legítimamente elegido pudiera haber perdido la guerra porque los rebeldes tuvieron ayuda de dos dictadores europeos y por la apatía de las democracias europeas.

Mientras la guerra progresaba y nosotros en el País Vasco sufríamos bombardeos en Guernica y Durango, era obvio que se tendría que evacuar a los niños para evitar los horrores de la guerra e incluso sobrevivir. Se ha escrito mucho sobre la salida desde Bilbao; la terrible tristeza de decir adiós a nuestros padres y el viaje tormentoso por el Golfo de Vizcaya hasta Southampton, la llegada a North Stoneham, y la dispersión de los niños a varias partes de las islas británicas, y por fin nuestro asentamiento en Inglaterra por un periodo de tiempo más largo que los tres meses originariamente pensados.

A 56 niños nos llevaron a Caerleon, un pueblecito al sur de Gales, que había sido una fortaleza romana. Nos quedamos en Cambria House, donde la vida empezó y continuó como probablemente en otras colonias. Nos visitaban amigos de los niños vascos: uno de ellos, una profesora, se interesó por mí y me permitían visitarla para que aprendiera inglés más rápidamente. Fue un éxito: lo aprendí enseguida.

En el otoño de 1938 me ofrecieron una plaza en Badminton School. Cuando llegué, me sentía sola y triste, echaba de menos Cambria House, que había sido mi casa por mucho tiempo. También echaba de menos a mis amigos, pero pronto adquirí otros. Puse mucho interés en el trabajo que tenía que hacer. Era una escuela maravillosa. Tenía tres grandes edificios, uno para las mayores, otro para las pequeñas, el último para las del medio. Había una sala de descanso y una cocina donde enseñaban a cocinar. También había campos y una piscina al aire libre.

En el instituto español llevábamos ropa de calle, pero aquí llevábamos uniforme, un placer para mí, así éramos todas iguales y a mí siempre me ha atraído eso de la igualdad. Había internas de diferentes países y mi mejor amiga era alemana. Teníamos unas c l ases muy interesantes: "Noticias del Día" era el estudio de los periódicos y "Progreso y Civilización" era el estudio de la historia, no a través de las batallas sino del desarrollo pacifista. La vida en la escuela se hacía difícil por lo que pasaba en España – la derrota del gobierno – y el estallido de la Segunda Guerra Mundial. Algunos de los exámenes se hacían entre visita y visita a los refugios.

Volviendo la mirada al pasado, pienso que la disciplina, la amabilidad del conjunto docente y la alta calidad de la enseñanza fueron una magnífica experiencia y preparación para mi formación superior. Pero me pregunto todavía cómo todas las diferentes nacionalidades podían vivir juntas entonces, si hoy en día las diferentes nacionalidades no pueden vivir en armonía.*

Felix Amat Irazola

Mi primera memoria al llegar al campamento de Southampton es del altavoz llamándonos a la tienda de campaña principal para encontrarnos con una de las maestras, Srta Amada Renouard. Años después me enteré que era una amiga de mi hermano mayor y que él le había encargado nuestro cuidado.

Mi hermano menor, mi hermana y yo montamos en un autobús que nos llevó a Langham, cerca de Colchester. La emoción que sentimos al llegar a Basque House fue increíble ya que los niños no se suelen dar mucha cuenta de su entorno. La casa era enorme con habitaciones en las cuales cabían hasta ocho camas. Éramos unas 30 chicas, 24 chicos más las maestras: Srtas Celia, Berta, Amada, Peque y Deme, y Rafaela, la cocinera auxiliar. También me acuerdo de los directores: Mr Stirling, quién al cabo de unos meses nos dejó al ser nombrado a un puesto diplomático en Suramérica y Mr Darling. Después vino Mr Theo Wills como Director. Era un entusiasta de la fotografía y antes de marcharse me dejó la mayor parte de sus fotografías y negativos diciendo: "Sé que los cuidarás". Aún tengo muchas de estas fotografías y han sido bien empleadas en exposiciones.

Pero si la casa era enorme y cómoda ¡los jardines eran de otro mundo! Jamás habíamos visto algo parecido y no extraña que uno de los chicos gritara: "Esto es un paraíso". Canchas de tenis, un campo para jugar al cricket y jardines de céspedes, de rosas y flores preciosas, invernaderos, una casita para el jardinero y cuadras. Al principio solíamos jugar al fútbol en el campo de cricket (no conocíamos el juego de cricket) pero bajo las órdenes del jardinero, tuvimos que parar porque lo estábamos estropeando. Más tarde nos dejaron usar el campo colindante, que llegó a ser nuestro campo de fútbol. Supongo que nos daban clase - por eso estaban las maestras - pero el único recuerdo que tengo es de jugar al fútbol todo el día, cada día.

Basque House se cerró en septiembre de 1939. Junto a otros niños me enviaron a Nottingham. Nos acogieron miembros del Cooperative Movement y Peace Pledge Union que habían financiado nuestra estancia en Langham. Yo tuve muchísima suerte en ser acogido por un maestro de escuela y sus padres que me dejaron seguir estudiando 18 meses después de pasar la edad mínima para dejar el colegio. Así pude aprender inglés. Hice muchos amigos en el colegio y nos seguimos reuniendo dos veces al año.

He trabajado en la construcción toda mi vida, incluida la guerra mundial. Todavía, a la edad de 81, hago trabajos de mantenimiento en dos residencias de ancianos.

En 1987 hubo una reunión para celebrar los 50 años de nuestra llegada a Langham. Fue nuestro primer encuentro con amigos que habían viajado del País Vasco. En declaraciones al periódico *Essex County Standard* dije que nuestros dos años en Langham fueron los mejores años de nuestra vida, un sentimiento compartido por mis amigos de Bilbao con los cuales sigo teniendo contacto.*

Mari Carmen de Andrés Elorriaga

La comida era cada vez más escasa en Bilbao y era obvio que la madre de Mari Carmen se quitaba de comer para que a sus hijos no les faltara lo que hubiese de comer. Pronto surgió la oportunidad de enviar a los niños más mayores a Francia para alejarlos del peligro. Por edad, solo Andrés entraba en el cupo que se fijó para salir y así pudo marcharse con otros chicos hacia un lugar más seguro.

Más tarde decían que una señora inglesa había fletado un buque para evacuar a los niños más pequeños de Bilbao y llevárselos a Inglaterra. Muchos ya habían apuntado los nombres de sus hijos para que se los llevaran y el barco partía al día siguiente llevando a bordo a casi 4.000 niños para conducirlos a un lugar seguro. La madre de Mari Carmen decidió no correr ningún riesgo: Mari Carmen partiría en ese barco al día siguiente.

Esa fatídica mañana Mari Carmen salió caminando de la mano de su madre hacia el puerto. Su madre llevaba una maleta, no era más grande que una bolsa de la compra. Pronto pararon junto a un viejo furgón blanco que estaba parado al lado de la carretera. Un marinero que estaba sentado en el asiento del conductor sacó la cabeza por la ventanilla y dijo: "¿Señora de Andrés?" "Sí." El marinero salió de la furgoneta y abrió la puerta trasera. La madre se agachó para que su rostro estuviera a la par del de su hija: "Te vas a ir de viaje y quiero que seas buena y que te acuerdes de nosotros siempre." Con estas pocas palabras empujó a su hija dentro de la furgoneta junto con la maleta y cerró de un golpe la puerta. La furgoneta, que había tenido el motor en marcha durante todo este tiempo, emprendió su camino sin que la pequeña, que apenas tenía siete años, tuviese la oportunidad de asimilar lo que su madre le acababa de decir.

A los diez minutos la furgoneta paró, la puerta trasera se abrió y la cara simpática del marinero apareció. "Hemos llegado." Vio que estaba en el muelle junto al barco más grande que había visto en su vida. "¿Dónde vamos?" preguntó Mari Carmen. "Te vas de excursión en barco con un montón de niños. Te lo vas a pasar muy bien." "¿Dónde está mi mamá?" gritó Mari Carmen."¡No me voy sin ella! ¡Me quiero ir a casa!" El marinero le hizo una señal al otro hombre y, sin mediar palabra, la cogieron en brazos a ella y a su maleta y la llevaron a la escalerilla que subía al barco. Mari Carmen gritaba, pateaba y se retorcía en todas las direcciones, pero los dos hombres, con lágrimas en los ojos, la sujetaron firmemente hasta que de repente se vio en un gran salón en el que había cientos de niños y niñas, todos llorando.

El viaje fue una pesadilla… Cuando llegaron a Southampton fueron trasladados a un lugar llamado Eastleigh. Inglaterra parecía muy bonita. Al menos ya no había más mareos. El sol brillaba, y menos mal, pues iban a vivir y dormir en tiendas de campaña. Unas señoras simpáticas les lavaron y ayudaron a ponerse ropa limpia, entonces le dieron a Mari Carmen un líquido que se llamaba té. Mari Carmen le dio un gran sorbo e inmediatamente lo escupió todo. Desde ese momento sólo bebió agua, mientras que todos los demás bebían ese té. Lo que sí que le gustó fue la bebida de leche que le daban antes de irse a la cama: *Ovaltine* o *Horlicks*.

Al cabo de un mes se difundió la noticia de que los iban a trasladar de Eastleigh, lo cual generó gran excitación y anticipación por todo el campamento. Mari Carmen se había hecho amiga de una niña llamada Elena que le dijo apenada: "Tú vas a estar bien, te tocará una buena madre adoptiva en cualquier lugar, pero yo soy huérfana."

"¿Qué es ser huérfana?" preguntó Mari Carmen con curiosidad. Cuando supo lo que quería decir, suspiró con alivio: "Bueno, voy a decir que yo también soy huérfana y así nos enviarán al mismo sitio a las dos."

¡Y cómo se arrepintió de haber sido tan tonta! Descubrieron que mientras que a la mayoría de los hermanos y hermanas los habían enviado a familias de acogida individuales y a otros a centros de acogida en varias comunidades, aquéllos que habían declarado ser huérfanos fueron enviados a un orfanato en un convento en la lluviosa Manchester. Además, Elena ya se había juntado con otros niños y se apagó la amistad entre ellas. En general, el tratamiento que recibieron de las maestras y monjas del convento fue bastante malo. Castigaban a las niñas: les hacían estar de pie por la noche con las manos en la cabeza en una esquina del dormitorio; si no terminaban su comida, la servían con el postre en el mismo plato de la comida, durante varias comidas. Todas estas penalidades hicieron que Mari Carmen acabase sonámbula, hasta que una noche la encontraron intentando abrir una pesada ventana para escaparse. Una monja muy buena la encontró y, tras guiarla de nuevo a su dormitorio, la despertó suavemente y hablaron en voz baja durante un rato.

Aquel gesto de cariño fue lo único bueno que había experimentado Mari Carmen. Un día una de las monjas se dio cuenta de que Mari Carmen necesitaba ayuda de fuera y la llevó a ver al médico. En cuanto Mari Carmen vio a una persona con bata blanca, empezó a gritar y gritar. La sedaron rápidamente y cuando se despertó estaba en un hospital entre niños que sólo hablaban inglés. La chiquilla ya no volvió a ver a aquellas maestras y monjas nunca más. Años después, Mari Carmen recordaría con arrepentimiento el haber aceptado hacerse pasar por huérfana, preguntándose qué hubiera pasado si hubiera dicho la verdad. A partir de aquel día prometió que siempre diría la verdad cualesquiera que fuesen las consecuencias.

Cuando se hubo recuperado lo suficiente, mandaron a Mari Carmen a la colonia de Margate, donde habían enviado a unos 40 o 50 niños. El comité organizaba conciertos para recaudar fondos para la manutención de los niños; Mari Carmen conocía muchas canciones y danzas vascas y pronto jugó un papel central en el escenario. Al fin Mari Carmen se sintió feliz. Ya no mojaba la cama.

En 1939, muchos niños fueron regresando a España a medida que sus padres solicitaban su repatriación. Sin embargo, Mari Carmen no tuvo ningunas noticias de los suyos. En Margate una de las maestras, una joven galesa llamada Bessie dijo que le adoptaría. Mientras tanto, se declaró la guerra entre Inglaterra y Alemania después de que los alemanes invadieran Polonia. Como Margate estaba justo frente a la costa europea, se erigieron fortines en los acantilados y se colocaron alambradas de espino por todas las playas como medida defensiva a una posible invasión.

Al final Bessie vino a ver a Mari Carmen y le dijo que se iban al País de Gales al día siguiente. Por fin llegaron a la estación de Barry Dock, y fueron caminando hasta la casa donde vivía su familia. A la mañana siguiente, después de desayunar, una señora con aspecto amable, Mary Jones, que resultó ser la hermana de Bessie, y dos niños pequeños, entraron por la puerta trasera. El niño más pequeño, un crío de unos tres años, se llamaba Lynden y su hermano mayor, Morris. El más pequeño empezó a hacer preguntas inmediatamente y se sorprendió mucho al saber que ella no hablaba inglés. Más tarde acabó sintiéndose muy orgulloso de su hermana española y no paraba de repetir su nombre, María del Carmen Andrés Elorriaga, a cualquier persona que encontrase. Mari Carmen se sorprendió mucho cuando Mary Jones la cogió de la mano y la sacó a la calle porque creía que iba a vivir con Bessie. Con Lynden cogido de la otra mano, los tres comenzaron a caminar hasta lo alto de una colina en cuya cima se encontraba la casa en la que pasaría los próximos años.

Al cabo de uno o dos meses le presentaron a otra niña española, Espe, y las dos se hicieron muy buenas amigas. Mary Jones, que era completamente sorda, llegó a ser la madre adoptiva de Mari Carmen. Insistió en cambiarle su nombre por el de María, pues Mari Carmen le resultaba muy largo. A partir de entonces, y hasta ahora, todos la llamaron María. Pronto empezó a ir al colegio y, aunque al principio le resultó difícil integrarse en las clases, una vez que la profesora de inglés supo que era extranjera, hizo un esfuerzo especial para explicarle las lecciones a esta niña que parecía tan ansiosa por aprender y hacerlo todo bien. Transcurridos dos años, María había asimilado los elementos básicos de la gramática y de la ortografía inglesas y consiguió hacer amistades.

En esa época la guerra con Alemania ya duraba dos años y Mari Carmen se había acostumbrado a que todos la llamasen María. Acabó siendo parte de la familia Jones. Bill Jones estaba en la Guardia

Metropolitana[1] y trabajaba en la oficina del puerto. Su tiempo libre lo pasaba cuidando de una huerta que proporcionaba fruta y verdura a toda la familia. Mary Jones cuidaba de la familia con ayuda de María, y se esforzaba en que los niños asistiesen a la escuela dominical de la iglesia bien vestidos.

Cuando llegó el final de curso, María era la primera de la clase en inglés y recibió un libro como premio. Era una chica de trece años; fuerte, todavía un poco patito feo, pero que comenzaba a feminizarse en otros aspectos. Su amistad con Espe continuó y juntas compartieron muchas risas y buenos momentos, lo cual les ayudó a mantener la lengua española viva. Espe siempre insistía en que continuasen hablando en inglés si estaban cerca de otras personas. Así, poco a poco, el acento de los valles comenzó a impregnar sus voces hasta el punto en que resultaba difícil detectar que eran extranjeras.

Al cumplir 14 años María terminó el colegio. Su profesora estaba encantada con su progreso, pues no sólo había acabado siendo la primera de la clase sino también de toda la escuela. Resultaba increíble que en apenas cuatro años hubiese aprendido tanto.

Un año después, mientras que trabajaba como enfermera en el Hospital de los Mineros de Caerphilly, María recibió una carta del Basque Children's Committee en Londres donde la invitaban a pasar unas vacaciones en una de las últimas colonias. La hermana más joven de Mary Jones vino a esperar a María a Paddington y la llevó a The Culvers, una mansión muy grande cerca de Carshalton. A partir de ese momento se convirtió de nuevo en Mari Carmen y fue presentada a todos los jóvenes vascos que vivían allí. Como eran originarios de la misma zona del norte de España, todos se llevaban muy bien y a Mari Carmen le encantó formar parte de la vida comunal del grupo. Hablaban y cantaban en español y algunos hablaban la lengua vasca, pero todos conocían bien las danzas y canciones vascas.

Debido a los bombardeos en Londres se tomó la decisión de evacuar a las chicas y a los niños más jóvenes a Norfolk para que estuvieran más seguros. En cuanto se subieron al tren consideraron todo esto el comienzo de una nueva aventura. Cuando llegaron, se encontraron con un comité de recepción esperándoles que enseguida los dividió en grupos: chicas con chicas y chicos con chicos. A Mari

---

1. Nota de traducción: A la Guardia Metropolitana (*Home Guard*) originariamente se la llamó "Voluntarios de Defensa Local" pero a partir del 27.06.1940 pasó a denominarse como tal. Este cuerpo pseudo-militar lo integraban voluntarios civiles que no habían sido movilizados para el frente y que no obstante se sentían útiles.

Carmen la pusieron con su amiga Feliciana y a las dos se las llevó una tal Miss Lambert a su casa. Les dieron una habitación a compartir y al llegar la hora de acostarse, después de un día tan extraordinario, las dos se quedaron dormidas en apenas unos segundos. Miss Lambert era bastante severa; el único problema era que las chicas no comprendían muy bien lo que les decía. Al final del otoño llegaron noticias de Londres sobre la segunda arma secreta de Hitler: un cohete cargado de explosivos que no hacía ningún ruido y que al caer explotaba. Se alegraron de no estar en Londres para no tener que soportar esta nueva barbarie.

Entretanto, Bill Jones se mantenía en contacto con María todas las semanas por teléfono y por carta. María sabía que Mary Jones tenía que ir al hospital para una operación seria y a medida que se fue acercando la fecha decidió regresar a Barry Town. Durante el tiempo que Mary estuvo hospitalizada, María cuidó de la casa y se hizo cargo de la cocina, de la limpieza, de asegurarse que los niños fuesen al colegio y de que Papá Jones desayunase antes de ir a trabajar. Cuando Mary (a quien María ya llamaba "Mamá") llegó del hospital, María la cuidó hasta que se sintió totalmente recuperada de la operación.

Pronto llegó mayo de 1945 y se declaró la paz con Alemania. Los padres de Mari Carmen finalmente la localizaron en 1946 cuando ya tenía 16 años. Volvió a su trabajo local y se fue asentando de nuevo en Barry. Después de todos los años en que se sintió abandonada, la época de posguerra fue una época feliz para ella.

Mari Carmen se siente orgullosa de haber nacido vasca española y, tras haber sido criada y querida por la familia galesa que la acogió, también se siente orgullosa de ser ciudadana británica. De hecho, a finales de 1949 obtuvo la ciudadanía británica en Londres. En parte, esto lo hizo para poder regresar a España a visitar a sus padres, pues Franco no podía retener a nadie que tuviese un pasaporte británico. Por teléfono se mantiene en contacto con su familia de Bilbao pero su marido dice que el sentimiento de pérdida continúa todavía muy presente en ella.*

Mauri Antolín Cordovilla

Mauri nació en Ortuella, donde su padre trabajaba en el ferrocarril. La familia era pobre, tenían cinco hijos y los padres los querían enviar a Inglaterra, no sólo para ponerles a salvo de los bombardeos sino también para que se pudiesen alimentar adecuadamente, puesto que para la madre era difícil darles de comer a todos. Al final solo tres niños fueron a Inglaterra, Mauri, su hermana Victoria y Teo, que eran más pequeños que ella. La otra hermana, Juanita, se quedó con su madre, y el hermano mayor, que tenía 17 años, escapó a Francia donde le internaron en un campo de concentración. Su padre intentó escapar por los Pirineos pero le dispararon. Consiguió esconderse pero la madre lo pasó muy mal sin saber de su paradero.

En Inglaterra enviaron a Mauri a la colonia de Aston. Allí era una de las chicas de más edad. La "madre de casa" era una joven sumamente amable que se llamaba Pili Merodio. En la colonia había también una maestra española que había venido con los niños y que era muy dada a pegarles cuando se portaban mal. A nadie le gustaba. Una de las tareas de Mauri era limpiar su habitación, cosa que ella detestaba puesto que era muy desordenada. En una ocasión, un niño desobedeció a la maestra, quien le pegó con un paraguas y le rompió el brazo. Al final consiguieron sacar a la maestra de la colonia y entonces Pili y Ketty Maiz, una de las mayores, se hicieron cargo de la enseñanza de los niños, con la ayuda de Cora Portillo que venía de Oxford los fines de semana.

Tenían una cocinera inglesa, una señora mayor que también tuvo que irse porque la cogieron robando comida. Así que Mauri y otra chica tuvieron que hacerse cargo de la cocina y cocinar para todos, una tarea a la que no estaban acostumbradas. Ella recuerda cuando intentó cocinar arroz por primera vez en una cacerola enorme y cómo se derramó todo por la cocina cuando el arroz se hinchó al absorber toda el agua.

Cuando la colonia cerró en 1939, Mauri se mudó con el resto de las chicas mayores a una casa subvencionada por el ayuntamiento que el Basque Children's Committee había encontrado para ellas en Witney. Después Mauri se trasladó a Barnet para cuidar de un niño cuya madre trabajaba.

No tuvo noticias de su madre durante años. Ronald Thackrah, de la BCC, fue a Francia y consiguió sacar a su hermano del campo de concentración y enviarlo a Chile. En 1953 Mauri consiguió finalmente reunirse con sus padres en la frontera francoespañola en Irún.

A pesar de la incertidumbre con respecto al paradero de su familia, Mauri recuerda los años pasados en Aston como una época feliz y considera que los voluntarios ingleses trataron a los niños con mucho cariño.*

Josefina y Ma Carmen Antolín Pintado

Josefina: Vivíamos en una pequeña ciudad del País Vasco, Berango, paisaje idílico y bello, pero la Guerra Civil Española cambió nuestras vidas para siempre. Después del bombardeo de Guernica, nuestros padres pensaron que no estábamos a salvo y junto a miles de niños, llegamos a Portugalete el 20 de mayo 1937. Se oían lloros y sollozos; fue francamente horrible tener que dejar a nuestros padres. Recuerdo que no quería soltar la mano de Mamá. Iba a cumplir 10 años al día siguiente y estaba inconsolable sabiendo que la dejaba en España con todas las personas que quería. Zarpamos el 21 de mayo, y no podía imaginar que iba a ser mi último cumpleaños en tierras españolas. Así comenzó nuestro viaje, que nunca olvidaremos. En los años que han transcurrido desde entonces, nunca he vuelto a cruzar el Golfo de Vizcaya.

Carmen: El domingo 22 de mayo el *Habana* llegó a Southampton. ¡Qué cantidad de gente! Nos dieron dulces y helados. El Salvation Army tocaba música: el ver a las señoras con esos sombreros que llevaban y los autobuses de dos pisos nos hizo reír mucho y nos dimos cuenta de que la vida era distinta en este país. Nos llevaron al campamento en Eastleigh y cuando vimos las tiendas, todos dijimos "¡Indios!" Nunca habíamos visto tiendas y menos dormir en ellas. No estuvimos mucho tiempo allí.

Josefina: No nos quedamos mucho tiempo allí porque el Salvation Army se propuso a ocuparse de unos 450 niños y cuidarlos en una residencia en el este de Londres, Congress Hall. Cuando llegamos, nos subieron por unas enormes escaleras de hierro; todo era muy grande y oscuro, parecía una cárcel. Nos enseñaron nuestros dormitorios, cuatro chicas en cada uno. Había un olor horroroso, que más tarde descubrimos era jabón carbólico y se me ha quedado grabado para siempre. No fui feliz en Congress Hall; hacía frío y estaba atestado de niños. Los niños decían que había un fantasma, de una jovencita que se había suicidado y yo tuve mucho miedo.

Por fin, a algunos de nosotros nos mandaron a otro de los orfelinatos del Salvation Army en Brixton. Era un poquito mejor, pero yo no podía aguantar la comida. Mi hermana Carmen se comía la comida de las dos y así nos daban dos raciones de fruta, que ella me daba para que me las comiera. Era lo único que me gustaba y esto me recordaba a casa. Por desgracia, en Brixton perdí mi osito peludo: otra niña lo cogió y lo tiró al otro lado del muro, y como los ingleses al otro lado no nos entendían, me produjo una enorme tristeza.

Como iba pasando el tiempo, y como comía tan poco, me quedé muy débil, pues la niebla de Londres y el frío no me sentaban bien.

El 5 de noviembre, todos salimos al patio, vimos los fuegos artificiales y las hogueras. No comprendimos la razón de todo esto hasta muchos años más tarde. El humo y la niebla me hicieron sentirme enferma y no podía respirar bien. Esa noche fui al dormitorio de los profesores. Después solo recuerdo que estaba en una cama y que Carmen estaba a mi lado. No puedo decir cuánto tiempo estuve allí. Creo que casi me moría y al final decidieron que abandonara Londres y me mandaron a otra colonia.

Creíamos que íbamos a ver a nuestro hermano Ángel en la próxima colonia. A finales de noviembre de 1937, salimos de Brixton y cogimos el tren de Southampton. Nos dijeron que cierta Miss Vessey vendría a buscanos. Allí estaba, esperándonos y nos habló en españon. ¡Qué gusto sentimos! Nos dijo que íbamos a estar en una casa llamada Moorhill House, cerca de Southampton. Angustiadas, preguntamos si estaba Ángel, pero nos dijo que no había otro Antolín en la lista. Cuando llegamos a Moorhill House, Miss Vessey nos presentó a la cocinera Mrs Lewis, a las Srtas Carmen y Rita y a la Sra Eulalia. Los niños parecían tan simpáticos y contentos. Me encontré mucho más contenta aquí que en Brixton y poco a poco empecé a interesarme por ciertas cosas y a comer la comida que me parecía menos extraña. La vida retornaba a lo normal.

Carmen: Éramos mucho más felices en Moorhill House; se convirtió en nuestro hogar. Miss Vessey era muy estricta pero amable, todos la queríamos. Era como una victoriana típica, un poco estirada pero encantadora.

Por las mañanas una de las señoritas nos daba clase. Nos gustaba a las dos, pues no habíamos tenido ninguna desde que salimos de España. Había un jardín en la parte de atrás, árboles que trepar y campos que recorrer, ¡tanto que hacer! Los domingos íbamos a la iglesia con Miss Vessey. Volvíamos para la comida del domingo. Por la tarde un amable señor nos llevaba a unas cinco de nosotras a los muelles de Southampton para ver los barcos. A veces había barcos españoles, y nos divertimos mucho hablando con los marineros españoles.

Pasamos las Navidades de 1937 allí y a todos los niños les invitaron a una fiesta en Southampton. Fue en una sala muy grande y vimos el mayor árbol de Navidad que jamás habíamos visto, cargado de regalos.

Josefina: Empezamos a jugar el juego de las sillas musicales y el juego en el que no teníamos que estar en la estera cuando la música se paraba. ¡Qué juegos tan diferentes de los nuestros! Nos alineábamos y teníamos que cantar *The Lambeth Walk*, solo podíamos decir "¡oh!" Nos reímos mucho, pasamos unos momentos muy felices. Después de una merienda estupenda abrimos los regalos.

Carmen: En una ocasión Mr y Mrs Keys (Robert y Sybil) pidieron a Miss Vessey si podían llevarme de vacaciones. Dijo que sí pero a condición de que llevasen a mi hermana también porque las dos hermanas no podían separarse, así fuimos las dos y lo pasamos de maravilla. Durante nuestras segundas vacaciones nos llevaron a Bournemouth a ver a un señor que nos quería regalar un par de zapatos a cada una. Entramos en una habitación llena de cajas de zapatos, donde un señor simpático estaba sentado en un sillón. Este señor era el famoso fabricante de zapatos Mr Clark. Estábamos muy excitadas con nuestros zapatos nuevos y le dimos muchísimas gracias.

Josefina: Un buen día, Miss Vessey nos informó de que algunos niños iban a volver a España, y los otros tendrían que ir a otra colonia. Nos quedamos muy tristes al tener que decir adiós a nuestros amigos. Nuestro hermano Ángel nos escribió diciéndonos que nos preparásemos para ir a casa. Las noticias nos emocionaron. Esperábamos noticias de parte de Miss Picken, que era la secretaria del Basque Children's Committee. Angel nos informó de que el comité lo iba a a mandar a casa. Cuando Ángel llegó, mandó recado a Carmen y a Miss Picken de que no volviésemos. Nuestra madre estaba enferma en el hospital, nuestro padre estaba en la cárcel y no teníamos casa. No había para comer y el País Vasco estaba en una situación de pena después de la Guerra Civil.

Carmen: Cuando parecía cierto que Inglaterra participaría en la Segunda Guerra Mundial, todo cambió. Vivimos con Sybil y Robert Keys hasta Dunkerque; después de esto, los padres de Sybil pensaron que estarían más seguros viviendo con ellos en el campo, en el condado de Stafford. Con reticencia, contactaron con Miss Vessey, que nos encontró una casa con Mr y Mrs Miall en Brighton. Ellos también se mostraron muy amables con nosotras.

Josefina: En Brighton visitamos el Pavilion, íbamos a pasear, a los museos y sitios interesantes. Un día visité Londres y terminamos en el número 33 Victoria Street, la sede del Basque Children's Committee. Vimos a Miss Picken, y allí conocí a un amigo de mi hermano, Pepe Estruch.

La guerra continuaba y cada día y noche oíamos pasar los aviones alemanes por Londres y Brighton. Teníamos que dormir en los sótanos cada noche. Durante el día veíamos las batallas, creo que fuimos testigos de la *Battle of Britain*.

Mr Miall tuvo que trasladarse a Portsmouth para trabajar con el Almirantazgo. Pensó que era demasiada responsabilidad para su mujer el cuidar de tres niños y nosotras. Así que le escribió a Miss Picken y le pidió si podía buscar otra casa para nosotras. Sybil escribió que sus padres Mr y Mrs Fawcett nos acogerían y nos tratarían como a sus hijas. El 28 de febrero de 1941 viajamos al norte del condado de Stafford.

Fueron tan buenos y amables que llegamos a quererlos muchísimo. En el pueblo nos conocían como *"The Fawcett Girls"*, nosotras les llamábamos Mamá y Papá y nos educamos con Sybil, como nuestra hermana mayor. Era un lugar idílico en el campo, alejado del ruido y la contienda en Londres y el sur. A pesar de que veíamos y oíamos los aviones y escuchábamos los bombardeos, nos sentíamos bastante a salvo en el campo con nuestra nueva familia.

Carmen: Cuando terminó la guerra éramos unas jovencitas. Habíamos dejado España siendo niñas de 10 y 12 anos. En ese momento, en 1945, teníamos 18 y 20 años. La vida había cambiado para siempre.

Josefina: Conocí a mi marido en 1946, y nos casamos en 1949, en la vieja iglesia de Leek. De regalo de boda, mis padres ingleses nos pagaron un viaje a España. Mi "papá" vino con nosotros y así, después de 13 años en Inglaterra pude volver y ver a mis padres. Todo el pueblo salió a recibirnos. La gente bailaba y la banda tocaba. Papá y Mamá lloraban de verme, de conocer a mi marido y al hombre que yo llamaba "Papá".

No tenían suficientes palabras de agradecimiento. Nos quedamos un mes. Fue muy duro volver a partir, pero ellos sabían de corazón que mi vida estaba en Inglaterra. Volvíamos todos los años a verlos y ellos nos visitaban y estaban largas temporadas conmigo y con Carmen.

Llevamos 70 años en Inglaterra y nos gustaría agradecer a todos de corazón por su entrega y sus cuidados en una época muy triste de nuestras vidas. Pero en mi corazón llevaré siempre el pueblo de Berango

Carmen: Como ha dicho Josefina, nos acomodamos al estilo de vida inglés. Yo también conocí a mi marido aquí y nos casamos en 1953.

Nos instalamos cerca de Bournemouth, donde nos asentamos y todavía vivimos.

El día que embarcamos en el *Habana*, poco nos imaginábamos que nuestras jóvenes vidas iban a resultar tan afectadas. Para muchos de los niños la vuelta a España fue casi imposible. Para algunos de nosotros la repatriación era posible después de la Segunda Guerra Mundial. La vida como la conocíamos había cambiado, nosotras habíamos cambiado. Felizmente nuestro hermano Ángel volvió a la Madre Patria. Se casó y tuvo cinco hijos, que los abuelos disfrutan con alegría.*

José María Armolea Bustamente
Mirar atrás y reflexionar sobre los acontecimientos que convirtieron a un niño en un adulto no es fácil. Comenzaron como una viaje, diciendo adiós a los padres y a la familia y luego el viaje tan largo que nos esperaba. Y sin embargo, hay un elemento de aventura que te cautiva desde el principio. Nuestros padres hicieron un sacrificio al querer salvarnos de los bombardeos y de la guerra, pero claro, era "sólo por tres meses".

Mi hermano Martín y yo comenzamos nuestro viaje desde Portugalete, donde vivíamos, adonde se puede ir andando desde Santurce. Mi padre, que estaba luchando contra Franco y los rebeldes, se encontraba en casa de permiso y nos llevó hasta el *Habana*. Ya lo habíamos visto en el puerto unos días antes. En el camino nos paramos a decir adiós a nuestra madre por última vez pues ella estaba trabajando de cocinera en un hospital militar que había junto a la playa de Portugalete. En aquellos tiempos era muy difícil tomarse días libres pues todo el mundo estaba ocupado con la guerra. Al llegar a Santurce le dijimos adiós a nuestro padre y a la familia y nos subimos al barco. El viaje fue horroroso, y ya ha sido bien documentado por otros.

Llegamos a Southampton y después de otro examen médico, nuestro viaje al campamento fue muy extraño, con banderitas y fotografías de la familia real en todas partes. Pero nuestra aventura realmente empezó al ver la entrada del campamento, una imagen que se ha quedado grabada en mi memoria para siempre desde aquel día. Un día para recordar en nuestro aniversario, que pronto será el 70º en Inglaterra.

Tras organizarnos en varios grupos, la vida empezó a tomar forma cuando nos dieron la responsabilidad de convertirnos en buenos *boy scouts* españoles. Por ejemplo, había un concurso para la tienda de campaña más ordenada, elecciones para jefe de tienda o para aquellos que iban a traer la comida de la cocina principal. A veces la vida era dura, como cuando la lluvia no paraba y la tienda se inundaba, hasta que aprendimos a cavar zanjas alrededor de su perímetro. Como en esa época apenas teníamos clases, nos lo pasábamos muy bien revolviendo los montones de ropa y zapatos de segunda mano. Debimos de estar en el campamento durante casi tres meses y vimos que se llevaban a muchos amigos sin saber siquiera a donde.

No teníamos muchas noticias de España ni de nuestras familias. Me imagino que era difícil para ellos. Pero el día más negro de todos y los días que siguieron inmediatamente después, fue cuando nos dieron la noticia de la caida de Bilbao en manos de Franco y de los rebeldes. Nos lo comunicaron usando el sistema interno de altavoces sin aviso previo ninguno; nos pusimos como locos de ansiedad al ver nuestro mundo desbaratarse. Los chicos de más edad salieron del campamento y se fueron hacia el puerto para subirse en un barco, ir en busca de sus padres y luchar contra los rebeldes. Muchos voluntarios y la policía tuvieron que rastrear la zona para traerlos de vuelta.

Al poco tiempo se hizo más patente la necesidad urgente de ir dispersando a los niños, puesto que iban a cerrar el campamento. Cuando nos tocó el turno no sabíamos adónde nos iban a llevar. Tras un viaje muy largo llegamos a Brechfa en las afueras de Carmarthen, en el País de Gales. El paisaje era precioso, con un río que discurría por uno de los lados del campamento, perfecto para pasar el resto del verano.

Al bajarnos del autocar nos dimos cuenta de que estábamos solos, con un hombre solo a cargo de 50 niños y sin nadie que viniera a recibirnos. El campamento lo habían utilizado para albergar a mineros enfermos y desempleados. En medio del campamento había una vasija llena de cacao y un montón de sándwiches de carne en conserva que estuvimos comiendo durante varios días después.

Lo primero que tuvimos que hacer fue rellenar los colchones y las almohadas de paja y ponerlas en plataformas de madera para dormir. No había escuela, ni supervisión y a algunos chicos que se portaban mal los acabaron cogiendo en la tienda del pueblo robando caramelos. El dueño les dio un tirón de orejas a dos de ellos pero cuando volvieron al campamento contaron una historia diferente a los chicos más mayores quienes se marcharon hasta el pueblo para enseñarle al tendero que no se podía tratar mal a sus amigos. Sin saberlo nosotros, ni los chicos que marchaban hacia el pueblo, alguien en el pueblo había llamado a la policía y ya estaba esperando un furgón lleno de policías que habían enviado de Carmarthen y que llegó justo a tiempo para dispersar a los chicos e impedirles que entraran en el pueblo. Cuando regresaron al campamento vimos que la policía les había tratado mal. Algunos habían tenido que cruzar el río con la ropa puesta. La policía también nos persiguió hasta que nos metimos en las tiendas. Nos escondimos debajo de las camas y entonces empezaron a golpear las cubiertas de metal de las tiendas con las porras para asustarnos.

A partir de entonces las cosas empezaron a cambiar pues estos incidentes habían sido recogidos por la prensa nacional: en el Parlamento se planteó la cuestión de los chicos "rojos" y muchos parlamentarios querían que nos mandaran de vuelta a España. La gente de Carmarthen había oído hablar de nosotros y vinieron en autocares para ver lo que podían hacer para ayudarnos. Llegaron con regalos y nos ayudaron mucho a organizar un equipo de fútbol y a dar conciertos por todo el sur de Gales. Esto continuó hasta que con el principio del invierno llegó la hora de partir, pues el campamento era sólo para el verano. Recuerdo el último proyecto que nos dio pena dejar: habíamos atrapado el caudal del río cerca del campamento para que fuese más fácil nadar en él, sin darnos cuenta de que los pescadores se estaban quejando río abajo de la falta de peces. Eso fue otro recordatorio de nuestra estancia en el País de Gales.

Así que nos fuimos de nuevo, sin saber adónde íbamos a parar, y después de un largo viaje llegamos a la escuela de Laleham en Margate. Allí había una colonia bien organizada con una sección de chicas, supervisada por señoritas y otros trabajadores. Desgraciadamente teníamos muy pocas clases y al final empezamos a ir a las escuelas locales, pero nuestro conocimiento del inglés era muy básico, así que nos dieron libros con dibujos para tenernos ocupados. Así continuaron las cosas durante un tiempo y lo que más disfrutábamos eran los deportes – natación, atletismo e incluso el cricket, que se nos daba muy bien. Era muy difícil hacer las carreras de campo traviesa con botas con tachuelas, así que nos alegramos mucho cuando llegaron las maestras españolas y organizaron clases en serio.

Hubo un largo periodo de normalidad en la colonia, a pesar de lo que otros piensen. Se organizó danza vasca, se formó un buen coro y se dieron conciertos en muchas ciudades de Kent que tuvieron mucho éxito y atrajeron a mucho público y también fiestas de jardín, todo lo cual sirvió para recaudar el dinero que tanto necesitábamos.

La colonia de Margate era bastante grande, así que era difícil asignarnos responsabilidades aparte de arreglar nuestros propios dormitorios. Teníamos una huerta con hortalizas y todo tipo de árboles frutales. Los chicos de más edad estaban siempre a cargo de la huerta y por tanto disfrutaban de lo mejor del reparto. Los más pequeños nos divertíamos en marabunta, y así cogíamos nuestra parte. El fútbol fue siempre el mejor pasatiempo pues teníamos una buena cancha y un montón de chicos de donde seleccionar a los veintidós jugadores.

Un día recibimos noticias muy malas de nuestra hermana, que también era una refugiada en Francia, diciéndonos que nuestra madre había muerto. La pesadilla que había comenzado como un viaje se hizo realidad. Mi padre, que había cruzado desde Francia a Cataluña para continuar la lucha contra el monstruo que había destruido a nuestra familia, no sabía la triste noticia.

Las malas noticias continuaron sucediéndose. Mi hermano se puso enfermo y se lo llevaron al hospital en Margate. Poco después, coincidiendo con el inicio de la Segunda Guerra Mundial, la vida en la colonia fue a peor, quizá por la falta de fondos. El Sr Landa estaba encargado de todo y hacía todo lo posible por mantenernos controlados, pues éramos un grupo muy alborotador. Me acuerdo un día que volví de ver a mi hermano en el hospital: al acercarnos a la colonia nos dimos cuenta del jaleo que se oía desde fuera. El Sr Landa también me contó las quejas que había recibido a causa de nuestro comportamiento en general. Poco después trasladaron a los chicos y a las chicas a otros hogares. Mi hermano fue a parar a un hospital en la zona de Reading y luego a mí me mandaron a un sitio muy bonito en Barnet, Rowley Lodge. Era un hogar muy bien organizado donde había un grupo muy majo de chicos.

El dinero había sido la razón por la que nos trasladaron allí y después de un tiempo empezamos a trabajar y a contribuir a nuestra manutención. No era mucho: en mi primera semana gané 12 chelines y tres peniques. Así continuamos durante el duro invierno de 1939 a 1940. Íbamos a trabajar andando para ahorrarnos el dinero del autobús a Boreham Wood. Durante la guerra trabajé en una fábrica de medias. El joven con el que yo compartía labores me invitó a pasar una semana en casa de sus padres. Nos caímos tan bien que más tarde les convenció para que me adoptasen y así muy contento me quedé a vivir con ellos durante la guerra.*

Carlos Asensio Montenegro

El gobierno vasco a los setenta años nos ha homenajeado en el palacio de Ajuria Enea el cinco de septiembre de 2006 a los niños de la guerra que fuimos evacuados en 1937 a distintos países de Europa. Con tal motivo, fuimos saludados por el Lehendakari D. Juan José Ibarretxe con un apretón de manos y yo me sentí emocionado. Entre otras cosas nos dijo: "Vosotros y yo vamos a ver la paz en el País Vasco."

Me mandaron al Reino Unido en compañía de otros niños como yo. Para empezar diré que no sabía dónde estaba Inglaterra, fueron las circunstancias de la Guerra Civil Española las que nos alejaron de nuestras familias y causaron un cambio total en nuestras vidas. En la colonia de Hadleigh éramos 50 niños y se hizo cargo de nosotros el Salvation Army: era un lugar en campo abierto con unas vistas al mar donde solía fijarme cómo los barcos entraban y salían por la desembocadura del río Támesis. Recuerdo que un día viendo como navegaban hacia puerto o hacia el exterior pensé: "¿Cuándo volveré?" pero de esto no hablaba con nadie, recordaba los días pasados con mi familia y lo lejos que me encontraba ahora. No recuerdo tener quejas para justificar mi regreso, el trato era bueno y la comida también. Recuerdo que los domingos por la tarde nos daban un plátano y una manzana para no trabajar en días de fiesta; si comía la manzana, no podía terminar el plátano, si empezaba con el plátano, tampoco terminaba la manzana. Cuando se repartía el correo surgían penas y glorias, unos con mucha alegría abrían sus cartas y luego comentaban: "Mira lo que mi madre me dice", otros se quedaban tristes por no recibir noticias, pero otro día sí que recibían y todos se disponían a responder contando cómo lo estaban pasando en Hadleigh.

Mi hermano y yo también recibíamos correo pero no de nuestra madre. Nos escribía una tía que estaba en zona de Franco, nuestro padre estaba ilocalizable quizás como los de muchos más de los niños por las circunstancias de la cruel guerra. Mi madre fue víctima de la guerra por un bombardeo en Erandio de la aviación franquista, al querer recoger a una niña sola en el lugar del bombardeo. Éste fue el motivo que nosotros fuéramos evacuados a Inglaterra, fuimos los últimos de la expedición, con los números 4121, 4122, 4123, 4124, 4125.

Así empezó la nueva situación lejos de los seres queridos cuya presencia era tan necesaria a la edad que teníamos. Además estábamos sobre todo en las circunstancias de la guerra que se vivía con odios. Al desembarcar del *Habana* al campamento de Stoneham no sabía qué hacer dentro de la tienda de campaña donde nos alojaron: nos organizaron para comer en grandes filas y muchos niños que iban y venían como yo estaban muy despistados sin saber qué era tanto trajín, mi hermano mayor me orientó y juntos nos arreglábamos mejor. Eso fue el primer día, en adelante seguíamos las normas que se daban por el altavoz. El segundo día recorrimos el campo buscando a nuestras hermanas que como nosotros también estaban aturdidas y asustadas. Una hermana tenía siete años, no se la podía dejar sola, pero en el barco se nos perdió, recorrimos el barco y la encontramos muy asustada.

Me gustaban mucho los sándwiches que comíamos en las casas que nos invitaban a merendar. Tenían un trato con nosotros muy especial, cuando nos sacaban fotografiás pronto nos las daban como recuerdo. Podría decir que todo lo que estaba viviendo en esa familia era como me hubiera tratado en mi propio hogar mi familia. En Hadleigh el Salvation Army fue bueno en su trato con nosotros. En las navidades que pasé con ellos fuimos al pueblo a cantar las canciones que ellos nos enseñaron. De la colonia de Hadleigh nos llevaron a la colonia de Kingston Hill, un lugar cerca de Londres, para reunirnos con nuestras tres hermanas: era una villa con hermoso jardín, huerta, muchas grosellas, escuela, gimnasio. La responsable era Miss Winifred Newby, de feliz memoria por su dedicación a ayudarnos, en compañía de las auxiliares, tan dispuestas en mi opinión. Aquí no era como en Hadleigh donde todos éramos chicos, creo que no llegábamos a 50 los acogidos en Kingston, seríamos mitad unos, mitad otras. Todo fue muy distinto aquí. Te comunicabas bien con todos, jugábamos mucho en el jardín. Un día apareció un pájaro muerto en el jardín y una de las auxiliares que nos cuidaban nos reunió para hacerle un entierro al pajarito. Se le preparó una tumba cubriéndole con hierba. Esto me hizo recordar que en mi pueblo les tirábamos con tiragomas para matarlos, esto si que fue una lección que me hizo reflexionar. En la colonia había mucha actividad gracias al trabajo de las señoritas que nos acompañaron en nuestro viaje para ayudarnos. Sta Pili Masa, maestra, Ma Teresa González, encargada de ropero, Mertxe y Rosario Bilbao, y Auxilio que nos enseñó los bailes vascos, Ezma, también maestra, Isabel y nuestro cocinero Sr Ceballos, con su delantal y su gorro blanco que nos hacía limpiar su cocina los sábados. En el comedor se leían las cartas que se recibían, en voz alta algunas. Recuerdo una en particular porque era de una madre a sus dos hijos de apellido Anchia, yo sentía que era mi madre la que me escribía a mí. Era como si yo lo viviese en mi ser. Unas chicas me comentaban que formábamos en esta colonia una familia bien avenida y tenían razón, pues el motivo de estar aquí era la cruel guerra. Cuando estalló la Segunda Guerra Mundial cambió mucho la colonia: nos visitaban muy a menudo alemanes y polacos que habían escapado de sus países en guerra, y quedé muy confuso, pues nos saludaban con el puño en alto, no agresivos pero a mí me parecía que volvía a vivir lo dejado en nuestra Euskadi, de porque viviendo en Inglaterra no participábamos de las mismas situaciones que nos tocaron vivir en nuestra tierra.

Pronto regresamos a Euskadi al comienzo de la Guerra Mundial. Al cruzar la frontera en Irún, un soldado con su fusil al hombro me dijo: "Ay chaval, ¡qué putas las vas a pasar aquí!" y qué razón tuvo. Verdaderamente lo pasamos fatal al recordar los tiempos vividos en Inglaterra, si bien sobre todo nos faltaba la presencia de una madre, tan importante a esa edad.

Bittor Azkunaga Goikolea

En el campamento de Stoneham, los miembros de los *boy scouts*, que se encargaban del orden y del buen funcionamiento del campo, eran muy atentos, así como la Dirección. Había visitas de voluntarios ingleses deseosos de ayudar. Los altavoces nos despertaban a diario con una melodía que recuerdo perfectamente, después de 70 años, y nos daban avisos y noticias. Una de las noticias que más nos afectó fue la caída de Bilbao ante las tropas de Franco, lo que nos trajo perturbación y más lágrimas.

Desde Stoneham nos fueron distribuyendo por grupos a distintas colonias. A nosotros, un grupito de 13, todos con algún hermano, nos destinaron a un colegio de alumnos internos de familias de Londres, regido por religiosas dominicanas de la enseñanza. Se llamaba St Dominic's Priory y estaba en Ponsbourne Park, cerca de Hertford. Era una hermosa finca con parques y campos, al norte de Londres. Aquí permanecimos gran parte de nuestra estancia en Inglaterra.

El colegio nos dejó un grato recuerdo por su amable acogida, aunque no hablaban nuestro idioma. Una religiosa nos atendió al llegar y trató de consolarnos ante nuestra común llorera. Más adelante ya nos familiarizamos con los alumnos ingleses. Fueron tiempos más tranquilos. Destinaron una monja, Sister Josephine, para cuidar y atender especialmente al grupito de *Spanish boys*. Llamaban con frecuencia a unos sacerdotes españoles que tenían iglesia en Potters Bar, para que nos atendieran espiritualmente.

A finales del mes de octubre de 1937 nos trasladaron (yo creo que por un malentendido) al País de Gales, a un lugar cerca de Carmarthen. Era una gran casa, yo creo que alguna antigua abadía, por los lemas en latín sobre algunos marcos de las puertas. Pero antes de terminar la semana, nos hicieron volver a Londres, ahora a una casa bastante grande, al sur de la capital. Estaba junto a un hipódromo. Todos en la casa eran españoles y unas maestras dirigían la residencia. Habría allí unos 30 chicos. Aquí permanecimos hasta pasadas las Navidades, luego los chicos se fueron repatriando. Este centro, que ahora supongo totalmente absorbido por la ciudad, se llamaba The Grange, y estaba en Kingston Hill, Surrey.

Mi impresión sobre la acogida que nos dispensaron es de que el trato fue muy bueno y de que en todas partes nos mostraron su simpatía y deseo de ayudar, haciéndose cargo de nuestra situación con nuestros recuerdos y temores, sobre todo los mayorcitos.

Pasados aquellos tiempos, ya en Bilbao, hemos seguido teniendo correspondencia postal durante muchos años con las religiosas de Ponsbourne Park y con algunos de los compañeros ingleses del colegio y siempre con gran afecto.

María Dolores Barajuán Fernández

En el mes de julio de año de 1936, mi hermano y yo disfrutábamos de las vacaciones de verano sin siquiera imaginar lo que nos preparaba el futuro. Apenas pocos días después estallaría el infierno que transformaría, no solamente España, más todo el mundo, en un inmenso brasero.

Casi un año más tarde, después de la destrucción de Guernica, se organizó la evacuación de niños vascos. Mi hermano Ricardo y yo fuimos a Inglaterra. Yendo hacia el puerto el tren pasó debajo de un puente al dejar la estación de Portugalete, y parecía que toda la población de Bilbao se diera cita allí, amontonándose sobre las barandillas, agitando pañuelos y gritando palabras de cariño y despedida. Esa fue tal vez la imagen más fuerte que quedó gravada para siempre en mi memoria.

La llegada al navío y nuestra instalación en el mismo fue un terrible caos. Centenas de niños llegando sin cesar, todos asustados, sin rumbo, cargando sus paquetes de ropa y sin encontrar a nadie para darles una orientación sobre lo que tenían que hacer o para dónde ir. Mi hermano y yo, con mi prima Isabel y dos hermanos refugiados de San Sebastián, encontramos un camarote vacío y nos instalamos allí. Pero no fueron todos los que tuvieron nuestra suerte. Al salir por la noche para ir al WC me deparé con un espectáculo dantesco. Todos los pasillos del navío estaban cubiertos de niños, de todas las edades, durmiendo tirados por el suelo amontonados unos por encima de los otros.

Serían aproximadamente las cuatro de la mañana cuando de repente el navío pareció criar vida. Empezó a temblar extrañamente, ruidos sordos sonaban al ser izadas las anclas y la pequeña ciudad fluctuante, con su extraña carga de sufrimiento y esperanza empezó su viaje. Movidos por un único deseo salimos todos en disparada hacia la cubierta. Queríamos dar un último adiós a nuestra tierra querida donde dejábamos todas las cosas que amábamos.

Dos días más tarde, después de una travesía muy agitada, llegamos de madrugada a Southampton en una mañana lluviosa típicamente inglesa. Nos llevaron en autobús hasta Stoneham, un enorme campo en las afueras de la ciudad, donde habían montado varias centenas de tiendas de campaña. Nos tuvieron allí en cuarentena haciéndonos exámenes y aplicándonos todas las vacunas preventivas, y después nos distribuyeron en pequeños grupos por todo el país. Fuimos tratados maravillosamente, con muchísima atención y cariño.

El 19 de junio del 1937 los altavoces del campo pidieron nuestra atención para la siguiente noticia: "Bilbao acaba de caer en manos de los rebeldes." El desespero general fue patético. Para nosotros España era Bilbao, el mundo era Bilbao. Nuestro barrio, nuestra escuela, nuestra familia, toda nuestra vida era Bilbao. Allí estaban nuestros padres. ¿Por qué dejar algo de pie si para nosotros el mundo estaba en ruinas? Varios grupos empezaron a destruir todo lo que veían por delante movidos por toda la rabia que pueden sentir los niños de poca edad cuando son llevados al desespero. Los profesores y todo el personal inglés empezaron inmediatamente a reunir pequeños grupos y con mucha paciencia y cariño consiguieron calmar los ánimos y resolver la situación.

Pocos días después, Ricardo y yo, con un grupo de 100 niños, fuimos para la colonia de Ipswich. Allí estábamos muy bien; teníamos clases con nuestras tres profesoras y los dos profesores ingleses que venían a darnos clases de inglés. Los jueves no teníamos clase y solían llevarnos de paseo por los lugares interesantes de los alrededores. Las playas de Felixstowe eran unos de los sitios que más nos gustaban. Continuábamos sin noticias de nuestros padres y después del escándalo de Stoneham, no nos daban más noticias de lo que estaba pasando en España. Yo intentaba distraerme estudiando y me dedicaba con el mayor ahínco a aprender el idioma. Pero por la noche cuando nadie me veía dejaba salir mi desespero y lloraba bajito por horas hasta que el cansancio me vencía.

Cinco meses después, en octubre, me avisaron de que Miss Vulliamy me llamaba en el escritorio. Me entregó una carta y, sonriendo, me preguntó: "¿Sabes de quién es?" Reconocí inmediatamente la letra de mi madre y ella me explicó que un matrimonio inglés que estaba viajando en Francia visitó el refugio donde se encontraba mi madre y ella les pidió que entregasen aquella carta a la organización que nos había llevado para Inglaterra. Salí corriendo en busca de Ricardo y juntos leímos la carta. Nuestra madre contaba como al acercarse los rebeldes a Bilbao, consiguió ir para Santander y de allí embarcó, con un grupo de refugiados, para Francia. Nuestro padre se quedó y ella no tenía ninguna noticia suya.

Miss Vulliamy organizaba todos los jueves por la noche una fiesta a la que convidaba a los alumnos de un colegio próximo. Las chicas mayores íbamos desde la mañana temprano para ayudar a la cocinera a preparar los pasteles y refrescos para recibir a nuestros convidados. Para nosotras la fiesta empezaba allí. Nos divertíamos aprendiendo a hacer los pasteles y al mismo tiempo hacíamos planes de cómo nos entenderíamos con los guapos chavales sin saber casi nada del idioma. Pero Miss Vulliamy, que era una eximia pianista, se sentaba al piano y nos hacía bailar hasta la media noche cuando se terminaba la fiesta.

Se acercaban las Navidades y nosotras quisimos hacer alguna cosa para agradar a nuestros nuevos amigos y empezamos a ensayar algunos bailes y canciones de nuestra tierra. Miss Vulliamy se enteró y quiso saber cómo eran las ropas típicas. Al día siguiente llegaron a la colonia un montón de tejidos de los colores precisos para que pudiésemos hacer todas las ropas. Con la ayuda de las profesoras y una vieja maquina de coser, nos pusimos manos a la obra y pocos días antes de Navidad realizamos nuestro espectáculo.

El día siguiente, el 22 de diciembre, llegó a la colonia un matrimonio que quería llevar a una pareja de hermanos a pasar las fiestas con ellos en su casa de Londres. Miss Vulliamy me llamó y me preguntó si me gustaría ir con Ricardo. ¡Con las ganas que tenía de conocer Londres! Pasamos dos meses, con ellos y al empezar las clases, al final de febrero, volvimos a la colonia.

Al volver a Ipswich encontramos algunos cambios. Primero, nuestro espectáculo había sido un gran éxito y estábamos presentándolo en varias escuelas. Después, Miss Vulliamy nos reunió un día y nos preguntó si nos gustaría ayudar a nuestra patria. Ella nos explicó que como era época de recoger las frutas en las haciendas vecinas podríamos trabajar durante un poco de tiempo en aquellas labores y colaborar con algún dinero en la campaña. Fue una alegría general y empezamos inmediatamente a trabajar. Por la mañana temprano llegaban los autobuses que nos llevaban a los campos y nos traían de vuelta a la tarde. Cuando recibimos nuestro primer sueldo todos pensábamos en dejarlo integralmente para la campaña, pero Miss Vulliamy nos hizo quedarnos con la mitad para nuestros gastos personales. Yo guardaba aquel dinero sin gastar ni un céntimo, tenía un extraño presentimiento de que tal vez algún día fuese necesario para algo muy importante.

En junio de 1938 como la casa de Ipswich había sido prestada por doce meses, tuvimos que mudarnos a Wickham Market. El cambio fue terrible: salir de la bellísima casa de Ipswich y llegar a aquel antiguo hospital psiquiátrico. El estado de abandono era impresionante. Nos pusimos manos a la obra y en poco tiempo limpiamos y arreglamos de la mejor manera posible todo aquel caos. Doña Margarita Lanvin, profesora de los mayores, me pidió que la ayudara a pintar las varias salas de uso común y allí fuimos nosotras llenando aquellas paredes de dibujos coloridos para alegrar un poco aquellos ambientes tan tétricos.

En septiembre mi madre consiguió descubrir el paradero de mi padre y fue a encontrarse con él en Barcelona. Coincidió que Miss Poppy, hermana de Miss Chloë Vulliamy, fue la encargada de ir a llevar una ambulancia y accesorios de la campaña para Barcelona, y vino a la colonia para saber si alguien tenía parientes allí. Yo le di una carta y dentro puse las dos libras que había economizado. Después mi padre me confirmó que recibió no sólo las dos que yo le enviara sino cuatro. Gracias Miss Poppy. ¡Que Dios le bendiga! Pocos meses después, cuando tuvieron que refugiarse en Francia fue el único dinero que les sirvió de ayuda ya que el dinero español no valía nada.

En Inglaterra empezaron a prepararse febrilmente para la guerra.. La casa de Wickham Market fue transformada en depósito para máscaras de gas y títulos de alimentación que serían distribuidos entre la población civil. Por eso nos distribuyeron, en pequeños grupos, entre otras colonias.

Ricardo y yo fuimos en un grupo de 25 para Margate. Al estallar la guerra, el 3 de septiembre, ante la dificultad que el Basque Children's Committee de Londres anteveía para continuar manteniéndose, nos propuso que los mayores podríamos trabajar y colaborar con la manutención de los más pequeños.

A principio del mes de diciembre recibí una llamada del comité de Londres para que me presentase allí al día siguiente. Sin explicaciones. Cuando llegué era casi mediodía. Me mandaron esperar en una saleta del escritorio. Fueron pasando las horas. Yo muerta de frío y con hambre. Serían las siete de la noche cuando llegó un señor muy bien vestido y, después de hablar con la secretaria, me pidió que le acompañase. Después de tomar el metro y andar por las calles oscuras de la ciudad bajo la nieve, que caía copiosa, llegamos a la casa. Allí me comunicaron que trabajaría de niñera para ellos. La señora era una de las auxiliares que fue para Inglaterra con nosotros y se había casado poco después. Pidió al comité una niñera para su niño y me escogieron a mí.

No quiero extenderme mucho sobre el tiempo que estuve en North Finchley. El tratamiento que me daban era más parecido al de los antiguos esclavos: un control total sobre todo lo que hacía, el agua para lavar los cacharros, para mi aseo personal y la cantidad de comida medida en el plato. La cama era de lona, sin colchón y sin siquiera una mantita para cubrirme, apenas una colcha de algodón. El invierno del año 1939 a 1940 en Londres fue terrible, a punto de congelar el Támesis. Mis amigas me habían convidado para pasar la Nochebuena con ellas, pero Doña Carmen solamente me dejó salir el día de Navidad por la tarde, después de arreglar la cocina y con la exigencia de que estaría de vuelta antes de la hora de la cena.

Mis padres estaban en Francia. La Segunda Guerra Mundial acababa de empezar y con la propaganda que hacía el gobierno francés sobre lo seguro que eran las defensas de la Línea Maginot, mi padre imaginó que la guerra no pasaría de Paris. Así que nos reclamó y el 3 de febrero del 1940, me encontré con Ricardo y embarcamos en un trasbordador que hacía la travesía del Canal de la Mancha hasta Dieppe. Nuestro grupo de niños y el señor inglés que nos acompañaba éramos los únicos civiles a bordo, todos los demás ocupantes del barco eran militares. Aquél fue tal vez uno de los últimos barcos en transportar civiles por el Canal por muchos años.

Después de atravesar en tren toda Francia llegamos a Bayonne a las dos de la tarde. Bayonne es muy parecida a todos los pueblos del País Vasco, que estén de uno o de otro lado de los Pirineos y eso nos hizo sentirnos un poco más cerca de casa. Podíamos ver a lo lejos las montañas. Allí detrás estaba mi tierra. Todo lo que había perdido y que jamás volvería a encontrar. Eran la barrera que me separaba de mi infancia feliz, de un mundo de paz y amor perdido par siempre.

Al día siguiente llegaríamos a Toulouse y abrazaríamos a nuestros padres. Tras tres años de agonía podría ser el final de una historia triste. No podíamos ni imaginar los cinco años que nos esperaban. Pero eso ya forma parte de otra historia.

Rafael de Barrutia Calera

Teníamos como Administrador de la colonia de Faringdon a un hombre relativamente joven, supongo que de 25 a 30 años, creo que era un judío austriaco y hablaba correctamente español. Le llamábamos Leon. También teníamos a un inglés que nos daba clases de su idioma y a otro inglés polifacético que se hacía llamar "Skipper" y a nuestro cocinero, el buen "Camuñas". Aparte de ese personal, con mucha frecuencia nos visitaban profesores o estudiantes de español de la Universidad de Oxford quienes, algunos días, nos daban charlas culturales. También había otro grupo de personas que nos visitaban con mucha frecuencia. Entre ellas se encontraban la Dra Russell y el Dr Ellis, que fueron los médicos ingleses que estuvieron en la revisión que tuvimos en Bilbao previa a la evacuación. Asimismo la que debía ser la promotora del grupo, Miss Poppy Vulliamy. La recuerdo como una *British*, joven, rubia, enérgica, coja de un pie suplementado con una alta bota. Faringdon, para mí, tiene recuerdos muy gratos y también muy duros. Creo que aquel periodo en que transcurrió mi vida influyó mucho en la formación de mi carácter.

En una de las visitas de la Dra Russell a la colonia, me invitó a pasar unos días en su casa de Londres. El primer día fuimos al teatro. Por lo que oí del espectáculo, debía ser organizado en ayuda a la causa republicana en España y en el mismo actuaron artistas de fama mundial. De todo ello, lo que más me gustó fue el cantante negro, bajo, Paul Robeson. Todavía me suena su voz y creo oírle: "Oh by and by, I'm going to lay down my heavy load." El teatro estaba repleto de gente. Nuestra localidad estaba en el patio de butacas, hacia el centro y se veía todo muy bien. Recuerdo que la gente aplaudía mucho, sobre todo al cuerpo de baile andaluz y en especial las canciones del cantante negro, del que decían era el mejor del mundo.

Al día siguiente por la mañana, me llevó la Dra Russell a visitar el zoo de Londres. Después me llevó a Hyde Park y vimos y oímos a uno de esos conferenciantes improvisados. También estuvimos en el grande y famoso almacén llamado Harrods. Más tarde me llevó por toda Londres: para mí fueron unos días inolvidables y los tengo gravados en mi mente. La acogida que nos dispensó el pueblo británico no se limitó a arrancarnos de la tragedia de la cruenta Guerra Civil y proporcionarnos un lugar seguro para vivir en paz, alimentarnos, vestirnos, hasta educarnos; lo que hizo la Dra Russell conmigo es una demostración palpable del afecto humano, de calor, que es lo que más se aprecia en esos momentos.

Un día uno de los chicos pequeños de la colonia llamó a la puerta donde estábamos en clase de inglés, preguntando por mí de parte del Administrador, que subiera a su despacho. Cuando llamé a la puerta, Leon, con la amabilidad que le caracterizaba, me hizo pasar y me agarró por el hombro acompañándome hasta la silla donde me senté. Leon se sentó cerca de mí en la mesa de su despacho y sin preámbulos me dijo: "Tengo unas malas noticias que darte. Me acaban de llamar del comité de Londres para que te transmita que han recibido noticias de que los franquistas han fusilado a tu padre y a tu hermano." Me quedé petrificado, era incapaz de articular palabra. Por unos instantes me quedé como muerto, hasta que reventé a llorar desoladamente.

Recuerdo que Leon me hacía caricias en la cabeza y trataba de consolarme, de tranquilizarme. Yo no hacía más que invocar: "Ama, ama, ¿por qué, por qué?" Dios mío: ¡qué momentos tan angustiosos pasé! Siempre que recuerdo aquel momento, se apodera de mí una angustia tal que no puedo evitar que me broten las lágrimas. El Administrador no me preparó para esa noticia, no sé por qué no empleó una táctica más suave, más humana, a lo mejor en su cultura es normal trasmitir esas noticias sin preámbulo ninguno como lo hizo conmigo, pero lo cierto es que me dejó helado. Leon intentó llamar por teléfono a Bilbao para ponerse en contacto con mi familia y recabar más información. Yo quería estar solo y me despedí de Leon. Bajé las escaleras y crucé el hall en dirección a la puerta de salida. Los compañeros barruntaron algo y me preguntaban: "Rafa, ¿Qué pasa, qué pasa?" No les contesté porque no podía. Salí fuera y me fui al jardín. Sentí un gran alivio y noté que aquella angustia que me ahogaba cedía. Al cabo de un rato, oí voces que me llamaban porque era la hora de comer. La noticia de lo que me pasaba la sabían todos, la veía en las miradas tristes de mis compañeros. Todos me querían ayudar, compartir mi pena, mi dolor...pero Ay Dios, ¡qué solo me sentía! Me sentía muy incómodo, y me levanté y me fui a mi barracón. Allí estaba tumbado en la cama, a vueltas con mis pensamientos. Aquella noche dormí como un lirón. Estaba agotado por todas las emociones que había soportado. Al día siguiente me levanté como de costumbre e hice vida normal.

Pocos días después de la horrible noticia que me había dado, Leon me volvió a llamar con toda urgencia y me dijo que acababa de hablar con el comité y le habían notificado que la noticia que le dieron los días pasados del fusilamiento de mi padre y de mi hermano había sido un error. La noticia me produjo gran alegría, al mismo tiempo encontraba dificultad para hacerme cargo de esas noticias diametralmente opuestas. La nueva noticia me llenó de gozo pero también me quedó la duda. Poco tiempo después, recibí una carta de mis padres. Con todo eso, mis ánimos estaban calmados y podía jugar normalmente con mis compañeros.

Una de las cosas que más me extrañaron al llegar a Gran Bretaña fue que los domingos eran días de absoluta tranquilidad, no había partidos de fútbol o espectáculos similares, no había nada de nada. Todo el mundo estaba en sus casas, o paseando, precisamente todo lo contrario a lo que estábamos acostumbrados en nuestra tierra. Para nosotros, el domingo suponía un día de diversión, para ellos era un día de recogimiento religioso, de descanso.

Nos trasladaron a Shipton-under-Wychwood. Por esos días vino a nuestra colonia un señor de Madrid de nombre Luis Portillo, era un señor muy serio y muy amable. En las clases que nos daba, nos hablaba de todo y nos enseñaba canciones. Recuerdo que le gustaba mucho aquella cuya letra decía: "Todas las mañanas sale la Aurora y se lleva la noche triste y traidora."

Lo que más recuerdo de mi estancia en Shipton fue el interés que atrajo a los chicos ingleses de querer competir con nosotros en fútbol. Por nuestra parte qué más queríamos que jugar contra ellos, tanto jugar entre nosotros mismos llegaba a ser un aburrimiento. El primer partido lo jugamos un sábado por la tarde y les dimos una paliza como para avergonzarse, el resultado fue de 6 u 8 a 11. El siguiente fue contra los jugadores de un colegio de chicos de nuestra edad y el

230

resultado fue apabullante. Al finalizar la partida íbamos al centro del campo para despedirnos del público, con qué energía nos salía aquel: "¡*Hip, hip hurrah!*" Fuimos la comidilla del pueblo.

(Extracto tomado de Barrutia de, Rafael (sin fecha) *Desde Santurce a Southampton*, libro publicado por el autor.)

Fausto Benito Gómez

Ante el panorama tan peligroso de la guerra, mis padres como todos los demás, no tuvieron más remedio que tomar una decisión, por dolorosa que fuera y decidieron apuntarnos para alguna expedición al extranjero, que el gobierno vasco estaba aconsejando a los padres. Nosotros éramos seis hermanos, tres chicas y tres chicos y decidieron enviarnos a los tres chicos.

Cuando mi padre se enteró de dónde había que apuntarse, no sabía exactamente para dónde nos enviarían. Coincidió que abrieron la expedición para Inglaterra y parece ser que mi padre llegó en el momento oportuno, porque resultó que fuimos los primeros niños expedicionarios. En el cartón hexagonal que llevábamos colgado al cuello y que ponía "Expedición a Inglaterra" y el número de cada uno, mi hermano Juan de 12 años llevaba el número 1, mi hermano Angel de 11 años el número 2 y yo Fausto de 9 años llevaba el número 3.

La despedida en aquellas circunstancias fue algo inenarrable, los muelles y el puerto estaban abarrotados de familiares, pañuelos, gritos, lloros y abrazos que no terminaban nunca, acompañados de los últimos consejos y recomendaciones: portaros bien, cuidaros, escribir, etc. Mi madre y mis hermanas lo pasaron muy mal en las despedidas; sin embargo mi padre era más fuerte, su serenidad y control de sus sentimientos y preocupación apenas los dejaba traslucir, pero la emoción la llevaba por dentro, a nosotros nos daba confianza y evitaba que pensáramos en algo más preocupante.

El barco era inmenso, más que un barco nos parecía un gigantesco hotel lleno de salas, pasillos y ventanitas, era un verdadero laberinto. Cuando el barco empezó a moverse y una vez en alta mar, enseguida se empezaron a ver en cubierta cantidad de niños y niñas devolviendo. Había una fila de sillones grandes de mimbre con cojines y todo, y mi hermano Juan me dijo que mejor que nos quedaríamos un rato en aquellos sillones a ver si con la brisa de cubierta se nos pasaba el mareo y así lo hicimos, pero yo debí quedarme dormido y cuando abrí los ojos, mi hermano no estaba en el sillón de al lado y yo me encontraba solo sin saber que hacer.

No encontré a mis hermanos en los dos o tres días que duró la travesía. Menos mal que tuve la suerte de que me vio una señorita y me conoció porque era de Basauri y su tía Encarna era amiga de mi madre. Al verme solo y como perdido y apurado, decidió que me quedara con ella hasta que encontrase a mis hermanos y me habilitó una litera en la zona de los camarotes de chicas. Trató de buscar a mis hermanos pero no lo consiguió, así que al llegar al puerto y bajar del barco me dejó con un grupo de niños y me dijo que no me separara de ellos hasta que encontrase a mis hermanos.

Al llegar a Southampton, nos llevaron a un gran campamento; yo seguía perdido de mis hermanos, estaba solo, me metieron en una tienda con chicos de 14 ó 15 años que no conocía. A mis hermanos no pude encontrarlos, pero un día deambulando por el campamento oí que alguien me llamaba: "¡Fausti!" Me volví y vi que era Manuel Landazuri, un chico del barrio. "¿Qué haces despistado por aquí?" me dijo, "Tus hermanos te están buscando todos los días, ven conmigo que estamos juntos en la misma tienda." Ví los cielos abiertos y me fui con él. Estaban todos los del barrio juntos, los dos hermanos Bautista y Ángel López, Manuel el que me encontró, mis dos hermanos Juan y Ángel y otros dos o tres más que no conocía, uno se llamaba Rodolfo.

Bautista que era el mayor de nosotros, tenía 14 ó 15 años. Era el jefe de la tienda, el que mandaba y nos organizaba para limpiar y tener la tienda bien ordenada. Había premios para las tiendas más ordenadas y vistosas, nosotros creo que ganamos algún premio una vez, porque Bautista era además de ordenado y curioso, muy listo y muy buena persona. Con nosotros se portó siempre muy bien y nosotros le respetábamos y obedecíamos.

El mayor disgusto que nos llevamos en este campamento fue el día que nos comunicaron por los altavoces que Bilbao había caído en manos de las tropas franquistas. Se desencadenó un pánico colectivo de gritos histéricos y desconcierto, unos corrían sin control, sin saber para dónde ni para qué, muchos se iban hacia el campo de aviación que estaba cerca. El mayor desconcierto era que no sabíamos nada de nuestros padres y hermanos, si estaban vivos, heridos o muertos: la angustia era total. Los lloros y gritos nos contagiaban a todos los pequeños y terminábamos todos llorando.

Aquellos momentos han sido los más tristes y angustiosos que pasamos en nuestra estancia en Inglaterra y que jamás se pueden olvidar, porque aunque a esa edad hay muchas cosas que no recuerdas, sin embargo esas tragedias se te quedan grabadas para siempre. A pesar de mi poca edad y de no comprender la trascendencia que pudo tener para nuestro futuro, sí recuerdo aquellos momentos como algo tremendo, muy triste, de gran angustia, de algo muy malo que estaba ocurriendo. Pasados unos días nos iban dando noticias y se iban recibiendo cartas, la cosa se fue calmando y por la capacidad de la juventud de sobrevivir, se fue normalizando la situación.

Pasadas un par de semanas se empezó a correr la voz de que nos iban a distribuir por toda Inglaterra en grupos pequeños. A nosotros, los seis de Basauri, con 50 niños, nos enviaron a un pequeño campamento también en tiendas de campaña, llamado Diss. Allí estuvimos poco tiempo.

De pronto nos llevaron a otra colonia en los alrededores de una ciudad llamada Great Yarmouth en la costa este. Era un gran caserón, con un campo de fútbol y unos alrededores muy bonitos de campo y árboles. Calculo que estuvimos en esta colonia unos cinco meses y fue el sitio donde mejor lo pasamos, teníamos hasta un equipo de fútbol bastante bueno, formado por los mayores y venían a jugar contra nosotros equipos ingleses y aficionados jóvenes que venían en bicicleta a ver el partido.

El resto de nuestra estancia en Inglaterra hasta que nos trajeron para España fue en Tythrop House. Era tambien una gran residencia de dos plantas con unas escaleras muy anchas para subir al primer piso; cuando llegamos allí ya estaba ocupada por otra colonia de chicas y chicos. Hasta entonces siempre habíamos estado solos los 50 chicos. Esta colonia estaba mejor organizada y creo que se estaban dando clases, pero yo no recuerdo que al menos de forma continua haya acudido a clases.

Volvimos a España en enero del 1938. Nada más pasar la frontera de Francia a España, nos dijeron que cantásemos el *Cara al Sol* y como no sabíamos nos preguntaron qué sabíamos cantar y empezamos a cantar *La Internacional* y enseguida nos mandaron callar. Nos llevaron hasta Bilbao en dos autobuses al Colegio del Amor Misericordioso en Iralabarri. Los familiares tenían que ir allí para recogernos.

El momento más grato y emocionante que recuerdo fue al encontrarme con mi madre. Yo iba asomado a la ventanilla en un autobús, mis hermanos iban en el otro, mirando a la gente para ver si veía a mis padres o alguna de mis hermanas. De pronto oí: "Fausti, Faustito". Era la voz inconfundible de mi madre, me había visto ella a mí antes que yo a ella. Me bajé del autobús, nos fundimos en un largo abrazo, como sólo se puede sentir el abrazo de una madre. Todavía tiemblo de emoción al recordar este episodio de mi vida infantil, aquel momento, sin duda uno de los más felices de mi vida.

Una de las cosas más importantes fue conocer a una extraordinaria y excelente persona, Henry Jeffery, que tenía 26 ó 27 años. Más tarde supimos que era pastor protestante anglicano. Le conocí en el primer campamento de Stoneham. Vino este joven señor, me ofreció unos caramelos, y puso gran interés en saber si tenía algún hermano mayor, y le dije que sí; entonces me dijo que fuera a buscarles. Sólo encontré a mi hermano Ángel que estaba con Manuel Landazuri y vinieron conmigo y allí estaba el señor esperándonos y les dijo que el fin de semana iba a venir a buscarles. Desde entonces muchos fines de semana se los llevaba a los dos, pero algunas veces también nos llevaba a Juan y a mí.

Cada vez que íbamos a otra colonia, él también venía a buscarnos los fines de semana. Unas veces nos llevaba en autobús o taxi, y otras en una motocicleta con sidecar. Nos llamó mucho la atención la niebla tan espesa de Londres cuando íbamos en la moto: daba miedo porque no se veía nada. Nos llevaba al cine, y una vez dimos un paseo por el Támesis en los barquitos de recreo.

Algunos fines de semana nos llevaba a misa. Henry celebraba la misa vestido de paisano que a nosotros nos llamaba la atención porque no se vestía como los curas de España. Nosotros como no entendíamos nada, aguantábamos de mala gana y Manuel que era bastante mal hablado, protestaba y hasta decía tacos. Henry le decía: " ¡Oh Manuel! no decir eso, ser palabra fea".

Nosotros siempre estuvimos muy agradecidos por lo bien que nos trataba y las atenciones que tenía con nosotros y comprendíamos que le debíamos contestar con respeto. Para Navidad, nos llevó a los cuatro a su casa en Londres a pasar dos días. Vivía con sus padres en una bonita zona, creo que era en Kensington.

Empezó a correrse la voz de que volvíamos a España. Aunque la guerra no había acabado, la propaganda franquista decía que no estábamos bien atendidos, que andábamos desperdigados y sin control. A través de los medios de comunicación animaban a los padres a reclamar a sus hijos. Las primeras expediciones de vuelta empezaron en noviembre. Nosotros volvimos el día 4 de enero de 1938.

Cuando nuestro amigo Henry Jeffery se enteró de que nos enviaban a España se llevó un gran disgusto: estuvo con nosotros hasta el último momento de embarcar para España. Nos trajo algunas golosinas y juguetes, y en la despedida final no pudo contenerse y se le saltaban las lágrimas y a nosotros también, y no dejaba de abrazarnos. Era muy sensible y humano, yo todavía después de más de 60 años le recuerdo con gran cariño por lo que supuso para nosotros en aquellos tiempos tan difíciles sin nuestros padres: él fue quien se preocupó de llenar de alguna manera aquel hueco irreemplazable y hacernos posible la sensación de que teníamos como mínimo un hermano mayor que se preocupaba por nosotros. Con qué ilusión esperábamos los fines de semana a ver si por los altavoces oíamos: "¡Atención! ¡Atención! Los hermanos Juan, Angel y Fausto Benito que se presenten en recepción que les espera Mr Henry Jeffery para pasar el fin de semana en su compañía."

Cuando vino a España a visitarnos en el mes de junio del año 1940 (la guerra había terminado el 1 de abril de 1939) estuvo en nuestra casa unos ocho días. Un día le llevamos a la plaza de toros a ver una novillada. Al empezar cualquier espectáculo, había que levantarse mientras tocaban el himno nacional y permanecer con el brazo derecho extendido porque era el saludo franquista y no se podía bajar hasta que acabara. Nuestro amigo Enrique-Henry se negó a levantarse y menos a saludar con el brazo en alto, decía: "Yo ser inglés y no ser franquista", y permaneció sentado. Pasamos un mal rata temiendo lo peor, pero afortunadamente no ocurrió nada, por suerte ningún policía lo vió. Le hemos tenido un gran cariño y siempre nos decía que nos tenía presentes en sus oraciones.

Mi conclusión es que mi estancia en Inglaterra fue muy buena. Otra cosa es lo que hubiera sido si no hubiera habido guerra, sin ninguna duda hubiera sido mucho mejor para la inmensa mayoría de los evacuados. Tres cursos perdidos, no haber podido estudiar, empezar a trabajar antes de los 14 años, etc. Hambre y tuberculosis en los años 1940 a 1960, falta de libertades, 40 años de dictadura. Conservemos la memoria historica.

Teodora Bueno Fernandez

No recuerdo mucho de mi estancia en la colonia de Langham, cerca de Colchester, pues tenía sólo 7 años. De lo que sí me acuerdo es de comer salchichas y puré de patatas los sábados al mediodía y de jugar muchísimo. De los mayores solamente recuerdo a la Srta Peque, siempre muy alegre y buena con los pequeños.

La Peace Pledge Union apoyaba a la colonia de Langham, pero cuando ésta tuvo que cerrar se pusieron anuncios en el periódico *Peace News* del PPU buscando casas que acogieran a las dos niñas más pequeñas, Espe y yo.

Tenía 9 años y primeramente, una señora de Dagenham me acogió. No estuve muy feliz, pues me trataban como la sirvienta. Recuerdo especialmente un día que su hijo adolescente me dijo que hiciera algo y yo contesté que no era su criada y el me empujó escaleras abajo. Muy pocos días después se llevaron a la señora al hospital y me dijeron que sufría una enfermedad nerviosa, así que tuvieron que buscarme otra casa.

Mrs Emily Ranson, que también vivía en Dagenham, había oído en su iglesia que necesitaban hogares para los niños refugiados del País Vasco. Su hija Irene le dijo a su madre que le pagaría lo que fuera necesario de su sueldo si ella me acogía. La señora vino a recogerme a la primera casa, juntas caminamos, yo con mi maleta que tenía un agujero y varias cosas se cayeron por el suelo, pero yo no me atreví a decir nada.

Los Ranson vivían en el número 257 de la calle Hedgeman. El marido se llamaba Ernest y trabajaba en el British Museum, en Londres. Tenían dos hijas, Irene, de 20 anos y Vera de 18. Ambas trabajaban en una oficina. Toda la familia era muy amable conmigo y yo me sentía muy feliz con ella. Siempre estaba con Mrs Ranson, me encantaba abrazarla y darle besos. Le ayudaba en las tareas domésticas, puesto que en la colonia todas las chicas de cualquier edad habían ayudado con la limpieza de la casa, así que yo estaba acostumbrada y seguía a Mrs Ranson sacando el polvo y trabajando con ella.

La familia pertenecía a la secta religiosa baptista. Nunca iban al cine, era como un pecado, pensaban que si Dios venía y te veía con los pecadores, no te llevaría al cielo. Pero a mí me encantaban los domingos. Cuando tenía 10 anos me bautizaron en su rito por total inmersión en el agua. Vestía un traje blanco y recuerdo como el pastor me sumergió en el agua. Sentí que pertenecía a Jesús y que se me perdonaban todos mis pecados. Recité este poema delante de toda la congregación:

Soy un rayito de sol
Sólo tengo 10 años
Me encanta brillar por Jesús
Y lo amo todo el día
Seré su pequeño rayo de sol
Lo dice la Biblia

Toda la familia iba a la iglesia todos los domingos. Mr Ranson salía unos 15 minutos antes de terminase la misa para hacer los preparativos de la comida y tener todo dispuesto al llegar nosotros. Los domingos por la tarde, yo volvía a la iglesia para dirigir un grupo en el "Sunday School". Les contaba a los pequeños historias de la Biblia. Toda la familia volvía de nuevo por la tarde a la iglesia y se compartían los alimentos traídos para cenar.

Fui a la escuela local hasta la edad de 14 años. No me acuerdo de mucho, sólo de una pelea con alguien que me había llamado "*Spanish onion*" (cebolla española). Después trabajé en la guardería como ayudante de la maestra, encantadora, Mrs Hughes. Los pequeños tenían que dormir la siesta en sus camitas, y cada uno tenía una manta con el distintivo de un animalito dibujado. Una de las niñas me quería a mí mucho, se llamaba Mavis, pero Mrs Hughes me dijo que no podía tener favoritos. Era muy amable conmigo y a veces me llevaba a Londres a ver el ballet. Al volver a casa Mrs Ranson preparaba bocadillos de *Marmite* y mantequilla de cacahuete. Esa era la cena, y luego un tazón de chocolate caliente antes de ir a la cama.

Tenía una amiga que vivía en la casa de al lado. Se llamaba Lily y yo siempre llamaba a su puerta al volver del trabajo. Su familia era muy pobre y nunca me dejaba entrar en su casa. Nos gustaba saltar a la comba y aprendimos malabarismo con tres pelotitas. Había otra vecina, cuyo marido estaba muy enfermo de los pulmones, y su mujer me pedía que sacara al perro. Se llamaba Spot.

Mi día favorito era el sábado: Mrs Ranson me llevaba a Londres todos los sábados. Íbamos a las tiendas o a Hyde Park o al Speakers' Corner a oír a los oradores. Comíamos en un café y algunas veces íbamos a ver a su marido al British Museum donde él trabajaba. Recuerdo sobre todo haber visto las momias

Durante las tardes de invierno nos sentábamos junto al fuego. Mr Ranson leía la Biblia, Irene bordaba, Vera tocaba el piano y yo cantaba. Había muchas fotos de la familia encima del piano, incluidas muchas fotos que me habían sacado a mí. Yo les llamaba "Papá" y "Mamá".

Querían adoptarme pero no pudieron porque mis padres estaban vivos.

Los terribles bombardeos sobre Londres hicieron que Mr Ranson construyera un refugio en el jardín con unas camitas, y cuando caían las bombas nos precipitábamos hacia el refugio. Teníamos máscaras de gas, y nos dijeron que si oíamos aviones enemigos, nos teníamos que tirar al suelo. Mrs Ranson tenía miedo por mí y me mandó con otros niños ingleses evacuados a Bristol. Así que otra vez yo era evacuada. Las dos señoras que me acogieron no me trataron bien. Era como una sirvienta, tenía que servir la comida. No estaba nada contenta allí: lo único bueno de esa experiencia fue que aprendí a escribir a máquina y pude escribir la primera carta a mis padres.

Cuando se enteró Mrs Ranson de como me trataban, vino a Bristol a buscarme y se quejó a las señoras. Al volver a Dagenham, ellas escribieron una carta muy dura, diciendo incluso mentiras sobre cómo me había portado, incluso que había dicho que Mrs Ranson me había pegado. Vi a Mrs Ranson cuando recibió la carta y vi que estaba llorando. Pero ella sabía que yo no hubiera dicho tales cosas.

En diciembre de1945 mi familia, a la que la Cruz Roja había encontrado en Francia, en Famel en el departamento de Lot et Garonne, me reclamó, con mis dos hermanos y mi hermana que también estaban en Inglaterra. Cesario era aprendiz de carpintero, Carlos estaba en Shrewsbury ayudando en una granja de pollos, Herminia había estado ayudando a la Srta Peque, ahora casada, con sus dos bebés, Sonia y Natalia.

La primera vez que vi a mi familia después de tantos años todo fue bien y nos reunimos hermanos y hermanas. Comimos muchísimo aunque aún había racionamiento: más tarde supe que mis padres pidieron prestado para poder darnos esa gran comida. Todos hablaban español, pero yo no entendía ni una palabra.

Como necesitábamos dinero, yo empecé a trabajar en una fábrica de cerámica en el Lot. Le daba todo lo que ganaba a mi madre, trabajaba horas suplementarias para poder llevarnos un bocado a la boca. Mrs Ranson me escribía a menudo y yo leía las cartas a mi madre. Ella decía: "Esa no es tu madre, soy yo". Pero yo siempre le escribía a vuelta de correo. La correspondencia continuó durante mucho tiempo.

En 1956 me casé con otro refugiado español y dos años después tuve un hijo, Tubal. Le envié una foto y una carta a Mrs Ranson, pero me la devolvieron, «dirección equivocada». Nunca supe lo que le pasó. Más tarde tuve un hijo discapacitado y requería mi atención 24 horas al día. No tenía tiempo para indagar lo que le había pasado a la familia Ranson. Este es el mayor pesar que tengo. *

Vicente Cañada García

Llegué al campamento de Stoneham con siete años recién cumplidos. Llevaba en mi solapa la tarjeta número 1702, número que nunca he olvidado y que actualmente conservo como número de la puesta en marcha de mi teléfono móvil, al resultarme fácil de recordar.

Tengo recuerdos del campamento, como las escapadas al pueblo dirigidas por el jefe de grupo, un tal Armando Santos. Su segundo nombre era Blanco y tenía el número 2584. Le recuerdo todavía con gafas, lo cual no era muy corriente en niños de nuestra edad; era delgado y con bastante iniciativa para hacer trastadas. Tenía entonces diez años. Recuerdo muy bien las llamadas por los altavoces, como éstas: "¡Atención, atención! Correspondencia recibida esta mañana", seguido de los nombres que se leían, o "¡Atención, atención! Que se presenten en la cabina médica Armando Santos, Vicente Cañada etc."

De Dymchurch recuerdo sobre todo su playa, desde la que creíamos ver Francia, y los proyectos que teníamos para reparar una destrozada embarcación que había en el lugar y con la que soñábamos regresar para ver a los nuestros. También tengo en la memoria la existencia allí de un tren miniatura en el que montábamos en un corto recorrido. Posteriormente, estando en España, leí en algún periódico que ese tren, pese a su reducido tamaño, prestó un gran servicio durante la guerra, trasladando tropas y armamento a las defensas de la costa.

Después fui a Scarborough, siempre acompañado de dos primos con los que pasé todo ese tiempo. Nos relacionamos con una tal Elsie Robinson que fue nuestra madrina y de la que todos trajimos a España un cariñoso recuerdo. Elsie era una chica joven, muy buena persona como todos los que encontré allí. Y sé que no todos los ingleses son de primera calidad (como pasa en todo el mundo), pero yo tuve la fortuna de encontrarme con los mejores.

Nuevo destino: Bradford, 245 Manningham Lane. Bradford es lo que recuerdo con más ilusión, pues fue allí donde pasé mis mejores momentos, aunque toda mi estancia tiene para mí buenos recuerdos. Fue un buen cambio porque así como en Scarborough éramos muchos, en Bradford éramos más o menos una docena. Allí conocí a Harry

Seed: este hombre fue lo mejor que yo vi en Inglaterra: amable, cariñoso, buena persona hasta más no poder. En fin, yo le he querido tanto como a mi padre (incluso creo que más). Nos sacaba los días de fiesta y nos llevaba en su coche con todas las atenciones que se pueden imaginar. En Navidad dormíamos en su casa y esperábamos nuestros regalos. Su esposa era también un encanto y no tenían hijos. Después de mi regreso a España supe que su esposa falleció, y que se volvió a casar con una hermana de aquélla con la que sí tuvo dos hijos. Le vi por última vez en una visita de una semana la primera vez que volví a Inglaterra después de mi exilio. El encuentro fue muy emocionante y puedo decir que mi querido Harry quedó llorando cuando nos abrazamos para despedirnos. Yo he recordado a este hombre muchísimas veces y todavía lo hago.

Ángeles Cubas Piñera

Mi hermana Susana y yo llegamos a la colonia de Brampton. Habría por lo menos cien niños vascos recogidos por Lady Cecilia Roberts, una señora adinerada que nos llevaba a su palacio para merendar y que nos enseñaba los bailes antiguos, lo pasábamos en grande. También quiero recordar a la hija de Lady Cecilia Roberts. Era una pintora que nos daba clases dos días a la semana. Recuerdo su nombre - Mrs Nicholson; era muy agradable y una gran pintora. Las gentes del pueblo nos llevaban a sus casas a merendar, hicimos amigos. Pero después de un tiempo todo cambió por la guerra y tuvimos que empezar a trabajar, y formamos un grupo de baile que nos servía para poder sobrevivir en la colonia. Recorrimos diferentes pueblos, y fue durante uno de esos viajes cuando conocí a Mr. Livingstone. Algo le debió gustar de mí, creo que le caí en gracia, porque me adoptó, pagando todos mis gastos. Vivía en Escocia y nos escribíamos. Le di a conocer que tenía una hermana y se hizo cargo de ella también.

Cuando estaba de vacaciones nos llevaba a su casa de Escocia. Hacíamos muchas excursiones, recorrimos la Región de los Lagos en Ambleside, y pasamos unos días inolvidables. También solíamos hacer camping, algo que me encantaba por estar al aire libre. Al regresar a la colonia, contábamos lo bien que lo habíamos pasado y el señor mandaba cajas de bombones para repartir entre todos.

Cuando regresamos a Euskal Herria, fue un regreso triste. El pueblo había pasado muchas miserias. Nosotras seguíamos carteándonos con Mr. Livingstone, y fue él mismo quien nos propuso regresar a Inglaterra. Fue una decisión dura pero mi hermana tomó esta decisión. Cuando aprendió el idioma, se puso a trabajar y se quedó para siempre en el país al que tanto queremos y que en momentos difíciles tanto nos ayudó.

Cuando fue el 60 aniversario de la evacuación, regresamos a nuestra colonia de Brampton. Hicimos una placa conmemorativa. El alcalde y otras personalidades nos recibieron; fue un momento verdaderamente emocionante. La televisión hizo un pequeño reportaje y tengo una foto de aquel momento, nunca lo olvidaré.

Alfonso Delgado Alava

Un día, nos dijo un señor de aspecto rechoncho y pelirrojo que un grupo de una quincena de niños sería trasladado a Bath. Una vez todo preparado y reunidos en el comedor, me alivié al encontrar entre ellos a mi hermana. Hechas las despedidas de los compañeros, nos dirigimos al autocar. Nos quedaba un consuelo en aquellos momentos del adiós, promesas lejanas al volvernos a encontrar, promesas que se evaporan al no ver en ellas un vislumbro de claridad. Era aquella una edad tierna en cierto modo y cercana a la pubertad, edad indefinible donde el cerebro infantil trabaja sin un objetivo pero en busca de él. No sé por qué pero aquel viaje fue interminable. ¿Dónde estaba aquella colonia de Bath?

Alrededor de las ocho de la noche abandonamos el autocar aquel puñado de niños refugiados españoles. Encontrándonos en las aceras frente a una manzana de casas esperando las órdenes o instrucciones de nuestro profesor, nos encaminó hacia una casa donde se podía leer en grandes caracteres y en lengua inglesa Basque Children's Home, es decir, en nuestro idioma, "Hogar de los niños vascos". El estilo de aquel edificio pertenecía a la época victoriana: mirador y ventanales al estilo. Al traspasar el umbral de la casa, cuál no sería nuestra sorpresa al cruzar un amplio pasillo y encontrarnos con la presencia de chicas españolas, ellas, sorprendidas a la vez y curiosas, nos observaban según pasábamos junto a ellas. Ellas estaban arregladitas y con lacitos en el cabello de diferentes colores, predominando el verde, azul y rojo, lo que nos cohibió por lo desastroso de nuestro ropaje, algunos con ropa de invierno, otros en manga de camisa. La señora encargada de nosotras nos advirtió que las chicas mayores se harían carga de nosotros con el objeto de que nuestra ropa estuviera limpia, así como nuestra asistencia a la escuela que había en la colonia. Enterados de los reglamentos de la casa sobre nuestro bienestar, nos comunicó que dentro de unos meses ingresaríamos en la escuela inglesa. Cuando algunos de nosotros hacíamos preguntas, ella nos atendía con maternal cuidado, dentro de la severidad que correspondía a su cargo. Su aspecto, mujer alta, gruesa, de cutis pálido y cabello endrino y rizado motivó en mí un concepto de persona seria y altiva pero, más tarde con el trato, pude comprobar su fondo, encontré en ella una mujer cariñosa y confidente. Ahora que los años han pasado, comprendo el error que es catalogar a una persona por la primera impresión.

Por la mañana, a primera hora, nos hacían levantar de madrugada, es decir, método empleado con los internados con el fin de habituarnos a una vida disciplinaria y saludable. Aquí nos anunciaban la hora de abandonar la cama con el toque seco de tres campanadas, ni más ni menos.

Recuerdo el caso de un niño que encontramos en el dormitorio haciendo las maletas; al preguntarle el motivo de su tarea, nos respondió: "Voy a solicitar permiso a la Directora para volver a España." Algunos trataron de consolarle diciéndole que no era motivo para tanto pues estábamos seguros que la Directora no le permitiría marchar.

Era la hora del desayuno. En cada mesa nos encontramos con una chica española encargada del servicio de comedor. Ellas nos recibían con los buenos días en la dulce voz de la mujer vascuence. ¡Qué días y recuerdos más felices! Apareció por la puerta de la cocina la Directora de la colonia. Al pasar revista sobre las mesas, se inclinó con ternura sobre los más pequeños haciéndoles preguntas sobre su estado de salud, estado de ánimo, pues era la mujer más maternal que he conocido en mi vida. Para mí representaba algo sublime como mujer. Una vez terminado el desayuno, descansábamos quince minutos como estaba reglamentado.

(Alfonso Delgado falleció en 2003. Extracto tomado de un manuscrito inédito encontrado por su hija María en el desván de su casa.)

Flori Díaz Jiménez

Soy una de las niñas que fueron evacuadas a Inglaterra en 1937 durante la Guerra Civil Española. Yo tenía 10 años. Tengo un grato recuerdo del tiempo que permanecí en el campamento en Eastleigh. Estuvimos muy bien atendidos: limpieza, visita médica y alimentación. En aquellos días sólo sentía la alegría de no ver los aviones que venían a bombardear y de no tener que ir corriendo a los refugios.

No se me olvida que a mi madre siempre le decía que me comprara unas botas katiuskas para el agua y ese momento no llegó nunca. Estando en el campamento se desató una gran tormenta. Nos dieron calzado para el agua y qué alegría tan grande cuando me dieron aquellas botas tan deseadas por mí.

No me acuerdo de cuando me llevaron a la colonia de Mrs Manning en Theydon Bois, pero aquello fue como un cuento de hadas. En mi casa nos bañábamos en un balde grande: cuando llegué a dicha colonia nos enseñaron un cuarto de baño con toallas y bolsitas para cada una conteniendo jabón, cepillo de dientes, pasta dentífrica y colonia, después el dormitorio, cuatro camas para las pequeñas, edredones y cortinones. Cuantas veces he pensado cómo pudimos tener tanta suerte después de lo mal que habíamos pasado en España durante el período de la guerra que nos tocó vivir.

La vida en aquella colonia fue de lo mejor. Los 21 niños parecíamos todos hermanos, los mayores nos daban mucho cariño a las cuatro más pequeñas. Mrs Manning fue maravillosa, con ella no faltó cariño ni atenciones. Recibíamos visitas de ingleses e inglesas que nos llevaban a Londres al cine o a tomar el té. También venían dos matrimonios que creo eran valencianos. Siempre digo que fueron los días más felices de mi vida.

Ahora viene lo peor. Mi hermano tenía tres años más que yo y para mí no sólo fue hermano sino también padre y madre, por eso el día que me dijeron que yo tenía que regresar a España y que mi hermano se quedaba no quiero recordar lo que sentí. Me dijeron que sólo era para visitar a mis padres y que después podía volver a Inglaterra. Infeliz de mí que me lo creí.

Al llegar a España en la frontera de Irún nos recibieron unas personas encargadas de hacernos llegar a nuestros respectivos destinos. Su trato fue hostil y su comportamiento fatal. No se daban cuenta de que solo éramos unos niños y niñas que nos habían enviado fuera de España por temor a los bombardeos y al hambre y no pensaron en el sufrimiento de nuestros padres al tener que separarnos de ellos por tales motivos y en beneficio nuestro. Mis padres no sabían que yo volvía, además era mi hermano el que figuraba en la lista y no yo.

En Bilbao la vida fue totalmente distinta. Era la posguerra y estábamos a falta de muchas cosas. Me encontré con familiares muertos, a otros les habían privado de sus hogares y les habían dejado en la calle sin nada. Mi abuela, por parte de mi padre, tuvo que ser internada en un sanatorio ya que se volvió loca al conocer la muerte de uno de sus hijos. Como resultado de esta locura falleció un tiempo después.

Para mí todo ello fue un trauma tan grande que empecé a vivir con tristeza. Por circunstancias de la vida no pude volver a Inglaterra, pero el recuerdo que tengo de mi estancia en Inglaterra es tan bueno que no lo he podido olvidar. Esto sólo lo puede comprender quien haya estado allí.

De mi hermano diré que él regresó a España año y medio después que yo y sin haber sido reclamado por nuestros padres. Tampoco lo fui yo y tanto en mi caso como en el de mi hermano no sabían que habíamos llegado a Bilbao. Se enteraron de forma casual.

Mi hermano tenía 16 años pero tuvo muy mala suerte porque para conseguir trabajo tenía que afiliarse al Frente de Juventudes que se trataba de una organización juvenil franquista. Como no quiso pertenecer a dicha organización se le negó todo derecho al trabajo. Pasaron los años y tuvo que incorporarse obligatoriamente a la Marina de Guerra Española para cumplir el servicio militar. Le licenciaron antes de cumplir la totalidad del tiempo de servicio por una malformación en un pie. Como en su mente estaba latente su deseo de volver a Inglaterra, intentó marcharse, pero con tan mala fortuna que le cogieron en la frontera con Francia y le acusaron de ser miembro de los *maquis*. Las torturas y vejaciones a las que fue sometido en comisarías de policía y cárceles le quitaron la vida a los 24 años. A pesar de los años transcurridos no puedo olvidar lo que hicieron con mi hermano y lo que él sufrió.

María Victoria Dominguez Elías

Ahora que lo recuerdo me parece que fue un sueño, cuando en el año 1937, un 20 de mayo, embarcábamos en el puerto de Santurce en un gran barco llamado el *Habana*. No olvidaré el pan blanco que nos

244

daban para comer, y el bizcocho para desayunar. En la travesía, como éramos tantos niños no había camarotes para todos. Mis hermanas y yo (éramos tres) tuvimos mucha suerte de tenerlos.

La llegada al puerto de Southampton fue de madrugada. Antes de bajar a tierra nos reconocieron unos médicos, después nos llevaron a Stoneham, un campamento con tiendas como las de los indios que se ven en el cine.

El tiempo en el campamento duró unos dos meses, hasta que nos trasladaron a una colonia. Nos llevaron a Birkenhead, donde lo pasamos muy bien el año escaso que estuvimos hasta regresar a España.

En honor a la verdad, la estancia en la colonia fue muy agradable; éramos 30 niños y 30 niñas en una gran casa señorial de verano en el campo. Nos cuidaba un matrimonio inglés y tres señoritas españolas, una maestra y dos auxiliares. Dábamos clase de cultura general con la maestra, y un día a la semana un profesor de inglés nos enseñaba su idioma. Las exploradoras nos solían llevar a la piscina; también nos agasajaban con alguna u otra fiesta que hacían para nosotras. Los domingos solían venir los discípulos del profesor de inglés para practicar con nosotros el español, que él a la vez enseñaba a los ingleses.

Los chicos de la colonia formaron un equipo de fútbol. Solían jugar los sábados contra equipos ingleses. A pesar de que cuando volví a España y a los pocos meses entré en un colegio interno en el que estuve siete años, de mis recuerdos de la niñez no se ha borrado mi estancia en Inglaterra de hace 70 años.

María de los Angeles Dueñas Montes

A pesar de que los padres de mi madre se marcharon a Francia, decidieron mandar a sus hijas a Inglaterra por las relaciones de mi abuelo con la compañía de ingeniería Brown Boveri.

La colonia de Sutton-on-Hull, donde les mandaron, se llamaba Elm Trees, edificio victoriano de ladrillo rojo en una esquina del pueblo de Sutton, con un gran jardín donde jugaban los niños. Su dueño era Mr Herbert Sewell, un constructor local, metodista de religión y filántropo.

Otra persona que estuvo en contacto con los niños fue Mr. Hudson, un joven hombre de negocios, popular porque tenía coche y sacaba a los niños a pasear en él. Estaba también Mr Priestman, dueño de una fábrica de ingeniería, que recogió a algunos niños como aprendices. Él y su esposa eran cuáqueros y se interesaban por mi madre y su hermana, y las invitaban a tomar el té. Les servía una criada que tenía un palatosquisis y no comprendían lo que decía.

Los niños no tuvieron lecciones de inglés, aunque fueron a la escuela local Chapman Street School. Cuando mi madre llegó, encontró que se podía comunicar en francés. Mi madre siempre nos comentaba su sorpresa cuando llegó a Sutton y vio los faroles de gas. Su padre había sido el encargado de una fábrica de hidroelectricidad en Burcena que alimentaba al norte de España, y esas luces le parecían muy primitivas.

Mi madre hablaba poco de sus años de jovencita en Sutton. Su hermana Lola y ella se fueron a vivir con Mr y Mrs Sewell y su hijo adoptivo, Douglas, en Chestnut House. Era una granja, con sección de carpintería y de construcción. Tenían invernaderos, gallinas, árboles frutales y huerta de verduras y así que eran autosuficientes.

Antes de casarse, Mrs Sewell había sido profesora y creía firmemente en el valor de la educación. Mi madre tuvo suerte, pues esta señora reconoció su potencial, y ellos pagaron para que estudiase en el Hull College of Commerce. También pagaron la educación de los hijos de otros empleados.

Un día, mi madre y Douglas llevaban un banco pesado y él dejó caer su lado y el de mi madre subió, la golpeó y le quitó unos dientes, así que tuvieron que ponerle una funda. Pienso que mi tía y mi madre no consideraban a los Sewell como padres, porque los suyos estaban en Francia y las dos chicas estaban en contacto con ellos, pero para mí eran como mis abuelos.

Cuando mi madre terminó sus estudios en el instituto, trabajó en la secretaría de asuntos de ciudadanía. Su papel era escribir cartas de los familiares de Hull a los soldados en Francia. De 1942 a 1945 estudió enfermería en el hospital de Hull, el Royal Infirmary. Nada más empezar como enfermera, dejó a los Sewell y vivió en la casa de las enfermeras. Su hermana Lola se quedó con los Sewell otros seis años, hasta que sus padres volvieron de su exilio en Francia. Se reunieron en Sevilla. Mi madre trabajó de enfermera de noche durante seis años, luego en otros departamentos en el Western Hospital de Hull. También trabajó de asistenta médica para visitas a domicilio y finalmente en una escuela y luego se jubiló.

Entre los años 1950 y 1960 la llamaban como intérprete en la Audiencia, en el hospital y en el puerto de Hull, pues había algunos marineros españoles. Mi madre visitó a sus tíos en París en 1947, se casó y visitó a su hermana en Sevilla, con su marido y conmigo en 1955. No volvió otra vez hasta 1975 y después visitaba a su padre y a su hermana todos los años hasta que su salud ya no la permitió viajar. Pasó su vida en Hull, hasta que pidió que la trasladaran a Edimburgo para estar cerca de mí.

Mi impresión sobre la actitud de Lola y de mi madre de su estancia en Sutton fue de total agradecimiento a las buenas gentes que abrigaron a los indefensos niños extranjeros, que habían pasado sus últimas semanas en Bilbao evitando los bombardeos. *

(María de los Angeles Dueñas falleció en 2004. Su hija María del Carmen ha escrito este relato.)

Celia Elduque Jaime

Mi madre nació en 1923 en la ciudad de San Sebastián, a donde sus padres, aragoneses, se habían trasladado a vivir a principios de los años 1920, permaneciendo en aquella ciudad hasta el inicio de la guerra. Contaba que su padre había acudido, como otros muchos, a alistarse para defender a la República, pero le dijeron: "Si no tenemos armas para los jóvenes… ". Como entonces pensaban que iban a ganar la guerra, decidieron salir de San Sebastián hacia Bilbao.

Cuando llegaron, hacia el 24 de abril de 1937, les dieron acomodo en un piso situado al comienzo de la Gran Vía, próximo al Banco de Comercio, que contaba con sótanos usados entonces como refugio cuando daban la alarma. De aquel mes hasta su evacuación a Inglaterra, los recuerdos que quedaron, tal como nos los contó, siempre eran referidos a lo mismo: el hambre y los bombardeos.

Hasta que un día, sería a comienzos de mayo de 1937, se enteraron de que se estaban organizando evacuaciones de niños hacia otros países. Cuando supieron que iba a salir una para Inglaterra, sus padres no se lo pensaron dos veces: corrieron a apuntar a ella y a su hermano Eduardo que contaba 11 años de edad, y recordaba mi abuela las colas que se habían formado para inscribir a los niños. Esto contrasta con la idea que luego extendió la propaganda de Franco de que "se habían llevado a los niños arrancándolos de sus padres". De regreso a España, después de la guerra, algunas personas le preguntaron si se los habían llevado a la fuerza o, por el contrario, voluntariamente por decisión de sus padres, a lo que respondían contándoles las largas filas que había para apuntarlos.

Llegado el día de la partida, hicieron "las maletas" (en realidad cajas de cartón sujetas con cuerdas) y fueron a la estación de Lanaja a tomar el tren para Santurce, donde ella y su hermano se despidieron de sus padres a quienes no vieron hasta enero de 1940.

Una vez el *Habana* hubo salido de puerto, mi madre se sintió muy mal a causa del mareo. Le contó su hermano que el barco iba protegido por el buque de guerra *José Luis Díez* hasta que llegasen en alta mar cuando continuaron escoltados por dos barcos ingleses. Cuando se retiró el *José Luis Díez* para ceder la escolta a los navíos británicos, formó su tripulación en cubierta, saludando al Habana, puño en alto, y justo entonces una ola los derribó.

Cuando desembarcaron en Southampton les llevaron al campamento de Stoneham. Como mi madre siempre había vivido en un ambiente urbano, nunca antes había dormido en tienda de campaña. Uno de los primeros cambios que experimentó fue que a los pocos días de campamento, el cabello se le volvió rubio.

Sería hacia el final del verano de 1937 cuando se formó el grupo de unos 20 niños que irían a la colonia denominada The Oaks, situada en las afueras de Carshalton en Surrey. Una vez en la colonia, comenzaron a darles clases de inglés, además de las clases impartidas por las señoritas. Era una vida apacible con la cercanía del campo y de los parques, también de viajes a Londres, donde iban de vez en cuando, y otros ocasionales como uno que hicieron a la Isla de Wight. También organizaban espectáculos con bailes folclóricos vascos (su hermano Eduardo aprendió por entonces a bailar el espatadantza) y con varias canciones. Al final de las representaciones solían cantar *"John Brown's body lies a-mouldering in the grave...Glory, glory, alleluia...",* lo que arrancaba muchos aplausos del público.

Solían llevarlos a un cine llamado The Plaza a sesiones matinales en sábados alternos, de tal manera que un sábado iba el primer grupo y el segundo grupo al siguiente. Muchas de las películas eran cómicas, con actores como Chaplin, Laurel y Hardy. Al ser actores británicos, el conocimiento del inglés adquirido por las clases que les daban, así como el tiempo que llevaban viviendo allí, era suficiente como para entender los diálogos, excepto cuando proyectaron una película de los hermanos Marx. Los niños no podían comprender el acento americano.

Otros recuerdos de mi madre eran relativos al contacto con la vida inglesa, por ejemplo las visitas a las casas o las invitaciones a comer. Aunque a veces se sentían cohibidos pensando en que quizás no sabrían comportarse adecuadamente en un país con otras costumbres, reaccionaban de diferente manera cuando les mostraban inventos o avances que suponían desconocidos en España. Por ejemplo, una vez les dijeron que les iban a mostrar lo que era el "teléfono automático", es decir un teléfono en el que no se necesitaba comunicar previamente con la operadora sino que llamaban marcando los números en el dial directamente. "Cuál fue su sorpresa cuando les contestamos que en España ya se conocía, lo cual era cierto". En otra ocasión y con motivo de un viaje a Londres, la persona que los llevaba les quiso enseñar Tower Bridge, explicando como una novedad, al menos para los niños, el sistema de elevación del puente que permite el tráfico fluvial y el tráfico terrestre. Los niños contestaron, con auténtico orgullo, que como aquel puente en Bilbao había tres iguales, nada menos. Había surgido la necesidad de responder a un "orgullo británico" con otro "orgullo español".

En otras ocasiones los niños iban a zonas de juegos con columpios y toboganes y, en cuanto llegaban, lo ocupaban todo de tal forma que ya no quedaba más sitio para los niños ingleses. Sobre cosas así, me decía mi madre: "Entonces nos creíamos con todos los derechos, pero ahora cuando lo pienso me doy cuenta de la paciencia y generosidad que tuvieron con nosotros los ingleses".

Hacia el verano de 1939, mi madre y su hermano fueron trasladados de la colonia de Carshalton a una casa particular en Lymington, donde vivía una señora llamada Mrs Williams. Una vez, Mrs Williams les preguntó si conocían cocinas de la clase que ellos tenían, porque había estado en España y había visto que se cocinaba en el suelo. Mi madre quedó muy sorprendida por esa observación y casi no podía creer lo que le estaban diciendo, hasta que la señora aclaró que ella lo había visto en un pueblo de Galicia.

Mientras duró la Guerra Civil Española, mi madre y su hermano no fueron reclamados por sus padres. Al caer Santander, ellos habían regresado a San Sebastián, donde su padre permaneció un tiempo en la cárcel hasta que fue liberado, después de vicisitudes, y una vez ya terminada la guerra, reclamaron a sus hijos. Poco antes de la Navidad de 1939, embarcaron desde el puerto de Newhaven hacia Francia. Era de noche, el barco era pequeño, con las luces apagadas a causa de los submarinos alemanes. El mar estaba muy agitado y mamá se mareó, de tal forma que ante los vómitos que comenzaba a tener, la subieron a cubierta y, sujetándola, un marinero le sacó la cabeza por la borda, sobre la negritud del mar. Tan fuerte quedó el recuerdo de aquellos malos momentos, al igual que sus mareos en la travesía tres años antes, que ya no volvió a subir jamás a un barco.

Una vez en Francia, fueron en tren a París donde, en el transbordo entre estaciones, les atendieron unas monjas facilitándoles comida. Desde París en otro tren fueron hacia Irún. Al llegar a la frontera de Irún, lo primero en que se fijó al entrar en España fue en unos guardias civiles y su primer sentimiento fue de tristeza al pensar que volvían, pero con la guerra perdida. Una vez allí quedaron internados en una especie de albergue de Auxilio Social en Irún o Fuenterrabía, permaneciendo allí durante unas dos semanas hasta que sus padres tuvieron conocimiento de su regreso.

Sus padres, que por entonces se habían trasladado a Madrid, no se habían enterado de su regreso. Sin embargo un día, un inglés, que muchos años después nos enteramos que se llamaba Ronald Thackrah y que pertenecía al Spanish Aid Committee, encontró a sus padres en Madrid, ya que iban comprobando la situación en la que se encontraban los niños que regresaban a España. Al preguntar por los niños, respondieron con sorpresa que aún no habían regresado de Inglaterra, a lo que el inglés les informó de que llevaban nada menos que quince días en la frontera. Rápidamente fue a buscarlos un tío suyo que vivía en Madrid y de esta forma se produjo el reencuentro hacia los primeros días de enero del año 1940. Uno de los contrastes que se daban en las primeras semanas, además de los previsibles cambios habidos durante la separación, era la costumbre que tenían de pedirlo todo "por favor", lo cual a veces casi llegaba a importunar a sus padres. Regresaron justo a tiempo, puesto que su padre falleció sólo tres meses después del reencuentro.

Sólo cabe citar entre las personas que conoció, entre otros, de los niños: los hermanos García Aldasoro (Helvecia, Delia y Elvio), José Sorozábal, los hermanos Sancho, Teresa David y todos los demás. De los británicos, personas como Mr Croft o Mr Lawrie, Mr Alan Hunter, el cual, según nos dijo, tanto les atendía y se preocupaba por ellos. También citaba y se carteaba con Charles West, o Ken Dow quien había tenido buen cuidado de advertirles que no era inglés ¡sino escocés!, y que tiempo después se casaría con una de las señoritas, Pili, que al igual que las otras dos, Ana María González y Carmen Díaz, continuaron viviendo en el Reino Unido.

Durante toda su vida, mi madre mantuvo vivo y permanente el

recuerdo de aquellos años, relatándonos tanta y tantas veces el porqué y el cómo había ido allí, el viaje, las anécdotas, todo. A pesar de tratarse de hechos vinculados a una guerra, no dejaba de notarse la alegría con que contaba su estancia en Inglaterra, hasta el punto de que sus recuerdos han pasado a formar parte de los nuestros.

(Celia Elduque falleció en 2004. Su hijo Miguel Ángel Cubero Elduque ha escrito este relato.)

Angelita, Paulita y Rosita Felipe Gómez.

Angelita, Paulita y Rosita Gómez eran tres hermanas que llegaron a Inglaterra en el *Habana* en 1937. Vivían en la Calle de la Semana en Portugalete-Sestao.

Ambos padres estaban muertos, las cuidaba su tía Marcelina y su hermana mayor Paquita. Pasaban la mayor parte de su tiempo en los refugios y sufrieron terriblemente por la falta de comida provocada por las acciones de Franco que impedía llegar comida al norte de España. Al cabo de poco tiempo tuvieron que comerse los animales domésticos y gorriones. Las tres hermanas salieron de España en 1937 en el *Habana*, dejando atrás a Paquita, que más tarde escapó a Francia para volver después de terminar la guerra.

De la colonia de North Stoneham, se marcharon a una colonia en Bristol y por falta de auxiliares, de allí a Cambria House en Caerleon, País de Gales. Allí las colocaron bajo la custodia de una señora española, Sra Fernández, de Dowlais, cuyos antepasados habían venido de Bilbao a trabajar en las minas de hierro de Merthyr Tydfil, a principio del siglo veinte.

Cuando la mayoría de los niños volvieron a España, las hermanas se quedaron, pues no tenían casa adonde regresar. Las separaron y las llevaron a diferentes casas en el sur del País de Gales. Las tres recuerdan cómo las trataron las autoridades, no se les permitió hacerse británicas hasta que se casaron. Angelita recuerda tener que pedir permiso oficial para trabajar en Metal Box Steel Works en Neath. Tenía también que informar a la policía si iba a Swansea.

Angelita volvió a España 15 años más tarde y se reunió con su hermana Paquita. Paula tuvo que esperar 25 años antes de regresar, y su visita fue muy emotiva. A pesar de sentirse galesas, el vínculo con su país de origen es muy fuerte.

La hija de Paulita le hace preguntas a su madre y a Angelita:
¿Qué recuerdos tenéis de vuestra estancia en España durante la guerra?
Paulita: Recuerdo pasar todo el día en el refugio mientras mi hermana mayor iba a buscar comida. Recuerdo el ruido de los aviones, estar hambrienta; cuando vivía mi padre, salía a cazar pájaros y conejos para comer, pero desde que murió, y con nuestra madre muerta también, nos fuimos a vivir con una tía, que también tenía hijos y faltaba comida. No tenía ni juguetes ni muñecas para jugar. Cuando tuve mis propios hijos disfrutaba haciendo vestidos para las muñecas o muebles para la casa de muñecas. Cuando tienes tan poco en tu infancia te haces muy ingenioso y nunca quieres gastar nada.
Angelita: Recuerdo sentir que era la hermana mayor y que tenía que cuidar de los pequeños cuando yo era también una niña.

¿Qué recuerdas de la travesía?
Paulita: Nos mareamos mucho, pero estoy segura de que era porque comimos demasiado de una vez, pues estábamos acostumbrados a comer poco. Tuvimos mucha suerte, pues uno de los camareros, que nos conocía, nos procuró un dormitorio. Cuando desembarcamos en Southampton, los muelles estaban llenos de gente de la Salvation Army, tocando música. Pensamos que los ingleses se vestían todos así, con esos uniformes. Había muchas banderas y decoraciones por todas partes y pensamos que era para recibirnos. Más tarde nos dimos cuenta de que habían sido colocadas para la coronación del rey unos días antes.

Recuerdo tener miedo de dejar España, pero nuestra hermana mayor Paquita había dicho que sería como unas vacaciones y que volveríamos muy pronto de nuevo, de alguna manera era como una aventura. Pero resultó que yo no volví a España hasta que tuve unos 30 años y ya tenía dos hijos.

¿Qué os gustó más de vuestra estancia en la colonia de Caerleon?
Paulita: Me encantaban los fines de semana porque íbamos todos a nadar y más importante, a veces tomábamos *"pudding* de cristal", un lujo especial, era lo que llamábamos *jelly*. Era muy agradable pues había muchos niños, siempre alguien con quien jugar. Dábamos conciertos para sacar fondos y bailábamos la jota. Era divertido y lo pasábamos muy bien. Los mineros venían los domingos y nos traían golosinas.

Angelita: A mi me gustaba cuando a todos nos contaban historias de fantasmas. Te daba seguridad y nos abrazábamos. Una vez fuimos a robar manzanas del jardín de al lado; cuando volvimos, no sabíamos dónde esconderlas, intentamos ponerlas en la ventana y de allí a las canaleras, pero de repente empezaron a rodar y no podiamos alcanzarlas, así nunca las recuperamos, nos estuvo bien empleado.•
(Angelita murió en 2008)

Isabel Fernández Barrientos

Cuando empezó la Guerra Civil Española, mi madre, que era viuda, tenía una casa de huéspedes. Antes había sido cocinera. Vivíamos muy bien las dos porque yo soy hija única, pero teníamos miedo de las bombas. Entonces, unos tíos le convencieron para que me mandara a Inglaterra con dos primos, algo mayores que yo, ya que sólo tenía siete anos.

Embarcamos en el *Habana*. Cuando llegamos, nos reconocieron a todos y nos pusieron unas cintas de color en la muñeca. Eran de colores: blanca, roja, y azul. A mí me pusieron la blanca aunque me gustaban más las de colores. Luego me dijeron que las de colores eran porque tenían piojos y otras enfermedades.

Nos llevaron a un campamento con tiendas de campaña y allí pasamos unos meses, hasta repartirnos por colonias. Sufría mucho de las muelas y como me dolía una mucho tuve que ir al dentista a sacármela. Mientras estaba en el dentista, se llevaron a mis dos primos al norte de Inglaterra, y yo me encontré muy sola, no conocía a nadie. Sólo conocía a la maestra que tenía en Bilbao que se llamaba Doña María de Dios.

Después de unos días me llevaron al sur del País de Gales. La colonia se llamaba Cambria House y estaba en Caerleon. La casa era enorme. Las salas eran grandísimas porque en una cabíamos todas las niñas y los niños en otra. El patio era enorme donde jugábamos y además teníamos toda clase de juegos: ping-pong, rompecabezas, libros y muchas más cosas. Conocí a muchos niños que eran de Vizcaya y Guipúzcoa. Los fines de semana, venían matrimonios que nos llevaban con ellos.

En la colonia, las niñas mayores cuidaban de las más pequeñas. Nos peinaban y nos ayudaban a vestirnos. Lo más divertido era cuando llegaba Navidad y nos escondían los regalos para darnos una sorpresa.

Fueron unos años muy felices. Lo único que llevaba muy mal era la hora de las comidas, pues no comía apenas nada, siempre dejaba en el plato y encima los chicos mayores llenaban mi plato con sus sobras. Entonces, a quien comía mal, le daban una cucharada de aceite de hígado de bacalao, y siempre me tocaba a mí. Para merendar nos ponían un gran trozo de pan con abundante mantequilla y cuando estaban encendidas las chimeneas, quitábamos la mantequilla y tostábamos el pan, que nos gustaba mucho.

Unos meses antes de reclamarme mi madre, vino a la colonia un matrimonio que no tenía hijos a llevarse a una niña y me eligieron a mí. Estuve muy bien con ellos, me querían como a una hija. Se llamaban Trevor e Iris Berry. Esta época que viví con ellos fue la más feliz en Inglaterra. Me daban todos los caprichos y como no me gustaba el té, Iris me llevaba a la cama el desayuno: zumo de naranja y cacao con galletas. Me mandaron a la escuela inglesa y aprendí mucho. Quien lo diría ahora, se me ha olvidado todo.

Al acabar la guerra mi madre me reclamó para ir a España con ella. Pero Mr y Mrs Berry no querían separarse de mí y pensaron en reclamar a mi madre para que viniera a Inglaterra. Entonces había empezado la Segunda Guerra Mundial y no la dejaron pasar. Nos despedimos con mucha pena, pensando que no volveríamos a vernos.

El mismo día que llegué a España cumplí once años. Mi llegada a España fue muy triste. No había más que miseria, se veía a los perros abandonados, muertos de hambre, por la calle. Me causó mucha impresión, acostumbrada en Inglaterra a ver a los animales domésticos muy bien cuidados por sus dueños. Estaba recién terminada la guerra y no había trabajo.

Nos habían quitado el piso donde vivíamos, así que tuve que ir con unos tíos que vivían en Logroño, hasta que mi madre encontrara trabajo. Mr y Mrs Berry me escribían muchas cartas, mandándome en ellas muchos besos, se acordaban mucho de mí. Yo también les contestaba. Pero no recuerdo cómo dejamos de escribirnos. Eran unos tiempos muy difíciles. Pero nunca les he olvidado y les sigo recordando con mucho cariño. He guardado unas fotografías de ellos y de la colonia.

Siempre he tenido mucho cuidado de no perderlas a pesar de haber cambiado de domicilio un montón de veces. He estado casada cerca de 50 años, pero hace seis años murió mi marido. Ahora vivo en Bilbao con mi hija, su marido y sus dos niñas.

Carmen Fernández Learra

Nací el 24 de noviembre de 1927 y me acuerdo de que empecé a ir a la escuela a los seis años. La guerra empezó en el 36 y entonces no hubo clases. Tenía nueve años cuando fui a Inglaterra en el *Habana*, fuimos tres hermanas (Manola, la mayor, Asun, la pequeña, y yo, Carmen, la mediana) y un hermano (Loren). Mis padres nos mandaron para huir de las bombas y de los horrores de la guerra. Al principio en el barco lloré mucho, pero luego ya no. Te vas haciendo. Una chiquilla se hace.

Me acuerdo de que en el barco nos miraban los médicos ingleses, y lo que también recuerdo siempre es que nos daban unos huevos cocidos pintados de colorines, y eso nos alegraba mucho, nos ponía muy contentos.

Llegamos a Southampton a un campo lleno de tiendas de campaña blancas: era la primera vez que veía tiendas de campaña en mi vida. La verdad es que estaba muy bonito porque había muchas tiendas. Allí nos dieron unas botas, porque llovía bastante. Allí estuvimos poco tiempo; despues de dos ó tres días, me parece, un señor muy simpático al que llamaban Señor Urra nos llevó en autobuses hasta Clapton, la colonia del Salvation Army. Allí estuvimos muy poco tiempo, a lo mejor un mes o podría ser algo más. Entonces nos llevaron a Brixton. Creo que en Brixton no había chicos, los mandaron a otras colonias. Mi hermano fue a Scarborough.

Allí estuvimos unos tres meses. Las comidas eran tan distintas de las nuestras que era un problema muy grande. Sobre todo a mi hermana la pequeña, Asun, no le gustaban. Nosotras no éramos de carne, y claro, nos daban una carne como picada y no nos gustaba. A Asun le tuvieron una semana con la misma comida. Como ella no la comía metían la carne en el frigorífico, volvían a sacarla, no la comía, otra vez al frigorífico… Mi hermana la mayor y yo sí la comíamos, pero la pequeña no la quería.

De Brixton nos mandaron a Laleham School en Margate en el condado de Kent. Había sido una escuela y la dejaron a los niños que veníamos evacuados de la guerra. En esta colonia había chicos tambien. Allí es donde verdaderamente ya fuimos felices. Ya nos íbamos adaptando a la vida inglesa. Allí tuvimos suerte porque aparte de estar bien, nos adoptaron. A mí me adoptó una familia de dos señoras, a mi hermana la pequeña una familia con una hija y a mi hermana la mayor otra familia. En realidad no es que nos "adoptaran", sino que pagaban los gastos del colegio, la ropa, etc. Dormíamos en la colonia, pero yo solía ir con las señoras, igual pasé un mes con ellas, pero no viví con ellas todo el tiempo.

Nos trataron muy bien a todos, con mucho cariño. Nos íbamos haciendo un poco más a la vida en la colonia. A mi hermana la pequeña, Asun, le costaba, pero nosotras dos nos íbamos acostumbrando. Además a nosotras nos gustaba tomar mucha leche y allí nos la daban en buenas cantidades. Teníamos una profesora que era hindú que nos daba clases de gimnasia y también teníamos una profesora de piano, Srta Bonasera. Me gustaba todo, sobre todo la gimnasia. Había un gimnasio, que luego volví a ver con mi marido, cuando me casé, en unas vacaciones que pasamos en Inglaterra. En la habitación teníamos doce camas. Yo por las noches les solía leer a las chicas.También hacíamos fiestas, carreras de sacos, etc. Iba aprendiendo inglés, como iba al colegio, no tenía más remedio, pues todo era en inglés, pero con otros niños en la colonia hablaba en español. Creo que los otros niños de la colonia no iban al colegio, y les daban clases allí mismo en la colonia.

No llegamos a perder contacto con mi hermano que estaba en Scarborough. Él solía llamarnos a las hermanas a la colonia y hablábamos un poco. Me acuerdo de que se le estaba poniendo ya la voz de hombre. Parecía un inglés, pues era rubio y tenía los ojos claros. Nos contaba que jugaba al fútbol y que estaba muy contento, aunque no estaba tan bien como nosotras: donde nosotras estábamos fue mejor, tuvimos mucha suerte. Ninguno de los pocos que he visto después de los que estuvieron en la colonia ha hablado mal de ella.

También hacíamos teatro, bailes de los nuestros, típicas danzas vascas, o nos vestíamos de marineros. Siempre íbamos a Londres. Recuerdo que cuando empezábanos los conciertos, todos se callaban y se cantaba el himno nacional *God Save the King*.

Había ingleses, no los que nos habían adoptado, que iban a la colonia y querían llevarse algún niño de vez en cuando de vacaciones. Una vez llamaron a la colonia para invitar a alguien a la Isla de Wight y el Señor Palomba, que era un profesor madrileño, dijo que me llevaran a mí.

Salimos de algún puerto de por allí, ya no me acuerdo. Era un sitio en el que había máquinas tragaperras. Los que me llevaron tenían una casa en la isla y tenían una hija que estaba estudiando declamación. La niña tenía un año más que yo y era hija única. Estuve en su casa tres días con ellos. Me dieron mucho dinero y a la vuelta llevé regalos a los de la colonia.

Creo que en total pasé dos años y medio o tres en Inglaterra. Me acuerdo de que antes de marcharnos, en la colonia nos estaban probando las máscaras antigás. Todavía no había empezado la Segunda Guerra Mundial, pero estaba a punto de estallar. Mis padres se habían escapado a Francia, y después de pasar por varios sitios diferentes, llegaron a París, porque allí vivía un hermano de mi padre desde antes de la Guerra Civil.

Nosotros todavía estábamos en Inglaterra pero mis padres se enteraron de donde estábamos y de las señoras que nos ayudaban. Mis padres, sobre todo mi madre, querían que nos mandaran a París, pero las señoras inglesas querían que nos quedáramos y les ofrecieron a mis padres trabajo en Inglaterra. Yo prefería quedarme, igual que mis hermanas. Quería ver a mis padres, pero me hubiera gustado que mis padres viniesen a Inglaterra, en vez de ir nosotros a Francia. Al final nos mandaron donde estaban mis padres, me parece por mediación de la Cruz Roja. A la vuelta traíamos dos cestas grandes con regalos de las señoras y regalos que me habían hecho en el colegio. Había dinero, cosas para mi padre (unos catalejos), fotos y un montón de regalos para todos, pero justo antes de cruzar la frontera de Hendaya nos robaron una cesta.

En la aduana había muchas colas, gente que volvía y un soldado le preguntó a mi madre a ver si pensaban entrar con Lenin. Mi madre, que tenía mucho carácter, le dijo: "No, venimos a nuestra tierra, que es Euskadi, que ¿quizás usted no sea de aquí?". Entonces yo que tenía miedo le digo:"¡Ama!" y mi madre, ¡zaca! me mete una bofetada y dice: "¿Ante éstos hay que agacharse la cabeza? ¿Ante éstos yo voy a agachar la cabeza? Ni se os ocurra a vosotras!" Y allí empezó ya la posguerra…

Llegamos a Irún. En Irún nos metieron en un sitio que era una nave en la que no había ni para ir a los servicios ni para nada. Bueno, ya de allí fuimos en tren a casa, a Erandio. Luego los horrores del hambre, lo que pasa después de las guerras… Cuántas veces dijo mi padre: "María, ¿qué hemos hecho con estos hijos? ¿Por qué no los dejaríamos en Inglaterra con lo bien que estaban allí?"

Un día, cuando llevábamos un tiempo de vuelta en casa, un vecino le dijo a mi padre: "Balbino, estas chicas han cambiado mucho, porque cuando vinieron de Inglaterra, cómo les gustaba decir "perdón" y "gracias", y entonces le contestó mi madre "¡Pues no será porque nosotros les hayamos educado mal!" Lo que pasaba es que lo mismo que con el inglés, íbamos perdiendo lo que habíamos aprendido. Luego despues de cierto tiempo, al ver lo que pasaba en España, empezamos a decirles a mis padres: "¿Por qué habremos venido? ¿Por qué no habéis ido vosotros a Inglaterra?" También lo que pasa es que uno idealiza todo. Cuando vas a un sitio y eres niña, lo ves todo bien: no nos fijábamos en lo malo, sino en lo bien que nos trataban, lo amables y educados que eran. Luego a la vuelta, según íbamos perdiendo el inglés, pues nadie lo hablaba entonces, nos acordábamos sólo de las canciones y también las íbamos olvidando. Lo mismo que lo aprendimos de niños, lo volvimos a olvidar por la falta de práctica.

(Transcrito por Susana Sabín, hija)

Rafael Flores Siosalido

Mi vida es prácticamente pasarme los días haciendo cola para obtener un poco de tocino o un poco de jabón o cosas por el estilo y correr al túnel más cercano cuando vienen los aviones alemanes o italianos a bombardearnos.

En el número 5 de la calle Zabala de Bilbao en el primer piso vive la familia Salcedo. El padre habla con mi padre y dice que él quisiera mandar a Irene, su única hija, a Inglaterra si mi padre manda a Rafa, el mediano de sus hijos, y piensa que no sería por mucho tiempo. Del sexto piso van Andresi, José Luis y Lorenzo de Bilbao. Y así pues se arregla para que los cinco vayamos como hermanos.

Mi padre junto a su mesa de cortar, pues era sastre, y trabajando en aquellos días con uniformes de las milicias vascas, me dice que pronto estaré de vuelta, que la normalidad en España sería cosa de unos pocos meses. Ya no le volví a ver más. Me enteré de su muerte en 1940. Mis abuelos en la puerta de la casa se despidieron de mí y mi abuelo me entregó un duro de plata, acuñado en el siglo anterior. Tampoco volví a ver a mis abuelos. Mi hermana mayor Ester, recién casada con Agrupino, el cual me dice que nunca me olvide de la República Española mientras que me encuentre en la rubia Albión. Este hombre fue encarcelado nada más entrar las fuerzas franquistas en Bilbao y estuvo tres años en la cárcel, por lo que dice la sentencia, "por hablar". Tenía una hermana recién nacida, Maite, que volví a ver 22 años después. Vi a mi madre otra vez diez años después, cruzando el puente de la frontera en Hendaya, gritando "¡Rafa! ¡Rafa!" y corriendo como una loca.

El viaje en el *Habana* y nuestra llegada al campamento de Eastleigh sin duda han sido descritos por otros. Estábamos un poco desilusionados porque no entendíamos por qué teníamos que estar en tiendas de campaña. Es aquí donde nuestro mundo y nuestras vidas cambiaron completamente.

El pan blanco era nuestra obsesión: no lo habíamos visto en más de un año. Un día un chaval que llevaba una bandeja llena de pan de molde se cayó al ser empujado. El pan se cayó al suelo y recogimos todo lo que pudimos, metiéndolo debajo de la camisa y volvimos a las tiendas. ¡Pensábamos que pronto podríamos volver a Bilbao con el pan! La comida era sopa de cebada o sopa de cebolla y carne de vaca en conserva. Comida sencilla pero nos alimentó y poco a poco nos repusimos. Había una cola constante para la bebida *Horlicks:* al terminar una taza de la bebida hacíamos cola otra vez.

Hizo un tiempo estupendo ese verano en Inglaterra y la vida en el campamento se hizo más y más soportable al paso del tiempo. En el centro del campamento se veía a las chicas que lavaban la ropa de sus hermanos y hermanas, colgándola a secar al sol.

Pronto llegó el día en el que tuvimos que dejar el campamento, unos dos meses después de nuestra llegada. Dos autobuses de dos pisos pertenecientes al ayuntamiento de Walsall llegaron al campamento. Un señor con un bombín se bajó de uno de los autobuses. Era el concejal del partido laborista en el ayuntamiento de Walsall, John Whiston. Más tarde sería el alcalde de Walsall.

Éramos 50 niños, tres señoras, dos maestras, Lucita y María Luisa, una auxiliar y asistente social, Paquita. Nuestra destinación era Aldridge Lodge, cerca de Walsall. Sería nuestra casa para los próximos dos o tres años. Subimos la carretera entre dos campos verdes pertenecientes a la granja de productos lácteos de Mr y Mrs Adams y finalmente llegamos a la casa. Estoy seguro de que cuando vimos la casa dimos un suspiro de alivio y nos sentimos a salvo. Era un sitio precioso, rodeado de campos verdes con vacas. Enfrente de la casa había un aeródromo que se usaba principalmente para vuelos de instrucción.

Acontecimientos a resaltar en el aeródromo: primero cuando Amy Johnson, la famosa aviadora, participaba en un concurso de planeo un domingo por la tarde. El ala de su planeador tocó nuestra valla al aterrizar. La máquina se volcó y ella se quedó colgando del cinturón de seguridad... pero salió ilesa. La conmoción era tremenda. Creo que los 50 niños y todos los adultos se quedaron observando hasta que los del aeródromo pudieron soltarla. El segundo acontecimiento fue en 1939. La Segunda Guerra Mundial había empezado y un bombardero Lancaster tuvo que aterrizar de emergencia en el aeródromo, pero la pista era demasiado pequeña. El avión aterrizó en Walsall Road.

Mr Whiston era un personaje público, presidente o miembro de comités y organizaciones dedicadas a asuntos sociales. Los señores Whiston con sus cuatro perros vinieron a vivir con nosotros. Creo que su pasatiempo era llevar a sus perros a exposiciones caninas. Sus dos hijos, Tom y Ron, y las novias, Ivy y Winnie, pasaban muchos de sus ratos libres con nosotros, los fines de semana y las vacaciones. Mr Whiston no aprendió ni una palabra de castellano excepto "curar" (que creía que quería decir "primeros auxilios"). Antes de ir a la cama se formaba una cola de niños a la puerta de su oficina y él y su mujer untaban ligeramente con iodo todo lo que se les presentaba - heridas, cardenales, arañazos. Mr Whiston era un actor natural y representando con gestos alguna palabra inglesa comprendíamos lo que quería decir.

Tom nos enseñó artesanía y nos llevaba en coche a clases de noche de arte, carpintería y ebanistería. Transformó en taller una dependencia del patio trasero y vendíamos lo que hacíamos a los visitantes. Nos hizo ver la importancia de estar ocupados todo el tiempo. Años después me di cuenta de que era un hombre con ideas muy progresistas y que la Guerra Civil Española le había afectado muchísimo políticamente.

Peggy Gibbins de Birmingham fue una de los primeros en visitarnos. Era una señora maravillosa. Nos invitaba a merendar y nos presentaba un verdadero banquete. Tenía un coche, un Morris 10. Un día se quedó atascado en el barro a la entrada de Bosty Lane. Vino a la casa y dijo: "¿Podéis sacar el coche? Aquí tenéis las llaves." Nos metimos en el coche, arrancamos y de alguna manera el coche salió disparado del barro. Cuando nos vio, sonrío y dijo: "Os voy a enseñar a conducir". Y así hizo. Una o dos veces a la semana nos llevaba a la piscina en Walsall. Un hombre nos dio un libro con dibujos e instrucciones sobre cómo nadar. Tomamos parte en un concurso de natación con un colegio inglés. Yo gané una de las pruebas y todavía tengo la medallita que me dieron.

Thomas W. Wooley de Tipton era un gran amigo de la colonia. Un fin de semana, él y su hermana me llevaron con José Luis Bilbao a Londres. Visitamos todos los lugares de interés turístico. Thomas también nos llevaba al cine en Walsall: veíamos una película y merendábamos en el restaurante: huevos fritos con patatas fritas, ketchup y té, con pan, mantequilla y mermelada. ¡Fue un verdadero lujo¡ Era una persona maravillosa y más tarde se hizo clérigo.

Mrs Whiston y dos de las chicas mayores llevaban la cocina pero Mr Whiston tenía dos tareas. A la noche tenía que preparar la avena para la mañana. Se ponía sólida durante la noche y a la mañana se cortaba, de verdad se cortaba, se ponía en tazones y se añadía leche y azúcar. Los domingos tenía que ocuparse del asado. Entraba a la cocina con un delantal y con un cuchillo de trinchar grande y un tenedor. Cortaba la carne en tajadas mientras Mrs Whiston y las chicas servían los vegetales.

Nos animaron a construir una casa para los pájaros y montarla sobre un tocón. Nos enseñaron a querer a los pájaros y a no hacerles daño. Pero sí hacíamos daño a los centenares de ratones. Al anochecer nos sentábamos en la cocina con palas y con las luces apagadas. Esperábamos cinco minutos antes de encender las luces. Cada vez que hacíamos eso cogíamos 14 ó 15 ratones pero durante el día no veíamos ni uno.

La vida en Aldridge Lodge empezó a cambiar cuando llegó Manuel Lazareno, un músico y compositor. Vino de Francia como refugiado. Formó un coro y usando el libro *Canciones de los niños vascos* nos enseñó a apreciar la música folclórica española. Yo me divertí muchísimo. Con la ayuda de un chico que tocaba el *txistu,* aprendimos bailes vascos como la *espatadanza* y la *jota vasca* y bailes de otras partes de España.

Cadbury's, el fabricante de chocolate, suministraba a Aldridge Lodge chocolate. Cada día a la tarde Mr Whiston nos daba una pastilla de chocolate con leche para la merienda. Nos invitaron a Bourneville, sede de Cadbury's, durante las Navidades de 1937 ó 1938 y lo pasamos muy bien. Interpretamos nuestras canciones y bailes para la familia Cadbury. Nos enseñaron la fábrica y nos cargaron con distintos tipos de chocolate, ofreciéndonos todo lo que se hacía. ¡Esta es otra visita que jamás olvidaré!

El inglés era difícil. Tom Whiston intentó enseñarnos en la colonia y escribió la palabra "enough" en la pizarra pero no podíamos pronunciarlo. Él la pronunciaba con una "i" y nosotros queríamos decir "e". Recuerdo pensar que jamás aprendería el inglés. Pero claro, poco a poco iba aprendiendo.

La familia Whiston nos enseñó nuestra primera canción en inglés titulada *Canción de un vagabundo* e iba así:

Ésta es la canción de un vagabundo,
Un vagabundo que se queda en tu habitación.
Yo soy el vagabundo y ésta es mi canción,
Una canción para hogar dulce hogar.
Canto una canción a los viejos,
Estén donde estén,
Canto a tu madre y a mi madre,
Aunque estén lejos la una de la otra.
Canto a los viejos en casa,
Dondequiera que sean.

¡Cuando cantábamos esta canción en público, la gente lloraba!

El taller tenía una ventana pequeña a través de la cual podíamos ver un poco de la granja de Mr Adams. Un día nosotros, los chicos mayores, tuvimos una clase de anatomía natural. Mr Adams y su hijo llevaban las vacas al toro y vimos todo por primera vez en nuestras vidas. ¡No lo podíamos olvidar! Creo que fue una clase de naturaleza muy buena y que todo niño de cierta edad lo debería ver.

Desde el comienzo de 1938 a la hora del desayuno Mr Whiston leía la lista de niños supuestamente reclamados por sus padres. Cuando oía mi nombre le decía: "Yo no vuelvo". Por fin un día Mr Whiston dijo que si Raf (así me llamaba) no quería volver entonces Raf se podía quedar con ellos. Y así sucedió. Me quedé con la familia Whiston hasta que se cerró la colonia y fui a vivir con ellos a Walsall.

Viví con la familia dos años más hasta que quedamos sólo cuatro en la región central de Inglaterra. No nos quedamos más tiempo porque cada vez que íbamos a Londres sentíamos la necesidad de estar más cerca de los refugiados españoles que se estaban estableciendo en Londres. Me encontré con Valeriana, que también era una de los niños del *Habana*. Nos casamos, tuvimos dos hijos y ahora tenemos cinco nietos - todos viven en Londres.

Ahora vivimos en Denia, Alicante. Damos clases de inglés voluntariamente a las Aulas de la Tercera Edad. Estas clases están organizadas por el ayuntamiento. A la gente les gusta oír nuestra historia y algunas veces comparamos nuestra vida en Inglaterra con los de nuestra edad que tuvieron que vivir bajo la dictadura. Comparar las dos experiencias forma una parte muy interesante de la historia española de esos años. *

Helvecia García Aldasoro

Mi padre se había muerto en 1933 a los 56 años de edad y se había quedado mi madre con cinco hijas y dos hijos. Mi hermano Óscar, el mayor, que hacía de padre desde entonces, estaba en el frente. Vivíamos en un pueblo minero llamado La Arboleda, muy cerca de Bilbao. Cuando hacía ya 10 meses que la sublevación había comenzado, y habíamos pasado hambre y mucho miedo durante los bombardeos, mi madre nos dijo que me había apuntado con mis hermanos pequeños, Elvio de nueve años y Delia de ocho, a ir a Inglaterra donde no caían bombas y había mucho que comer. Yo tenía 14 años.

Cuando llegamos a Southampton nos llevaron en autobuses a un campo enorme; a los pocos días de estar en el campamento empezaron a salir grupos destinados a colonias en diferentes partes del Reino Unido. En agosto se acercó una señorita que no conocía y me preguntó si quería ir con ellos a una colonia pequeña, pues necesitaban a tres más que fueran hermanos y yo dije que sí. Fuimos en tren a Carshalton en el condado de Surrey. La colonia se llamaba The Oaks, y éramos nada más 20 niños (12 niños y 8 niñas), una maestra y dos auxiliares. Había una cocinera y una ama de llaves que vivían con nosotros y otra persona que venía diariamente a ayudar. Las hermanas mayores teníamos que cuidar de los pequeños, lavar y planchar su ropa, etc. Además de eso, teníamos turnos para ayudar en la cocina.

Era una mansión suntuosa con torres de castillo, pero nosotros no la habitábamos toda. En la otra parte vivía un matrimonio inglés con dos hijos; el padre era el guardián y se encargaba de que todo fuera bien. La casa estaba rodeada de jardines y árboles. Nosotros teníamos un patio grande para correr y jugar y además el uso de un campo para jugar al fútbol. Estábamos muy bien y nos llevábamos como una familia. Pero en el invierno hacía mucho frío, pues en aquellos tiempos no había calefacción central y había un pasillo muy largo y frío para llegar a los aseos. Por la noche nos echábamos los abrigos encima de la cama.

La administración corría a cargo de un comité local y la manutención de lo que voluntariamente daban asociaciones locales e individuos que habían contestado al anuncio puesto en algunos periódicos laboristas, donde se decía que con diez chelines a la semana podrían apadrinar y mantener a un niño. Uno de los que respondieron al anuncio fué Mr Cadbury de la familia de fabricantes de chocolate, y le asignaron a mi hermana.

Al cabo de un tiempo los Cadbury se enteraron de que éramos hermanos y nos sacaban de vez en cuando, ya bien al centro de Londres o a su casa. Ellos teñían dos niñas encantadoras, una era un bebé de meses y la otra de unos dos años. En enero de 1939 arreglaron con el comité para que fuera yo a su casa a pasar un mes, con idea de mejorar el poco ingles que sabía. En la casa, en el noroeste de Londres, vivían también una cocinera y una niñera, así que Mrs Cadbury tenía tiempo para conversar y ayudarme con el idioma.

Oíamos las noticias por la radio todas las noches y un día las noticias de España fueron tan malas que me puse a llorar y les conté, como pude, que mi familia no quería que volviéramos por el momento. (Franco nos estaba reclamando desde que cogió Bilbao.) Me consolaron y prometieron que ellos se encargarían de nosotros hasta que mi madre quisiera nuestra vuelta y empezaron los trámites para adoptarnos. Pensaron que lo mejor era que fuéramos a un internado coeducacional, para no separarnos, a mí me pareció muy bien con tal de que pasáramos las vacaciones en la colonia con los otros niños.

Visitamos tres escuelas cuáqueras y nos decidimos por la más cercana a Londres, The Friends' School, Saffron Walden, en Essex y en abril de 1939 ya estábamos instalados en las clases. Para no humillarme me pusieron en una clase con niños de mi edad (16 años) que iban a hacer lo que entonces se llamaba *matric*. La manera de enseñar era muy diferente de lo que estaba acostumbrada y entendía muy poco, pero me dijeron que siguiera lo que pudiera, que lo importante era que aprendiera el idioma escuchando. El maestro de matemáticas encontraba curiosa mi manera de hacer divisiones y el de geografía estaba contento porque aquel año estudiaban España y me preguntaba la pronunciación de las ciudades y ríos que él trataba de imitar. Al principio echábamos mucho de menos a los amigos de la colonia. A mis hermanos, siendo tan jóvenes, no les afectó tanto el cambio y se adaptaron bien.

Estábamos en las afueras del pueblo, rodeados de campos y jugábamos al hockey, cricket y tenis. Una tarde mirando como jugaban al hockey los chicos mayores, me pegó la pelota (que es muy dura) en el ojo derecho y tuve una moradura tremenda por dos semanas. El culpable del accidente vino corriendo a pedirme perdón y desde entonces siempre fue muy amable y simpático conmigo. Lo curioso es que dos o tres años después jugando un partido con el equipo de hockey de la compañía donde trabajaba la pelota me pegó en el ojo izquierdo mucho más fuerte esta vez. Temía haber perdido el ojo y me lo tapé con la mano fuerte y no la quería quitar –nunca se me olvidará– hasta que me llevaron del campo y me forzaron a quitarla. ¡Qué alivio sentí al ver que estaba equivocada!

Todos los domingos por la mañana, nos llevaban al pueblo en fila a compartir la asamblea con los cuáqueros de Saffron Walden. Se sentaban en un cuarto con una mesa en medio, la Biblia encima de la mesa, y sin ningún adorno; estaban en silencio hasta que el espíritu les movía y entonces se levantaban y daban el mensaje. Se volvían a sentar y continuaba el silencio: y eso duraba por lo menos media hora. Era una experiencia muy espiritual. Después de la cena los domingos, siempre teníamos alguna visita que daba una charla: alguien que había estado enseñando en Africa o algún misionero. Al que más recuerdo es a Mahatma Gandhi, con su vestidura tan extraordinaria.

Un día, hablando del futuro, le dije Mr Cadbury que lo que yo quería era hacerme taquimecanógrafa para estar preparada para trabajar y ayudar a mi madre cuando nos llamara. Al cabo del año académico arregló todo para que fuera a Birmingham a estudiar en un colegio comercial y viviera con una señora amiga viuda y su hermano soltero inválido de la primera guerra mundial. Eran muy buenas personas que me querían mucho.

Antes de mi viaje a Birmingham, el Señor Cadbury se puso en contacto con el Basque Children's Committee en Londres, y se enteró que en Birmingham y sus alrededores había varios niños vascos trabajando en fábricas y que un adulto se encargaba de su bienestar. Hizo una cita con él para los tres y entonces me enteré de mucho más. Su nombre era Walter Leonard, pero le llamaban León; nacido en Alemania, había vivido en España, hablaba muy bien el castellano y además había sido director de una colonia de niños vascos. Me dijo que en Birmingham vivían cinco chicos vascos, un matrimonio catalán con una niña, dos de las asistentas que vinieron con nosotros, y que en los alrededores esparcidos en varias ciudades había unos quince, dijo también que su futura suegra abría su casa para todos los españoles que quisieran ir el primer domingo de cada mes y que daba una merienda. Yo prometí ir y así lo hice.

Cuando fui por primera vez estaban León, su novia Peggy y su madre, Mrs Gibbins, y algunos de los que vivían en Birmingham. Como hacía bueno, pasamos la tarde en el jardín, pero teníamos también a nuestra disposición una sala con gramófono, mesa de jugar al ping-pong, libros y revistas. En las próximas visitas acudieron más y poco a poco llegué a conocer a todos. No sé de dónde salió la idea pero formamos un club que llamamos *"The Midland Boys' Club"* y yo era la secretaria. Más tarde, con ayuda de Mr Cadbury, me dejaron usar el campo de deportes y la caseta que pertenecía a la compañía Cadbury. Yo vivía allí cerca, en Bourneville, y me era fácil abrir y cerrar. Decidimos reunirnos allí todos los domingos quien pudiera venir. Si había suficientes chicos, jugaban al fútbol y hacíamos una merienda en la caseta. Teníamos contacto con los niños vascos de Londres y todos los españoles que pasaban por Birmingham nos venían a ver.

Poco a poco se fueron yendo los chicos a Londres, incluso la familia catalana, pues le habían ofrecido el puesto de Secretario de la Fundación Juan Luis Vives al marido que se llamaba Domingo Ricart. Al poco tiempo recibí una carta del Sr. Ricart donde me preguntaba si yo quería ser su secretaria. Mencionó que usaría los dos idiomas, pues entonces sólo usaba el inglés. La idea de usar el castellano además del inglés y el hecho de haberme quedado sola en la zona de los Midlands hizo que le contestara afirmativamente. Vine un domingo por la tarde a una entrevista con Don Pablo de Azcárate. Me informó de que también habían fundado un Instituto Español en el mismo edificio y como las dos cosas acababan de formarse, no había mucho trabajo y querían que trabajara para las dos entidades: para el Sr. Ricart por las mañanas y para el Sr Salazar Chapela, que era el Secretario del Instituto, por las tardes. Decidí aceptarlo.

En el Instituto se daban todas las semanas clases de español y de literatura por las tardes y cada semana había una conferencia. También tuvimos varios conciertos, uno de estos por el gran violoncelista Pablo Casals que aceptó la invitación por ser un concierto privado. Cada tres meses publicábamos una revista compilando las conferencias que eran dadas por profesores hispanistas como J B Trend, diplomáticos de Sudamérica y otras personalidades.

Al llegar a Londres fui al Hogar Español en Bayswater, 22 Inverness Terrace, que era un centro de españoles republicanos exiliados donde había mucha actividad y encontraba a mis amigos. Había un coro y un grupo teatral; yo me apunté al grupo de teatro y ensayábamos una vez por semana. El director era un valenciano llamado Pepe Estruch. Un año hicimos La Zapatera Prodigiosa en un teatro pequeño de Notting Hill Gate y tuvimos mucho éxito.

En el año 1945, al acabar la guerra mundial, vinieron a Londres muchos españoles que habían luchado en el ejército inglés. Entre ellos estaba José Hidalgo con quién me casé.

Mi madre nos visitó en julio de 1948 cuando mi hija tenía cuatro meses. Elvio, Delia y yo fuimos a esperarla al aeropuerto de Northolt: entonces era un campo con una alambrada alrededor; detrás de ella estábamos nosotros. Al bajar del avión y vernos, mi madre se echó a correr hacia nosotros y un policía la seguía. Tuvimos que explicarle que tenía que ir con los demás pasajeros. Después me llamaron para traducir. La emoción fué tremenda. No la habíamos visto en once años y ya no éramos los niños que ella había despedido en el puerto de Santurce. La encontramos más pequeña de lo que recordábamos y nos extrañó mucho. Disfrutó con su nieta durante su estancia en Londres, bañándola y sacándola a paseo en su coche. Se quedó con nosotros hasta que nos mudamos de casa y me ayudó a hacer las cortinas. Al poco tiempo dijo que quería ir a su casa y se fue. Volvió de nuevo en el verano del año 1958 cuando ya tenía otro hijo, esta vez varón, que había nacido en marzo del 1952 y tenía seis años.

María Dolores Gómez Sobrino

Mi primer recuerdo es cuando me despedí de mi padre Timoteo Gómez en Santurce. "No os preocupéis," nos dijo. "Solo será para tres meses y estaréis de vuelta para Navidad." Fue la última vez que le vi. Era el mes de mayo de 1937 y yo tenía 12 años. Mi madre Ramona Sobrino, que era maestra, mi hermano mayor Ignacio, mi hermana menor Tere y yo nos embarcamos en el *Habana* rumbo a Southampton. (Mi hermana Luchi tenía 20 años y la consideraron demasiada mayor para ser uno de los niños vascos.)

El viaje duró dos días y el mar estaba muy agitado. Nos perseguía un barco franquista y todavía oigo el boom boom de sus cañones disparándonos al abandonar aguas españolas. Éramos unos 4.000, la mayor parte niños pero también curas y maestras, como mi madre, que nos cuidaban. Algunos chavales lloraban porque estaban solos o porque se habían perdido en ese barco grande. Había un cura vasco, grande y viejo, tocando su txistu y tambor para animarnos.

Al acercarnos a las costas de Inglaterra, vino un buque de la marina británica a escoltarnos. El 23 de mayo llegamos a Southampton. Desembarcamos y nos llevaron al campamento de North Stoneham, cerca de Eastleigh, donde nos alojaron a mi madre, mi hermana y a mí en una tienda de campaña grande junto con otras chicas.

Después de un par de semanas, 25 chavales bajo el cargo de mi madre fueron trasladados a Baydon Hole Farm cerca de Newbury, con 75 siguiendo unos días después. Uno de los chicos era Marcelo Segurola, también natural de Azpeitia en Guipúzcoa, que más tarde sería mi esposo. En Baydon vivíamos en barracas prefabricadas en forma de barril. El comandante Tomkins y su señora estaban al cargo del campamento y un joven enorme, llamado Tom, era el cocinero – en realidad la comida no era mala. El momento más drámatico para mí fue un día en el lavadero cuando empecé a chillar y vinieron todos deprisa y corriendo. Mamá estaba segura de que me había cogido el brazo en el escurridor. Me encontró refugiada medrosa en un rincón aterrorizada por una típula. (Todavía me dan miedo, después de 70 años.)

Permanecimos en Baydon hasta octubre de 1937. Fue un verano maravilloso pero con la llegada del invierno se necesitaba un sitio más adecuado. Así fue que mis primeras Navidades en Inglaterra se celebraron en Bray Court, Berkshire. Nos mudamos a una mansión enorme donde me acuerdo de un árbol de navidad gigantesco. Gracias en mayor parte al alcalde de Reading, Mr McIlroy, la casa sirvió para alojar a los niños vascos. Bray Court tenía una rosaleda, un campo de fútbol, canchas de tenis y una cuadra con caballos. Andábamos en bici por los jardines. Bray Court había sido un hotel y a causa de un escándalo tuvo que cerrar. Miss Burke era la directora. Era alta, delgada e irlandesa. Con su nariz larga y puntiaguda parecía un papagayo. El silencio todo el tiempo era su regla de oro y cada vez que bajábamos la escalera principal corriendo nos pedía en un castellano terrible que no hiciéramos tanto ruido.

Vivimos en Bray Court casi dos años y de todas las colonias fue mi favorita. Se celebraban días abiertos al público para recaudar fondos y me acuerdo de hacer un baile con sombrillas. El Sr Sánchez daba clases en castellano; era muy joven y muy guapo. La tienda del pueblo estaba muy cerca y algunos de los chicos pasaban por un agujero en el seta e iban a la tienda. Una vez vino el tendero para quejarse que alguien había robado unos caramelos: por fin tres chicos confesaron haber robado los caramelos. Se tienen que dar cuenta de que hacía mucho tiempo que no habíamos visto caramelos.

En el verano de 1939 se desmanteló la colonia de Bray Court: sin duda porque con la llegada de la guerra mundial no había dinero. (Años después nos enteramos de que se había abierto otra vez para dar cobijo a refugiados de Checoslovaquia.) Nuestra familia se separó:

mi hermano Ignacio, con otros chicos, fue a trabajar a la región central de Inglaterra cogiendo setas (más tarde se alistó en el Royal Air Force, el ejército del aire británico), mientras que a mi hermana Tere le encontraron una familia de acogida en Newbury donde atendió al colegio, porque era demasiada joven para poder trabajar.

Mamá y yo fuimos a una colonia cerca de Bray Court, en Camberley, Surrey. Otra vez nuestro alojamiento era una casa de campo bonita, pero no tan preciosa como Bray Court. Otra irlandesa, Miss Britton, estaba al cargo de la colonia junto con otra señora cuyo nombre se me ha olvidado. La colonia ya estaba establecida y tenía sus reglas. Es quizá por esta razón que la encontramos un poco presumida.

Ahora que tenía 14 años tuve que ir a trabajar. Mi primer trabajo fue en un hotel en Camberley, como fregona. Tenía que fregar cazos, algunos de ellos más grandes que yo (todavía soy pequeñita). Miss Britton se dio cuenta de que lo encontraba muy difícil y en 1940 me encontraron un puesto de criada interna con una familia en 71 Kenton Road, Harrow. Sola en el mundo por primera vez, lloré al principio. Los señores Axton tenían dos hijos - uno en el ejército y otro en la marina - y una hija. Ella me llevaba a patinar. Echaba de menos a mi madre y a los otros. Se había cerrado Camberley y mi madre ahora estaba trabajando en un hotel en Frimley. Necesitaban más personal y mamá pidió si me podían dar trabajo. Así que empecé a trabajar en el hotel de camarera.

En 1942 fuimos a Oxford a trabajar en el servicio doméstico: mamá de ama de llaves y yo de niñera de una niña llamada Patricia. La familia tenía una peluquería y Mrs Peggy Underwood me preguntó si quería ser peluquera. Así fue que me hice peluquera, trabajando en Bond Street, en el centro de Londres, cuando acabó la Segunda Guerra Mundial. Por estas fechas estábamos viviendo en Kensington donde nos reunimos con Marcelo y su familia (que se habían refugiado a Francia durante la Guerra Civil y habían conseguido llegar a Inglaterra a reunirse con Marcelo). Nos casamos en 1951.

Marcelo murió en 1978 a la edad de 53 años. Mi madre, Ramona Sobrino, murió en 1992 y mi hermano, Ignacio, en 2006. Mi hermana mayor Luchi se quedó en España y murió en enero de 2007. Mi hermana menor, Tere, vive en Hampshire. Yo ahora vivo en Wokingham, muy cerca de Bray, con mi hija.

En cuanto a mi padre, fue detenido y encarcelado en 1937. Puesto en libertad cuando estaba muy enfermo, murió en San Sebastián en 1942.

(El 12 de febrero de 2007, pocas semanas después de dictar estas palabras, Loli falleció en casa en Wokingham en brazos de su hija Tere. Sus cenizas serán llevadas a Azpeitia para ser enterradas junto a los restos mortales de su querido marido Marcelo.)

Benedicta González García

El bombardeo de Guernica impulsó a mi madre a sacarnos fuera del peligro de las bombas y se dirigió al Ayuntamiento para dar los nombres de sus hijos para que fuesen al extranjero. Éramos cinco hermanos; le dijeron que de momento sólo podían salir dos, y el 5 de mayo salieron los más jóvenes, rumbo a Francia. Quedamos tres en lista y a los pocos días, le comunicaron la salida de las tres para Inglaterra el día 20 de mayo de 1937.

Ese día amaneció gris con amenaza de lluvia, no parecía un día florido de primavera y menos para ser un día de felicidad para mí, un día de cumpleaños como otros años. Mi madre con la felicitación me dio varios consejos y recomendaciones para nuestra marcha y sobre todo repetía que esto sería por poco tiempo, quizá un mes. A la media tarde salimos de casa camino de la estación de Portugalete de Bilbao. Al llegar, unos encargados nos colocaron en el tren, nos despedimos de mi madre y vi tanta tristeza en su rostro que me sentí sola, pero me tuve que hacer fuerte, puesto que llevaba a mi cargo dos hermanas menores.

Ya casi era de noche cuando entramos al barco. Caía una débil lluvia que llamábamos sirimiri. Según avanzaba la noche, empezaron muchos niños a llorar y llamar a sus amachus. Recuerdo a mi lado a un niño, no más de seis o siete años, que llamaba a su madre. Yo le dije: "Calla, que pronto vendrá." Levantó su cara y me preguntó: "¿Conoces a mi madre?" Creo que le diría que sí, ya que no se separó de mí durante la noche. Creo que se sintió amparado. Qué pena, no lo volví a ver.

De madrugada, empezó el barco a moverse y salió del puerto, rumbo a Inglaterra. Por la mañana, sentí un mareo y casi todo el viaje fue mi compañero. Dos días más tarde, llegamos a Southampton. En el puerto nos esperaban muchos autobuses y nos trasladaron a un campamento, donde estuve tres meses antes de que me mandasen a Montrose en Escocia. No describo como era el campamento, ya que otros niños lo contarán, pero sí quiero decir (por ser una parte muy importante en mi evacuación) que pasé tres meses muy duros y negativos, pero no puedo dejar de mencionar a la primera inglesa que conocí. Se llamaba Miss Mary y fuimos invitadas a merendar en su casa una compañera de campamento y yo. Era una señora mayor, llena de ternura y delicada con nuestra tragedia. Ella me enseñó las primeras palabras en inglés como pan, leche, café, gracias, por favor y algunas cosas más. Ella fue como un bálsamo para mi vida en el campamento. Cuando nos comunicaron que salíamos del campamento, fuimos a decírselo y despedirnos de ella. Nos dijo que al día siguiente iríamos, porque quería sacarse una foto con nosotras para recordarnos, y cuando nos despidió, vi lágrimas en sus ojos. Jamás la he olvidado.

Después de una larga noche de tren, llegamos a la estación de Montrose en Escocia. Era una bonita mañana de septiembre y en la estación se encontraban muchas personas del pueblo, quizá por curiosidad, pero una señora al pie de las escaleras levantaba una caja de bombones, diciendo que este dulce entiende todos los idiomas.

El grupo se componía de 35 niños, Miss Wilson, una maestra, Doña Adelina Larraga y una auxiliar, María Blanco. Salimos a pie hacia la casa, ya que estaba muy cerca de la estación. Entramos en un parque y anduvimos varios metros, y apareció Mall Park House. ¡Qué bonita me pareció! En la entrada nos recibieron unos señores que pertenecían al comité de la organización de la colonia. Entre estas personas estaba el Cónsul español, Sr Izaguirre, quien traducía a los otros señores. Mall Park House era una casa muy señorial: la puerta de entrada daba a un gran hall cuyo suelo era de un mármol muy brillante. Las chicas y la maestra teníamos los dormitorios en el primer piso. Los dormitorios de los chicos estaban en el piso bajo cerca de la cocina. La casa tenía un parque muy grande, así que tuvimos mucho terreno para jugar.

Para mí empezó una nueva vida más tranquila, puesto que nada más llegar a la colonia, tuve noticias de mi madre y aunque fue una carta corta, me decía que pronto estaríamos en casa. Empezamos a salir al pueblo, pero siempre acompañados por Miss Wilson o la maestra: los domingos por la mañana, Miss Wilson nos llevaba a una iglesia anglicana y nos dieron a todos una Biblia. Una vez por semana nos llevaban al cine y el acomodador nada más vernos, decía: "¡Silencio!" en español y se quedó con ese nombre, que así le saludaban los chicos a nuestra llegada. Dos cosas me llamaron la atención al llegar a Escocia: ver a las mujeres con pantalones y fumar, y otra, ver a los hombres con la falda escocesa.

El personal a cargo de la colonia era principalmente el comité: se trataba de cuatro señores que nos visitaban una vez al mes. Ese día se quedaban a comer con nosotros y recuerdo que siempre querían tortilla de patata, que la cocinera hacía muy rica. Miss Wilson era la Directora y responsable. Tenía cincuenta años, era muy alta y fuerte, era pelirroja y en su cara tenía muchas pecas. Su carácter era fuerte y se hacía respetar y al mismo tiempo querer; era muy dulce y cariñosa con todos los niños y la queríamos mucho; para mí fue un poco el apoyo de la falta de mi madre. La maestra española se ocupó únicamente de sus dos hijas que llevó con ella, una de 12 años y otra de 8, nunca dio ni una clase. La misión de la auxiliar fue la cocina; ella nos hacía las comidas al estilo de nuestro país, cocinaba muy bien, era muy buena y cariñosa con todos.

Llegó el invierno y con él, la primera nevada antes de Navidad. Fue un gran acontecimiento ya que el parque llegó a una altura de nieve que no conocíamos en nuestra tierra, pero lo pasamos muy bien jugando y haciendo bolas para tirarnos unos a otros, era una manera de pasar el tiempo. Llegaron las primeras Navidades fuera de casa y yo me sentí preocupada, ya que eran siete meses desde que llegamos y no parecía que estuviese muy cerca la vuelta, la guerra seguía en nuestro país y no con buenas noticias.

Días antes de Navidad, empezaron a llegar cantidad de paquetes de las personas del pueblo, incluso de comercios. Nunca vi tantos regalos en el despacho de la Directora. La víspera de Navidad, mandaron pronto a la cama a los más pequeños y sólo quedamos las cuatro mayores; vinieron unos señores del pueblo con un árbol grandísimo y lo colocaron en el comedor y nosotras ayudamos a colocar las cajas con el nombre de cada uno, que escribía Miss Wilson. Por la mañana, al entrar todos en el comedor, fue muy bonito y se veía en la cara de todos, la emoción: para las niñas, pequeñas muñecas preciosas, para los niños, coches muy bonitos y para todos un recuerdo para siempre. Al llegar el año 1938, la estancia en la colonia se alargaba y las personas que la mantenían necesitaban ayuda, esto suponía que nosotros podíamos hacer algo de teatro y recaudar fondos. Preparamos unas funciones, hicimos vestidos vascos de hilanderas y actuamos en varios teatros en Dundee, Glasgow y Edimburgo principalmente.

Al llegar el verano de 1938, tuvimos que dejar la colonia libre durante quince días y a mí me mandaron con una familia a Edimburgo. Tenían dos hijos, un niño de diez años, llamado John, y una niña de siete años, llamada Elisabeth. Fueron días muy felices, tuvieron muchos detalles conmigo. Una de las cosas que no olvidé nunca fue que esta familia, después de la cena, tenía costumbre de reunirse para leer un libro durante una hora. El señor de la casa al llegar yo, para seguir la costumbre, me compró un libro en español, que era una obra de teatro cómica. Una noche leyendo, solté la risa y él me dijo: "Cuanto me alegro que así sea, el mío es muy triste".

A la vuelta a la colonia, retornamos a la vida rutinaria; yo tenía el encargo de lavar y peinar a una de las más pequeñas de seis años. Por la mañana después del desayuno, esperaba al cartero. Nos acostumbramos a vivir como si fuéramos hermanos. La vida en la colonia era bastante monótona y teníamos muchas horas de ocio. Yo echaba en falta algunas horas de estudio, que nada de eso tuvimos, a pesar de tener una maestra con nosotros para ese fin. No culpo a nadie, quizá todo el mundo creía que de un día a otro volveríamos a nuestro país, pero fueron dos años en blanco en este tema. El inglés lo llegamos a hablar a fuerza de tener contacto con personas inglesas, pero nada de escribirlo, !qué ocasión perdida!

Pasó el año y las segundas Navidades parecidas a las anteriores. Llegó 1939 y con la primavera las primeras noticias de que la guerra estaba ya casi terminada y con ello, las primeras listas de los niños que volvían a casa. Llegó la ocasión del primer viaje, pero no me tocó a mí. Un día vino a la colonia el Cónsul y me dijo que en pocos días salía otro grupo en el cual estaba yo, pero me dijo que con la edad que tenía (faltaba poco para los 17), podía quedarme en Escocia, que España estaba muy mal y la posguerra sería mala. Para mí fueron dos días de lucha interna. Por una parte me gustaba el país. Yo había notado la diferencia del mío: nivel más alto en educación y más avanzado en todo. Por otro lado me acordaba de casa, de mis padres y tenía dos hermanas de las que mi madre me recomendó no separarme de ellas, total, me decidí a volver y en la segunda expedición salimos diez.

Cuando volví, llegamos a Irún y nos dieron la comida en un centro de la Sección Femenina; nos trataron bastante mal, ya que nos dijeron que éramos los hijos de rojos. La llegada a casa y unos días después fueron de alegría y emoción, pasado esto vino la realidad. Bilbao estaba mal, la guerra había terminado, pero dejó mucha huella. La comida estaba racionada y para añadir un poco a esto, tenías que comprar de estraperlo. Yo pensé durante un tiempo que no hice bien con volver, pero esto duró sólo hasta que me enteré de que había estallado la Segunda Guerra Mundial y esto me conformó de mi vuelta.

Yo empecé unas clases nocturnas para recuperar algo de lo perdido, pero lo tuve que dejar y entrar a trabajar en un taller de costura, ya que en casa se necesitaba ayuda de los mayores, porque éramos muchos. Fueron años duros hasta 1943 y después empezó a mejorar.

Tengo que decir en conclusión que de Escocia me gustó mucho su gente, su educación, su cariño y su humanismo que nunca olvidé y dejaron en mí una huella positiva. Sólo una cosa negativa que se lo debo a la guerra, tres años perdidos en mis estudios, nunca recuperables.

Ernesto Grijalba Grijalba

Después de varias semanas en el campamento de Stoneham, fui enviado a una colonia en el norte sólo para chicos cuyas señas eran Harwood Dale, cerca de Scarborough donde permanecí hasta empezar el invierno. En Scarborough se formó otra colonia en la misma ciudad, pero yo fui enviado a otra cuyas señas eran Riddlesden Sanatorium en Keighley (Yorkshire). Nuestra primera ocupación allí fue adecentar el centro para la llegada máxima de niños, pues fue una de las colonias más numerosas. De allí y por voluntad propia, junto con otros cuatro amigos, conseguimos ser trasladados a otra colonia en Hutton Hall, Guisborough. Aquí estuve hasta enero de 1939 cuando partí para Londres con un pequeño empleo en una revista quincenal comunista llamada *Russia Today* con el sueldo semanal de un chelín, creo que pagaban mi manutención. La oficina estaba en Holborn.

El recuerdo de mi estancia en ese país – a parte de tener que estar lejos de mi familia – fue bastante placentera. Jugué al fútbol, hice teatro, hice amistades inglesas, una de las cuales con Harry de Carlisle, hasta su fallecimiento hace cuatro años.

Tengo varias anécdotas, la primera es la impresión que recibí cuando llegamos a ver el muelle de Southampton tan engalanado. Pensé que así nos recibían, y cuál fue mi desconsuelo cuando me enteré de que era debido a la coronación del nuevo rey inglés. Otra cosa que jamás se me olvidará es el día que las tropas franquistas entraron en Bilbao. Yo me encontraba tomando el té en una casa de Eastleigh cuando al volver al campamento oí un murmullo de voces y lloros. Eran los niños que al enterarse empezaron a hacer sus pequeñas maletas, a saltar las vallas y a salir andando para Bilbao: no había forma de pararlos. Esto es inolvidable.

Otra que recuerdo, encontrándome en Hutton Hall: a cinco niños, los mayores, para ocuparnos en algo, nos mandaron a cortar leña a un bosque cercano, pero allí hallamos otra ocupación. El bosque estaba lleno de conejos, así que nos dedicamos a su caza. Por suerte en una cabaña hallamos unos cepos que por lo fuerte que eran creo que serían para cazar zorros. Así pasaron bastantes semanas, hasta que un guardabosque nos vio y dio conocimiento a la policía, que se presentó en la colonia. No nos castigaron aunque estábamos cazando en un coto y en tiempo de veda. Consideraron que era una travesura de niños, pero no comimos más conejos, con lo buenos que sabían.

María Teresa Grijalba Subirón

Salimos del puerto de Santurce, en Bilbao, en los últimos días de mayo de 1937. Éramos cerca de 4.000 niños, varias asistentas, maestras y una cocinera. Una de las asistentas, recuerdo, era la señorita Cayetana Lozano. Llegamos a Southampton todos mareados y escoltados por barcos de guerra ingleses. Nos alojaron en cuarentena en unas tiendas de campaña tipo indio, muy bonitas. Permanecimos un mes y de allí salimos 30 chicas y 4 chicos pequeños para la ciudad de Worthing en la costa de Sussex. Nos alojaron en una bella casa llamada Beach House. Permanecimos varios meses y fuimos alojados definitivamente en Penstone House, Lancing, pueblo cercano.

Me siento agradecida a Inglaterra por la acogida tan calurosa y atenta dispensada por su pueblo. Fuimos niñas felices y lejos de la guerra. No fuimos atendidas directamente por el gobierno inglés sino por la ayuda del pueblo y donativos de voluntarios y amigos ingleses. Tampoco se ocupó el gobierno vasco. No fuimos a ningún colegio inglés porque no nos admitieron. Sólo venía una señora alemana refugiada, Mrs Truman, un día a la semana, quien supuestamente nos enseñaría inglés, pero hablaba mal, no le entendíamos. Yo por mi parte tenía estudios avanzados de bachillerato hechos en San Sebastián.

Me propuse aprender inglés y leía cualquier revista o libro que caía en mis manos. Procuraba traducirlos al español. Mi tarea era aprender diez palabras diarias. Llegué a escribir, leer y hablar el inglés bien.

La Directora de la colonia era la Sra Rosa Omegna y cuando su esposo, quien era ingeniero en los campos de naranjas, volvió de

Israel, también estuvo dirigiendo la colonia. Mantuve amistad con ellos a lo largo del tiempo por carta, teléfono y los visitamos posteriormente en 1984.

La casa en que vivíamos era hermosa, tenía tres plantas, sótano y un salón enorme con piano de cola. Este era un lugar para reuniones y todo tipo de actividades. Formamos un pequeño coro y nuestra maestra española, Felisa Velasco, buena pianista, nos dirigía. Las labores de la casa las hacíamos nosotras mismas divididas en grupos, yo era la campanera. A las 6:30 de la mañana tocaba una campana de bronce para despertar a las niñas. La cocinera era otra española y todo lo que hacía era aceptable. Los ingleses nos daban ropa y la arreglábamos. Allí vi la primera lavadora a gas. Me gustaba mucho la leche. Nos daban tarros de cerámica con la figura de los Reyes. El pan era muy blanco y no pesaba. Recuerdo que le enviaba a mi papá chocolate y pan blanco en unos paquetes de comida, pero no le llegaban. Él me enviaba libros.

Los sábados por la mañana nos llevaban en fila por la calle, íbamos al cine del pueblo. La playa estaba cerca y con buen tiempo nos bañábamos a menudo en el mar. Eso sí, llevábamos a la espalda la máscara anti-gas y en el bolsillo la cartilla de alimentación.

Teníamos un grupo de bailes vascos, nos hacíamos nuestros vestidos típicos. En una de nuestras salidas para presentaciones, así como para recaudar fondos para mantenernos, conocí a la Duquesa de Atholl, prima de la Reina Mary. Le dirigí un discurso en inglés que fue reseñado por los periódicos y le entregué un pergamino. Decía:

"In the name of all my compatriots, I ask the people of Lancing, the Mayoress of Worthing, our beloved chairman, Mrs Barber, and all here present to go and tell others that we, the future generation of Spain, will not forget what England has done for our welfare". ("En nombre de todos mis compatriotas, pido a las gentes de Lancing, a la alcaldesa de Worthing, a nuestra apreciada presidente, la Sra Barber, y a todas las personas aquí presentes que vayan y cuenten a todo el mundo que nosotros, la futura generación de españoles, no se olvidarán de todo lo que el pueblo ingles ha hecho por nuestro bienestar".)

Al deshacerse la colonia, ya que Franco hizo regresar a muchas compañeras, yo estuve en casa de la Alcaldesa de Worthing, hasta cumplir los 18 años. De allí me permitieron trabajar en el hospital del pueblo de Shoreham by the Sea, donde empecé la carrera de enfermera. Allí pasé dos meses, hasta que mis padres, quienes estaban en Toulouse, Francia, me reclamaron, ya que se iban para Méjico.

Viajé a Londres y de allí a Dover para embarcar rumbo a Francia el 17 de mayo de 1940.

Pasé muchas penurias hasta encontrarme con mis padres y hermanos. Mi familia había estado dispersa mucho tiempo. Mis hermanos de 4 y 10 años salieron en septiembre de 1936 del puerto de San Sebastián hacia Francia. Iban en un barco de pesca. Otro hermano de 8 años fue solo a Francia. Después seguí yo hacia Inglaterra. Mi mamá y dos hermanos mayores fueron hacia Bélgica. Papá apareció en Barcelona.

Por medio de la Cruz Roja, papá nos ubicó y reagrupó. De todas maneras no pudimos irnos a América y pasamos la Segunda Guerra Mundial en Toulouse. Sufrimos hambre, bombardeos, frío, todo en un país extraño. Por lo menos sobrevivimos y podemos contarlo.

En 1949 me casé con un joven exilado español y partimos para Venezuela. De esto hace 57 años y me considero ciudadana del mundo.

Eric Hawkins

El Basque Children's Committee de Cambridge era una sólida combinación de *"gown"* (miembros de la Universidad) y *"town"* (ciudadanos). Estaba apoyado por sociedades y clubes universitarios (incluida la tripulación de una de las barcas de competición de los colegios) y por familias que "adoptaron" a niños individualmente haciéndose responsables del pago semanal del coste de su mantenimiento. El problema del alojamiento de los niños fue solucionado de un golpe cuando el reverendo Austin Lee, párroco de Pampisford, a siete kilómetros al sur de Cambridge, ofreció vaciar su rectoría para que fuera usada como una colonia.

La Rectoría de Pampisford era un edificio espacioso situado en un gran jardín; disponía de edificios auxiliares muy útiles, pero no estaba en buenas condiciones de uso. Un grupo de voluntarios empezó a preparar el edificio en abril. La mayoría de las habitaciones estaban en estado de abandono ya que habían estado algún tiempo sin habitar. El suelo de madera, podrido en algunos casos, tuvo que ser renovado, ventanas y puertas fueron reparadas. Se requirió ayuda profesional para reparar las cañerías y los desagües e instalar luz eléctrica en el piso superior. Se barnizaron los suelos, se colgaron cortinas y se trajeron utensilios de cocina y vajilla.

Desde un primer momento de la planificación, se me pidió que estuviera preparado para instalarme en la colonia cuando los niños llegaran, como tutor residente y responsable voluntario de los niños allí alojados. Con 30 niños comiendo y durmiendo, trabajando y jugando en la rectoría, tuve que buscar un aula. Encontré una de ensueño en el desván que había encima de los establos al que se accedía por una escalera exterior. Bajo las bajas vigas de madera dos filas de pupitres se disponían de lado a lado de la nave.

Ocho de los niños y niñas de más edad destacaban como más preparados que el resto y se convirtieron en la clase de nivel superior. Unos ocho o diez se agruparon por sí solos como los "pequeños", dejando en el medio un grupo de muy variados niveles, pero con el que se podía trabajar como clase. Los "pequeños" fueron pronto la responsabilidad de nuestra enfermera, Srta Carmen, y empezaron a trabajar con sus primeras letras y números.

Nuestro horario empezaba a las nueve de la mañana, cuando las dos clases de los más jóvenes empezaban sus lecciones, mientras los mayores tenían una hora de trabajos en la casa antes de incorporarse a las clases matinales en la nave sobre el establo. Hacia media mañana había treinta minutos de ejercicios gimnásticos. El comité había decidido desde el principio que el entrenamiento físico debería tener un sitio importante y por ello se proveyó de pantalones cortos y camisetas para los niños y de túnicas sin mangas de estilo griego para las niñas. Hacían a menudo sus ejercicios rítmicos descalzos en el césped y los niños con gracia natural hicieron rápidos progresos. A continuación había dos horas más de clase antes de la comida a la una de la tarde. Después había una hora de descanso y a continuación la tarde se dedicaba a actividades de pintura, música o trabajos manuales con la ayuda de una paciente y dedicada banda de trabajadores voluntarios.

En las clases de la mañana lectura y escritura eran al principio nuestra principal preocupación. Recitar versos ayudaba a mejorar la expresión oral y cuando el sol apretaba nos sentábamos bajo un árbol con el libro de Tornor: *El folklore en la escuela.* El estudio intensivo de inglés fue pospuesto en Pampisford porque pensamos que el conocimiento del español, aunque fuera rudimentario, debía de ser adquirido primero (a los niños se les había dicho, después de todo, que su estancia sería "sólo por tres meses"). Con los alumnos mayores se comenzó con algunas charlas sobre historia y geografía, a pesar de que teníamos continuamente el problema de la falta de libros en español para que pudieran investigar por sí mismos. Teníamos que tener constantemente en cuenta que los alumnos padecían de una neurosis de guerra severa. Sus mentes, según el Profesor Ryle, presidente del comité, parecían estar todavía vibrando por sus experiencias durante los bombardeos, de manera que sólo se conseguía momentáneamente su atención como si fuera el péndulo de un reloj. El descanso y el silencio tenían que hacer su trabajo antes que el estudio formal pudiera tener éxito, como ocurriría después. Mientras tanto, nos concentrábamos más en los "intereses"de cada uno, la parte del currículo que se hacía durante las tardes.

En cuanto a esto los alumnos respondían enseguida con gran entusiasmo a la simpatía y a los métodos cuidadosamente planificados de Mrs Youngman, que les inspiraba para que pintaran en un estilo dramático y libre, con libertad para elegir colores brillantes, y de Dr Hertz que les proporcionó otra salida a sus sentimientos a través del modelado en barro, recortables de colores y plastilina. Al principio las obras de los niños eran de un único tema: aviones de caza y bombardeo, barcos de guerra y armamento fueron pintados y esculpidos semana tras semana hasta que el trauma de guerra empezó a ceder ante el ambiente de paz y tranquilidad del entorno. Entonces, poco a poco, árboles y flores empezaron a surgir y las bombas empezaron a perder interés; empezaron a plasmar sus hogares ideales y a modelar sus castillos en España.

También la música jugó un importante papel en Pampisford. Tuvimos desde el principio la suerte de contar con el apoyo de una ferviente republicana, Rosita Bal, una joven concertista de piano que había tenido la distinción de ser una de las pocas alumnas que había estudiado bajo la tutela de Manuel de Falla. Abría sus lecciones interpretando el himno de la República. Después seguía una hora y media de trabajo dedicado a las canciones del folklore español. Los niños aprendían de oído y en tres lecciones la música y las letras de las canciones fueron perfectamente aprendidas.

Una vez que el currículo y las esferas de interés quedaron claramente establecidos era obvia la necesidad de una revista escolar. En una reunión de los alumnos mayores la propuesta fue acogida con entusiasmo y pronto encontraron un título para ella: *Ayuda*. Con el asesoramiento de Mrs Youngman se hizo un diseño para la portada en el que se veía el "barco de la ayuda" surcando las olas. *

Eulalia Ibáñez Gómez

Durante todo el tiempo que pasé en Inglaterra estuve con mi hermana mayor, María Teresa. Ella todavía no tenía los diez años, y yo contaba con ocho. Estuvimos en dos colonias, Lancing y Upton, pero no recuerdo en cuál primero y en cuál después.

Puedo acordarme del viaje en el *Habana*, pero no del momento de la llegada a suelo inglés. Pero lo que sí nunca olvidaré fue la llegada a la colonia: había un montón de muñecas y cada niña cogió una, pero a mí no me dejaron hacerlo, cosa que me entristeció. Pero cuando todas las muñecas se terminaron, sacaron una preciosa, la más bonita de todas, y para mi sorpresa me la dieron a mí, pues yo era una de las niñas más pequeñas del grupo.

En la colonia había un matrimonio mayor, los señores Owen. Tenían dos perros, Tim y Mark. Tim era blanco y muy cariñoso y todos los niños lo queríamos mucho, no así a Mark, de color negro y malas pulgas. La casa de la colonia era muy grande y tenía mucho terreno y árboles frutales, sobre todo manzanos, cuyos frutos nunca llegaban a madurar del todo, pues nos los comíamos verdes. Los viernes nos hacían revisión y nos daban dos monedas para comprarnos dulces. Los fines de semana salíamos con la familia que lo solicitaba, cosa que pasaba a menudo. Una vez un matrimonio nos llevó a mi hermana y a mí a unos grandes almacenes, donde pasamos todo el día. Por cierto, que al salir, no podíamos encontrar el coche, pues el señor no se acordaba de dónde lo había dejado. En esa tienda a mi hermana le compraron una muñeca preciosa, y a mí un oso amarillo de peluche, que me gustó tanto que lo conservé durante muchos años.

Nos llevaron a muchos sitios. Recuerdo la visita a Londres, ciudad que no me gustó mucho, pues me pareció muy grande y sobre todo muy sucia, en comparación con todo lo que había visto de Inglaterra. También recuerdo la visita a Liverpool, donde atravesamos un túnel que pasaba por debajo del agua.

En el colegio de South Lancing lo pasé muy bien. Había una maestra, Miss Peskett, que era muy amable con nosotros. Como yo era muy buena en dibujo, me solían poner como distinción una estrella azul o roja, dependiendo de cómo lo había hecho.

No estoy segura de en qué colonia fue, pero me acuerdo de que los martes llegaba un chico con un proyector y nos pasaba películas por episodios, lo que nos encantaba, por supuesto. Justo cuando la chica estaba ya atada a los rieles y parecía que el tren estaba a punto de arrollarla, la película se terminaba y teníamos que esperar a la semana siguiente. Pero lo más emocionante fue cuando nos llevaron a todos al cine a ver Blancanieves y los siete enanos. ¡Qué emoción ver aquello, con sonido y en colores!

Todos los martes íbamos a la piscina de las exploradoras, que tenía un agua helada. Quizás por eso es que al salir del agua nos daban una galleta como premio, cosa que a mi hermana le encantaba. Hasta que murió, en el año 1990, solía recordar aquella galleta que le esperaba luego de pasar un rato muy divertido, pero también bastante frío.

Cuando comenzó la Segunda Guerra Mundial tuvimos que empezar a llevar a todas partes una careta antigás. Ésta iba dentro de una caja de cartón, que a su vez contaba con un cordón y había que portar en bandolera. Si la policía te veía sin ella, te hacía volver a buscarla. Todavía recuerdo ver pasar los aviones y los simulacros de alarma nocturna que teníamos que hacer.

En la primera colonia había un chico –uno de los que nos cuidaban- que me quería mucho. Lamentablemente, no recuerdo su nombre. Pero sí que me acuerdo de las visitas que me hacía, y de los regalos que me llevaba. El día que nos avisaron que nos teníamos que ir a otra colonia y me di cuenta de que no iba a poder despedirme de él, decidí irlo a buscar para decirle adiós. Mi hermana y dos niñas más me acompañaron. En realidad no teníamos ni idea de donde vivía, pero en nuestra ingenuidad creíamos que al llegar al pueblo lo encontraríamos. Pero la cosa no fue tan fácil. Salimos de la colonia sin decir nada y comenzamos a caminar sin rumbo, hasta que dos policías de a pie nos encontraron y al enterarse de quiénes éramos y de dónde veníamos, nos escoltaron de vuelta. Ese fue el final de la aventura, y para mi pesar tuve que irme sin despedirme del chico que tanto cariño me tenía.

(Transcrito por Margarita Gil, hija.)

Fidela de Juan Quintana

Mi hermano y yo, con otros niños, fuimos a la colonia de Camberley donde nos trataron muy bien. Allí conocí la democracia, no me cansaré de decirlo. La colonia era una finca muy grande. (¡Cuánto me gustaría verla ahora!) Tenía una huerta y unos jardines preciosos con fruta y flores, lo recuerdo como divino. Estaba rodeada de un inmenso campo donde jugábamos como queríamos. El edificio era también grande con habitaciones hermosas, las niñas distribuidas a un lado, los niños a otro. La alimentación era la propia a nuestra edad, teníamos dos cocineras y una auxiliar, dos profesoras para las clases de estudios en español. Este personal era español; había también una inglesa y otra irlandesa para las clases de inglés, y además un profesor irlandés para las clases de química. Una vez vino un grupo de enfermeros para enseñarnos primeros auxilios, también había un sacerdote para los que querían ir a misa. A parte de este personal, teníamos una Directora que se ocupaba de todo el resto.

Yo guardo un buen recuerdo de la vida allí porque el trato con todos fue muy bueno. Había familias inglesas que de vez en cuando nos llevaban de excursión. Por ejemplo, a mí me llevaron con ellos de vacaciones y estuve quince días o más; me trataron muy bien, como una de la familia. Yo seguí comunicándome con ellos una vez de vuelta en España, yendo a verles en Londres varias veces con mi marido y mis hijos, hasta que fallecieron. Mi hermano, que tiene cinco años menos que yo, guarda buenos recuerdos. A él le operaron de apendicitis y según él, le trataron con mucho cariño en el hospital. Volvió a la colonia hecho un inglés, hablando el idioma como un nativo aunque también se le olvidó por no usarlo. Yo, como lo aprendí estudiándolo (teníamos buenas profesoras), todavía me defiendo hablándolo, aunque he perdido mucho.

A mí me ha quedado para el resto de mi vida una experiencia nada mala. Si algo lamento es el no haber tenido a mi familia, ya que yo siempre pienso que perdí a mi madre cuando embarqué para Inglaterra, porque cuando volví, falleció al poco tiempo.

Luis Lavilla San Vicente
Salimos de Bilbao el 20 de mayo de 1937 y el viaje para mí no fue nada agradable, ya que me mareé y tuve que dormir donde encontraba sitio. Solo me curé cuando llegamos a Southampton, y por cierto que encontré la cocina y me dieron de comer todo lo que pude tragar, ya que los días anteriores no había comido. Al desembarcar, me separaron de mi hermano y con otros me llevaron a ducharme, cortar el pelo y cambiar de ropa. De allí al campamento.

No habían pasado muchos días, creo que alrededor de seis, cuando anunciaron que había una expedición para Londres y a ella me apunté.

El destino era Congress Hall en Clapton , que fue administrado por el Salvation Army. Fuimos muchos y nuestro comportamiento no fue nada de contar. Pocos días después a un grupo nos trasladaron a Hadleigh en la desembocadura del Támesis. Nos localizamos mi hermano y yo y me convenció para ir con él a Diss. Siempre que íbamos de excursión, cantábamos, y estas dos canciones fueron inventadas en Diss:

Allá en el campo de Diss
hay una hermosa cocina
donde guisa Lucerito
para el Chato y compañía
Allá en Diss
hemos dejado
al pobre Lucero
medio enamorado

y

Yo soy un muchacho elegante
intrépido y galante
mi afán es de correr
tras de una mujer
aunque el mundo me llame tunante
De España me vine a Inglaterra
tras de una hermosa inglesa
hermosa y gentil
cual rosa de abril
que perfuma la bella mañana

Era verano y hacía buen tiempo, pero cuando empezó a cambiar, nos trasladaron a Rollesby cerca de Great Yarmouth. El siguiente cambio fue a Tythrop House, donde estaba un grupo mayor que el nuestro. Había también chicas, cosa que no había habido hasta entonces. No duró mucho la estancia y otra vez cambiamos, esta vez a Farringdon. Desde luego, no se quedó ninguno de los de Diss, por el contrario, vinieron otros.

Aquí terminó mi vida en las colonias, ya que me buscaron ocupación y me trasladaron a Londres con un empleo en un hospital, en el laboratorio del Departamento de Patología. El hospital se llamaba

Guy's Hospital, estaba cerca de London Bridge. Al principio, me acomodaron con familias inglesas, la primera vez en New Kent Road y luego Balham, pero como había ya más muchachos como yo, nos fuimos a vivir en West Kensington. Aquí terminó mi vida en Inglaterra, este fue mi último domicilio hasta el 12 de diciembre de 1939 en que volví a España.

El recuerdo que me ha quedado ha sido y es muy agradable, de simpatía y cariño que guardo y no olvido. Actualmente no he perdido oportunidad de ir a Inglaterra y sigo esperando que se presente una para volver aunque sea por pocos días.

Colin Leakey

Mi madre, Frida, abandonada por su marido Luis en 1936, vivía con dos niños pequeños. Tenía un círculo de amigos entre los que se encontraban Jessie y Hugh Stewart en Girton Gate, Francis y Frances Cornford y mi padrino Hugh Heywood, decano del colegio Gonville and Caius de la Universidad de Cambridge. Unas casas más arriba en Pepys Way vivía Anna Hertz, que con su madre había salió de Alemania cuando subieron al poder los nazis y se refugiaron en Inglaterra y ella ejercía como pediatra.

Hijo del catedrático Cornford, John fue la primera víctima mortal británica de la Guerra Civil Española y para 1937, Cambridge estaba a tono con las necesidades de los refugiados del País Vasco. Mi madre y su círculo de amigos tenían conciencia de esta situación . Muchos tenían ideas un poco izquierdistas. Mi madre no, ella se describía como "mini capitalista" y había comprado la casa en la que vivíamos con su subvención de ropa. De todas maneras, no era la izquierda solamente la que se preocupaba con el alza del nazismo y su extensión por España.

Hugh Heywood se hizo secretario del Basque Children's Committee local. Anna Hertz era el médico que ayudaba a cuidar a los niños vascos y sus problemas médicos. Mrs Youngman, que era otra amiga, les enseñaba arte y dibujo. Pero en particular, Dr Stewart y su esposa recibían con cariño a los niños en su casa, Girton Gate que se convirtió en un permanente centro internacional. Sobre todo, Jessie Stewart y sus hijas Jean, Frida, Katherine y Margaret estaban muy involucradas.

Cuando fue el momento oportuno para que ciertos de los niños vascos fueran repatriados y la colonia cerró, algunos que eran huérfanos se quedaron con familias en la vecindad. Ya hablaban buen inglés y estaban acostumbrados a los dos estilos de vida, vasco e inglés. Carmen Moreno se quedó con nosotros como otra hermana y miembro de la familia. Por esta época mi madre había decidido que la enseñanza en casa era desde muchos puntos de vista una buena idea y contrató unas institutrices, para ayudar en casa y ser acompañantes y al mismo tiempo para darnos clase a mi hermana mayor Priscilla y a mí, junto con otros niños de amigos que estaban fuera trabajando para la guerra y ellos compartían el coste de las clases particulares con mi madre. Carmen se adaptó muy bien al sistema y vivió con nosotros hasta que tuvo 16 años y entonces se fue a la escuela cuáquera The Friends' School, en Saffron Walden; nosotros también fuimos cada uno a internados y después nos dispersamos.

Carmen nunca perdió contacto con mi madre. Después del instituto, empezó a estudiar fotografía con la conocida fotógrafa de Cambridge, Lettice Ramsay, que dirigía el Ramsey and Muspratt Studio cerca de la iglesia de San Andrés. Más tarde conoció y se casó con José Mari Villegas y volvió a España. Ella y algunos amigos vascos continuaron su relación con mi madre y mi hermana, menos conmigo. Ella y su marido visitaron Cambridge varias veces, la última vez, creo, siendo viuda, cuando vino con su hija Sonia. *

Manuel Leceta Ortiz

A los pocos días de llegar a Southampton, fuimos trasladados a Langham, en un autobús de dos pisos que era el primero que yo veía. Llegamos a Langham al atardecer. Nos fueron distribuyendo por edad a las habitaciones y viendo los jardines, nos pusimos muy contentos ya que además había frutales.La vida diaria para nosotros consistía en levantarnos a las ocho y después de asearnos, íbamos a desayunar; a continuación nos daban clases en español y alguna en inglés. Por las tardes después de clase teníamos juegos.

Poco después de nuestra llegada a Langham, las tropas de Franco tomaron Bilbao. La noticia nos la dieron en el comedor, los lloros que nos costó, dejamos de comer y por la tarde nos llevó Mr Stirling a pasear por los campos cercanos a la casa.

Mr Stirling formó un coro y un grupo de teatro que solía actuar en varias ciudades, también se hizo un equipo de fútbol que solía jugar contra equipos ingleses. Por la noche teníamos música con baile hasta la hora de acostarse. Los domingos nos daban la "paga" según las edades y nos hacía mucha ilusión. Al principio nos veíamos con los chavales ingleses por entre los setos y hasta cogimos confianza.

Las fiestas de Navidad, los dos años que pasamos en Inglaterra, tanto mi hermana como yo las pasamos en Watford en casa de Mr y Mrs Russell y Eva Hartley, así como el verano. En la Navidad de 1938, nos sorprendieron llevando a otra pareja de hermanos de una colonia de Oxford, dando la casualidad de que íbamos juntos a la escuela. Los nombres de éstos eran Ma Angeles y Santiago Elorza.

En el año 1939, al regresar de las fiestas de Navidad en el tren a Colchester, mi hermana y yo cuidados por el interventor del tren, tuvimos la sorpresa en la estación de que ese día no había autobús para Langham. Un matrimonio que estaba allí se brindó a llevarnos, ellos para ir a su casa pasaban cerca de la colonia.

En nuestra visita a Langham en el año 1989, esperando para ir a visitar Langham, vino una señora, y señalando a mi hermana y a mí, nos llevó en su coche y se aclaró por qué nos había elegido a nosotros. Tenía una fotografía de ambos montados en un caballo y de un día que nos llevaron a su casa a merendar.

También fue muy emotivo el día que me encontré con la Srta Celia. Yo no sabía que había regresado a Bilbao y en un autobús la reconocí. Después celebramos junto a ella la comida anual de los niños de Langham. Con Leonard Read tuve contacto hasta su muerte.

Quiero señalar que el comportamiento de los ingleses con nosotros fue superior.

Valeriana Llorente Guerrero

1936, ¡qué fecha tan significativa para el pueblo español, igual para miles de niños españoles que evacuaron para salvaguardarles de las bombas y la malnutrición!

Me separaron de mis padres, mis hermanos y mis amigas de pocos años, pues solo tenía diez. Atrás se quedó mi pueblo, Portugalete, con su puente colgante, hoy declarado Patrimonio de la Humanidad. Portugalete, con su plaza hermosa, que tiene un quiosco desde donde tocaba la banda y se bailaba todos los sábados. Los viernes, las aldeanas llegaban con sus productos frescos, verduras y frutas, huevos y también pollos.

Inglaterra supuso un cambio muy grande para todos nosotros niños – un país muy distinto – sus gentes muy diferentes y una lengua extraña. Hoy, a veces, me paro a pensar, ¿cómo aceptamos ese cambio tan profundo en nuestras vidas infantiles tan naturalmente? Algunos tuvimos más suerte y muchos otros lo pasaron muy mal. Yo estuve poco tiempo en Stoneham y, en mi tienda de campaña éramos diez chicas y a todas nos llevaron a la colonia de Langham, cerca de Colchester, una casa grande con unos hermosos jardines y con muy buena gente mayor al cuidado de los 50 a 60 niños que habitamos allí.

En Langham hice muy buenas amigas. Tere, Mariluz, Luisa y Berta eran hermanas; Asunción, Begoña y Aurora también. Algunas de estas amistades duraron mucho tiempo: nos separamos en 1939 y en 1946 me reencontré con algunas de ellas. Nuestras queridas maestras, Celia y Berta Echevarría, ¡qué cariñosas fueron con nosotros! Me acuerdo de Otto, que nos arreglaba los zapatos, de Leonard Read, el Director, con su barba pelirroja y tan buen hombre, siempre atento con los niños.

En el verano de 1938 conocí a quienes se ocuparían de mi educación – el grupo de Streatham del Peace Pledge Union. Estos grupos se pronunciaban contra la guerra y la participación en ellas. Ese mismo verano fui para unas vacaciones a la casa de "*Auntie Bee*", como yo la llamaba. Ella también era del PPU de Streatham. Tenía dos hijos ya mayores y trabajando. Mary, la hija, era soltera. Desconozco el trabajo del hijo, Philip. Vivían en el barrio de Norbury, Londres, en una casa muy bonita. *Auntie Bee* fue muy cariñosa conmigo. En su jardín tenía dos colmenas y cosechaba su propia miel. Según escribo estas letras, la estoy viendo con su sombrero con una red para protegerse de las abejas. ¿Cómo nos comprendíamos? Pues no sé, mi conocimiento del inglés era muy limitado. ¡Que duda cabe que me encuentro muy agradecida a todas estas buenas personas del PPU de Streatham! Su gran generosidad me pagó unos seis meses en una escuela privada. Aquí aprendí a defenderme mejor con el inglés y también a tocar el piano. En un concierto para los padres, toque una pieza de música llamada *The wind in the trees*. La música es igual que andar en bicicleta, nunca se olvida.

Volví a Langham, no sé para cuanto tiempo, pero antes del comienzo de la Segunda Guerra mundial fui a vivir con otra familia del mismo grupo del PPU, Mr y Mrs King. Ellos tenían dos hijas, Barbara más joven que yo y Eileen, mayor, y también un hijo que se llamaba John. Con Barbara y Eileen comencé a estudiar en Streatham Secondary School, sólo para chicas. Ya sabía más ingles – así pensaba yo. Mrs King fue como una madre para mí, además era buena cocinera y hacía unos postres deliciosos. Me encontré muy a gusto con ellos, eran una gran familia.

La Segunda Guerra Mundial supuso otro cambio. Tenía 13 años y en 1940 evacuaron nuestra escuela a Chichester, Sussex, debido a los bombardeos sobre Londres. Nos dieron a todos una máscara de gas, y nos enseñaron cómo utilizarla. No recuerdo mis sentimientos pero seguro que estaría muy confusa. En Chichester me alojaron con una familia jóven, Mr y Mrs Sweet, muy majos conmigo. Ellos tenían una nena. Iba a la escuela y seguía con mis estudios.

No recuerdo en qué año pero la escuela regresó a Londres y fui a vivir con mi tercera familia, Mrs Dignasse, su hijo David y su hija Muriel, los dos ya pasados sus 40 años y los dos solteros. Muriel, "Minky" como yo la llamaba, había perdido a su novio durante la guerra y creo que para ella yo era como una hija. Lo cierto es que quiso adoptarme pero mis padres no dieron su consentimiento.

Con el apoyo de esta familia – a quienes siempre he estado agradecida – conseguí matricularme en la misma escuela donde había estudiado desde 1939. Seguidamente hice un curso de secretaría y contabilidad, lo cual me permitió conseguir buenos empleos.

Había perdido todo contacto con la gente de mi colonia y no hablaba el español. Tanto así que la correspondencia con mis padres era en inglés, y ellos consiguieron su traducción. Mi hermana se encargó de este problema y me envió la dirección de un chico vasco, Antonio Tudela. Fui a ver a Miss Picken y finalmente me reencontré con muchos de los niños vascos del 1937, entre ellos, amigos de mi colonia de Langham.

Muy importante para mí, conocí a Rafael, mi marido y tuvimos dos hijos, Rubén y Raimundo. Rafael y yo viajamos en el *Habana* y Londres nos unió. Sin el respaldo de nuestros padres, conseguimos salir adelante, con nuestros problemas pero también con tiempos muy felices.

Somos parte de una gran familia – los niños vascos del '37.

Eduardo López Sanz

En el mes de mayo de 1937 si la despedida era triste, el día también lo era porque recuerdo que llovía. Iba a la expedición a Inglaterra acompañado de mi hermano Alberto, dos años mayor que yo. Entonces yo tenía diez años recién cumplidos y él cumpliría 13 años en agosto. Aún recuerdo los números de expedición: mi hermano tenía el 2.500 y yo el 2.501. En el mismo viaje con nosotros iba también un vecino llamado Delfino del Olmo. Los tres vivíamos en Urioste, pueblo que pertenece al municipio de Ortuella, en el territorio de Vizcaya.

En el tiempo que estuvimos esperando en el muelle, y hasta el momento de embarcar, estuvimos con nuestras madres, que nos arropaban desconsoladas entre lágrimas y sollozos, como es natural en estas circunstancias, porque nadie sabía como sería nuestro futuro. Estos momentos de la espera y del embarque se reflejan muy bien en una película documental realizada in situ y en la que aparecemos los tres junto a nuestras madres.

Una vez que embarcamos, en la misma cubierta, nos encontramos con un niño como nosotros que estaba solo y llorando. Entonces mi hermano Alberto le consoló y le animó a que se uniera a nosotros, y de esta forma hicimos todo el viaje y la estancia juntos. Su nombre era Gumersindo González y vivía en Uribarri-Bilbao.

De la travesía que hicimos no recuerdo nada, no sé si es porque fui todo el tiempo mareado. Solo recuerdo que tardamos en llegar dos días y medio desde el puerto de Santurce hasta el puerto inglés de Southampton. Después de desembarcar nos llevaron a un campamento, no muy lejos de allí, donde nos juntamos 4.000 niños y niñas, con maestras y algunos sacerdotes.

En este campamento estuvimos unos tres meses, aproximadamente, hasta que nos destinaron a distintos puntos del país. Nosotros tuvimos mucha suerte porque nos mandaron a Guildford, en el condado de Surrey, junto a otros 40 niños y niñas.

Todos los días nos levantábamos a las 8 de la mañana. Lo primero que hacíamos, si hacía buen tiempo, era una caminata bastante aceptable por las afueras de la ciudad. Si el tiempo era lluvioso hacíamos gimnasia en la misma colonia. Después desayunábamos y acto seguido teníamos unas horas de clase. Después de comer nos obligaban a echar la siesta. Por la tarde salíamos a dar un paseo por la ciudad o nos quedábamos jugando en el jardín, al balón, con bicicletas y muchos otros juegos. Los viernes nos invitaban a un gimnasio y los sábados por la mañana íbamos al cine Odeon de Guildford donde veíamos la película que tocaba esa semana.

Los domingos por la mañana nos llevaban a misa en fila de dos, y la tarde la dedicábamos a pasear. En época de verano nos solían llevar a una piscina que había en las afueras de Guildford y que se llamaba el Lido, por cierto muy hermosa. También tuvimos la suerte de veranear durante una semana en una playa.

Además de todo esto, nos enseñaron a cantar y a bailar nuestro propio folklore, y solíamos actuar para el público inglés. Una de estas actuaciones se realizó en un teatro del condado de Kent, y en el intermedio repartieron una revista sobre la guerra de España. Nosotros pudimos aprender todo esto porque teníamos a dos mujeres que se responsabilizaron completamente de todas y todos nosotros. Una de ellas era asistenta y se encargaba de cuidar de nuestros enseres: se llamaba Purificación Vela. La otra era maestra y se llamaba Juanita Aizpuru. Se casó con un inglés que cuidaba también de todos nosotros y que se llamaba Mr Jenkins.

Esta situación duró aproximadamente dos años. Después yo fui trasladado a otra colonia en Camberley, Aldershot. Allí había un número bastante mayor de niños y no se estaba tan bien como en la colonia anterior. Sin embargo a mi hermano Alberto y a otros tres compañeros más, como ya tenían 14 años, les buscaron trabajo y no tuvieron que ser trasladados porque tenían un sueldo del que podían vivir. Los cuatro estaban integrados también en una sociedad de *boy scouts*. Pero mi hermano para no dejarme venir solo de vuelta a España, decidió volver conmigo.

El 15 de diciembre de 1939 llegó la fecha de regreso a España. Atravesamos el Canal de la Mancha y recorrimos toda la costa de Francia hasta llegar a Hendaya donde desembarcamos. Después atravesamos el puente internacional de Irún. Yo creí que se caía el cielo al ver la destrucción y la suciedad que allí había. Pobreza por todas partes. Aquella noche la pasamos en un colegio de Hondarribia, y al día siguiente cogimos un tren que nos acercó hasta Bilbao donde nos esperaban nuestros familiares.

Para finalizar este pequeño relato de mis recuerdos sobre un tiempo tan excepcional e importante para nosotros, deseo expresar que no tengo palabras suficientes para agradecer y alabar todo el trabajo, el esfuerzo y el amor que depositaron los ingleses en todas y todos nosotros.

Pilar Magdalena Iglesias

Llegué a Southampton cuando tenía 11 años, junto a mi hermana Julia de 15 y mis hermanos, Fermín de 14 y Federico de siete. Después de poco, a Julia, Federico y a mí nos trasladaron a Hutton Hall en Guisborough. Dos hermanos, Carmen y Maurice Short, de ascendencia española, nos acompañaron desde Southampton, Maurice a cargo de los niños y Carmen de las niñas.

Puesto que el comité de Hutton Hall había decidido que las familias estuvieran juntas, Fermín se unió a nosotros y también nuestro primo Pepe. Como Federico era tan pequeño lo recogió una familia mientras nosotros tres y Pepe nos quedamos en la colonia hasta el comienzo de la Segunda Guerra Mundial.

Unos 30 niños y niñas de Bilbao vivían en Hutton Hall. Era una casa enorme y grandiosa. A mí me pusieron en una habitación con otras cinco niñas. Yo estaba bastante entusiasmada de vivir en una mansión tan espléndida, después de haber vivido en tiendas de campaña en Southampton. Todos los niños menores de 12 años iban a la escuela; las clases tenían lugar en el comedor, transformado cada mañana en un aula de clase. Como yo había cumplido 12 años, ayudaba con las tareas domésticas. Trabajaba en la cocina, donde estuve todo el tiempo. La cocinera se encaprichó conmigo y yo disfrutaba ayudándola, aunque las horas eran muy largas y el trabajo pesado. Otras niñas trabajaban en la lavandería, fregando, planchando y remendando ropa; los chicos trabajaban duro en el jardín, cortando leña y se ocupaban del fuego de las chimeneas.

Para poder pagar nuestra estancia se organizaban bazares. Las chicas hacían punto de media y bordaban y los chicos cestas de mimbre. También dábamos conciertos. Los organizaba Ruth Pennyman, un miembro del comité, que vivía en Ormesby Hall. Cosimos trajes de gitana para los conciertos y bailábamos y cantábamos canciones tradicionales. Teníamos mucha imaginación y hacíamos trajes de torero y recreábamos las corridas de toros. Recogíamos narcisos y campanillas blancas y los vendíamos al público para recaudar fondos.

Los fines de semana la gente venía a ayudar y nos sacaban a pasear. También nos daban ropa que podíamos arreglar y llevar. Había dos hermanas, Doris y Frances Oates, de unos 20 años que solían visitarnos. Dejaban seis peniques para mí y para otras chicas, y así podíamos tomar el tren de ida y vuelta a Middlesborough. Tomábamos el té con ellas y sus padres. De vez en cuando Doris nos llevaba al cine o a la playa. Recogían dinero para nosotras; eran tan simpáticas, lo hacían con mucho gusto. He mantenido una amistad de toda la vida con estas hermanas. La hija de Frances fue mi paje junto a Doris en mi boda. Desgraciadamente, Frances murió, pero Doris y yo seguimos carteándonos, aunque no goza de buena salud.

Al comienzo de la Segunda Guerra Mundial, Hutton Hall fue requerido por el ejército y desgraciadamente los chicos se dispersaron. Algunos volvieron a Bilbao, entre ellos mi primo Pepe. Nuestra pequeña familia no pudo volver, pues nuestros padres estaban en un campo de refugiados en Francia. Mi hermana Julia se casó con Maurice Short, el que cuidaba a los chicos, y vivieron muy felices. Mi hermana Julia y mi hermano Fermín han muerto. Siempre he mantenido el contacto con mi hermano Federico y somos los únicos que vivimos en el noreste de Inglaterra de todos los que fueron a Hutton Hall. *   (Pilar murió en 2007)

Enriqueta Maíz Esteban
Yo tenía 15 años y vivía en Bilbao la Vieja Con mis padres y mis dos hermanas, Carmen y Felisa. Cuando la Guerra Civil empezó en 1936, ya había terminado la escuela. Mi padre era camionero. Las autoridades (o sea, el gobierno republicano que había sido elegido) requisaron el camión y como él era miliciano lo destinaron a Aloeta, un pueblecito pequeñito donde mi padre se alojaba en la casa del cura con otros cuatro. Las tropas de Franco habían avanzado hasta Vitoria y la misión de mi padre era proveer a los milicianos del frente de comida y munición.

Un día mi padre vino a hacernos una breve visita. Me extrañaba la manera en que se olía las manos todo el tiempo y le pregunté por qué. Lo que nos contó entonces a mi madre y a mí fue horroroso. El día anterior, un domingo, tras haber terminado sus entregas en el frente él había vuelto a Ochandiano. Hacía un día bonito y soleado y la gente había estado disfrutando del paseo de la tarde. Entonces se aproximó un avión que pensaban que era "de los nuestros", soltando regalitos. El entusiasmo inicial se convirtió rápidamente en un sentimiento de horror mientras las bombas caían en medio de la plaza. La destrucción de las casas, el ver cuerpos por todas partes, era aterrador. Los más afortunados ayudaban a los heridos que habían conseguido escapar de la carnicería. Entre mi padre y otros voluntarios empezaron a cargar el camión de cadáveres y cuerpos desmembrados. El olor de la sangre, nos dijo, no se le iba de las manos por mucho que se las lavara… y por eso no dejaba de olérselas.

Felisa, la más pequeña, estaba tan petrificada que se enfermó. Había oído que estaban evacuando a niños a Francia y no dejó a mi madre en paz hasta que consintiera en dejarla partir. Los bombardeos se hicieron más frecuentes y destructivos y el número de víctimas aumentó. Me enteré de que iban a evacuar niños a Inglaterra y no me costó mucho convencer a mis padres para que dieran su consentimiento para nuestra evacuación. Para mí no era tanto el peligro lo que me empujaba sino la perspectiva de pasar tres meses de vacaciones y la oportunidad de visitar otro país. ¡Qué emocionante! Una no se podía perder semejante oportunidad. Ahora siento vergüenza y arrepentimiento pues no tuve consideración de los sentimientos y pena de mi querida madre. Nunca se me pasó por la cabeza que ya no la pudiera volver a ver.

Al embarcar en el *Habana*, Carmen y yo nos perdimos y con tantos niños era imposible encontrarla. Al llegar a Southampton, nos agruparon y nos pusieron en fila para que nos hicieran un examen médico. Allí me reuní de nuevo con Carmen, pero fue una reunión muy traumática. En el examen médico le vieron la cabeza llena de piojos y le afeitaron su hermosa melena. En cuanto me vio rompió a llorar desconsoladamente y todo lo que decía era que qué iba a decir Mamá si la viera ahora, sobretodo cuando lo último que nos había dicho era que nos cuidáramos el pelo y lo mantuviéramos limpio.

Después llegaron unos autocares y al final llegamos a un campamento enorme lleno de tiendas de campaña grandes. Me acuerdo de una noche, después de un día precioso soleado y caluroso, nos despertó una tormenta de truenos estruendosos con un viento fuertísimo. De repente la tienda se derrumbó encima de nosotros. Para tranquilizar a los niños, los reuní y tal como estábamos, salimos corriendo en busca de abrigo. La tormenta no duró mucho pero al amanecer vimos el caos que había dejado tras de sí. Apenas quedaban unas pocas tiendas en pie.

Carmen y yo escribimos cartas a nuestros padres pero no recibíamos respuesta. Llevábamos en el campamento un mes cuando nos mandaron a empaquetar nuestras cosas: nos llevaban a otro lugar. Cuando llegó el autocar se subieron 41 niños y dos auxiliares y nos llevaron a Aston en Oxfordshire. No nos lo podíamos creer cuando nuestros ojos vieron la casa tan grande y bonita que iba a ser nuestro hogar. Nos bajamos del autocar y entramos en el gran recibidor, desde el que una imponente escalera conducía hasta el piso de arriba.

Dos miembros del Basque Children's Committee estaban allí para recibirnos. Pilar Merodio se presentó. No nos habíamos visto nunca antes, pero el nombre Merodio era bien conocido en Bilbao y su hermana vivía casi al lado de nuestra casa. No conocíamos a la maestra. El comité nos hizo un recorrido de inspección de la casa, que era muy espaciosa. En la planta de abajo había dos habitaciones grandes, un comedor y un salón. Desde el recibidor se accedía a la cocina, a una habitación anexa a ésta y a una pequeña sala. En la parte de arriba había un pasillo tan largo como la casa desde donde se entraba a dos habitaciones enormes, tan grandes como las de abajo, que eran los dos dormitorios. Estaban habilitados con colchones en el suelo y mantas rojas, un regalo de la fábrica de mantas en Witney; las camas llegaron más tarde. También había tres habitaciones individuales y un cuarto de baño grande. Afuera había un jardín muy grande con árboles frutales. Para nosotros, niños acostumbrados a vivir en manzanas de pisos altos con habitaciones pequeñas, era un verdadero lujo.

A partir de aquel día era cuestión de acostumbrarnos al lugar, de ir conociéndonos unos a otros y de aprender a vivir juntos. Había una mujer en el pueblo que se había comprometido a venir a cocinar todos los días, pero no duró mucho. No nos gustaba su comida, y aún menos el cigarro que siempre colgaba entre sus labios mientras trabajaba. Así que Pili se convirtió en nuestra cocinera. No había agua corriente en la casa, sino una bomba de agua manual instalada en la habitación anexa a la cocina que se usaba para sacar el agua con la que se llenaba el tanque del ático. Dos muchachos del pueblo venían para realizar estas tareas y también para cortar el césped. Mi trabajo era cuidar de los más pequeños, ayudarles a vestirse y lavarse. Los de más edad se encargaban de hacer las camas y limpiar los cuartos.

No llevábamos mucho tiempo en Aston cuando nos dimos cuenta de que la maestra era más bien una carga que una ayuda. Pili habló con Mrs Dalgleish del comité y un buen día la maestra se marchó. Entonces empecé a dar clases por la mañana a los más pequeños. Sólo había una cosa que nos estropeaba la existencia: la ausencia de cartas o de noticias de nuestros padres; siempre era mañana, mañana.

Recibíamos mucha atención del mundo exterior. Algunas organizaciones, como el Women's Institute, Toc H y el Rotary Club organizaban meriendas en las que los niños actuaban para los niños de la localidad cantando y bailando danzas tradicionales vascas. Los niños de Witney empezaron a venir en bicicleta.

Los días y las semanas pasaban y una mañana llegó finalmente una carta de mi madre. Era una carta breve: nos decía que había conseguido nuestra dirección llamando a la embajada española en Barcelona. No daba noticias de Papá. Contestamos a vuelta de correo. Pasaron dos o tres semanas hasta que recibimos una segunda carta, la cual abrí con un presagio de terror. En esa carta mi madre había vertido su alma y su corazón. Cuando Franco entró en Bilbao, mis padres ya habían salido, primero camino de Santander y luego hacia Gijón, en Asturias. Las tropas de Franco avanzaban, destruyendo desde el aire y bombardeando todo lo que encontraban en su camino. Mi madre se había quedado en un piso y mi padre llegó para recogerla con el camión. Mientras bajaba las escaleras oyó una explosión y cuando llegó al portal se encontró con el cuerpo ensangrentado y muerto de mi padre. Nos contaba que mientras sostenía sobre su regazo la cabeza de mi padre rogaba a Dios que cayera otra bomba y se la llevara a ella también. Mientras escribo esto, 69 años después, se me saltan las lágrimas. Nuestro padre era nuestro ídolo y para él las cuatro éramos su "harén". Leer aquella carta casi me destruyó. No podía comer, no podía dormir y sé que durante un mes todos estuvieron muy preocupados por mí. Pero yo era joven y poco a poco empecé a recuperarme.

En septiembre los niños empezaron a ir a la escuela, los menores de 11 años a la escuela del pueblo y los mayores de 11 a la escuela de Witney. A mi hermana Carmen se le daba muy bien el arte y le consiguieron una plaza en la Escuela de Bellas Artes de Oxford. Las tres chicas mayores que se quedaron fueron de gran ayuda con el funcionamiento de la colonia.

Debo rendir homenaje a nuestro fantástico comité: Mrs Lee, la esposa del ferretero, Mrs List, la esposa del carnicero, Mrs Dalgleish, la esposa del médico y, cómo no a Rosemary y Patrick Early de la fábrica de mantas de Witney. Mrs Dalgleish solía llegar en un bonito Riley verde; Patrick era un hombre joven, de unos treinta años, y tenía un auto sedán muy grande negro.

Una de nuestras excursiones más memorables fue a la fábrica de automóviles Morris donde nos habían invitado a tomar el té. William Morris – a quien más tarde le hicieron Lord Nuffield - nos dio una cariñosa bienvenida y nos acompañó en nuestra visita a la planta. La primera parada fue la nave de pintura, donde estaban sumergiendo los capós de los coches, las puertas y los guardafangos en tanques de pintura y sacándolos para que se secasen. Después fuimos a ver una gran banda transportadora donde las ruedas y otras partes se transportaban para colocarse en el chasis. Luego nos llevó al taller de costura, donde se hacían y se colocaban las cubiertas de los asientos. A medida que la cadena transportadora continuaba su camino se iban montando el motor, el volante, los frenos y los asientos y cuando llegamos al final había un conductor que nos estaba esperando con un coche para que lo lleváramos a probar. Después de una experiencia tan maravillosa, nos llevaron a la cantina para tomar un delicioso té inglés.

Los meses fueron pasando y un día una joven llamada Cora Blyth llegó a Aston. Cora era una escocesa de Kircaldy encantadora y enseguida nos caímos muy bien. Era mayor que yo y se convirtió en mi profesora de inglés. Para Pili, que era más o menos de la misma edad, se convirtió en una gran amiga y colaboradora. Cora se quedó en Aston y más tarde en Witney con los niños vascos hasta que fueron formalmente repatriados o trasladados a otros hogares. Fue en Aston donde Cora conoció a Luis Portillo, un profesor de universidad español que estaba también siendo perseguido por Franco. Después se casaron y uno de sus hijos fue el antiguo ministro conservador Michael Portillo.

Una de las chicas de Aston, Mauri, y mi hermana Carmen fueron a vivir a Londres. Carmen conoció más tarde a otro evacuado vasco, Jesús Alcón, y se casó con él. Teodoro, el hermano de Mauri, y yo nos quedamos en Witney. Cuando empezó la Segunda Guerra Mundial, como todas las mujeres jóvenes y solteras, tuve que contribuir con mi trabajo. Mi puesto era en la fábrica de uniformes de Compton and Webb en Witney, donde producíamos toda clase de gorras y artículos para la cabeza para las tropas británicas e incluso rusas. En 1941 me casé con un chico de Witney y tuvimos a nuestra hija Carmen, que nació en 1943. Ahora tengo tres nietos y 10 biznietos con edades comprendidas entre los tres meses y los 15 años. Mi nieta más joven ahora vive en el sur de España con su marido y sus tres hijos.

En cuanto a mi queridísima madre, nunca volvimos a saber nada de ella y no sabemos lo que le pudo haber sucedido después de haber llegado a Barcelona. Sabemos que bombardearon a muchos barcos que transportaban refugiados desde España a Francia y nos imaginamos que eso era lo que pudo haberle sucedido.

Desgraciadamente, mi hermana Carmen murió en 1947, seis meses después de dar a luz a su hijo Marcos, al que yo cuidé hasta que su padre se casó de nuevo tres años más tarde. Mi hermana más joven, Feli, lo pasó bastante mal en Francia. La familia con la que estaba la trataba como a una criada, pero cuando empezó la Segunda Guerra Mundial la repatriaron a Bilbao y al final se casó y tuvo dos hijas.

Y esta es mi historia, llena de felicidad y de tragedias, pero al igual que todos los que volvieron a España y los que se quedaron en Inglaterra, nunca olvidaré la alegría de nuestra colonia de Aston. *

Leonor Marcos Prieto
Nací el 1 de febrero de 1925, en Erandio, Vizcaya, la mayor de cuatro hermanos. Al empezar la guerra nos mudamos a Bilbao. Frente al avance de las líneas de batalla y los tremendos bombardeos fascistas, mis padres decidieron que las dos hermanas mayores, Mari Carmen (10 años) y yo (12) iríamos a Inglaterra. En Bilbao, con la guerra y las bombas encima, con las amenazas sobre mi padre por sus predilecciones intelectuales y políticas socialistas, quedaron papá, mamá y los dos hermanos menores.

Nuestra salida fue en un día hermoso y claro, diría que de los mejores de aquella primavera, pero tristísimo al momento en que todas las familias debían separarse de sus hijos. Viajamos por tren desde Bilbao a Santurce. En la estación del tren y en el puerto, el ambiente era de gritos y lloros desgarradores, ¡qué despedida más horrible! ¿Volveríamos a ver a nuestras queridas familias? A Mari Carmen y a mí, como niñas inocentes, la salida nos pareció una diversión al principio, aunque llegado el momento de separarnos de nuestros padres y hermanos, todo fue terrible. Algo que por más años que pasen, me será imposible olvidar.

Subimos finalmente al *Habana*, y cuando llegamos a Southampton, nos llevaron a un campamento en Stoneham, donde estuvimos 22 días y diría que lo pasamos bastante bien. Después de un tiempo nos distribuyeron en colonias por toda Inglaterra. La primera fue en Thame, Oxford, donde nos llevaron a 50 niñas. Allí estuvimos muy bien, todos nuestros antojos al momento eran saciados, todo era tratar de alegrarnos para olvidar las tristezas pasadas. Aquí conocí el corazón noble de la gente inglesa. Nunca podré olvidar a las personas de esta ciudad y en particular a Mrs Michaelis, Directora y protectora nuestra. En el verano, después de dormir la siesta, nos llevaban a pasear a los campos y jardines cercanos, en donde los niños ingleses no hacían otra cosa sino acogernos en sus juegos como personas de su familia.

Recuerdo una travesura que allí hice. Había unos aparatos por los que se echaba el dinero y salían distintos dulces; yo como tenía una perra española, la eché con toda malicia y allí no salió ni dulce ni dinero. Entonces, entré a la tienda y le dije a la encargada que había echado mi dinero y no salía su equivalente. Ella me preguntó si había metido dinero español y le contesté negativamente. A esta respuesta la pobre mujer me tuvo que dar lo que no me pertenecía.

El primer viaje que hice a Londres fue estando en Thame. Me causó gran impresión el ver aquella magnífica ciudad, primera en grandeza en el mundo, con grandes rascacielos, una cantidad de público inmensa, grandes comercios con muchísimos niveles. Una ciudad con un movimiento intenso de vehículos y especialmente de autobuses de dos pisos, que como era la primera vez que les veía, me causaron gran impresión. Pero lo que más me extrañó, es que a eso de las tres de la tarde, se puso una niebla tan intensa que era imposible distinguir a una persona de otra por cerca que estuvieran. El tráfico tuvo que cesar, porque era imposible continuar caminando.

En esta colonia de Thame, estuvimos durante siete meses, hasta que pasadas las primeras Navidades, en el día de los Santos Inocentes, nos comunicaron la triste noticia de que la colonia se cerraba y que teníamos que ir a otras colonias.

Nosotras fuimos enviadas a Langham, cerca de Colchester. Ahí sí que estuvimos bien. Era una casa preciosa, con gran extensión de jardín y árboles frutales, especialmente manzanos cuyas frutas comíamos directamente del árbol. El trato fue muy bueno, y la comida rica y abundante. En Langham nos pusieron padres adoptivos a mi hermana y a mí, que nos visitaban periódicamente. Afortunadamente nos tocaron lindas personas, que nos trataban como hijas verdaderas mientras las escasas noticias que teníamos de la familia y de la guerra eran normalmente malas y muy preocupantes.

Mis padres adoptivos eran un matrimonio joven de recién casados, los Purling, que vivían en Norwich y que me visitaban periódicamente. Los de mi hermana eran un matrimonio sin hijos, como de 50 años, Mr y Mrs Clark, que la querían mucho.

Mantuvimos la relación con nuestros padres adoptivos incluso después de terminar la guerra en Europa y nos escribimos hasta muchos años después, estando ya en México, hasta que un buen día las cartas dejaron de llegar. A los Purling les guardo un recuerdo muy especial y me encantaría saber qué fue de ellos.

Más tarde nos tocó ir a Margate, ciudad hermosa y alegre, y una de las más elegantes de Inglaterra, con una gran playa, como nunca había visto. En esta colonia no puedo decir que lo pasábamos mal, pero por primera vez nos hallábamos conviviendo con gente que resultaba un tanto fría en comparación con la que habíamos tratado hasta entonces. ¿Dónde estaban aquellas adoradas señoritas Peque, Gloria, Elena y Virginia?

Debido a la falta de cariño, comparando con nuestra estancia en Thame, y la no tan abundante comida, nos era difícil soportar la estancia allí. Además, como la iglesia anglicana era quien nos mantenía, teníamos que ir a misa todos los domingos.

Volvimos a Bilbao al terminar la guerra en España y perfilarse la entrada de Inglaterra en el conflicto mundial. En esos años a mi padre lo habían metido preso al regresar a Bilbao desde Barcelona y ser denunciado por uno que suponía buen amigo. Lo denunció por rojo y por tener muchos libros... Salió de prisión después de casi un año e irónicamente, con la ayuda de un capitán de la guardia civil que lo conocía de años atrás y que intercedió por él antes de que su situación se tornara todavía más difícil.

Al poco tiempo de nuestro regreso nos fuimos a vivir a San Sebastián por casi dos años. Regresamos a Bilbao y después de sufrir muchos miedos por la persecución y presiones de las que era objeto mi padre, decidimos exiliarnos a México, y salimos de España el 10 de junio de 1947. Desembarcamos en Nueva York y viajamos en autobús Greyhound a la ciudad de México, llegando el 3 de julio.

En México fuimos recibidos por un hermano de mi madre y comenzamos una nueva vida. Aquí encontramos nuevas amistades y conocí a José Ángel Gutiérrez Sánchez, médico cirujano de profesión, con quien me casé y tuve un matrimonio maravilloso. Criamos juntos a 8 hijos, tres chicas y cinco chicos, hasta que en 1977 y de manera sorpresiva y dolorosa murió mi querido José de una leucemia fulminante. Hoy tengo una familia grande y maravillosa, contando a mis 19 nietos y un bisnieto.

Ahora, después de tantos años, me doy cuenta de que mis raíces están repartidas en tres lados. Mi natal País Vasco, Inglaterra que me cuidó durante la guerra y claro, el maravilloso lugar que me recibió con brazos abiertos y que me ha dado tanto, México.

Por otro lado y desafortunadamente, veo con tristeza y decepción como se repiten en todo el mundo los errores de aquellos años y las injusticias quedan sin solución. Me queda siempre la esperanza de que algún día aprendamos a vivir en paz y buscando el justo bienestar de todos.

Con ésta quiero también enviar unos abrazos para todas las compañeras y compañeros que salimos de niños refugiados a Inglaterra. Mi agradecimiento a Natalia Benjamin por emprender este esfuerzo para registrar algunas de nuestras historias, pero sobre todo, por su maravillosa madre, a quien recuerdo con enorme cariño.

Herminio Martínez Verguizas.

Los años después de la guerra habían sido muy perturbantes. Muchos de nosotros jóvenes estabamos nadando entre dos aguas. No éramos ni británicos ni españoles. No podíamos acceptar el régimen franquista y regresar a lo que todavía considerábamos casa.

Hacia 1960 ya estaba echando raíces. Daba clases y me me había casado con Verena, una suiza, que se dedicaba a la enseñanza de los que tienen problemas de oído. También había solucionado mis problemas de nacionalidad. Me habían negado la ciudadanía británica pero ahora tenía un pasaporte español en vez del documento de viaje apátrida de la ONU. Por esas fechas el gobierno español ofreció a los exiliados como yo un indulto. Esto nos permitió regresar a España y quedarnos por menos de cuatro semanas. De esta manera no tendríamos que cumplir el servicio militar en las fuerzas armadas franquistas.

Así que por la primera vez desde 1937 fuí a España con Verena para pasar dos semanas. Llegamos en tren a Irún. Enseñé mi nuevo pasaporte español. Se lo llevó el oficial. Me sentí inquieto. Mi amigo, Manolo Andrés, había regresado y había pasado gran parte de sus dos semana en la cárcel. Al cabo de poco tiempo el oficial volvió y me preguntó en tono bajo: "¿Pero que hace Ud. aquí?". Tenía una ficha con mis datos personales en la que constaba mi condición de exiliado político. Le dije que me había ido del país cuando tenía siete años y que a esa edad carecía de toda ideología política. Ahora, por supuesto que sí la tenía. Me dió la impresión de que era una buena persona. Me dijo: "Pase unas buenas vacaciones, pero tenga mucho cuidado". ¡Estábamos dentro!

Cambiamos de tren en San Sebastián. Sin ninguna razón un guardia civil nos apartó de los demás viajeros y revisó nuestro equipaje, sacando todo. Le pregunté en tono burlón que buscaba y si lo teníamos se lo diría. Sólo frunció el cejo. Llegamos a Bilbao. Mi madre y una señorita nos esperaban en el andén. Pensaba que la señorita era mi hermana Mari que había nacido un poco después de nuestra salida para Inglaterra y la saludé como tal. Pero era mi cuñada Ester, la mujer de mi hermano mayor.

Mis padres vivían en una huerta que mi padre había descubierto en una ladera algunos años antes de que mi hermano Víctor y yo dejáramos España. La huerta estaba resguardada en un barranco cubierto de zarzamoras achaparradas que parecía no pertenecer a nadie, aunque posteriormente descubrimos que era propiedad del ayuntamiento. Era tiempo de depresión económica, cuando mi padre halló la huerta, y estaba sin empleo tras haber trabajado en las minas de hierro y la metalurgia. Eran días de hambre, en los que no teníamos medios de subsistencia. Mi padre solía ir a Baracaldo para mendigar un poco de pan de puerta en puerta. Durante aquel tiempo vivíamos en El Regato, un pueblo de mineros situado un poco más allá de la ladera donde estaba la huerta, en Arnabal. Alquilábamos el primer piso de una casa en la que no había agua ni saneamiento. Teníamos gallinas, un burro y una vaca que pastaban en el campo.

Mi padre trabajaba en la huerta y poco a poco la limpió de maleza y asentó el terreno. Creó un paraíso. Yo solía llevarle la comida al valle desde casa, a unos tres kilómetros, montado a lomos de nuestro burro. Tendría alrededor de seis años. Mi padre encontró un manantial de agua que salía de la roca y lo canalizó. Plantó higueras, albaricoques, cerezos… Al tiempo plantábamos todo tipo de vegetales. Esto nos salvó y les salvó a ellos, una vez que Víctor y yo nos habíamos ido, durante los horribles años de hambre que siguieron a la caída de Bilbao, y en los que mi padre fue llevado a prisión.

Cuando volví en 1960, Verena y yo nos quedamos en la huerta con mis padres y mi hermana pequeña, Mari, que tenía 23 años y a la que nunca había visto. Nacida justo después de que Víctor y yo llegáramos a Inglaterra, había vivido una infancia hambrienta y llena de carencias. Era una mujer amargada, y llena de rencor hacia mí por haber tenido una vida mejor en Inglaterra… si ella supiera… Mis otros tres hermanos y Begoña, mi hermana mayor, ya estaban casados, aunque vivían cerca. Antes de ir a prisión, mi padre había extraído a mano piedra de la ladera y mis hermanos construyeron una casa en la huerta mientras él estuvo preso. Había luz eléctrica pero no agua. Todo era muy básico y rudimentario.

Nos reunimos con mis hermanos, Santi, Manuel y Félix, y con sus mujeres e hijos. Los 23 años de separación nos habían convertido en extraños, sobretodo con mis hermanas. Verena aceptó la situación. Para ella, acostumbrada a la vida segura y ordenada de los suizos, tuvo que ser mucho más impresionante que para mí. No tenía problema con la comida –comiendo caracoles, cada uno metiendo la cucharra en la cazuela y untando el pan. Verena dio una buena impresión y mi padre le tomó cariño. Verena tenía buen apetito y pies grandes – requisitos para trabajo duro.

Mi recuerdo de mi padre es que era muy cariñoso conmigo. Otrora un hombre físicamente fuerte, era ahora un hombre roto y lisiado, quien, a pesar de todo, seguía trabajando la huerta de sol a sol. La vida tan terrible y dura que les tocó vivir a él y a los demás les había pasado factura a todos, pero sobre todo a él. Su condena por acusaciones de las que no era culpable y el trato feroz que allí recibió, le convirtieron en un hombre retraído. Me gustaba sentarme con él y hacerle hablar pero no era fácil. Mis hermanos no querían hablar del pasado y la miseria y a mi madre no le gustaba cuando hablaba con mi padre de sus experiencias después de su encarcelamiento.

A mi padre lo habían denunciado por activismo y lo arrestaron. Pero él no era un activista. Mi madre sí. Ella organizaba a las mujeres del pueblo para que tejieran ropas para los milicianos del frente. Nunca supimos quién denunció a mi padre. Lo llevaron a una prisión-barco en la ría del Nervión, donde le pegaron. Lo condenaron a muerte, según la costumbre del momento, aunque más tarde le conmutaron la pena por 30 años de prisión y trabajos forzados. Mientras estuvo en la cárcel de León, se alimentaba a los prisioneros con comida preparada con aceites industriales. Unos 60 de ellos sufrieron parálisis e, incapaces de trabajar, fueron liberados.

Mi familia estaba segura que había sido la maestra quien había denunciado a mi padre, para vengarse de mi madre. Explicaré. Empecé el colegio a la edad de cuatro años. Iba a un colegio que había abierto la República en El Regato. Aprendí a leer y escribir pero mis padres eran analfabetos. Mi padre no era educado pero podía juntar palabras – le había enseñado un maestro cuando se alojaron juntos cuando mi padre vino a trabajar a Vizcaya. Mi madre no tenía pelos en la lengua. Era, como ella decía, socialista. No iba a misa, no necesitaba curas para ayudarla a hablar con Dios. Mi maestra, al contrario, era muy beata. Me echaba la culpa por cualquier travesía. Para vengarse de mi madre, me castigaba mandándome a través de la plaza y poniédome de rodillas en la iglesia. Sentí la injusticia. La enmistad entre mi madre y mi maestra siguió y yo me vengaba de forma discreta. Mi maestra tenía que pasar nuestra casa al ir la suya. Yo me escondía entre los arboles y le echaba piedras. Esto empeoró la situación.

Verena y yo descubrimos un estado de miedo permanente entre mi familia. Me recomendaron que no me metiera en problemas con la Guardia Civil, que no cantara las canciones del pasado y que no me fiara de nadie ni me relacionara con nadie de fuera de la familia. Temían que con cualquier indiscreción les pudiese traer problemas o causármelos a mí. Me llevó un tiempo entender por qué se sentían tan amenazados, aunque pronto descubrí que su miedo estaba justificado.

Mi madre era una mujer pequeña pero de gran carácter, muy determinada, práctica y trabajadora, con un sentido del humor malicioso. Mantuvo a la familia junta durante los años duros en los que mi padre estuvo en la cárcel. Santi tenía 15 años. Era listo, capaz y sostén principal de la familia. No había trabajo, así que trabajaba la huerta para sobrevivir. Manuel, 14, encontró trabajo como pastor. Begoña tenía 10 años cuando encarcelaron a mi padre y cuando mi madre dió a luz. Tuvo que criar a Mari, nuestra hermanita, durante esos años de hambre. Félix tenía cinco años. Años después cuando mi padre salió de la cárcel, Félix le acompañaba a la Guardia Civil donde se tenía que presentar periódicamente. Félix temía estas ocasiones desconociendo que iba a pasar. Sobrevivieron ¿pero a qué coste? ¡Qué desastre hubiera sido si Victor y yo hubieramos vuelto en diciembre de 1939! Mi madre rechazó firmar el formulario de repatriación aunque la visitó un cura y un oficial que la amenzaron con encarcelamiento y llevarse a los otros niños. Sostuvo que si volvíamos nos moriríamos todos de hambre. A pesar de que su firma fue falsificada para hacernos volver, la intervención en el último momento de la Cruz Roja impidió que regresáramos.

Mis hermanos trabajaban largo y duro. En esa época, estaba ocurriendo una transición en el estilo de vida, de la vida rural a la industrial. En muchas familias el marido trabajaba en las fábricas de Baracaldo, Burcena o Zorroza, mientras todavía conservaban algunas gallinas, cerdos o vacas. Había mucho trabajo y la vida empezaba a mejorar, después de muchos años de hambre y recesión. Había sed por prosperar y la industria floreció. Era como un salvaje oeste industrial, sin controles ni seguridad. Más adelante, esto tuvo consecuencias trágicas para mi familia, cuando mis dos hermanos mayores, Santi y Manuel, murieron en sendos accidentes laborales en plazo de un año. Nos devastó a todos, dejando a dos viudas y sus hijos en la familia.

Todos hablaban de los años de hambre. Mi hermano Félix me contó lo que había pasado. Dijo que gente mayor en la aldea había muerto de hambre. La familia había sobrevivido a base de vegetales, sobretodo berza, por eso tenía la obsesión con comer bien y comer carne.

Verena y yo percibimos que la gente era muy conformista y que estaba muy preocupada por las apariencias y el qué dirán. Había reglas absurdas sobre cómo el hombre no podía ir en mangas de camisa sin chaqueta, excepto que la camisa tuviera un bolsillo, o sobre como las mujeres debían cubrir siempre sus brazos y llevar medias, y los trajes de baño eran muy victorianos. Al margen del papel que jugaba en todo esto la Iglesia, enseguida entendí que el alcalde de Baracaldo era un artífice importante de estas tonterías. También descubrí que la gente, y entre ellos mi familia, tendía a creer a pies juntillas la palabra de los periódicos. La estricta censura tenía un efecto evidente y las ideas que yo traje del mundo exterior chocaban abiertamente con las concepciones con las que habían sido adoctrinados. Esto causó problemas entre nosotros. Mi familia no podía aceptar que, tanto sus vidas como sus ideas, habían sido restringidas.

Estábamos con mi familia para la fiesta de San Roque –la fiesta del pueblo. Nos invitó mi hermano a su casa. Las familias empezaron a llegar por la mañana, andando desde Baracaldo, Retuerto y otros pueblos. Todos se juntaron con sus niños y hubo comida en Las Arraguas, una campa al otro lado del río en frente de nuestra antigua casa. Había mucho árbol y la gente buscaba la sombra. Pronto se encendieron los fuegos y las mujeres empezaron a cocinar. Salieron las botas de vino y los hombres jugaron a las cartas. Los niños bajaron al río para mojarse los pies y para coger pececillos entre las rocas.

Bajé para ver si había alguién que yo hubiese conocido de chaval. Me encontré con Felisa, una de los socialistas. Tenía un hijo que era miliciano y había muerto en el frente. Todavía tenía toda su pasión y pronto me estaba preguntando sobre la vida fuera de España. Ella me dijo lo que había pasado bajo el franquismo, lo que había pasado a mis amigos. Ella estaba muy resentida porque algunas familias habían acogido a los Nacionales, colgando banderas de sus balcones. Me contó que la familia de los hermanos Ricardo y Jaime había tenido problemas con la Iglesia. Sus padres no se habían casado por la Iglesia y los chicos no habían sido bautizados. Cuando entraron los Nacionales les vino a ver el cura. Les dijo que la huerta donde trabajaban ahora era de la Iglesia. Si no se casaban y bautizaban a sus hijos no podrían cultivar la huerta. En esos días de hambre esto hubiera sido un desastre. ¡Se casaron y bautizaron a Ricardo y Jaime! Felisa también me contó que la hija de La Sorda, que ahora era monja, estaba visitando a su hermana menor, La Morena. Me acordaba muy bien de esta familia. Vivían al otro lado del río en una chabola encima de una cuadra en lo que había sido un henil. Siempre había querido saber lo que le había pasado a esta familia, a los dos chicos que habían sido mis amigos.

El padre trabajaba en las minas. Me acuerdo de cuando bajaron al padre encima de una tabla. Había muerto en un accidente. Esto fue un desastre para la familia. La vida se hizo imposible para La Sorda, la madre. Unos vecinos se llevaron a la hermana menor, La Morena, y la hermana mayor y los dos chicos desaparecieron. No he podido olvidar su vuelta al pueblo para pasar unos días con su madre. Jugaban con nosotros. Como siempre nos peleábamos y soltábamos tacos. La reacción de los dos hermanos fue increíble. Nos dijeron que no debíamos usar palabrotas, que era un pecado. Escuchamos mientras describieron el infierno con Satanás y los demonios tendiendo las calderas de fuego donde se cocía a los malos. Esto me causó una fuerte impresión como a ellos cuando las monjas les amenazaron con el infierno. Cuando fueron separados de su madre les habían llevado a una institución religiosa. ¡Las monjas les habían enseñado muy bien!

Encontré a la hermana mayor en casa de La Morena, la misma casa a donde la llevaron los vecinos. Salió a verme en el hábito gris sencillo de monja. Se acordaba de mí. Era encantadora. No tuvimos ningún problema en recordar esos años terribles de sufrimiento. Me contó que sus hermanos ahora vivían en Vitoria. Ella estaba en un convento en Bélgica. La orden era bastante liberal y mantenía contacto con su hermana y sus hermanos. Hablaba francés y estaba educada. Sí, estaba contenta pero sentí una tristeza. ¿Qué hubiera pasado si la vida no hubiese sido tan dura? Estaba claro que ella estaba en paz consigo misma. Le gustaba visitar a su hermana La Morena que tenía dos niños pero yo me preguntaba si quizá la vida en el convento no satisfacía sus instintos naturales. Este encuentro fue una alegría, que de tanta miseria había salido un poco de felicidad.

San Roque era un día para comer. Comimos demasiado. Hubiera sido fácil convertirse en vegetariano después de comer tanta carne. Las mujeres estaban trabajando como mulas con las las sartenes grasientas en las chapas intentando suministrar a todos con comida. A los hombres solo les interesaba ser servidos. Gritaban: "¡Pan!" y llegaba más pan: "¡Agua!" y se llenaba la jarra.

La gente no estaba acostumbrada a tratar con extranjeros. Cuando íbamos a la plaza del pueblo, la gente le gritaba a Verena porque, obviamente, si no entendía, es que era sorda. Andamos mucho porque apenas había transporte público. Cogíamos el autobús de Baracaldo a Retuerto y andábamos el resto del camino a la huerta en Gorostiza. Para Verena esto era un martirio. El autobús estaba a tope y lleno de pulgas. Ella sentía las "bestias" en todo su cuerpo pero no se podía mover. Las picaduras se hinchaban y eran muy dolorosas. Yo, como el resto de mi familia, estaba inmune a las picaduras.

Nos aconsejaron tener mucho cuidado con lo que decíamos y no meternos con gente fuera de nuestra familia. Nos dimos cuenta de que había algo raro en la actitud de la gente de Gorostiza hacia nosotros. Era agosto. Al andar por el pueblo, los lugareños estaban sentados fuera de sus casas en banquillos o sillas de rejilla. Los perros disfrutaban de la frescura del atardecer. Mientras cruzábamos el pueblo, los ojos de los lugareños y sus perros se giraban para observarnos. No saludaron ni reconcieron nuestra presencia. No contestaban a nuestro saludo de: "Buenas". Esto nos extrañó. Recibían a mi familia de la misma manera. Paulatinamente advertimos que el resentimiento de esa gente hacia mis padres se remontaba al tiempo en que mi padre había encontrado la huerta y había empezado a trabajarla 30 años antes. Tenían ojeriza hacia un forastero que había usurpado sus dominios. Se nos consideraba unos inmigrantes. Semejante terrible comportamiento hacia mis padres era del todo despreciable.

Pasándolos sentados a las puertas de sus casas, me paraba, les miraba y decía: "Hola, buenas tardes". De mala gana respondían: "Buenas". Al paso de tiempo venía la respuesta sin confrontarles. Años después les vine muy útil. Vivía en Londres y como había tanto interés en aprender inglés, venían jóvenes de Gorostiza a Londres. Se quedaban con nosotros o las chicas iban a ciudar niños después de pasar un rato con nosotros. Algunas veces los padres me trataban de confianza y pedían mis consejos, sobretodo en un caso. Durante esas dos semanas en España viajamos mucho. Alquilamos un Fiat 500 para ir a Santander y a la meseta de Burgos.

No sé como nuestro regreso a Inglaterra no acabó siendo un desastre. Todavía no me lo explico. Las dos semanas volaron. Cogimos el tren de Bilbao a San Sebastián. La despedida no había sido difícil - sabíamos que volveríamos. Cambiamos de tren en San Sebastián y cogimos El Topo (porque había muchos túneles) – el tren que iba a la frontera francesa parando en todas las estaciones.

El tren estaba formado de vagones abiertos. Estábamos a la entrada de uno de los vagones. La gente montaba o bien con mercancía que supongo habían comprado en las plazas o con fardos o equipaje atados con cuerda. Nuestro equipaje en la rejilla era nuevo y parte de ello era el equipaje suizo de Verena. Vaya contraste con lo de los otros pasajeros. Verena y yo también contrastamos con los otros pasajeros. Era claro que Verena con su pelo rubio era extranjera. El vagón se llenó y muchos estaban de pie. En uno de las estaciones montó un hombre pequeño. Me dí cuenta de que al entrar en el vagón levantó la solapa de la gabardina. Era insignificante –aparte de la gabardina y un bigote delgado – el bigote de la Falange. No dijo nada pero enseguida hubo silencio. Las mujeres empezaron a buscar en sus bolsos y los hombres sacaron sus carteras. Me dí cuenta de que este señor era un policía de civil. La gente sacaba los permisos que necesitaban para viajar de una provincia a la otra, aunque había terminado la Guerra Civil hace 21 años. Habíamos cruzado de Vizcaya a Guipúzcoa.

Todavía me pregunto qué me pasó aquel día. Uno de las cosas que nos sorprendió a Verena y a mí fue el miedo que la gente tenía a la Guardia Civil y a la policía. Armados hasta los dientes y siempre en pareja parecían disfrutar del miedo que provocaban y su papel represivo. Parecían estar en todas partes. Me molestaba que este pequeñín asumiera que la gente iba a responder a su posición de autoridad. "Hazte la tonta," la dije a Verena. Yo estaba sentado en la primera fila del vagón. Como no respondí el policía me preguntó: "Documentación". Le miré, me encogí los hombros y sonrié. Hubo silencio. Se dió cuenta de que eramos extranjeros y preguntó otra vez muy despacio: "Yo, ustedes, documentación". No entendía palabra. Los otros pasajeros nos rodearon intentando ayudar diciendo en voz alta "¡Él, quiere, su, documentación!". Si yo no entendía era porque estaba sordo. Intentó otra vez con gestos. Por fin entendí. Le contesté en inglés también con gestos. Le dije a Verena de darme su pasaporte

–rojo con una cruz blanca. Todos gritaron: "Suizos". Se lo dí al señor, lo revisó y me lo devolvió con respeto. Me tocó a mí. Tardé mucho tiempo en sacar el pasaporte del bolsillo de mis pantalones y por fin se lo ofrecí, mi pasaporte español. Todos se echaron a reir, una explosión como si se hubiera roto un dique. Ni lo miró. Se largó. No hubo inspección de permisos para viajar.

Muchas veces me pregunto como pude ser tan estúpido y cómo no me llevaron al cuartel para darme una paliza. En esa época los españoles, aparte de los que formaban parte del régimen privilegiado, tenían dificultad para viajar al extranjero. Supongo que el policía se vió con un buen señor con un pasaporte español y encima casado con una suiza y que tenía que ser un jefazo, un pez gordo, alguien que se podía permitir estas bromas y que él no necesitaba problemas con una persona semejante. Aparte del miedo a la Guardia Civil que la gente tenía, nos habíamos dado cuenta de la corrupción en como se hacían las cosas y el poder y la influencia del privilegio. ¡Quizás había tenido mi ángel de la guarda a mi lado!

Javier Martínez Castillo

Llegué a Inglaterra con mis dos hermanos, José Mari y Tirso. Mi familia era muy pobre, vivíamos en Bilbao en el barrio de Ochurdinaga, cerca de Santuchu. Llegamos a Inglaterra en el buque *Habana* con otros 4.000 niños y niñas españoles. No recuerdo muy bien el viaje, pues solo tenía 10 años en aquel entonces y estaba muy asustado, pero sé que fue un viaje duro. Al llegar nos llevaron a un campamento lleno de tiendas de campaña. Sólo recuerdo que un día que descansaba, alguien me golpeó con un palo y me trasladaron a la casa de socorro del campamento.

De Southamtpton, mis hermanos y yo nos fuimos a una colonia llamada Bray Court en Maidenhead, y de allí pasamos a Brighton en 1938. Un año más tarde, a mis hermanos y a mí nos separaron. A mí me acogió una familia de Coventry (Mr y Mrs Keeley), junto a otro niño español llamado Pepito. Nos montaron en el tren en la estación de Victoria en Londres, donde nos presentaron a Miss Picken, secretaria del Basque Children's Committee. Era una señora muy simpática y ella nos puso en el tren de Coventry. Allí nos esperaban los Keeley, que nos llevaron a su casa. Tengo unos recuerdos muy gratos de mi estancia con ellos. Fui por primera vez a una escuela inglesa, pero no sabía hablar inglés, así que me costaba comunicarme con los otros.

Cuando terminó la guerra en España, los padres de Pepito lo reclamaron. Yo me quedé solo, pues mis padres se habían escapado a Francia con mi hermano pequeño Valentín. Mis padres lo pasaron muy mal durante la ocupación nazi de Francia. Nunca volvieron a España, los dos murieron en Francia.

Mientras tanto yo continuaba en Coventry. A Mr Keeley le gustaba el senderismo: pertenecía a una asociación y me llevaba con él y los socios y disfruté muchísimo. En 1940 cuando los alemanes bombardearon Coventry, los Keeley decidieron que yo no estaba a salvo y me llevaron a la colonia de Barnet, en el condado de Hertfordshire. Continué en Rowley Lodge unos dos años y participaba en muchas actividades con los niños españoles. En Barnet, nos bombardearon otra vez y nos llevaron a Cambrian Lodge mientras reparaban Rowley Lodge.

Cuando cerraron Rowley Lodge me llevaron a The Culvers, en Carshalton, la última colonia que permanecía en Inglaterra. Allí me volví a reunir con mi hermano mayor, José Mari, a quien no había visto en muchos años. A mi hermano menor, Tirso, lo recogió un señor, Mr Polling de Brighton y se quedó allí muchos años.

Yo me sentí muy feliz en The Culvers. Entonces tenía 14 años y empecé a trabajar de mecánico en un taller en Cheam en el condado de Surrey. Pero me evacuaron a Perth en Escocia con la cocinera, Mrs Somerset, originaria de esa cuidad. Fue muy amable con nosotros y nos cuidó muy bien. Estuve allí dos meses donde trabajé en la empresa de tintorería Pullens. De Perth volvimos a Carshalton, y luego con mi amigo Herminio Martínez estuve un año trabajando en una granja en Colchester. En 1945, después de Colchester, fui a vivir a Reigate, en el condado de Surrey. Mr West, que estaba ayudando a los niños vascos, me encontró trabajo y alojamiento. Me encontraba muy feliz trabajando con mis amigos Manuel Larraz y Tomás Martínez haciendo sierras Multico. Fue una etapa buena de mi vida.

De Reigate me fui a Londres, que no me gustó mucho, pues siempre había disfrutado más el campo. Allí me encontré con muchos de mis amigos vascos. En una verbena vasca que se celebró en The Firs School en Notting Hill Gate, conocí a mi querida esposa, Josefa. Esto cambió mi vida. Era andaluza, de Jerez. Nos casamos en 1954 y después de vivir en Londres un año, nos mudamos a Luton donde hemos vivido 40 años. Tenemos tres hijos, dos chicos y una chica y cuatro nietos. Gracias a Mr Keeley, me hice socio de la Asociación de Senderistas. Esta fue la mejor etapa de mi vida, pues con la asociación visité muchos países incluido España.

En general he tenido una buena existencia en Inglaterra, y no me pesa nada. Inglaterra nos ha tratado bien y ahora somos una pareja de viejetes, y ¡tenemos más tiempo para discutir!*

José Maria Martínez Castillo

1937 – North Stoneham Camp, Eastleigh

Concentración de 4.000 niños vascos más médicos y *boy scouts* en un bosque de campamento de tiendas de campaña nosotros tres hermanos José María Javier y Tirso abrigados protegidos por una barrera de alambre encerrando este campo abierto extenso que durante la mayor parte de nuestra estancia llovía a cántaros formando crecidas inundando nuestra residencia de tiendas con colchones que se convertían en balsas bajo nuestros cuerpos que me recordaba la travesía del Océano Atlántico de Santurce a Southampton en ese atestado barco de travesía Habana viaje épico en mar borrascoso mareo y lágrimas a través del Golfo de Vizcaya en los estómagos hambrientos lamentando la salida de la patria bombardeada

No lejano de North Stoneham un campo de aviación un avión murmuraba como esos bombarderos alemanes que diseminaron bombas incendiarias del cielo en Guernica - Bilbao trayendo memorias retrospectivas de inseguridad a este paisaje solitario verde pero el campo hormigueaba con niños pero entonces yo andaba solo y había atestiguado la devastación el hambre del sitio de Bilbao durante un año… lo peor fue cuando anunciaron la entrega a las tropas fascistas nuestros corazones pisoteados y en el campo de North Stoneham hubo una tristeza silenciosa las nubes negras de la perdición pronto se manifestaron en cada cara ¿y nuestros padres? esta agonía acongojada era contagiosa a través del campo pensando a nuestras familias dejadas atrás en la desesperación y preguntándose qué había pasado a sus niños en una isla tan alejada de la patria Euskadi

1937 – Baydon Hole Farm y el cuartel del ejército

De Eastleigh Southampton a un corral de granja pollos patos gansos cerdos vacas perros nos cortaron el pelo no más picaduras irritantes de pulga nuestros cuerpos sumergidos en una bañera para ser desinfectados fregados en caso de sarampión una repetición del repaso médico en Stoneham y decidieron prender fuego a todo nuestro equipaje con el contenido sentimental de España... todavía huelo los malolientes montones de excremento de vaca de antaño corral que se repite periódicamente en mi vida especialmente de noche ese olor a través del dormitorio de los cuarteles dominaba las ventanas de mi nariz desde entonces un perfume apestante

1937 – Bray Court Maidenhead

El más lujoso hotel hogar que nosotros tres hermanos encontramos y posiblemente la colonia de niños vascos más grande del Reino Unido esta mansión victoriana construida en los 1800 por la familia John Haig los del whisky tardó cuatro años en construirse tenía 365 ventanas una para cada día del año jardines fabulosos bordeados con canchas de tenis cercados por una franja de árboles una felicidad idílica para la multitud de niños vascos que habitan su esplendor espectacular e instalaciones aprender a bailar en los terrenos abiertos comiendo suculentos platos tradicionalmente ingleses a la hora de comer maravillada forma de vida después de las experiencias traumáticas de la guerra civil bombardeo de la aniquilación en Bilbao-Euskadi 1936-37

Algunas veces los benefactores anglo españoles venían a Bray Court y llevaban a los niños de excursión en sus coches y a menudo autobuses lo que era muy agradable meriendas y paseos por cercano Windsor esta impresión me dio un gusto para las agradables comodidades y tranquilidades de estándares de vida inglés a fines de los años 1930 como mis pasatiempos infantiles pastorales en mi pueblo de la montaña de Navarra de alguna manera el futuro no existía en esos años formativos en Albión había una tranquilidad de espíritu dentro de este panorama exquisito que es Inglaterra y sociedad tolerante anfitrión de nosotros los niños vascos con los sentimientos serenos de la gente

1938 – Girton House, Brighton

De Maidenhead a la playa de Sussex de nuevo ligando aguas del océano a memorias que flotan de suelo español que el conocimiento no es absoluto pero el condicional subconsciente memorias alejadas ligado por el cordón umbilical que conecta la onda cerebral a memorias pasadas-presentes-futuras ... en este hogar al lado del mar aire punzante ozono fortaleciente nadamos a menudo o tomamos el sol en los guijarros y a veces el Padre Cirilo nos invitaba a merendar en Lyons Corner House en la explanada marítima

Finalmente se cerró la casa y nosotros tres hermanos separados Tirso fue a vivir con Dick Polling organizador activo de Girton House quien acogió a cinco niños vascos y mi padre acogedor Charles Gildersleve me llevó a vivir con su familia en Hove Poplar Avenue Javier enviado al norte a Coventry... mi gratitud abunda la generosidad de Mr Gildersleve (ingeniero inventor) su esposa e hija mientras viví con ellos asistí a Hove Grammar School mis primeras clases de inglés comenzaron con el cuidado paternal y una intimidad tierna familiar que previamente estaba ausente desafortunadamente llegaba el punto culminante de la segunda guerra mundial y hacia el invierno nevoso de 1939 decidieron transferirme a la seguridad de The Culvers Carshalton

1940 – 1946 The Culvers, Carshalton

Con la segunda guerra mundial en plena marcha aterricé
en esta casa victoriana The Culvers Surrey entre muchos
niños vascos internos y encuentro extraño después de ser
aislado sociable en la colonia de Hove Sussex aunque el
personal era muy acogedor Mrs Somerset Miss Vulliamy
Mrs Temple Mari Cruz y Pepe gran comunidad
administradores idealistas todos inspirando cooperación de
los niños vascos de la casa y queridos por su atención hacia
nuestro comportamiento leal y respetando su sabiduría…
En este domicilio de Carshalton permanecí seis años
adolescentes y era el despertar más difuso estético dinámico
cultural aparte de los bombardeos incendiarios constantes
por los nazis y la batalla de Gran Bretaña feroz en el cielo
debajo en el abrigo de los sótanos de las casas el temblor
cada vez disparaban las baterías antiaéreas y la misma
agonía torturada de las noches sin sueño de Guernica-
Bilbao de bombas truenos y después bombas voladoras
más cohetes V1 V2 cinco años de esto de Hitler y tres de
Franco ocho años abominables de guerras al llegar a los
19 años 1945 mundo loco de la masacre y autodestrucción
del hombre para siempre conflictos mundiales hostiles

La única consolación era una cierta correspondencia
frecuente con mi nueva madre acogedora americana e hijas
a través del Foster Parents' Plan (Women's International
League for Peace and Freedom) 1940-47 la familia de Rose
Comora entonces una beca de la fundación Juan Luis Vives
para estudiar arte en la escuela de arte de Croydon 1942-
1945 ayudó a aliviar los años de guerra atormentados
bombardeos psicotraumáticos yendo en bici al colegio
cuatro veces al día pasando el aeropuerto de Croydon con
refriegas aéreas arriba y balas silbando como flechas
mientras que andaba en bici volviendo a casa por el parque
de Beddington…racionamiento del alimento otro problema
y cupones para ropa además de bombas incendiarias que
apagábamos con las tapas de los cubos de basura cuando
llovían sobre el césped delantero de Culvers House en la
orilla del río Wandle la supervisión tutorial de Pepe y de

Chloë hizo de esta última colonia vasca residencial la empresa más progresiva y talentosa educacional que jamás he vivido esos seis años de domicilio también fueron un período creativo inventivo en mi erudición formativa celebrando mi primera exposición en el Instituto Español 58 Princess Gate London SW1 en 1944 seguida por otras exposiciones en Archer Gallery Westbourne Grove London W11 1946-1951 y muchas exposiciones personales en el centro de Londres en 1993 dibujos pinturas escultura que habían sido mi impulso constante desde que nací en abril de 1926 y creo que es el único resto del logro final de la civilización de tiempos históricos-prehistóricos desde el origen de la especie ... todo esto y la poesía yendo en paralelo con 69 años de exilio vine vi permanecí ad interim y en 2007 nuestro setentavo aniversario expatriado en el Reino Unido el último refugio-consecuencia-1936-1946-2006-2007 de la supervivencia (José María murió en 2009)

Álvaro Martínez Olaizola

Álvaro vino a Inglaterra con su hermana mayor, María Luisa; la hermana mayor escapó a Francia con su madre después de que su padre muriera luchando contra Franco. Tras pasar un tiempo en el campamento, los llevaron a Pampisford, a una rectoría en las afueras de Cambridge; eran 29 niños. Los pequeños permanecieron en la rectoría, donde recibían clases de profesores y estudiantes de la universidad. Después de unos meses los niños tuvieron que abandonar la vicaría y se trasladaron a una casa en Station Road en Cambridge. Aprendieron a cantar y bailar y dieron conciertos para recaudar fondos.

Todos los niños creían que la Guerra Civil terminaría pronto y que regresarían a España. Cuando estalló la Segunda Guerra Mundial, los niños estaban de vacaciones en Hunstanton y tuvieron que volver a Cambridge.

Álvaro tuvo mucha suerte pues le acogió una familia que tenía dos hijos, Mr y Mrs Stearn, y le trataron como a un hijo más. Papá Stearn era el jardinero principal en la casa de una familia aristocrática de Cambridge y solía llevar a Álvaro a los jardines, donde aprendió mucho sobre la profesión de jardinero. Álvaro también fue a la escuela en Cambridge, pero le resultó difícil aprender la lengua; sin embargo consiguió aprender lo suficiente como para defenderse.

Su mayor deseo era ver Londres, así que se marchó de Cambridge y se fue para allá, donde conoció a muchos niños vascos de otros grupos y del suyo, pues solían compartir viviendas. Después de un tiempo encontró trabajo en una empresa de ingeniería llamada Light Alloys donde se especializó en la fabricación de herramientas. Se fue a vivir a Ealing, donde se hizo amigo de una pareja argentina que se instaló en el piso de arriba. Tenían un hijo, Ñato, y una hija, Lale, y el padre trabajaba en la Embajada Argentina en Londres. El padre le dijo a Álvaro que si le interesaba había un puesto vacante en la Embajada, así que Álvaro lo solicitó y lo cogieron. El trabajo consistía en descodificar mensajes y transmitirlos a los argentinos residentes en Inglaterra. A Álvaro lo acogieron como parte de la familia. Lo invitaban a todas las comidas, e incluso hasta hoy en día Álvaro y yo nos hemos mantenido en contacto con Ñato y su familia. Él era capitán de un porta contenedores y siempre nos invitaba a subir a bordo cuando atracaba en Londres. Vivimos en España durante diez años en la década de los noventa y cada vez que venía a España le visitábamos y nos quedábamos a bordo del barco. Nos trataban como reyes: que vida tan maravillosa, pensábamos nosotros. Claro que después de la guerra de las Malvinas ya no podía anclar en Londres así que solíamos ir a Francia, a le Havre a verle.

Álvaro y yo nos casamos en 1958 y para nuestra luna de miel nos fuimos de acampada por los Pirineos. Viajamos allí en lambretta. Como Álvaro no podía ir hasta San Sebastián a ver a su madre, puesto que Franco todavía estaba en el poder, yo hice el viaje sola para conocer a su familia.

Tuvimos tres hijos y en 1965 nos mudamos a Somerset, donde Álvaro se puso a trabajar de ingeniero en la Westland Helicopters. En 1988 cogimos la jubilación anticipada y nos marchamos a Torrevieja, cerca de Alicante, donde teníamos una casa preciosa con piscina. En esa época solíamos tener un almuerzo anual conmemorativo con los *niños* que vivían cerca de Alicante. Volvimos a Inglaterra diez años más tarde para estar más cerca de nuestros nietos. Mirando atrás, pienso que la vida de Álvaro ha sido rica en experiencias y que él es uno de los niños que ha aprovechado al máximo las oportunidades después de unos comienzos tan modestos en otro país.

María Luisa Martínez Olaizola

Mataron a mi padre. A mi hermano y a mí nos mandaron a un orfanato en Bilbao. Nos separaron de nuestra madre y hermana mayor, las cuales se marcharon a Santander y de allí pasaron a Francia por los Pirineos.

Fue muy diferente llegar a Inglaterra. Íbamos en un barco como sardinas en lata, éramos un grupo que nos conocimos en el orfanato. Al llegar a Southampton nos pusieron en un campamento donde organizaron a qué colonia habíamos de ir. Tuvimos suerte: todos los de Bilbao fuimos a Cambridge.

Según lo que dicen, fue la mejor colonia. Primero nos mandaron a la rectoría en Pampisford, a las afueras de Cambridge. Estábamos muy contentos y nos cuidaron muy bien. Era una casa muy grande con campos de tenis y un gran jardín y los establos eran nuestras aulas. El catedrático Eric Hawkins, que acababa de terminar su licenciatura, solía venir a dar clase. Fue maravilloso verlo hace dos años cuando descubrió la placa conmemorativa, me trajo muchos recuerdos.[1]

También recuerdo a un marinero, cuyo padre era catedrático de universidad. Venía a arreglar el jardín, y yo me llevaba muy bien con él. Me escribía desde el Antártico y me contaba sus experiencias, muy interesantes. Continuamos nuestra amistad, pero por desgracia murió el año pasado.

Durante nuestra estancia en Pampisford solíamos hacer gimnasia al aire libre. Cuando mis hijos eran pequeños, encontraron las fotos de nosotros haciendo ejercicios muy divertidas. Mi hermano Álvaro y yo enseñábamos a bailar la jota y dábamos conciertos con canciones vascas para sacar dinero para nuestra manutención, viajábamos a Londres y al condado de Lincoln.

Mi hermano y yo fuimos los primeros en recibir cartas. Nuestra hermana Titi solía escribirnos mucho, ella sabía como hacer que nos llegaran las cartas. Fue una cosa muy acertada que ella se quedara con nuestra madre, pues ésta hubiera estado perdida sin ella.

Cuando tuvimos que marcharnos de Pampisford, Jesus College generosamente nos dejó una casa en Station Road en Cambridge. Estábamos muy contentos y los profesores de la universidad y los voluntarios nos cuidaron fantásticamente allí. Cuando empezó la

---

1. En mayo de 2005, Professor Eric Hawkins descubrió una placa azul en la colonia de Station Road, Cambridge, de parte del Basque Children of '37 Association UK.

Segunda Guerra Mundial se cerró y los mayores tuvieron que ir a trabajar y los menores a la escuela. Como yo ya tenía 14 años y era la edad límite, me mandaron a vivir con un miembro de la comunidad vasca. Allí fui con Amparo Moreno, que era seis meses menor que yo, así que ella iba a la escuela. Pero yo tuve que hacer las tareas domésticas, me pagaban muy poco, dos chelines y seis peniques, y era muy duro para mí.

De allí fui a trabajar a casa de una aristócrata. Me pagaba siete chelines y seis peniques y tenía que llevar un uniforme por la mañana y otro uniforme por la tarde. Estuve muy infeliz allí. Pero la suerte llamó a mi puerta porque mi amiga Carmen Belón, que cuidaba niños en una buena familia, se marchaba a Australia y me habló de ese trabajo. Así fui a trabajar con esa familia y me quedé unos cuantos años, muy feliz. Empecé como niñera y terminé como la hija mayor. Hasta me casé desde su casa.

Conocí a mi marido Brian en Cambridge. Era un estudiante de Gonville and Caius College. Terminé rehaciendo mi vida allí, me casé, tuve hijos y nietos. Aunque soy británica de papel, mi corazón es aún español, aún vasco. Voy a España cada año y me siento como en casa. Se dice que las raíces del terruño tiran, sin embargo después de muchos años aquí me llevaría mucho tiempo acostumbrarme a vivir allí otra vez.

Tomás Núñez Toledo

La situación anterior a mi emigración a Gran Bretaña la denominaría de terror, porque yo sentía un horror desmesurado a los bombardeos de la aviación del dictador, pasando horas e incluso pernoctando en un túnel de un ferrocarril habilitado como refugio. Este fue el motivo por el que mi madre, viuda con dos hijos, el mayor de 17 años que estaba en el frente, se decidiera a enviarme, a los 11 años, fuera de Euskadi ante el miedo que yo sentía por los bombardeos. A pesar de quedarse sola, decidió solicitar mi evacuación a un país amigo.

Al cabo de pocos días se ordenó que pasáramos un reconocimiento médico. Cuál no sería la sorpresa de mi madre cuando le notificaron que me enviaban a la URSS, cuando se suponía que sería a Francia o a Inglaterra. Se negó a enviarme, y no sé por qué medios o en qué forma consiguió pocos días antes de la salida a Gran Bretaña que me incluyeran en dicha expedición.

Salimos de Bilbao el día 20 de mayo de 1937 para Santurce, puerto donde embarcamos en el vapor el *Habana*. Recuerdo la despedida de los familiares de los que emigrábamos que se hizo entre sollozos, lamentos y recomendaciones de nuestros padres que en aquellos momentos pensaban que igual no nos volveríamos a ver...

Anteriormente al embarque nos colocaron en la solapa dos etiquetas, como si fuéramos paquetes a enviar, aunque reconozco que algún distintivo teníamos que llevar para poder reconocernos a los 4.000 niños y niñas que viajábamos.

Emprendimos nuestro viaje por mar y por primera vez sin temor por ignorar por nuestra edad los peligros que este viaje pudiera tener. Lo cierto es que hice un buen viaje, pues con sinceridad, me mareé pero muy poco ya que comí con buen apetito y correteé por el barco por todos aquellos lugares que nos permitieron.

El viaje duró tres días y creo que fue al segundo día nos salió al encuentro un barco de guerra, y la verdad pasamos miedo porque sabíamos que no era barco amigo. Se cruzaron algunas señales de Morse con un destructor inglés que llevábamos de escolta y de pronto el barco enemigo viró a babor del vapor *Habana* y no nos volvió a molestar.

Nuestra llegada al puerto de Southampton fue espectacular porque se encontraba el puerto lleno de personas que nos recibieron con grandes muestras de alegría, y con gran expectación desembarcamos. Nos condujeron a unos autobuses que llamaron mi atención y curiosidad ya que eran de dos pisos y yo nunca había visto semejantes moles. Nos llevaron directamente a un campamento habilitado con tiendas de campaña, metiendo en cada tienda 8 ó 10 personas.

Lo cierto es que lo pasé muy bien. Nos venían los ingleses a ver desde el exterior, ya que el campamento estaba rodeado con alambre de espino, y nos hablaban y nos regalaban golosinas y se portaban con cariño con nosotros. A los tres meses de mi estancia en el campamento tuve un ataque de apendicitis y me llevaron a un centro fuera del campamento que era para los inmigrantes. Me auscultaron e inmediatamente en un turismo me trasladaron al hospital de la ciudad de Winchester, donde nada más llegar, me operaron. Estuve un mes en dicho hospital, pues al parecer hubo alguna complicación de tipo infeccioso. El trato del personal médico, enfermeras, pacientes y familiares de los mismos fue de lo más cordial y atento que se pueda desear. Guardo un grato recuerdo de dicha estancia. Al darme de alta y regresar al campamento, me trasladaron a otra sección porque los chicos con quienes había estado antes habían sido trasladados a una colonia.

Recuerdo un día que discutiendo con otro compañero nos peleamos y me dio un golpe con tal fuerza en el pecho o en el hígado que me tuvieron que llevar a la enfermería porque no podía respirar. (Por cierto, el niño que me golpeó se ve que tenía ya buenas aptitudes y buen *punch* pues luego al correr de los años fue un boxeador de bastante nombre en Bilbao: se llamaba Zulaga) A raíz de esto, conocí a la doctora o enfermera que me atendió que se llamaba Mrs Winifred Russell y vivía en Southampton. A mí y a otro muchacho que se llamaba Juan José Anda y que nos conocíamos por haber estado estudiando en Bilbao en el mismo colegio, nos llevaba a su casa todos los fines de semana, al cine, a parques infantiles para que no nos aburriéramos. En el jardín de su casa, su esposo, que se llamaba Dennis, nos ponía en el respaldo de una silla una moneda de un penique y con una escopeta de aire comprimido tirábamos al blanco y si acertábamos, la moneda era para nosotros. Como a estas edades el dinero es muy goloso y como nosotros no disponíamos de él, afinábamos al máximo y con tal ilusión que casi siempre hacíamos blanco.

Un buen día, encontrándome en el campamento, se acercó la Srta Celia Echevarría, que era la monitora que había tenido antes de operarme, y me preguntó: "¿Tú eres Tomás, sí? Mira, nosotros estamos en viaje como premio de fin de curso de los estudios de este año concedido a los que han conseguido los primeros puestos. ¿Quieres venirte con nosotros a la colonia?" Yo, bien por la novedad o por conocer otros lugares, acepté, y me fui a Langham cerca de Colchester donde fui muy feliz hasta el punto de no querer volver a Euskadi como después explicaré.

En la colonia de Langham pasé los mejores meses de mi estancia en Gran Bretaña. Teníamos unos directores, Mr Stirling, Srta Celia Echeverría, profesores Mr Theo Wills, Srta Amada, monitores Mr Leonard, Otto y alguno más que no recuerdo, que fueron nuestros segundos padres en nuestra segunda patria. Estudiábamos todos los días laborables español e inglés. Teníamos muchas diversiones: jugar al tenis, al hockey sobre hierba, al fútbol. Íbamos a un riachuelo cercano a nadar, se organizaban excursiones a playas y competiciones balompédicas con otras colonias. Se hacían e intercambiaban obras teatrales con otras colonias y sociedades para sufragar gastos. Se hacían muñecas con trajes típicos andaluces. Tarros de mermelada grandes se pintaban con alegorías para usar como floreros: todo para beneficio nuestro. Bailábamos entre nosotros en el salón de actos, teníamos un coro en el cual cantábamos un repertorio de canciones regionales y alguna inglesa. En fin, éramos inmensamente felices. Tanto que quizás por mi edad y poco conocimiento de la vida, ni añoraba mi patria chica ni mi familia aunque escribía periódicamente a mi madre y a mi hermano que cayó preso por los franquistas.

Cuando se me comunicó con unos días de anticipación que tenía que regresar a Bilbao, estaba tan feliz en Langham que un compañero apellidado Rivera y yo cogimos dos bicicletas y nos escapamos. En cuanto notaron la falta, avisaron y a las pocas horas la policía nos devolvió a la colonia. Por cierto que no nos castigaron.

En fin, muchas cosas podría contar pero la memoria falla. Una cosa muy curiosa: en mi habitación en la que dormíamos cuatro, Recaredo, Félix, Eloy y yo, Eloy era sonámbulo y nos pasamos las grandes juergas cuando se levantaba dormido a dar paseos por los pasillos o dependencias.

El regreso fue más triste. Atravesamos el estrecho de Calais y nos metieron en un tren hasta Hendaya. Al llegar allí y según íbamos pasando todos agrupados por el puente internacional, se subió sobre el pilar de sustentación de la barrera un señor uniformado y con una boina roja, gritando: "¡Viva España! ¡Viva Franco!" y la verdad todos estábamos un poco asustados. Nos pasaron a la aduana donde nos revisaron y nos preguntaron si llevábamos dinero inglés y nos dieron dos bocadillos hermosos y dos plátanos. Nos metieron al tren y nos llevaron al Colegio del Amor Misericordioso en Bilbao, donde nos recogieron nuestros padres. Yo por cierto, a pesar de estar con mi madre, estaba cohibido y extraño por tanta aglomeración y luego, acostumbrado a oír inglés y aquí el castellano, lo extrañé mucho.

Esperanza Ortiz de Zárate

Cuando estalló la Guerra Civil en España yo tenía nueve años. Vivía con mi familia (éramos cinco hermanos: tres chicas y dos chicos, yo quedaba en medio) en Zaldívar, un pueblo pequeño de Vizcaya. Nuestro padre era institutor del pueblo. Nuestra vida tranquila paró repentinamente cuando estalló la guerra en julio de 1936. Después del bombardeo de Guernica el 26 de abril de 1937, la situación empeoró y mis padres abandonaron nuestra casa para trasladarse a

Bilbao. Cuando el gobierno vasco anunció que había organizado una evacuación de niños a Inglaterra, supongo que mis padres vieron la salvación y decidieron apuntarnos a mi hermana y a mí. Mi hermana Pili que tenía dos años y medio más que yo, no quería ir. Yo, sin embargo, estaba contenta, pues todo me parecía una aventura.

La noche antes de nuestra partida nos dimos cuenta de que faltaba mi hermana. La buscamos por todos los lados, incluso en la calle, y por fin la encontramos escondida en el armario ropero. Lloraba desconsoladamente y mis padres pasaron horas persuadiéndola y diciéndole que íbamos sólo por tres meses.

El 20 de mayo de 1937 amaneció triste y sombrío, como todos los días desde que llegamos a Bilbao. Mi madre nos dijo que nos llevaría mi padre a Santurce porque ella no podía ir con los pequeños. El momento de despedida fue horrible. Cuando llegamos a la estación para ir a Santurce el andén estaba repleto de padres y niños. En el momento de despedirnos mi padre nos abrazó, nos prometió que nos escribiría mucho. Vi que se le humedecieron las gafas: era la primera vez que veía llorar a mi padre.

Todo lo que me acuerdo del viaje es que el barco estaba abarrotado con tanta gente.

La llegada a Southampton fue para mí como un cuento de hadas. Las casitas que se divisaban a lo lejos me hicieron pensar que entrábamos en el País de las Maravillas, tan distintas a los bloques de pisos de Bilbao.

Nos llevaron a un campamento enorme con tiendas de campaña en Eastleigh. Mi primera impresión de los ingleses voluntarios en el campo, con sus pantalones cortos, fue que eran larguiruchos y delgados, tipos muy distintos a los hombres del País Vasco. Había que hacer cola para todo, excepto para los retretes – unas zanjas en la tierra con tablones de madera cruzados – muy precarios, sobre todo para los pequeños.

Semanas después de llegar al campamento nos trasladaron a una escuela católica de las Hermanas de la Caridad en Manchester. Éramos un grupo de 15 a 20 chicas, yo era de las más jóvenes. Me fascinaba la vestimenta de las Hermanas – tocas blancas como la nieve, muy almidonadas, parecían que iban a coger vuelo en cualquier momento. Asistíamos a las clases y, aunque no hablábamos la lengua, en las asignaturas que no requerían inglés, como, por ejemplo, geografía, sacábamos buenas notas. Recuerdo también que las monjas se quedaron extrañadas de nuestro método de hacer la división. Varias veces recibimos estrellas que decían "*Excellent*" que colocamos con mucho orgullo en el cuaderno.

Un día una de las Hermanas nos dijo que saliéramos a la entrada del convento donde nos esperaba un grupo de periodistas y fotógrafos. Nos hicieron muchas fotos y nos pedían que levantáramos el puño, sin duda para continuar la propaganda que algunos periódicos estaban perpetuando de que éramos hijas de rojos. Esto enfureció a las chicas mayores.

Después nos llevaron a la colonia de Bray Court, una mansión bastante abandonada entre Maidenhead y Windsor, donde residían ya alrededor de 100 niños y niñas vascos. Solían venir ingleses a la colonia para invitar a los niños a pasar el día. Así conocimos a Mr y Mrs Rickards, un matrimonio que nos sacaba a mi hermana y a mí todos los miércoles. Nunca olvidaré mi impresión al llegar a su casa. Me parecía enorme, estaba rodeada de jardines preciosos. Cuando nos sentamos a comer, la mesa estaba tan elegante, con una vajilla preciosa y tantos cubiertos de plata, que ni mi hermana ni yo sabíamos con qué cubierto empezar. Tenían tres niños más jóvenes que nosotras y nos sorprendió mucho su buen comportamiento en la mesa. Parecía que los niños ingleses no hablaban en la mesa como nosotros estábamos acostumbrados en casa.

En la colonia de Bray Court nos sentimos más felices, a pesar de que la comida era bastante pobre y en el invierno hacía mucho frío, pues no había calefacción. Teníamos clases pero no con regularidad porque había otros quehaceres como ayudar en las tareas de la casa y ensayar para los muchos conciertos de bailes vascos que presentábamos en Londres y sus alrededores para recaudar fondos para nuestra manutención.

Cuando se cerró esta colonia, nos trasladaron a The Oaks, en Carshalton, Surrey, a una hora aproximadamente de Londres. The Oaks era una mansión deshabitada donde habían acomodado a unos 20 niños y niñas en una ala que hicieron habitable. La llegada a The Oaks después de la colonia de Bray Court fue como llegar al Ritz. La comida era excelente, el cocinero usaba sombrero alto de chef y nos hacía unos postres que quitaban el hipo, con el resultado que yo inmediatamente engordé varios kilos.

Cuando se declaró la Segunda Guerra Mundial el 3 de septiembre de 1939, un día de mucho calor, nos encontrábamos de vacaciones en tiendas de campaña en Hayling Island, al sur de Inglaterra. Estaba a nuestro cargo Mr. Edgar Philips, miembro del comité, quien inmediatamente hizo los arreglos para nuestro regreso a la colonia. Mr Philips era un hombre con gran simpatía a la causa republicana que dedicaba todo su tiempo libre a los niños vascos y a mejorar nuestras vidas.

Pocos días después, nos informaron de que el gobierno inglés no estaba dispuesto a que continuáramos en Inglaterra. El comité empezó inmediatamente a apuntar a los niños que podían regresar, pero se opuso a que aquellos cuyos padres habían fallecido o estaban encarcelados fuesen repatriados. Mi hermana y yo éramos las únicas en la colonia que no podíamos volver: nuestro padre estaba preso y nuestra madre había sido desterrada del pueblo y vivía en Eibar con una hermana que le acogió con mis dos hermanos pequeños.

Al quedarnos solas, nos trasladaron a otra colonia muy cercana, The Culvers, también en Carshalton, Surrey, donde ya residía un grupo no muy numeroso de niños. En esta colonia el régimen era parecido al de la anterior pero la comida no como en el Ritz. Teníamos clases, pero tampoco con regularidad pues había que ayudar con la limpieza de la casa. Yo estaba encargada de lavar y planchar la ropa de los chicos.

Una catástrofe que jamás olvidaré fue mi primera experiencia culinaria. Mi hermana y yo preparábamos la comida, espaguetis a la boloñesa. Estábamos en la pequeña cocina. Mi hermana había llenado de agua el enorme puchero y al hervir el agua, había metido los espaguetis. Segundos antes de empezar a hervir los espaguetis, mi hermana fue al retrete, encargándome que cuidara de la olla. Cuando empezó a hervir el espagueti no había forma de pararlo. Me asusté de tal manera que estaba paralizada y en unos segundos el fogón y el suelo de la cocina estaban cubiertos de una alfombra de espagueti. Salí gritando de la cocina y alguien que me oyó vino a socorrerme. Apagó el gas y logró parar el "volcán". El suelo estaba tan resbaladizo que tardamos horas en limpiarlo. Nunca más me delegaron nada en la cocina, pero ¡tuve que aguantar muchas bromas por largo tiempo!

En esta colonia el ambiente era feliz. Recuerdo especialmente a la Directora, Miss Chloë Vulliamy, una señora rechoncha que hablaba el inglés con ese acento superior que en Inglaterra clasifica enseguida a las personas de alto nivel social, y a Pepe Estruch, español exiliado, de ideas progresistas y muy culto, que nos introdujo a la literatura española, a las obras de teatro de Unamuno y de Lorca y, en general, despertó en nosotros la curiosidad y las ganas de aprender que por años habían estado latentes.

Los años iban pasando y el comité de la colonia decidió enviarme a Pitman's Secretarial College en Londres, para prepararme a la vida activa. En el colegio hice un curso de un año. Me levantaba temprano para coger el tren de Londres, con mis libros y bocadillos que llevaba para la comida. Siempre recordaré con gran afecto a Mrs Somerset, la cocinera escocesa de la colonia, que con tanto cariño me preparaba los bocadillos, con su cigarrillo en la boca, mientras yo desayunaba. Casi diariamente teníamos interrupciones en clase a causa de las bombas.

Más tarde, el gobierno republicano en el exilio, encabezado por el Dr Juan Negrín, creó la Juan Luís Vives Trust para la educación de los niños vascos y otros refugiados, y un número de chicos y chicas fuimos beneficiarios de becas. Recibíamos £3 por semana para renta y manutención, una cantidad no muy generosa, considerando que vivíamos independientemente en Londres donde compartíamos un piso con otras tres amigas vascas. Estudiábamos en Regent Street Polytechnic, Londres, también con muchas interrupciones en las clases pues Londres seguía siendo el objetivo de los aviones alemanes. Afortunadamente no sufrimos ningún daño, aunque una bomba volante cayó en Earl's Court, cerca de nuestra casa. Una noche fuimos a dormir al metro para evadir las bombas, como lo hacían muchos londinenses, pero fue una experiencia tan desagradable que preferíamos quedarnos en casa cuando sonaba la sirena.

Durante los años de la guerra se formó en Londres el Hogar Español, un centro subvencionado por el gobierno republicano en el exilio donde se reunían muchos refugiados de la Guerra Civil. Para los chicos vascos, ya adolescentes, aquel centro fue un verdadero hogar, donde pasábamos todos nuestros ratos libres. El ambiente era muy político, como es de esperar. Se celebraban conferencias y conciertos y se organizaban manifestaciones contra el régimen franquista. Allí se formó nuestra organización "Amistad". Bautista López, que más tarde llegó a ser mi marido, fue por algún tiempo presidente. Los domingos se celebraba baile donde nos encontrábamos con otros amigos que venían de fuera. Así conocí a Bautista. Él había vivido en Londres pero al comienzo de la guerra se había desplazado a Stafford, en el centro de Inglaterra donde, con un grupo de chicos vascos, trabajaba en la English Electric donde se fabricaba material de guerra.

En el Hogar Español, bajo la dirección de Pepe Estruch, se formó un grupo artístico y representábamos obras de teatro y conciertos.

Manuel Lazareno, otro exiliado, dirigía un excelente coro en el que muchos de los chicos vascos tomábamos parte. Celebramos conciertos en el Albert Hall y en la BBC. El año después de finalizar la guerra hicimos una gira por Francia y Checoslovaquia para recaudar fondos para los presos en España. En Praga conocimos a Dolores Ibarruri, la Pasionaria.

Mi padre nos escribía muchas cartas y poesías en los siete años que estuvo preso, siempre dándonos consejos que fuéramos honradas, que estuviéramos agradecidas a las personas que nos cuidaban y que no olvidáramos a España, pronto vendrían tiempos mejores. Estoy segura de que estas cartas nos ayudaron a conservar vivo nuestro grato recuerdo de España.

Durante nuestra niñez topamos con gente muy buena que nos cuidaba lo mejor posible, a quienes estaré eternamente agradecida. No obstante, me veo obligada a decir que nuestra educación estuvo muy abandonada, probablemente por falta de recursos y porque nuestra estancia en Inglaterra iba a ser corta. La guerra en Londres fue dura pero a mí, personalmente, me afectó mucho más la Guerra Civil y sus consecuencias. El haberme separado de mis padres a tan tierna edad y el sentirme abandonada me afectó mucho. Sé que todo fue por salvarnos, pero si ahora volviera a ocurrir algo semejante, mi consejo a mi hija sería que no se separara de sus niños.
(Espe Lopez murió el 28 de marzo de 2007.)

Agustina Pérez San José

Salí de Bilbao a los siete años en mayo de 1937; me acompañaban mi hermana mayor, Asun, que tenía entonces 13 años, y un hermano más pequeño, Antonio (Tony), que tenía cinco. Atrás quedaron mis padres, dos hermanas mayores y nuestros dos hermanos más pequeños.

Tan pronto como nos subimos al barco, que iba abarrotado de niños, perdí de vista a mi hermano y a mi hermana y ya no los volví a ver hasta que llegamos al campamento de Eastleigh el 23 de mayo. Todavía recuerdo vagamente a la señora que me dio una cinta blanca y me dijo que me la pusiera en la muñeca. A otra niña de la que me hice amiga le dieron una cinta roja. Como el rojo había sido siempre mi color favorito nos cambiamos las cintas. ¡Qué poco podía yo imaginar el significado de las diferentes cintas de colores! Sin embargo, no tardé mucho en averiguarlo. A los que llevaban cintas rojas nos separaron de los que las llevaban blancas. El autobús al que me subieron nos llevó a los baños públicos. Me acuerdo de la sorpresa y del miedo que sentí cuando nos mostraron la piscina. Yo nunca había visto una. Me acuerdo de que me llevaron a un cubículo, me cortaron el pelo y después me dieron un baño. Me llevaron al campamento y descubrí que la maleta pequeña que había traído conmigo de Bilbao con la única muda de ropa que nos dejaron llevar y un pequeño libro que me había traído habían desaparecido y ya no los volví a ver más.

No nos quedamos mucho tiempo en Eastleigh. Fuimos unos de los primeros grupos que se marcharon del campamento. Nos trasladaron a Brampton, una pequeña ciudad en la región de Cumbria. El viaje duró todo el día y llegamos por la tarde y nos llevaron a una casa muy grande que parecía una mansión. Dormí en un dormitorio muy grande con otras seis niñas de mi edad. Tenía una gran chimenea en una de las paredes y una puerta que conducía a un servicio. En Brampton me sentí feliz y segura. Era maravilloso no tener que oír las sirenas de los bombardeos, ni el ruido de disparos que en aquellos momentos era tan normal en Bilbao.

En la colonia había unos cuantos maestros y ayudantes españoles que habían venido con nosotros. De vez en cuando recibíamos la visita de un cura español. También estaba un tal Mr Froelich, un refugiado judío austriaco que había conseguido escapar de su país. De todos los maestros y adultos que había, Mr Froelich era mi favorito. Él era profesor de física y hablaba perfectamente español e inglés. Nos leía y nos contaba historias a menudo. De vez en cuando nos llevaba a Carlisle.

Mi hermano y yo a veces pasábamos hambre en Brampton, lo cual nos recordaba a la Guerra Civil. Por suerte, una de las tareas de mi hermana era preparar y servir la cena en el comedor de los adultos. Cuando le tocaba a ella servir, Tony y yo corríamos desde el jardín y nos escondíamos debajo de la ventana del comedor antes de que llegaran los maestros para comer. Asun nos pasaba una salchicha, una patata, un trozo de pan. A la hora del té era una galleta o un trozo de pastel.

La casa en la que vivíamos pertenecía a Sir Wilfrid Roberts, que en esa época era un diputado del Parlamento por el partido Liberal. Recuerdo a su madre, Lady Cecilia, que para nosotros era alguien muy especial. A veces venía a vernos y pasaba tiempo con nosotros u otras veces nos invitaba a su hermosa casa de campo, que para nosotros era como un palacio. Me acuerdo de un día en que nos mostró sus pequeños tesoros. En otras ocasiones nos llevaba a pasear por su lindo jardín. Siempre que íbamos allí nos llevaba y nos traía de vuelta su chófer. Su hija era artista y solía venir a la colonia a enseñar a los niños mayores a pintar.

Poco a poco algunos niños iban volviendo a España. Nosotros no podíamos volver porque mi madre y mis dos hermanos pequeños estaban en un campo de refugiados francés. A mis dos hermanas, que se habían quedado en Bilbao cuando nos evacuaron a nosotros, las acogieron unas monjas en un lugar cerca de Bilbao. Mi padre, que había luchado con los Republicanos en la defensa de Bilbao antes de ser capturado en Santander en el verano de 1937, era ahora un prisionero de guerra en España.

Años más tarde mi padre me contó que cuando le capturaron los soldados de Franco lo llevaron, junto con otros miles de soldados republicanos, a la plaza de toros. Allí esperaban ser fusilados, tal como lo habían sido otros Republicanos que habían sido ejecutados en la plaza de toros de Badajoz al comienzo de la guerra. Sin embargo, lo que les salvó la vida fue un contingente de soldados italianos que recibieron órdenes de su oficial de interponerse entre los prisioneros republicanos y las tropas de Franco y que rehusaron moverse hasta recibir garantías de que los prisioneros no serían fusilados.

Permanecimos en Brampton durante dos años, hasta mediados de 1939, cuando a mi hermano y a mí nos enviaron a vivir con Mr y Mrs Nichol en el área de Knightswood, en Glasgow. Esto supuso la separación de nuestra hermana Asun, pues las autoridades no pudieron encontrar una familia que pudiese cuidar de los tres. A ella la enviaron a vivir con Mr y Mrs Phillips y sus tres niños en Clyde Park, que también estaba cerca de Glasgow.

A mi hermano y a mí nos gustaba vivir con la familia Nichol. El hijo Billy estaba estudiando para maestro. Nos enviaron a la escuela local en Knightswood, donde aprendimos rápidamente el inglés con acento escocés. Esto tuvo un gran impacto en mí, pero incluso más en mi hermano Tony, que debía de tener seis o siete años por entonces. Incluso hoy en día, Tony habla inglés con un acento escocés muy fuerte.

Los sábados por las mañanas íbamos al cine de Annisland con nuestros nuevos "primos", Archie y Nichol McLean. "*Auntie Mary*", su madre, era hermana de Mr Nichol. Los domingos íbamos a su casa a cenar. Jugábamos al Monopoly y a otros juegos de mesa. También nos enseñaron juegos de cartas con barajas inglesas. El abuelo Nichol, que vivía con ellos, a veces jugaba con nosotros. Era un personaje encantador y un gran hombre. Había sido ingeniero y había trabajado en los Estados Unidos. Nos fascinaban sus historias sobre la vida americana. Tenía fuertes convicciones antifascistas y odiaba con pasión a Franco, Hitler y Mussolini.

Mr Nichol trabajaba en el ayuntamiento de Glasgow. Nos llevó allí una o dos veces a echar un vistazo. Tristemente, nuestra estancia con ellos no duró mucho tiempo. De 1940 a 1941 la Luftwaffe bombardeó ferozmente Glasgow y Clydebank. Varias escuelas, y entre ellas la nuestra, fueron evacuadas al suroeste de Escocia. A la mayoría de los niños de nuestra escuela nos llevaron a Gatehouse of Fleet, que está en Kircudbrightshire, un pequeño condado en el suroeste de Escocia.

Gatehouse es un pequeño y precioso pueblo del Solway Firth. Tony y yo vivimos con Mr y Mrs Halliday y su hija Betty que era peluquera. La mayoría de los jóvenes fueron llamados a servicio y algunos nunca volvieron. Unos pocos se quedaron trabajando la tierra. Tanto la comida como la gasolina fueron racionadas. Aún recuerdo que nos permitían ocho onzas de caramelos por persona al mes. El racionamiento duró hasta 1952 o 1953. La leche y el pan no estaban racionados, tampoco el pollo, ni el pescado. Mrs Halliday siempre tenía comida en la despensa, por eso nunca pasamos hambre. Debo añadir que no faltaban los conejos o las liebres, y para el caso, los cazadores furtivos.

Íbamos a la escuela del pueblo y pronto hicimos amigos. Al mismo tiempo que aprendíamos inglés, íbamos perdiendo el español, hasta el punto que cuando salí de Gatehouse para Londres en 1946 lo había olvidado completamente, lo mismo que mi hermano Tony, que se reunió con Asun y conmigo uno o dos años después.

En el pueblo a mi hermano le llamaban "el pequeño escocés" porque de vez en cuando se vestía con falda escocesa. Un domingo volvió a casa después de jugar al cricket en el parque y Mr Halliday se dio cuenta de lo que había estado haciendo y le gritó: "¡Pequeño pagano!" Mr Halliday tenía unos principios presbiterianos muy fuertes y los domingos nunca se le veía ni siquiera leer un periódico.

En Gatehouse íbamos a misa los domingos. También nos apuntamos al movimiento de los *boy scouts*; Tony se hizo *scout* y yo guía. Una vez al mes se organizaba un desfile desde la iglesia. Para los jóvenes participar en el desfile era el punto álgido del mes. Después de misa salíamos de la iglesia y nos incorporábamos a nuestros puestos. Participaban en el desfile la Guardia Metropolitana[1] , que allí estaba formada principalmente por granjeros y peones de granja, así como por hombres que trabajaban en la Comisión de Bosques y en el Servicio Social Voluntario, y luego estábamos nosotros – los *scouts*, guías y exploradoras. El encargado de organizar el desfile era el carnicero local, que había sido capitán en la guerra de 1914 a 1918. La mayoría de los hombres de la Guardia Metropolitana también habían participado en esa guerra.

Con los uniformes teníamos un aspecto brillante y elegante. El capitán, o mejor dicho, el carnicero, se colgaba todas sus insignias y se paseaba de arriba y abajo pasándonos revista. Después llegaba el momento de marchar por la calle principal. Allí nos daba órdenes: "¡Descansen!" "¡ Firmes!" "¡Derecha, Izquierda!" y también decía muchas más cosas.

En enero y febrero, después de ir a la iglesia, iba con unas mujeres y algunas chicas al campo a coger campanillas. Las cogíamos, las empaquetábamos y las enviábamos por tren a la Cruz Roja de Glasgow, donde las vendían para reunir fondos para la guerra. En la primavera, hacíamos lo mismo con los narcisos y las prímulas. En verano cogíamos un musgo llamado *"sphagnum"*, del que había mucha demanda porque servía para hacer vendajes.

A veces siento un poco de melancolía cuando me doy cuenta de lo agitadas que han sido nuestras vidas. Me casé con un refugiado vasco. Los dos hemos trabajado muy duro. Hemos tenido una familia maravillosa y dos nietos que son la alegría de nuestras vidas.

Aunque he sido feliz en el Reino Unido a veces me pregunto cómo hubieran sido nuestras vidas si no nos hubiésemos separado de nuestras familias tan temprano. Los echamos mucho de menos y no podíamos evitar preocuparnos por ellos. El primer año tras nuestra llegada no tuvimos ninguna noticia de ellos. Después, una señora inglesa escribió a mi hermana en Brampton diciéndole que había estado visitando los campos de refugiados en Francia y que había hablado con nuestra madre y con nuestros hermanos y que los tres estaban bien.

---

1. Nota de traducción: A la Guardia Metropolitana (*Home Guard*) originariamente se la llamó "Voluntarios de Defensa Local" pero a partir del 27.06.1940 pasó a denominarse como tal. Este cuerpo pseudo-militar lo integraban voluntarios civiles que no habían sido movilizados para el frente y que no obstante se sentían útiles.

Si pudiera vivir mi vida de nuevo, y sabiendo lo que sé ahora, creo que hubiera preferido arriesgarme a lo que fuera y permanecer con el resto de ellos. La mayoría de nosotros éramos demasiado jóvenes para que nos separaran de nuestras familias a una edad tan temprana, porque eso te marca para el resto de tu vida. Al mismo tiempo creo que, debido a las experiencias que hemos compartido, he hecho muchos amigos entre mis compañeros los niños vascos, amigos que lo han sido para toda la vida. Algunos, como yo, eran de Brampton, pero la mayoría de los que conocí acabaron viviendo en Londres después de la guerra.

He conocido a personas maravillosas en este país, pero siempre sentiré un cariño especial por los escoceses. Fueron siempre agradables, alegres, cálidos y con un gran corazón. Nunca olvidaré su cariño y la amabilidad que tuvieron con nosotros.*

Cora Portillo

Mientras cursaba mi carrera de estudios hispánicos en la Universidad de Oxford no pude realizar mi año de prácticas en el extranjero puesto que a partir de 1936 ya no se podía entrar en España. Así que mi tutor encontró a una señora mayor de Valencia para que me diera clases de conversación. Un día, conocí a una joven de Bilbao que se estaba alojando en casa de esta señora; era una de las voluntarias que había acompañado, con una maestra, al grupo de niños evacuados a Inglaterra en mayo de 1937. Se llamaba Pili Merodio y era la "madre de casa" en la colonia de Aston, a cinco millas de Witney en Oxfordshire. Así que el sábado siguiente cogí el autobús y me dirigí allí. Esto fue el principio de toda una etapa nueva en mi vida.

La colonia era un lugar alegre. Era muy pequeña, y estaba organizada por una sección local del Basque Children's Committee que era excelente. La dirigía la familia Early, que eran dueños de la fábrica de mantas de Witney. Al llegar los niños, le dieron a cada uno una manta de lana roja. Entre las personas de la comunidad que también se involucraron en la vida de la colonia figuraban la esposa del médico, la señora Dalgleish, y el dueño de una tienda de bicicletas en Witney, el señor Tidy, que proveyó a los niños de bicicletas. El día a día de la colonia lo organizaba Pili con la ayuda de Ketty, que era la mayor entre las chicas adolescentes que habían llegado. El ambiente de la casa era de compartir: las penas, las alegrías y las cosas materiales.

La casa tenía un jardín precioso que a los niños les encantaba, sobretodo habiendo salido de un Bilbao destrozado por la guerra. Pero por dentro las condiciones eran muy austeras: no había agua corriente y apenas una cocina de carbón para calentar el agua. La única habitación que tenía calefacción era la cocina; en la parte de arriba, hacía muchísimo frío.

A los niños les gustaba mucho recibir visitas y los fines de semana cuando alguien venía se agolpaban bajo las escaleras entre chirridos de alegría. Aparte de mí, entre los visitantes más frecuentes se encontraba Geoffrey Turner de la Universidad de Oxford quien a pesar de andar con muletas a causa de la polio, llevaba siempre bajo un brazo un gramófono y bajo el otro una caja de discos de canciones y danzas españolas, los cuales eran imprescindibles pues los niños tenían que dar conciertos para recaudar fondos que asegurasen su manutención. Otro visitante regular era un joven de 19 años, Edwin Edwards, que trabajaba en la biblioteca de Oxford. Había aprendido español por su cuenta y era uno de los personajes más simpáticos que he conocido. Los niños le llamaban 'Eduardísimo'. Era como un hermano mayor para ellos. ¡Solía bombear agua durante horas para llenar el tanque para el baño semanal!

A medida que la Segunda Guerra Mundial se iba gestando y Franco empezaba a exigir la repatriación de "sus" niños, las colonias se empezaron a cerrar y al mismo tiempo se organizaban los viajes de retorno. Aston fue una de las últimas colonias en cerrar y un sábado cuando llegué me dijeron que nos habían enviado a un profesor español. (Obviamente, los refugiados adultos permanecieron exiliados y a muchos académicos e intelectuales españoles se les ofreció asilo provisional en las residencias del personal universitario) Nuestro visitante, Luis Portillo, había sido profesor auxiliar de Derecho Civil en la Universidad de Salamanca antes de unirse al ejército republicano. A causa de esto fue cesado en su puesto. Entonces sirvió en el departamento jurídico del ministerio de guerra a cargo del ministro vasco Manuel de Irujo. Pili y yo nos dimos cuenta de que aunque llevaba un anillo de casado, en realidad no estaba casado pero tenía una prometida en Vitoria …Yo me sentí inmediatamente atraída a este personaje tan romántico y cuando trasladaron a las últimas chicas que quedaban, a Pili y a otra "madre de casa" a una vivienda social en Witney, Luis y yo continuamos visitándolas. Él encontró una habitación modesta de alquiler en Oxford en la esquina de St Hilda's College por cinco chelines a la semana y ganaba dinero pelando patatas en una cafetería once horas al día.

Al final nos prometimos: en vez de mis padres fue mi hermana quien "inspeccionó" a Luis quien tuvo que superar la prueba de visitar a mis padres conmigo para que lo examinaran de arriba abajo. A su favor jugaba el que fuese un profesor con exquisitos modales, pero …¡ sin un penique, un católico, un extranjero!

A pesar de todo, Luis pronto aprendió a defenderse en inglés (sobretodo a base de leer el *Times*) lo suficiente como para conseguir un buen trabajo con Reuters, traduciendo los discursos de Churchill ¡menuda responsabilidad! Nos casamos en marzo de 1941, en la cripta de la catedral católica de Westmimster (ya que yo soy protestante) pero se permitió que un cura vasco Onaindía participara junto al cura residente en la ceremonia. La recepción fue en la Embajada Vasca, por invitación de Don Miguel de Irujo y mis hermanas se encargaron de servir las bebidas mientras que yo acompañaba a Luis a registrarse como extranjero para obtener un documento de viaje que le permitiera ir de luna de miel. Cuando volvimos a la recepción apenas nos dio tiempo de un brindis pues inmediatamente después salimos a coger el tren para Oxford. Una vez allí, fuimos andando a campo traviesa, Luis cargando con una pesada maleta, para llegar a una modesta granja que nos habían recomendado unos amigos españoles. Seguro que no hay mucha gente que haya tenido una boda tan austera. Sin velo, sin vestido blanco…

Tuvimos cinco hijos y aunque pasaron diecinueve años antes de que Luis pudiera volver a visitar a su familia en España, yo sí que pude llevar a los chicos a ver a sus parientes españoles. Sus padres nos visitaron una vez, cuando se atrevieron a viajar en avión. Luis murió a los 86 años.*

Paco Robles Hernándo

Pasamos en el *Habana* tres noches muy malas de vómitos, y sin poder dormir, porque no encontrábamos camas. Por fin en la mañana del 23 de mayo vimos que habíamos llegado a Southampton, Inglaterra, y en cubierta había varios médicos con chaquetas blancas, que nos daban a todos inyecciones antes de desembarcar. La ruta del puerto a Eastleigh, adonde nos llevaban, estaba llena de banderas y decoraciones: yo creí que era para nosotros pero luego entendí que eran las banderas que pusieron los ingleses para celebrar la coronación del Rey Jorge VI de Inglaterra.

En el campo de Eastleigh nos metieron a casi todos en tiendas de campaña. Éramos ocho personas, no nos desnudábamos y muchos cogieron pulgas, piojos y lo peor que cogimos la mayoría era sarna, que llevamos con nosotros a las colonias. Venían a vernos los ingleses en bicicleta, y nos traían caramelos, pasteles y muchos bizcochos. Claro, muchos de nosotros cogimos diarrea porque no habíamos comido eso desde hacía casi un año; sólo habíamos comido pan negro y carne de caballo, y en algunos casos, yo había visto a vecinas pelando sus gatos para comerlos. En Eastleigh, todas las mañanas nos tocaban música en los altavoces, tocaban *Land of Hope and Glory*. Ese toque a mí se me quedó marcado para el resto de mi vida, y es una de mis canciones favoritas.

Yo fui destinado a Wherstead Park, Ipswich, y en esa colonia estábamos muy contentos. Había jardines grandes y un pequeño bosque y en otoño los dueños de las propiedades venían a cazar. Nosotros los chicos buscábamos los pájaros para ellos, haciendo el trabajo de los perros de caza, y los amos nos daban seis peniques por cada pájaro que encontrábamos. Después de unos meses en Wherstead Park, nos llevaron a Wickham Market; la colonia estaba en un hospital viejo, muy antiguo, que había cerrado años antes y lo abrieron para nosotros. A mí no me gustaba esa colonia, porque sufríamos de sarna que trajeron unos niños que vinieron de otra colonia y además estaba llena de ratas.

Poco tiempo después de llegar allí nos trajeron maestros para enseñarnos el inglés: yo no quería aprenderlo porque lo encontraba muy difícil de pronunciar, y además como nos dijeron que volveríamos a España en meses, ¿para qué iba yo a aprender la lengua? Por fin decidí interesarme en el inglés, porque hay una frase que me gustó, y se me quedó grabada en la mente porque era fácil de pronunciar, y esa frase era: "*I think so*". De todas formas tuve mucho interés en aprender el idioma con un amigo Pedro Encinas: salí yo primero en inglés y él segundo y como regalo nos llevaron a Londres por una semana de vacaciones.

Después de varias colonias, como Margate, me adoptó una familia de Birmingham y pasé dos años con ellos. Lo pasé muy mal, porque sólo me querían para trabajar en una pequeña granja que tenían donde me tenía que levantar a las 6 de la mañana a dar de comer a las cabras y los cerdos, limpiar la cuadra, y luego tenía que ir a la escuela a cinco millas de distancia. En la escuela yo era uno de los más listos porque lo que enseñaban yo ya lo había aprendido en los Salesianos de Baracaldo, así es que los maestros me apreciaban mucho. A los dos años volví a Margate, y luego nos llevaron a Carshalton. Terminamos mi hermana y yo en Rowley Lodge en Barnet. Yo empecé a trabajar en una fábrica de guerra en Boreham Wood y de allí fui a trabajar en una panadería en Barnet High Street.

Como nuestra colonia estaba en línea recta con las fábricas de Boreham Wood, y además nuestros vecinos eran un cuartel de soldados, caían bombas cerca, y una mañana a eso de la una, nos cayó una bomba de 1,000 kilos en el jardín de la casa y mató a todos los animales que teníamos. Tuvimos la suerte de que ninguno de nosotros salimos muertos o heridos. Al caer esta bomba, la policía organizó autobuses y nos llevaron a unos salones de ancianos cuidados por monjas, y para nosotros había dos salones, uno para las chicas y otro para los chicos, esto era en High Barnet.

Seguíamos yendo a trabajar, y después de dos semanas nos dijeron que ya tenían otra casa para nosotros a unas tres o cuatro millas de distancia. Eso fue un viernes a eso de las seis de la tarde: nos dijeron que el sábado por la mañana pondrían dos autobuses para llevarnos a esta casa en New Barnet, pero que si nosotros queríamos, nos daban las señas de la casa nueva y podíamos ir esa misma tarde. Todos decidimos irnos el viernes, ¡y menos mal! porque a eso de las tres de la mañana del sábado cayó en ese mismo centro lo que llamaban una mina aérea que caen en paracaídas con mucha potencia explosiva y arrasó todo donde habíamos estado viviendo por casi un cuarto de milla cuadrada, matando a monjas y ancianos que habían quedado viviendo allí. Luego después de New Barnet, fuimos a otra colonia en Woodside Park. Y de allí fuimos a Landsdown Walk, Holland Park. Después de poco tiempo nos distribuyeron en casas particulares; a mí y a otro chico amigo mío que se llamaba Imanol Iriondo, nos llevaron a Kensington Gardens Square en Bayswater hasta después de la guerra.

Maria Jesús Robles Hernando

Mi primera impresión de Inglaterra no fue nada extraña. Podría haber llegado a cualquier parte, se hablaba español, y me rodeaban caras familiares. Fue en Wickham Market donde noté que hablaban inglés.

Este idioma me impactó fuertemente, lo que me duró mucho tiempo. Para mí sonaba monosilábico y sin tono. La gente hablaba bajito y sin expresión en la cara. Volviendo a aquel entonces, el inglés me parecía insípido, incoloro e inanimado. Desde luego no lo podía expresar así entonces. Uno tiene que comprender que las razas latinas hablan tanto con las manos, con sus caras y el tono de voz como con sus palabras. Sin embargo, tres años más tarde mi opinión no fue la misma. Esa lengua se arraigó en mí, con su loca gramática y aprecié su diversidad de dialectos.

Mis recuerdos de las diferentes colonias donde estuve son fragmentados, y algunas escenas son muy nebulosas, son como relieves con las diferentes capas. Tal es mi recuerdo de Chloë Vulliamy. Ella está grabada en mi mente, aunque estuvo con nosotros en otras colonias, su presencia se destaca y pertenece a mis recuerdos de la primera colonia exclusivamente, Wherstead Park, cerca de Ipswich.

Miss Vulliamy, como la llamábamos, era en ese momento una señora muy atrevida. Tenía el pelo negro con raya en medio, recogido severamente en un moño. Llevaba los labios pintados de rojo fuerte, y su pelo negro y los labios contrastaban con su piel blanca. Fumaba en boquilla, tenía una voz muy culta (me di cuenta de eso muchos años más tarde) y una sonrisa siempre en los labios. Nos hacía reír con su risa contagiosa. Ella y sus amigas se reunían en una de las salas cerca del vestíbulo, maquilladas como muñecas, vestidas con trajes vaporosos, solían bailar al ritmo de los sonidos del Charleston y de otros bailes populares en esa época.

Creo que fue probablemente en Wickham Market que empezaron a llegar las primeras cartas de nuestra madre. En aquel tiempo, nuestro padre era prisionero de guerra. Nunca supimos cómo mi madre se puso en contacto con nosotros y pronto empezamos a escribirnos con regularidad.

La colonia en Wickham Market era como en los libros de Dickens, un edificio feo, de ladrillo rojo, que se extendía kilómetros y kilómetros. Mis recuerdos son siempre de días calurosos cuando íbamos al río y pasábamos la tarde entera bañándonos. La colonia tenía otras dependencias y a menudo las chicas mayores estaban allí arreglándose el pelo con las pinzas eléctricas, yo miraba fascinada como cambiaban de apariencia.

También recuerdo a la cocinera: era una mujer grande y desaseada, tenía una hija de 18 años y un hijo de ocho años. Un día fuimos todos al parque de columpios y tiovivos. Ese chico chocó con un columpio y se dio en la cabeza. Uno de los profesores que nos estaba acompañando le llevó a la colonia. Yo no recuerdo volverlo a ver, pienso que se murió.

Mi primer encuentro con la literatura española fue en esta colonia: un joven nos leía extractos del libro *El cantar del mío Cid*. El español sonaba algo raro, pero la belleza y fluidez de la lengua me cautivó, y a pesar de entender poco de lo que se leía, yo ponía mucha atención. Había visto a este cuenta cuentos en una moto, vestido con un abrigo largo y marrón y una gorra en la cabeza, pero tengo la impresión de que no pertenecía al profesorado.

Algunas veces nos invitaban a visitar a unas familias inglesas. En general yo iba sola, es decir, mi hermano no venía conmigo. La primera vez me recibió una familia con cinco niños y una niña. Ésta tenía más o menos mi edad; se llamaba Patty, y era la menor de la familia. Me saludaron con el puño en alto, la señal de los comunistas, que yo nunca había visto. Resultó que el padre había sido miembro de las brigadas internacionales, de las cuales no había oído hablar. Este hombre, Mr Sines y yo nos comunicábamos en un mal español y un peor inglés. Me informó de como perdió un dedo y como algunos de sus camaradas sufrieron heridas y algunos murieron.

Después a mi hermano y a mí nos llevaron a Birmingham. La familia tenía una hija de unos 20 años, y su hermano había muerto un año o así antes. La idea era que mi hermano ayudara a Mr Thomas en su huerta y que yo trabajara en la casa, y así la hija y la madre se podrían ocupar de la tienda de ultramarinos. Por primera vez en mi vida supe lo que era pasar hambre. Tenían un perro y me tocaba a mí darle de comer lo que sobraba de la comida. Su perro comía mejor que yo. Cuando iba a la perrera, le quitaba comida hasta que me pillaron. Nos fuimos de allí y fuimos a Margate.

Hacía mucho frío y unas semanas más tarde me mandaron a casa de dos señoras mayores, que les gustaba mucho a los niños y que habían recibido en su casa a 12 niños ingleses evacuados. Su impresionante mansión estaba situada al final de una alameda. Pertenecía a Miss Isabel Fry, de la familia cuáquera Fry, e iba a ser mi casa durante 18 años. Llegué en febrero y tengo un recuerdo muy fuerte de ser llevada por el ama de llaves a una gran habitación que tenía una enorme chimenea.

Por un corto tiempo fui a la escuela del barrio pero Miss Fry decidió ser mi profesora ya que había escrito un libro de gramática y había sido directora de una escuela en el País de Gales donde enseñaba a los hijos de familias pobres, en particular de las familias mineras. Después de dos años, me dijo que yo estaba preparada para ir a un internado. Me encantó ser interna y, claro, pasaba las vacaciones en casa. Tanto en casa como en el colegio nos alentaban a pensar por nosotras y expresar nuestras opiniones.

Las dos hermanas Fry tenían muchos amigos invitados, y de los cuales he sabido que eran famosos tales como los Bonham-Carter y el profesor CM Joad. Nos animaban a estar presentes en sus conversaciones, aunque mucho de lo que decían no lo comprendía. Me preguntaba a menudo Miss Fry: " María ¿tú qué piensas de eso?» Nadie se reía de mis opiniones ni me hacían sentir inferior.

Todas las tardes sonaba una campana y todos, incluso las criadas, nos reuníamos a escuchar a una de las hermanas que leía la Biblia, o un capítulo de un libro o algo del periódico. Hacíamos comentarios y después nos daban tiempo para pensar y luego discutíamos el tema. Antes de salir se nos sugería que los niños reflexionáramos sobre lo bueno y lo malo y que reparáramos lo roto antes de ir a la cama. Las disputas o malentendidos entre nosotros se arreglaban amigablemente, pero a veces un adulto tenía que actuar de árbitro.

Teníamos lo que llamábamos la "sala silenciosa" donde podíamos ir si queríamos tener un momento de tranquilidad sin ser molestados. Éramos 13 niños entre 8 y 10 u 11 años, estábamos todos separados de nuestras familias y de vez en cuando añorábamos a nuestras madres. Más tarde en mi carrera de enfermera recordé esa habitación y la importancia de esos momentos. En esa habitación nos desahogábamos, nos quitábamos nuestras frustraciones o aireábamos nuestra tristeza. Allí se guardaban los aparatos de deportes, incluso los guantes de boxeo al aire libre. Nadie veía lo que hacíamos, y salíamos de allí refrescados y nuevos. ¿Qué hubiera pasado si no hubiéramos tenido ese cuarto? ¡Imagínense 13 niños llorosos y un grupo de jóvenes chillones peleándose!

No recuerdo cuando los otros evacuados empezaron a marcharse, pero un día me quedé sola. Creo que Miss Fry me protegía, quizás porque yo era extranjera y tenía dificultades con el idioma. Mientras ella leía yo escuchaba, haciendo punto o cosiendo, o nos paseábamos, ella hablando de las maravillas de la naturaleza o contestando mis infinitas preguntas.

De una forma tranquila y sin yo darme cuenta me iba enseñando los principios de la vida, los que a su vez yo pasaría a mis hijos.

También me enseñó a cuestionar lo que leía y las "verdades" que me decían, las cuales podrían ser sólo ideas del hombre. Esto lo recordé más tarde cuando estudié filosofía.

Terminé la escuela a los 17 años y medio, y empecé mi carrera de enfermera pediatra en Hackney, en el este de Londres. Miss Fry me inscribió en un curso a distancia sobre filosofía y literatura, que hoy día llaman lingüística, bajo la supervisión de una de sus amigas que enseñaba en un colegio de mujeres relacionado con la Universidad de Cambridge. En esos días tenía la idea de volver a España y enseñar inglés, pero después de un año me di cuenta de que lo que quería era ser enfermera. Pasé de enfermera pediatra, enfermera de hospital, comadrona, de tuberculosis y finalmente de oncología. Después de unos doce años cuidando a mis hijos, volví a ser enfermera de cáncer y lo he hecho durante toda mi vida laboral.

Miss Fry me alentaba a visitar las colonias para estar en contacto con mis raíces españolas. Así que me quedé en The Culvers en Carshalton, Rowley Lodge en Barnet y en un lugar en Finchely, en el norte de Londres. Pero visitaba las colonias cada vez menos frecuentemente, por la presión del colegio, de mi trabajo y de los estudios. Mi hermano y yo nos escribíamos y nos visitábamos de vez en cuando, sin embargo perdí de vista a todos esos niños con los que me crié.

No eran tiempos fáciles para nosotros. Perdimos y a la vez ganamos mucho. Para mí, perdí mi identidad. No soy ni española ni inglesa. Cuando volví a ver a mi madre ya era una adulta. Se había perdido la relación madre-hija, pero nos hicimos buenas amigas. Yo había ganado una segunda madre que me entendía mejor que yo misma, me enseñó a ser una ciudadana respetuosa, llevando a cabo todo lo que podía. Estoy muy orgullosa de mis dos madres que querían lo mejor para mí. Las felicito. *

Vicente Rodríguez Elorza

Hay recuerdos que perduran, que se quedan con nosotros para siempre, que están prestos a nuestra llamada y a los que no podemos ser insensibles. Intentaré escribir una pequeña parte de esos recuerdos imborrables.

Tenía 13 años y fui uno de los niños evacuados a Gran Bretaña. Nuestro exilio comenzó el día 20 de mayo cuando embarcamos en el transatlántico *Habana*. Al dejar el puerto y adentrarse en mar abierto, el barco empezó a balancearse y pronto todos empezamos a sentir mareos. A medida que pasaba el tiempo, la situación se hacía insostenible y empezamos a vomitar. Todo eran lamentos, lloros, la imagen era desgarradora; yo en aquel momento sentí una gran soledad, una gran tristeza se apoderó de mí. Recordé a mis familiares y me pregunté si hubiera sido mejor quedarme con ellos.

Por fin el barco atracó en el puerto de Southampton el día 23. Nosotros llegamos extenuados, desorientados, pero por otra parte alegres de haber terminado el viaje por mar. Nos llevaron en autobuses al campamento de North Stoneham en Eastleigh. Allí nos habían preparado muchas tiendas de campaña con capacidad para ocho niños y que fuimos ocupando por orden. Llevábamos tres o cuatro días en el campamento, yo estaba en el interior de la tienda de campaña cuando oí unos gritos. Salí y vi un grupo de niños rodeando a unos ingleses que estaban repartiendo el pan. Parte del grupo de niños se iba acercando y pude ver que una niña se separaba del grupo y venía en dirección donde yo me encontraba. Venía gesticulando y gritando algo que entonces no pude entender. Pronto lo comprendí todo: ella venía abrazando el trozo de pan blanco contra su pecho y gritaba: "Esto es para mi madre. Se lo guardo a mi madre." En aquel momento ella no pensaba en otra cosa que dar a su madre lo mejor que ella tenía, un trozo de pan blanco. Al pasar a mi lado, pude verla mejor. Era una niña de unos ocho años, morena, su rostro dejaba traslucir una profunda sensación de ternura, de felicidad, al mismo tiempo que unas lágrimas resbalaban por sus mejillas. Se fue alejando, abrazando el trozo de pan blanco contra su corazón y seguía gritando: "Esto es para mi madre. Se lo guardo a mi madre."

No la volví a ver más; a veces me pregunto que habrá sido de ella, si habrá recordado ese día y habrá podido contárselo a su madre. Todo aquello me afecta muchísimo, tanto que cuando lo recuerdo me emociono y no puedo evitar que mis ojos se humedezcan, porque lo mismo que ella, en aquel momento, yo también recordé a mi madre.

No recuerdo donde leí que la historia está hecha de instantes. Quizá tengan razón, no lo sé, pero supongo que mis relatos ofrecen la posibilidad de pensar en todas las consecuencias que originan las guerras, sobre todo a los más débiles, por lo cual debemos reafirmar que no hay ninguna guerra justa.

No llevábamos dos semanas en el campamento cuando tuve noticias que junto a 28 chicos y 29 chicas íbamos a ser trasladados a una colonia. Fue a primeros del mes de junio cuando llegaron dos autobuses a recogernos. Nos sentamos, los coches empezaron a alejarse del campamento; dejábamos atrás una pequeña parte de nuestros temores, nuestras tristezas, nuestros miedos y nuestras alegrías.

Una vez que los coches empezaron a circular por la carretera general, nos pusimos a cantar; no dejamos de hacerlo durante mucho tiempo. Estábamos contentos, pero el viaje se nos estaba haciendo largo y pesado. Llegamos a tener los ojos cansados de tanto mirar por las ventanas. Creo que llevábamos casi cinco horas de viaje para llegar a Colchester. Entonces fuimos al pueblo de Langham. Ante nuestros ojos apareció un gran edificio de piedra gris, The Oaks, que en aquel momento nos parecía un palacio.

Entramos, quedamos absortos y encantados con lo que vimos en el interior. Ardíamos en deseos de ver todo el terreno que abarcaba la colonia, fue una delicia contemplar unos campos verdes, separados por unos senderos un poco estrechos con unos árboles frondosos. Todo aquello daba una sensación de tranquilidad. Tuvimos suerte: Basque House, como llamábamos a The Oaks, fue reconocida como una de las mejores colonias de níños vascos en Gran Bretaña.

Muy pronto la dirección de la colonia nos distribuyó en grupos para la limpieza, ayuda en la cocina y para los otros trabajos que se requieren para el buen funcionamiento de la colonia. Empezaron las clases y los profesores se esforzaban en enseñarnos sus asignaturas. Al principio creo que no poníamos mucha atención pero las clases pronto nos resultaron más amenas e interesantes. Viene a mi memoria la insistencia de Mr Sterling de que recitáramos versos: era un amante de la poesía, pricipalmente de la de Federico García Lorca. En el salón había un piano, creo que lo tocaba Caridad, cuyas notas nos ayudaron a coordinar mejor nuestras voces y a iniciar nuestros primeros bailes. Más tarde aprendímos a bailar algunos bailes regionales que presentábamos cuando venía a visitarnos algún miembro del PPU y se hacía una fiesta en su honor.

También formamos un equipo de fútbol. El jardinero, muy trabajador y amante de su trabajo, se quejaba de que al finalizar los partidos el cesped no quedaba en buenas condiciones. Sus quejas duraron hasta que empezamos a utilizar otro campo con la hierba más fuerte. Ya habíamos jugado contra el equipo de la colonia de españoles en Ipswich con resultados aceptables, lo que nos animaba más en nuestros entrenamientos. Después de los partidos siempre celebrábamos una fiesta.

Para mí fue una gran alegría cuando me informaron de que una familia inglesa quería invitarme a pasar unos días con ella. Ya anteriormente otros chicos habían disfrutado de unos días junto a unos familiares ingleses. Cuando volvieron a la colonia se les veía muy alegres, no se cansaban de explicarnos hasta los más mínimos detalles de todas las cosas que les habían sucedido. Nosotros les escuchábamos, y me preguntaba si yo alguna vez podría tener la oportunidad que ellos tuvieron.

Era una mañana a finales del mes de julio. Me levanté muy nervioso. Me despedí de mis compañeros tan efusivamente como si mi ausencia fuera para mucho tiempo. Me llevaron a la estación de Colchester y llegó el tren con dirección Londres. Se hizo cargo de mi el revisor del tren, subimos, y él muy cortésmente me llevó a un asiento al lado de una ventana. Arrancó el tren al mismo tiempo que sentí una gran emoción al ver que por fin iba a lograr lo que tanto había deseado. Me asomé a la ventana; hacía una mañana soleada, una pequeña brisa amortiguaba el calor que llegaba a través de la ventana. Permanecí mucho tiempo viendo pasar hermosos paisajes, amplios campos verdes, alguna granja. De pronto se acercó a mi de nuevo el revisor del tren. Me dijo que estábamos a punto de llegar a la estación de Stafford donde me esperaba una familia para recogerme. Paró el tren, bajamos y él me presentó a un matrimonio con una hija que me recibieron muy amablemente.

Me llevaron en coche a su casa, un bonito chalet. Entramos a un amplio vestíbulo desde donde por una escalera de madera se subía al primer piso. La casa era elegante y me gustó mucho. Era la hora de la comida y nos sentamos a la mesa. Todos estaban pendientes de mí, quizá temieran que la comida no fuera de mi agrado. No fue así aunque yo no estaba acostumbrado a las comidas inglesas.

En el chalet había visto una máquina de escribir y me recordó la que yo había dejado en mi casa. Al día siguiente me llevaron en coche a ver la ciudad. Otro día fuimos a tomar el té con otra familia que nos recibió con mucha alegría. Me preguntaron muchas cosas de mi vida en Langham y también como vivía durante la Guerra Civil; naturalmente tenían que tener paciencia conmigo y hablarme despacio para que les entendiese. Al día siguiente me llevaron a ver el zoo. Entre tanto me puse a practicar algunas veces con la máquina de escribir.

Llegó el día de mi vuelta a Langham: estaba triste, habían sido unos días maravillosos para mí. Nos despedimos, ellos con su habitual amabilidad, yo seguramente con una mezcla de tristeza y alegría al mismo tiempo. Yo esperaba que alguna vez volviera a estar con aquella familia. Dos semanas despues de regresar a la colonia, redacté una carta que me tradujeron en inglés y la enviaron a Stafford a aquella familia. No tuve ninguna noticia de ellos. Siempre me he preguntado ¿Por qué? ¿Qué hice mal? ¿No supe adaptarme? Siempre me ha quedado la desilusión y la duda.

Era la primera vez que nos iban a llevar a una playa. Al conocer la noticia, hubo una gran excitación en la colonia. Era una mañana de verano. En el cielo se veían algunas nubes blancas como algodones que a veces dejaban pasar la luz del sol, lo que animaba a pensar que iba a ser un día caluroso. Ilusionados, montamos en un autobús y entre mirar por la ventana y más tarde cuando ya el autobús circulaba por la carretera principal, y empezar a cantar, casi no nos dimos cuenta de que habíamos llegado. El autobús se paró cerca de la playa. Bajamos y miramos al mar. La playa parecía casi como una alfombra tostada. Con gritos de júbilo corrimos hacia el agua, no había grandes olas y el agua no estaba fría.

Más tarde recorrimos toda la playa corriendo por la orilla dejando las huellas de nuestros pies en la arena mojada. Estaba cansado. Extendí la toalla sobre la arena y me senté. Empecé a contemplar el horizonte más allá del mar azul hacia donde empezaban a emigrar mis recuerdos, mi familia, mi pueblo, mis baños en la playa de Las Arenas, pero pronto pensé que no era la hora ni el momento de la nostalgia, de la soledad, sino de la esperanza, de la ilusión, de la alegría. Volví a nuestros juegos hasta que llegó la hora de marcharnos

Una tarde empezamos el camino hacia el río. Era un placer caminar por aquel paseo con árboles sombríos a sus lados cuyas hojas verdes dejaban filtrarse los rayos del sol. Nuestros cantos, nuestras voces jóvenes apasionadas resonaban. Llegamos, entramos en el agua despacio, muy despacio, porque el agua estaba fría. En la orilla había unos charcos donde chapoteábamos; nos divertíamos mientras nuestras voces rompían el silencio de aquel lugar. Llegamos cansados y muy ilusionados, con ganas de volver otra vez.

Nuestra vida en Basque House seguía desarrollándose felizmente, con nuestras clases, bailes y partidos de fútbol contra equipos de escolares de Colchester y de la colonia de Ipswich. El grupo de baile, compuesto por seis chicas y dos o tres chicos, ofreció una serie de actuaciones fuera de la colonia. De esa manera ayudar a su mantenimiento se convirtió en realidad. Teníamos trajes nuevos (preparados por las chicas) para los bailes que íbamos a realizar.

Llegó el día que nos llevaron a Northampton. La primera representación fue un éxito, el público nos aplaudió mucho, lo que nos permitió tener más confianza en nosotros mismos. En las siguientes actuaciones en Bradford, Rushden, Didsbury y en otros tres o cuatro distritos, nuestros temores habían desaparecido: el público no se cansaba de aplaudirnos y felicitarnos.

Agradezco muchísimo al personal: la Srta Celia Echevarría, (pienso que ella fue el alma de la colonia), Mr Stirling, Mr Darling, Srta Cecilia Gurich (la Peque, como cariñosamente la llamábamos), Srtas Berta, Amada y Deme, asi como a Theo Wills y a Leonard Read de Cornwall, con quíen mantuve correspondencia hasta unos días antes de su muerte.

Si tengo una crítica, pienso que estuvimos demasiado aislados de los habitantes de Langham, sin conocer su juventud, lo que nos hubiera permitido tener amigos ingleses, conversar y perfeccionar el idioma inglés. De todos modos quiero expresar mi agradecimiento a todos los habitantes de Langham por su hospitalidad durante aquellos tiempos y a todos los miembros del Peace Pledge Union que con tanto tesón y cariño trabajaron para que nuestra estancia en Basque House fuera lo más agradable possible. También a todos los ingleses que con su envío de donativos (que tanto necesitábamos) nos ayudó enormemente.

Pilar Rodríguez Izaguirre

Llegué el 2 de junio de 1937 a Rowley Lodge, Barnet con otros 20 niños y 19 niñas. Era un lugar muy bonito y bien llevado. Lady Tewson era la secretaria y nos invitaba a su casa a tomar té. Teníamos suerte en Barnet, pues no todas las casas eran buenas. Cuando algunos niños volvían a España, otros venían de diferentes casas, y así conocíamos a muchos otros y éramos como hermanos.

Fuimos felices en Barnet hasta que nos bombardearon. Nos enviaron dos días a Oddfellow Hall hasta que el comité nos encontró una casa más grande. Nos cambiamos ese día y por la noche una bomba potentísima cayo en el *hall*. Fue horrible. Todo el mundo en Barnet creyó que nos había matado. Cuando algunos chicos fueron al trabajo al día siguiente, los hombres no se lo creían ¡Qué suerte habíamos tenido!

Conocí a tres hermanos que venían de otra casa. Su apellido era Murga. Aquel día, sin yo saberlo, cambió mi vida. Me casé con el mayor en 1948 y vivimos en Barnet. Se llamaba Antonio, pero le llamaban Tony; los hermanos eran Julián y Jesús, mejor conocido por Chechi.

Se tenía a Barnet como una de las mejores de las colonias, como se llamaban las casas. Fue una de las últimas en cerrar, en 1942. Allí viví hasta el final. El comité me buscó trabajo y alojamiento. Empecé como aprendiz en el departamento de lencería y terminé como compradora. Tenía a mi cargo cinco departamentos y 18 empleados. Estaba muy contenta y me encantaba mi trabajo.

En el 2002 se murió Tony, y mi hermana y yo compramos una casa en el País de Gales para estar cerca de nuestra otra hermana y su familia. Pero echo de menos a mis amigos que solían venir a Londres donde nos reuníamos.*

Alfredo Ruiz López

Nací en 1923 en la preciosa ciudad de San Sebastián en el norte de España, el penúltimo de los seis hijos de Pedro y Felisa Ruiz López. Pasé mi infancia jugando y yendo al colegio, enredándome como hacen los niños, por ejemplo cuando el carro de mi tío me atropelló el pie. Mis amigos y yo nos burlábamos del policía que era patizambo. Gritábamos "¡No nos puede coger, ji, ji, ji!", habiendo olvidado que ese mismo policía siempre estaba en la esquina cuando íbamos al colegio y al pasarle nos cogía, nos daba una bofetada y decía "¿así que no os puedo coger, eh?" ¡Tiempos felices!

De niño no me di cuenta que empezaba la Guerra Civil Española. Cuando tenía unos 11 años nos mudamos a Bilbao porque tres de mis hermanos mayores estaban luchando por el gobierno legítimo.

En mayo de 1937 dos de mis hermanos y yo subimos a bordo del *Habana* rumbo a Inglaterra. Al llegar a Southampton nos pusieron en un campamento que había sido construido por los *boy scouts*. Al cabo de poco tiempo unos 100 niños fueron a Brampton, incluidos yo, mis dos hermanos Luis y Alfonso, maestros y un auxiliar. Nos pusieron en una colonia y vimos la nieve por primera vez: pensábamos que era algo mágico. La gente era muy amable e invitaron a los niños a sus casas para comer. Fue así como aprendimos inglés.

Después de dos años en Brampton se acabó el dinero y nuestra colonia, como muchas otras, tuvo que cerrar y algunos de los niños volvieron a España. Mi hermano mayor, Alfonso, se fue a Francia para trabajar con una organización que apoyaba los refugiados de la Guerra Civil Española. Luis y yo nos quedamos pero nos separaron. Luis fue a vivir con un médico y su mujer en Glasgow y a mí me mandaron a Coventry. El dejar nuestra colonia y a la Srta Lolita (Mrs Southern) – que todos queríamos – nos dejó muy tristes. Mantuve correspondencia con ella a lo largo de los años y cuando murió a finales de la década de los noventa Ricardo Martínez, Luis Porras y yo fuimos al funeral y llevamos una corona con los colores de la bandera española.

Llegué a Coventry a la edad de 16 años. Me encontraron trabajo en una fábrica de ingeniería y me alojé con Antonio Tudela y Juan y Víctor Cantalapiedra. Poco pensaba que me iba a enredar en otra guerra. Decidí ir de voluntario el 14 de mayo de 1942 y me llamaron a filas el 7 de junio de 1943.

Me alisté en la *Fleet Air Arm* (Marina Aérea) lleno de entusiasmo. Podía hacer todo lo práctico pero no sabía hablar inglés muy bien. Me transfirieron a *HMS Victory* en Portsmouth. Para poder ser marino tuve que aprender todos los nudos y saber cómo funcionaba el equipo y los cañones. Un poco antes de embarcar hice un curso corto de radar que más tarde resultó ser muy importante.

Mi próxima destinación fue Fort William en Escocia para adiestrarme en barcos pequeños. Esto duró dos semanas. Mientras estábamos allí una noche nos llamaron para controlar un fuego en el centro de adiestramiento de los comandos. Subimos al tejado para controlar las llamas pero no sabíamos que había municiones en el edificio y pronto estábamos evitando las balas. Al amanecer volviendo al cuartel se nos pusieron los pelos en punta – saliendo deprisa y corriendo durante la noche no habíamos visto ni las curvas de la carretera ni los precipicios.

Después de Fort William me fui a Lowestoft y me embarqué en el *ML 147*. Hicimos pruebas para asegurarnos que estaba en condiciones de navegar. Llegaron órdenes de volver a la base principal *HMS Hornet*. Nuestra tarea era escoltar buques que traían suministros a través del Canal de la Mancha. Después nos mandaron al Océano Atlántico, porque los submarinos alemanes intentaban emboscar los convoyes que venían de América. Usando ASDICS, [sistema de detección y localización de objetos por eco acústico] echamos dos cargas de profundidad: sabíamos que habíamos tenido éxito cuando vimos aparecer objetos en el agua. Pero los alemanes eran listos: solían poner objetos en los tubos lanzatorpedos para engañarnos.

Después de acompañar a los convoyes, volvimos a base y nos dimos cuenta que algo iba a pasar dado la cantidad de barcos y tropas. Y así fue cuando nos dieron la orden de zarpar a Normandía a colocar bajo el agua balizas con sonar para que los dragaminas pudiesen limpiar el canal para el desembarque. Diez días después del Día D, el rey George VI llegó a bordo del *HMS Arethusa*. Las órdenes eran de trasladarle a él y a sus oficiales de alto rango a un vehículo anfibio que les llevaría a la playa donde le esperaba el General Montgomery.

La única protección que teníamos en las costas de Normandía fueron unos buques mercantes hundidos cerca de la playa para dar cobijo a los barcos pequeños hasta que se construyó el puerto de Mulberry. Cuando nos atacaban por el aire, nuestra tarea era echar humo para proteger a los barcos más grandes. Aunque el desembarque procedía según los planes, el puerto de Le Havre seguía bajo control alemán. Las fuerzas canadienses cercaron la ciudad y nosotros bloqueamos la entrada y salida por mar. Así los submarinos alemanes no tenían acceso al puerto.

Después de cinco meses en las costas francesas volvimos a la base. En noviembre de 1944 esperábamos con ilusión un periodo de permiso, aunque fuese corto, pero nos dieron ordenes de escoltar un convoy de lanchas de desembarco a la isla de Walcheren en Holanda para la invasión. A mí me tocó relevar el timonel. Poco después llegaron los órdenes de cambiar de rumbo pero resulta que la orden se dio demasiado temprano. La noche era muy oscura y chocamos con la lancha de desembarco al frente del convoy. Pensábamos que habíamos perdido el cabo de artillería pero menos mal que resultó estar sano y salvo. El choque le había lanzado fuera de la lancha de desembarco. No pudimos continuar. Nos remolcaron a base y así terminó nuestra participación en la invasión. Por fin al volver conseguimos el permiso.

En noviembre de 1944 embarcamos en el barco nuevo, el *ML 913*. Nos mandaron a la base de Stornoway. Nuestra tarea era recoger todos los submarinos alemanes y llevamos nueve al puerto de Stranraer. No había donde alojar el personal alemán, así que quitamos todos los armamentos de los submarinos para usarlos como alojamiento. Llevábamos a los alemanes a las duchas y al médico si necesitaban asistencia médica. Uno de los oficiales alemanes que hablaba inglés mostró su frustración diciendo: "¡Ganasteis la Primera

Guerra Mundial, ganasteis la segunda pero a ver quién gana la tercera!" Una vez los alemanes fueron repatriados y los submarinos destruidos, volvimos al *HMS Hornet*.

Volvimos a Poole en nuestro barco y me ascendieron a contramaestre. Todos los barcos alemanes fueron concentrados en el puerto y yo iba con dos marinos a cada barco para vaciar los pantoques que se llenaban de agua. Cuando se cumplió esta tarea nos mandaron de vuelta a Peterhead.

Tras la liberación de París pedí un permiso especial para visitar a mis tres hermanos mayores que habían luchado con los Republicanos. Viajé a la Gare du Nord y como entonces no hablaba francés enseñé la dirección de donde tenía que ir a un hombre que fue muy amable y me acompañó. Le di las gracias dándole un paquete de cigarrillos ingleses. Estaba encantado. Se puede imaginar que mis hermanos estaban nerviosos pero contentos de ver a este marino joven en vez de un chaval de 12 años que llamaban "Chato".

Cuando nos licenciaron nos dieron un traje, sombrero, chaleco y un poco de dinero para poder empezar una vida nueva de civiles. Volví a Coventry y al mismo alojamiento que tenía antes de la guerra. Tuve suerte en poder volver al mismo trabajo.

En 1947 se juntó toda la familia en París. Mis padres habían conseguido permiso para cruzar la frontera española porque mi madre tenía cáncer y se reunieron con mis cuatro hermanos. Mi hermano Luis y yo vivimos y trabajamos en Paris durante un año y todos cuidamos a nuestros padres. Mi padre murió poco después de mi madre y los dos están enterrados en Paris. Luis y yo volvimos a Inglaterra.

Después de la guerra volví a la ingeniería y como muchas otras personas me casé. Tuve cinco hijos preciosos. 27 años después me casé otra vez y soy padrastro de tres, abuelo de 14 y bisabuelo de dos. Llevo casado de segundas 27 años. Y por fin he podido recuperar mi nacionalidad española.

Al reflexionar sobre mi vida me doy cuenta de que el pueblo británico que organizó la evacuación de tantos niños españoles en 1937 fue nuestra salvación. Sentía que era mi deber hacer algo y por eso me alisté como voluntario en la Royal Navy para luchar contra el fascismo. Tuve esta opción. He sido privilegiado en amar a dos países: el país de mi nacimiento que siempre lo llevaré en mi corazón y mi país adoptivo. Mantengo vínculos con mi pueblo natal y lo visito cuando puedo.

Tengo que mencionar a mi mujer. Desde que nos conocimos siempre hemos estado el uno para el otro. No podría vivir sin ella y ella sin mí ya que como cristianos sabemos que la vida continúa* (Alfredo murió en 2008)

Alfonso Ruiz López

Al amanecer del tercer día arribamos al puerto de Southampton. Está anclado en el puerto el gran trasatlántico *Queen Mary* y el *Habana* a su lado parece una cáscara de nuez. En autobuses, en muchos autobuses de dos pisos, nos llevan a un campamento inmenso, consta de más de quinientas tiendas de campaña, que a ocho por tienda hacen cuatro mil niños: muchachas y muchachos que ha traído el *Habana*.

También hay tiendas rectangulares muy grandes, que harán de hospital, cocinas, almacenes, todo esto muy organizado, como el país mismo. Cada tienda tiene una mesa con dos banquetas al largo, que será nuestro comedor. El campamento está instalado y organizado por *boy scouts*. La comida resulta un tanto extraña, pasta, pasteles y bocadillos, y una leche sintética, que sabe a cal. Nuestra tienda es la número 126.

Al mes, empiezan a salir niños y temo que vayan a separarnos, pero corremos la suerte de salir juntos, patrocinados por la marquesa Lady Cecilia Roberts, que adopta a 40 niñas y 40 niños, una gran suerte. Viviremos en el norte de Inglaterra, en un pueblecito llamado Brampton. Partimos todos juntos en dos autobuses y llegamos de noche. Es una casa enorne y espaciosa, tiene grandes jardines y un pequeño campo, que de él hacemos uno de fútbol. La casa está dividida en dos alas iguales, habitarán en una las niñas y en otra los muchachos.

Todo muy organizado, tenemos un Director, Don José María, dos maestras, Srta Lolita y Srta Kiny, personal de limpieza y cocinera españolas, que vinieron con nosotros en el barco *Habana*. Además tenemos un profesor de inglés, Mr Froelich, un profesor de matemáticas, Sr Calzada. Lo más singular para mí es la pintora Mrs Nicholson, nuera de Lady Roberts que comienza dándonos clases con acuarela y en la medida que progresamos nos pasa al óleo. Disfruto de estas clases, pues me entusiasma y deleita pintar. Por último, Harry Herrington viene en moto por las tardes a darnos clases de canto. Nos enseña las canciones inglesas, y él a la vez aprende de nosotros, adaptándolas al piano, las canciones populares españolas.

Mrs Nicholson nos muestra las posibilidades del color, nos enseña la forma de mezclarlos, y su condición, sobre todas, es la luz. Un día pinté una tormenta sobre una noche, al fondo unas luces simulando una aldea y un rayo atravesando el oscuro cielo de la tela. ¡Me felicitó! A partir de aquí, Alfonso Clemente y yo somos sus discípulos preferidos, y los jueves nos lleva en su tremendo coche a su estudio. Pintamos todo el día y tomamos té a cada hora, después nos devuelve a casa y siempre se despide con su frase: *"Be good boys."*

Pronto seremos conocidos en la región. A la Srta Lolita, muy culta por cierto, que observa nuestros ensayos de canciones en inglés y en español, se le ocurre que podríamos dar conciertos en las localidades alrededor en forma desinteresada, gratuita, como agradecimiento a la bella gesta de esta gran señora Lady Cecilia Roberts. Entusiasmados, empezamos a ensayar, y el resultado no pudo ser mejor.

Logramos formar un coro, *The Brampton Chorus*, y damos pequeños conciertos en la región: somos recibidos con mucho cariño, siendo agasajados y aplaudidos. La Srta Lolita me mete en el compromiso de hacer la manifestación de agradecimiento, una vez terminada cada sesión, ante el público. Yo era tímido a esos años, pero armándome de valor, me toca salir a escena, con la cara como un tomate: *"Thank you very much for all that you have done for the Basque children. Thank you!"*

Estos viajes cortos, además amenos, tienen un contenido espiritual y sentimental, porque si bien en todo momento recordar a nuestros padres y hermanos, que dejamos en la guerra, hace nuestra existencia un tanto afligida, con estas giras nos sentimos más unidos entre nosotros, transmitiendo a nosotros mismos la alegría que producimos al público.

Más tarde, la nieve, el fútbol, las clases, la pintura y la vida armoniosa y llena de afectuoso compañerismo que practicamos nos permite sobrellevar nuestra existencia, con una como nostálgica alegría, en estos años jóvenes, felices por naturaleza, pero un tanto amargos por el destino. Tuvieron que llegar las Navidades, era lo que no necesitábamos, y estaban allí. La casa de Brampton, que es una gran "familia", está triste, y todos, pequeños y mayores, nos sentimos meditabundos.

En el gran comedor, que ocupa el centro de la edificación, estamos todos presentes – ausentes - en la comida de la Navidad, porque aquí ni saben lo que es un villancico. Todos nos hallamos muy, pero muy lejos, con el pensamiento en nuestros padres y hermanos. El Director y la Srta Lolita tratan de alegrarnos el día. Tenemos todo el amparo que pudiéramos desear pero estamos muy lejos de nuestros seres queridos. Nos mostramos con el alma apagada, que cruel es cuando se apaga el alma en estos años jóvenes.

Nos retiramos a nuestras habitaciones para abrir nuestros sobres donde tenemos unas fotografías de nuestra familia, las vemos una y muchas veces, miramos a través de los grandes ventanales, y en ese cielo níveo fijamos concentrados la vista como deseando ver en él a los que tenemos en el pensamiento. Nunca había pensado que las Navidades ofrecerían tanta tristeza.

Nos llega una agradable noticia. El Basque Children's Committee anuncia que abrirá una exposición de pinturas de los chicos vascos y piden nuestra participación. Mrs Nicholson está entusiasmada, y nos pone a trabajar sin descanso. Irán 18 cuadros míos. Se venden todos en Londres, habrán ido a parar a hogares ingleses, con el fin de tener un recuerdo nuestro. Recibo £38 por la venta. Eso significa una fortuna para mí, y ya he pensado el destino que he de dar a ello. A nosotros nada nos falta, así que compraré ropas para mis hermanos en España, que carecen de ellas.

La Srta Lolita tiene que hablar conmigo. Me dice que han solicitado desde Barcelona a 18 jóvenes traductores del inglés, para que los niños patrocinados allí por los Cuáqueros americanos puedan leer las cartas que les escriben sus padrinos, y a la vez traducir las que ellos escriben del español al inglés. Decido ir. Sé que Alfredo cuidará a su hermano Luisito. Creo que estoy haciendo lo correcto. Brampton deja en mí un recuerdo encantador, transformante y en mis años futuros lo recordaré con mucho cariño, desearé regresar a él, y muchas veces lo haré espiritualmente.

Cuando he dejado a mis hermanos y estoy camino a España, presiento un destino oscuro y es inevitable acudir al recuerdo familiar para caer en un estado deprimente moralmente, en verdad me creo más solo que Fausto.

Estos 29 meses en Inglaterra me han hecho cambiar mucho, ha sido como un fermento que ha hecho que madure prematuramente, y deja uno de ser un adolescente.

(Extracto tomado de Ruiz López, Alfonso, 1989, *Cuando la sangre llama*, libro publicado por el autor. Alfonso murió en 2008.)

Valentín Sagasti Torrano

1936… y caían las bombas. Nos refugiamos en la Iglesia de Sta María, en la calle 31 de agosto, en San Sebastián. Se tenía como regla que los edificios religiosos fueran respetados por el enemigo y por esa razón las iglesias eran los grandes centros de reunión para refugiarse. Como los combates avanzaban hacia el norte mi familia se marchó de San Sebastián y todos nos fuimos a Baracaldo, un pueblo cerca de Bilbao. Mi hermana Carmen que tenía casi cinco años y yo jugábamos en las calles y oíamos las sirenas. Todo el mundo corría a los refugios y nosotros los seguíamos. El túnel nos llevaba a las laderas y todos estábamos como sardinas en lata. Carmen y yo nos cogimos de la mano. Siempre había pensado que existían dos vías y que nosotros elegimos la de la suerte, pero después de muchos años me enteré de que solo había una vía, y mi recuerdo confirma esto.

Los aviones invadían el cielo, y las bombas buscaban objetivos. Por la vía un tren, como si estuviera fuera de control, tomó velocidad hacia el túnel. El conductor evidentemente sintió pánico y con tal miedo se dirigió a salvarse. Personas muy valientes de pie en medio de la vía movían los brazos en señal de parada, pero sin éxito: el tren se metió en el túnel como un trueno, chocando y llevándose por delante a esas inocentes víctimas. Paró en algún sitio, dejando un panorama desolador. No me acuerdo de los detalles gráficamente, sólo de ver a los soldados dar los primeros auxilios.

Mis padres decidieron mandarme a Inglaterra. ¿Querían protegerme de los dolores de la guerra?¿Era quizás porque un chico era más vulnerable en época de guerra? La verdad es que querían que yo estuviese fuera de peligro. Fue una partida que duró toda una vida. Mi familia se dispersó, mi madre y dos hermanos se refugiaron en Francia. Mi padre que era policía municipal perdió su trabajo como muchos Republicanos vascos y le encarcelaron, primero en la cárcel de Santoña cerca de Santander y después en la cárcel de San Pedro de Cerdena, Burgos. Toda su vida tuvo que sufrir la indignidad de sobrevivir en una industria para la que no estaba preparado y buscar trabajo donde quiera que hubiera. Durante muchos años perdí todo contacto con mi familia

El buque *Habana* salió del puerto de Santurce el 20 de mayo de 19 37. Niños evacuados, los mayores y adultos llenaban el buque. Yo tenía siete años que era la edad más baja para viajar sin compañía. Carmen aún no tenía los cinco años y fue demasiado joven para acompañarme, porque yo casi no era bastante mayor para cuidarme.

No había nadie cercano a mi en el *Habana*. Era uno de la multitud acogida y protegida en el buque, sin reconocer a nadie. Pertenecíamos al mismo rebaño. Nunca sentí miedo, nunca estaba solo, pero conocía la soledad. Alguien tomaba mi mano y me llevaba hacia la compañía de otros: "Aquí, cuídelo."

Llegamos sanos y salvos a Southampton y del campamento en North Stoneham nos enviaron a varias casas. Mi primera colonia fue Brampton. Cuando llegamos a Citadel Station, en Carlisle, nos recibieron Lady Cecilia Roberts y Charles Roberts, y nos llevaron a la colonia en autobuses. En total éramos 100 niños, 33 niñas y 67 niños.

La casa, que era muy grande, estaba rodeada de un muro de piedra coronada con raíles de hierro. Y yo, como era muy activo, recuerdo que salté a las ramas bajas de un árbol cercano atado con guarniciones de cuerda, y aunque se enredaron en los raíles no me impidió volar pero resbalé de las ramas, me caí al suelo y terminé con el brazo izquierdo dislocado.

De vez en cuando invadíamos los campos vecinos y robábamos patatas, que asábamos al aire libre en el fuego. Otras veces tostábamos el pan que encontrábamos. ¡Cuánto nos ilusionaba ese botín! Algunos chicos perseguían gallinas y de la misma manera, nos perseguían a nosotros.

Por este tiempo, yo participaba en los espectáculos: había 14 chicas y un chico. Vestidos con trajes regionales del País Vasco, cantamos y bailamos en los diferentes centros culturales del lugar. El premio remunerativo servía para los fondos de la colonia. También nos daban regalos, que nos repartíamos entre nosotros. Uno de los regalos que yo escogí fue un melodeón. Éste, un par de pantalones y calcetines con agujeros, fueron material de risa para mi "padre"escocés, pues era lo único que poseía cuando llegué a su casa.

La llamada llegó para ir a Glasgow, aunque yo no sabía nada de mi destino. Se debió organizar con prisa. Alguien me trajo una maleta, colocó mis posesiones en ella y me llevó a la estación de Carlisle. El tren ya estaba en movimiento cuando llegué, me despachó con rapidez, diciendo: "Cuide de este niño", y me colocó en un compartimiento. No tenía carné de identidad y no sabía cuál sería mi destino en Glasgow. La indignidad final debió ser causada por la rapidez de la persona que me llevó a la estación: se le olvidó darme el billete.

Esto fue en agosto de 1939 y mi problema surgió cuando al llegar a la estación de St Enoch solo, bajé al andén y me encontré con el revisor que pedía el billete. Le dije en español: "Lo tiene un hombre". No había nadie para recibirme. El problema se solucionó muy pronto, me llevaron a la residencia del cónsul español en Park Circus, donde pasé la noche. Mi único recuerdo de este asunto fue que me enseñaron el retrato de Franco, que colgaba en una de las salas de recepción. Al día siguiente, Mr Blackwood, mi "padre" escocés, me recogió y llegamos a 392 Edinburgh Road, Carntyne. Era una familia de ideas socialistas y que ayudaba a los refugiados españoles.

Yo no sabía nada de inglés y no había recibido ninguna educación en Brampton. En Glasgow empecé a ir a la escuela a los 10 años, se llamaba Carntyne Primary School. Hacíamos ejercicios de dictado y ortografía, el profesor dictaba 10 palabras y nosotros las escribíamos. En general, yo escribía tres o cuatro, todas mal porque estaban escritas fonéticamente A pesar de los problemas de ortografía, después de un año hablaba correctamente inglés pero se me había olvidado por completo mi español.

Había llegado a Glasgow en agosto de 1939, y la guerra mundial había estallado ese septiembre. En 1941 la Luftwaffe penetró en los astilleros de Glasgow en el río Clyde y destruyó la zona en la llamada "Clydebank Blitz". Esto generó más evacuaciones y Mrs Blackwood y yo nos alojamos en un campo de vacaciones, tres millas al sur de lrving, donde continué con mi educación. Me adapté muy bien y recuerdo mi alegría y presteza por levantar la mano y contestar las preguntas. Al terminar mi educación volví a Glasgow.

Durante mi estancia en Brampton y Glasgow, no tuve contacto con mi familia, excepto por carta, yo en inglés y ellos en español. ¡Difícil comunicación! Así 13 años después de salir de España, decidí visitar a mi familia. Como era todavía ciudadano español y apto para el servicio militar, decidí ir a la frontera francesa.

El año era 1950. Salí de Glasgow con sólo 12 libras esterlinas, que me dio Mr Blackwood. Con un amigo me trasladé a Londres. Compramos billetes para París que nos costaron siete libras. Mi amigo se quedó en París. Yo compré un sencillo para Nantes, con la esperanza de hacer autostop hasta la frontera. Después de muchas aventuras, llegué a Bordeaux y compré un billete a Hendaye, en la frontera francesa. Le había escrito a mi padre con antelación, diciéndole que iba a venir pero no sabía cuándo llegaría: parece que no lo planeé muy bien. Sin embargo, al llegar a Hendaya esperaba un recibimiento por todo lo alto, lo cual no sucedió.

Caminé hacia el río, que era la frontera internacional. A un lado del río encontré a dos hombres que trabajaban en una barca, el mayor se llamaba Pedro Carasatorre, cuyos padres habían venido de España hacia tiempo y ahora vivían en Francia. Él trabajaba en una fábrica, y nos hicimos amigos. Todos los días yo hacía lo mismo, caminar hasta la estación, esperando ver a mis padres, luego de vuelta al río, luego durmiendo bajo los arbustos, consumiendo la poca comida que llevaba que duró unos cinco días. Lo único gratis era el agua de la estación.

Al quinto día estaba desesperado. Les escribí una carta a mis padres, contándoles mi desesperación. Se comerciaba entre los dos países al nivel local, y mucha gente iba y venía sobre todo para comprar pan, pues la doble nacionalidad era muy común. Le pedí a Pedro que echara mi carta a correos desde España, pero esa noche fue a casa de mis padres y les dio la terrible noticia. A su regreso por la noche, me despertó, y me dio el carné de identidad de mi padre y dinero para comprar comida. Temprano, a la mañana siguiente, en el café, desayuné de lo lindo, café, tocino, huevos y pan.

Más tarde vigilé el puente esperando a mis padres. Habían tenido dificultades para obtener autorización de cruzar a Francia. Por encima del parapeto, con dolor de cuello, tratamos de vernos hasta que nos reunimos y entonces vino el momento final.

Llegaron mi madre, mi padre, y creo que dos hermanas, no recuerdo cuáles. La alegría y el júbilo eran aparentes, abrazos, sonrisas y un amor perpetuo se escondían dentro de nosotros. Trajeron comida y bebida y fuimos a sentarnos a la orilla del camino, en la parte francesa del puesto de vigilancia, pues no les permitían ir más allá. Este primer encuentro duró dos horas. *

Miguel San Sebastián Perez

Del campamento de Eastleigh nos llevaron a Dorking (19 niños y niñas y dos señoritas, maestra y auxiliar). Allí conocimos a personas maravillosas como Mr Charles Duffield y su madre que nos llevaban con frecuencia a su casa a tomar el té y a pasar algún fin de semana con ellos.

Cuando la colonia de Dorking se cerró, nos trasladaron a Redhill, también en el condado de Surrey, donde estuvimos hasta el día de nuestra repatriación. Ascension House (era el nombre de la casa) fue comprada por Mr. Richard West, miembro del Basque Children's Committee para albergar a 20 niños y niñas.

A los pocos días de llegar a Redhill nos matricularon en la escuela pública de Cromwell Road. José Ramón Valentín y yo formamos parte del equipo de fútbol de la escuela. José Ramón jugaba de interior izquierda y yo de portero. Muchos de los asistentes a los partidos sabían que en el equipo de nuestra escuela jugaban dos niños vascos y en cierto modo éramos una de las atracciones de todos los partidos.

Un caso muy curioso que fue fiel exponente del trato que nos dispensó el pueblo inglés en general tuvo lugar en Londres. Mr. Fred Lilley que poseía una tienda de frutas y hortalizas, así como una pescadería en Merstham, Surrey, me llevó un día al mercado de Londres. Salimos temprano por la mañana y después de haber comprado la mercancía fuimos a desayunar a un bar cercano al mercado. Al ir a pagar los dos desayunos, la persona que nos había servido le dijo a Mr Lilley que sólo le cobraba su desayuno y que el mío no lo cobraba. Actitudes similares se repetían continuamente.

El día de la repatriación, las despedidas entre los que se quedaban y los que nos íbamos se sucedieron con tremenda emoción. Siempre he tenido la duda de por qué nos repatriaban a mi hermano y a mí si no habíamos sido reclamados. El momento de la despedida en el puerto de Newhaven fue altamente emotivo. Los abrazos y los besos entre los amigos ingleses que nos acompañaron hasta el puerto y los que regresábamos a España se sucedían con creciente emoción. Ronald Thackrah, otra excelente persona miembro del comité, estaba a cargo de la expedición.

Durante el viaje no paramos de pensar en las personas que dejábamos en Inglaterra y en cómo encontraríamos a nuestros padres y demás familiares, pero lo que no pasó por nuestras mentes fue el cambio tan radical con el que nos íbamos a topar nada más traspasar la frontera Hendaya-Irún. No es fácil explicarlo porque fue como si pasáramos de un mundo a otro completamente distinto en sentido negativo, agudizado aún más por el trato injusto que recibimos en la frontera española por parte de algunas personas. En Irún otra despedida hizo brotar lágrimas de nuestros ojos al despedirnos de quienes durante nuestra estancia en Inglaterra habían compartido con nosotros penas y gozos así como el cariño y el afecto de tantos buenos amigos.

Enseguida nos dimos cuenta de lo difícil que iba a ser para nosotros adaptarnos no ya a la vida de nuevo con nuestros padres sino a vivir en un ambiente de represión que existía. No era el ambiente de libertad al que estábamos acostumbrados, era una extraña mezcla de temor, incertidumbre y desasosiego. Constantemente nos decían que no fuéramos por tal o cual lugar y que no habláramos delante de la gente en inglés ni pronunciáramos ninguna palabra en Euskera (éste nuestro idioma estaba prohibido) por el riesgo que ello implicaba, dada la delicada situación en la que se encontraba nuestro padre. Se carecía de muchas de las cosas que nos sobraban en Inglaterra. Había escasez de alimentos y de artículos de primera necesidad.

El trauma que sufrimos a nuestro regreso de Inglaterra y los subsiguientes momentos difíciles e inquietantes que tanto nuestros padres como mi hermana y yo tuvimos que vivir han dejado una huella imborrable en nosotros.

Salvando los motivos por los que mi hermana y yo fuimos evacuados y el no estar con nuestros padres, podemos decir sinceramente que nuestra estancia en Inglaterra constituyó uno de los períodos más felices de nuestra vida.

Marguerite Scott

Me formé como enfermera infantil y estaba trabajando con una familia en High Wycombe cuando oí por primera vez hablar de los niños españoles refugiados en la granja Baydon Hole, cerca de Newbury. Una amiga mía había pasado una semana con ellos, así que cuando llegaron mis vacaciones anuales yo también fui a pasar dos semanas.

Disfruté tanto con el trabajo de proporcionar refugio a los niños que habían salido de sus hogares destrozados por la guerra que me despedí de mi trabajo en High Wycombe y regresé con los niños a Baydon Hole tan pronto como pude. Había mucho que hacer pero recuerdo como ayudé a los niños a aprender inglés llevándolos de paseo por la colina que había detrás del campamento y señalando las cosas que veíamos en inglés para que ellos me las dijeran en español. De esa manera aprendimos un poco de la lengua de cada uno.

Un poco después un benefactor, Mr McIllroy, que era dueño de unos grandes almacenes en Reading, y el comité de ayuda local, organizaron una colonia para los niños en Bray Court, cerca de Maidenhead en Berkshire. Yo no pude ayudar con el traslado porque tenía una infección de garganta que el médico pensaba que podía ser difteria, una enfermedad que por aquel entonces era bastante peligrosa, así que regresé a mi casa a recuperarme durante unos días. Por suerte no era difteria así que pude reunirme con los niños en Bray Court. Al poco de llegar a Bray, la señora para la que había trabajado en High

Wycombe nos visitó y me pidió que fuese a trabajar para una amiga de ella, pero yo sabía que los niños me necesitaban más, así que me quedé con ellos.

Había tres españoles, Doña María, Doña Rosario y Eduardo Sánchez. Eduardo era del sureste de España. Doña Maria me dio la receta de "leche frita", que todavía tengo. Maria, Rosario y Eduardo cuidaban de los niños más mayores mientras que yo cuidaba de los que tenían menos de 10 años y de los mayores que estaban enfermos. Además de mí, había otra voluntaria inglesa, Kathleen Hawes, que se había criado en España y hablaba español perfectamente.

Poco tiempo después de llegar a Bray hubo una epidemia de sarna entre los niños. ¡Odiaban el tratamiento! Una noche, una de las niñas, Teresa, se puso a gritar y a retorcerse en la cama durante horas con un dolor de estómago terrible. Kathleen y yo pensamos que podía ser apendicitis pero la enfermera jefa pensaba que no tenía nada malo y que lo hacía por llamar la atención, así que se negó a llamar al médico. Al final como a Teresa le dolía tanto, bajé corriendo las escaleras para llamar al médico local que ya había ofrecido a venir a la colonia a cualquier hora del día o de la noche. Me preocupaba que no fuese apendicitis pensando que la enfermera jefa se iba a enfadar conmigo, pero afortunadamente me encontré con Eduardo en el recibidor y él ya había llamado al médico, así que me evitó cualquier problema. El médico llegó y se llevaron inmediatamente a Teresa al hospital para operarla. Después pasó una semana de convalecencia en casa de mi madre en Twyford. La enfermera jefa se marchó al poco tiempo. Kathleen Hawes se convirtió en la nueva enfermera jefa y yo en su asistente.

De los niños, recuerdo especialmente a José Alberdi, que se quedó en lnglaterra tras terminar la guerra civil y se convirtió en un famoso escultor: él diseñó el toro del Centro Comercial Bullring (Plaza de Toros) en Birmingham.

Un bienhechor local, puede que fuese Mr McIllroy, compraba una vez por semana a los niños pescado ahumado, el bacalao, así que Doña María y Doña Rosario enseñaron a los cocineros cómo prepararlo. Este bienhechor también traía una caja de naranjas para que los niños se las comieran después. Otro benefactor ponía a nuestra disposición un autocar para llevar a los niños a misa los domingos.

Mi hermano, Cyril Scott, solía venir los fines de semana y hacía muchas fotos y diapositivas en color. Al final, Ronald Bates vino a ayudar a los chicos mayores cuando regresó de las Brigadas

Internacionales y se quedó hasta que la colonia cerró. Nos casamos en 1940.

Cuando la guerra civil terminó, muchos de los niños fueron volviendo a casa poquito a poco. Kathleen acompañó a dos grupos y a mí me tocaba llevar al grupo siguiente, pero la colonia se cerró y los niños que quedaban fueron enviados a otras colonias. Nunca fui a España hasta que mi marido me llevó para la conmemoración del 65 aniversario de la Guerra Civil que organizó la fundación en memoria de los caídos de las Brigadas Internacionales.

Miren Solaberrieta Mendiola

El 20 de septiembre de 1936, salió aita desde Zarauz hacia Bilbao, él solo con una pequeña maleta y con un grupo de amigos. Al poco tiempo las tropas de Franco encarcelaron a ama junto con un grupo de mujeres cuyos maridos también habían huido, dejándonos solas a las dos hermanas de 9 y 12 años.

Nuestra madre había sido canjeada por presos de la oposición que estaban en la misma ciudad, así que el 4 de diciembre de 1936, nos llevó a mí y a mi hermana Begoña a Bilbao donde estaba mi padre. Durante nuestra estancia en esta ciudad sufrimos varios bombardeos, incluso el de Guernica. En este tiempo, nuestros padres decidieron enviarnos a Gran Bretaña, no sin antes consultarnos si deseábamos hacerlo o no.

El 20 de mayo de 1937 salimos desde Santurce en el barco *Habana*, llegando a Southampton a los tres días. No podré olvidar mientras viva, y creo que tampoco lo harán todos los niños que estaban con nosotras en el campamento en aquella época, el despertar de la mañana del 19 de junio con la noticia de la caída de Bilbao a manos de los franquistas. Ninguno de nosotros conocíamos el paradero de nuestros padres. Aquello fue un lamento continuo. Mis padres tuvieron que escapar de Bilbao en barcos separados, y saliendo de distintos puertos llegaron a Francia, donde pasaron varios meses sin saber uno del otro. Cuando por fin pudieron juntarse se dedicaron a trabajar e intentar salir adelante hasta que nos pudieran reclamar.

Llevábamos en Southampton unas dos semanas cuando nos comunicaron a mi hermana y a mí, así como a nuestros amigos y compañeros de viaje de Zarauz, Elisabete, Lore y Pirmin Trecu, que junto con otros 16 niños nos conducían a una residencia llamada

Shornell´s. Esta era una antigua y hermosísima mansión como las descritas en las novelas inglesas, rodeada de grandes bosques. Pertenecía a la Royal Arsenal Co-operative Society en Abbey Wood, Londres, a corta distancia de Woolwich y a unos 20 minutos de Londres en tren. El lugar era idílico, no nos lo podíamos creer. La dirección y personal del centro nos recibieron estupendamente. Los primeros días su gran empeño fue quitarnos el hambre.

Acudíamos a un colegio llamado St. Joseph´s Convent Secondary School en el mismo Abbey Wood y a unos cinco minutos andando. El primer curso nos dedicamos a aprender inglés para después integrarnos en las clases de las alumnas inglesas y seguir con ellas dos cursos más. Recuerdo perfectamente como estuvimos a primeros de septiembre atentas a la radio para oír a Mr Chamberlain anunciar el estallido de la guerra entre Gran Bretaña y Alemania. Fueron momentos muy tristes, sin saber qué iba a ser de nosotras y sin noticias de nuestros padres.

Considerando la Dirección del colegio que aquel era un lugar peligroso en caso de bombardeo, ya que vivíamos a muy pocas millas del arsenal de Woolwich, trasladaron a todas las colegialas, entre ellas a nosotras las niñas vascas, a Canterbury, donde nos siguieron impartiendo las clases. (A los chicos no les llevaron, había pocos.) Fuimos alojadas en casas particulares, donde también nos acogieron las familias como hijas suyas. La estancia en Canterbury fue muy interesante y provechosa. Nos daban clases por las mañanas y por las tardes nos llevaban las profesoras a conocer los lugares históricos, que hay en abundancia en ese lugar. Recuerdo muy bien aquella época en la que hice muy buenas amistades, con una de las amigas aún me escribo. Ambas tenemos ya 82 años. Durante todos estos años nos hemos visto varias veces, bien en Bilbao o en Canterbury. A mediados de diciembre de 1939 volvimos a Shornell´s. Paradójicamente en aquel tiempo Woolwich no fue tan castigado por las bombas como Canterbury.

El 2 de febrero de 1940 nos reunimos con nuestros padres en Biarritz, en plena guerra mundial. Al acercarse a Biarritz las tropas hitlerianas, nuestra madre y las dos hermanas tuvimos que regresar a Bilbao y empezar nuestra vida, pero aita que aún no podía volver por cuestiones políticas se quedó 10 años más en el exilio. Tuvimos contacto pero no con mucha frecuencia, ya que la frontera estaba cerrada. No había correspondencia pero nos arreglábamos por medio de amigos o gente que pasaba la frontera de forma clandestina.

Esta es mi historia desde el comienzo de la Guerra Civil el 18 de julio de 1936, día inolvidable. Mi experiencia en Inglaterra ha sido uno de los acontecimientos más gratos e interesantes que he vivido, habiéndome marcado muchísimo en mi manera de ver la vida y comenzar a conocer la democracia. Gracias a los conocimientos de inglés que adquirí he podido trabajar en Bilbao como secretaria bilingüe para una empresa importante de Vizcaya.

Una vez de regreso a Bilbao y después de haber transcurrido varios años, conocí al que fue mi marido Juan José Mancisidor, pasajero con expedición número 1054 también del buque *Habana*, y que admiraba Inglaterra igual que yo. Ambos hemos recordado durante nuestra larga vida juntos los momentos felices que vivimos en Inglaterra, a donde hemos vuelto con bastante frecuencia.

La zona en la que le tocó vivir era al norte de Inglaterra, en un pueblecito llamado Gainford, en Durham. Tengo entendido que era zona minera de carbón, cerca de Darlington. Fue acogido junto con otro grupo en una residencia para niños huérfanos católicos. En un viaje que él y varios amigos hicieron después de mucho tiempo a ese lugar bastante triste e inhóspito por el clima, llevaron una estatua de la Virgen de Begoña en agradecimiento por la acogida que en aquellos difíciles momentos les hicieron. Estuvo asimismo en Scarborough, en una colonia muy numerosa a la que llamaban The Old Hospital.

Los hermanos Trecu fueron a Biarritz al volver de Inglaterra. La hermana mayor se casó con otro de los niños vascos y aún vive en Inglaterra. Lore volvió a Zarautz donde se casó, tuvo varios hijos y es abuela. Y Pirmin volvió también a su localidad natal a vivir con otros de sus hermanos al retirarse, después de haber ejercido como profesor de ballet en la academia que fundó en Oporto. Fue el pequeño del grupo y le tratábamos todos como tal, nos convertimos en sus cuidadoras. Fue una época muy bonita.

Fernando de la Torre Fé

Mis padres y yo llegamos a Inglaterra el 26 de marzo de 1939. Llegamos habiendo seguido la "vía dolorosa" de Barcelona, Figueras, La Junquera, Le Perthus y Vernet-les-Bains, donde estuvimos unas pocas semanas hasta que tuvimos el primer contacto con los niños. Recibimos una carta de Mrs Jessie Stewart, echada al buzón el día 2 de marzo de 1939, desde Girton Gate, Cambridge, invitándonos a vivir con ellos aunque no nos habían visto nunca ni nos conocían.

Carmen Martínez Lorite, una amiga de mi madre y muy involucrada con la colonia de Cambridge de Station Road, había mencionado a Mrs Stewart que mi padre deseaba venir a Inglaterra, por eso la carta, el comienzo de ese nunca olvidado gesto: "Somos grandes amigos de la Señorita Martínez y de los niños vascos y los recibiremos a usted y a la Señora de la Torre con mucho cariño. Confíe en mí, Mrs Stewart". Tal es el final de esa maravillosa carta y nuestra introducción a la existencia de ese pedacito de Euskadi que se estableció en esa tierra verde y placentera de Inglaterra.

La familia de mi padre es originaria de Balmaseda, Vizcaya (donde yo todavía voto) desde hace muchas generaciones. Mi abuela materna nació en San Sebastián, así que el sentimiento vasco ha estado muy arraigado en nuestro corazón. No es entonces sorpresa que mis padres encontraran cierta afinidad con los niños vascos de Cambridge, particularmente dentro del contexto de la tragedia que fue la Guerra Civil Española.

Yo tenía 13 años cuando llegué a Inglaterra y lo más importante para mí era ir a la escuela y aprender ingles. Empecé en Girton Village School, después en Impington Village College y luego completé mi educación en la Perse School. En todas estas etapas se nos hacía muy fácil por la total aceptación y amabilidad de todos los profesores y niños ingleses supuestamente de carácter frío y distante.

Mis recuerdos de los niños vascos son limitados, pues por necesidad nuestras vidas siguieron diferentes caminos, sin embargo nos vimos en Girton Gate, la casa de Mrs Stewart, pues tengo una selección de fotos, la mayoría tomadas por mi padre. Yo me uní a los niños en un partido de fútbol que jugamos en Jesus Green y recuerdo que llevábamos camisetas de cuadros rojos y azules. No recuerdo contra quiénes jugamos, pero mucho me temo que el resultado fue 11-11, pero pudiera ser algo diferente. ¡Fue el primero y el último partido que jugué!

La gran ocasión en la que mis padres y yo nos unimos al grupo completo fue en unas vacaciones en un molino de viento en Burnham Overy, en la costa de Norfolk, en agosto de 1939, un poco antes de comenzar la Segunda Guerra Mundial. La mayor emoción que recuerdo fue el ensayo de emergencia contra el incendio, en el que descendimos desde una gran altura en la parte externa de la torre del molino. También recuerdo un concierto coral, dado en el quiosco de la banda en Christ's Piece, cerca de la estación de autobuses y mi padre ensayando en la colonia de Station Road y yo me sumé a ellos para aumentar el número más que por otra razón.

Una conexión temprana y casi inexplicable ocurrió mientras yo estaba en la Perse School. El profesor de arte, Cecil Crouch, que había llevado a grupos al ballet en Covent Garden, y al que yo había mencionado los niños vascos, me dijo que uno de ellos, pero no de Cambridge, se había convertido en bailarín y bailaba con el Royal Ballet. Este se llamaba Pirmin Aldebaldetrecu. Más tarde y con mucha razón se hizo llamar Trecu.

Me llegaron noticias de segunda mano sobre los niños vascos a través de Carmen Lorite, mis padres o Mrs Stewart. Supimos que Domingo Arana, que trabajaba en Cambridge Instruments, había tenido un accidente, posiblemente de tráfico, y le pusieron una placa de metal en la cabeza. Menos mal, salió bien. Sé que Enrique Murgia era boxeador porque lo vi una vez en una feria en Cambridge. Por desgracia murió en un incendio de su taller. Recuerdo que Carmen Lorite me dijo que Benito Tomé había sido nombrado comandante en el ejército británico.

Mi madre, Caridad, se hizo muy amiga de Luisa Gallego, la madre del clan Gallego, que después de un traumático periplo por toda Europa como refugiada, se pudo reunir con sus cinco hijos supervivientes en Cambridge en 1947. Recuerdo haber visitado su casa, No. 34 de Trafalgar Road. Allí estaba José con su hijo, jugando a la pelota y le decía: "Usa la izquierda". Ambos, José y Antonio, portero y extremo izquierda, llegaron a ser futbolistas profesionales.

Vi a Carmen Lorite durante mi primera visita a España en 1953, en su casa de Madrid, Juan Bravo 12. Hablaba mucho sobre sus niños vascos todavía en Cambridge y espero que algunos hayan mantenido contacto con ella. Más tarde me encontré con Salomé Moreno y su esposo Juan y con Ascensión Belón y su esposo Miguel Ramira, quien luchó en España y en Noruega con el ejército francés. Me dijo como mi madre les instaba a conseguir la mejor educación y objetivos sociales.

Estoy muy contento de que la Basque Children of '37 Association haya tomado la decisión de mantener la memoria histórica de esos oscuros pero gloriosos días, cuando la amabilidad de los británicos era como un elixir contra los horrores de la brutal Guerra Civil.*

Carmen Uribarri Bilbao

Mi hermano Juanito y yo fuimos unos más de los miles de niños evacuados de la guerra en 1937. Embarcamos en el *Habana* el 21 de mayo rumbo a Southampton. Yo sólo tenía 7 años y llevaba la tarjeta número 2879. Era muy pequeña y tengo un vago recuerdo del viaje. Una vez que llegamos a Inglaterra, nos instalaron en el campo de Stoneham donde los niños estaban separados de las niñas, así que no estaba con mi hermano. Después de estar un tiempo en el campamento, fui con otras niñas a la colonia de Weston Manor en la Isla de Wight, hasta septiembre del 38, cuando mi tío José Antonio Bilbao me trasladó a Bélgica. Mi hermano Juanito estuvo en la colonia de Cardiff.

Una de las vivencias que mejor recuerdo fue estando en el campamento. Hubo una gran tormenta, y nos pasamos muchísimo tiempo sujetando los palos de la tienda de campaña para que el viento no la tirase abajo. Otra anécdota que recuerdo de la colonia de Weston Manor fue que asistíamos a misa en la capilla, a diario. Todas las chicas iban a comulgar, y yo también. Lo curioso era que yo no había podido hacer la primera comunión en mi país. Antes de ser evacuados, mi hermano y yo estábamos preparándonos para recibir la comunión pero no hubo tiempo para celebrarla. Así que allí mismo me organizaron mi primera comunión. Conservo una foto del momento con un velo y vestido blanco y un rosario en la mano.

También me dejó un grato recuerdo mi tío: era marino y la guerra le sorprendió en Inglaterra. Se preocupaba mucho por nosotros. Vino varias veces a visitarme con mi hermano. En una de estas ocasiones me compró ropa y calzado. Aún conservo la fotografía con mi ropa nueva, recién estrenada. En otra de las visitas nos regaló una muñeca a cada niña. En una de las fotos aparecemos todas las niñas con las muñecas y nuestra *anderreña* en el centro.

Como niñas que éramos también hacíamos alguna que otra travesura; junto a la colonia había un huerto tapiado, y dentro unos árboles frutales, no sé por qué hueco nos adentrábamos pero cogíamos fruta como manzanas e higos. El jardinero era un señor de poca estatura y regordete y le llamábamos "Barriguita". Cuando se daba cuenta de nuestra presencia, soltaba frases en inglés que no entendíamos y seguidamente escapábamos a toda prisa con la ventaja que corríamos más deprisa que él. Algunos días se acercaban hasta Weston Manor matrimonios ingleses y nos invitaban a sus casas a tomar el té. A pesar de que han transcurrido setenta años de aquella experiencia, me haría mucha ilusión pasar por aquellos lugares algún día.

Durante mi estancia en Bélgica fui acogida junto con mi hermana en la casa del Sr Jean Pierre Jansen que se preocupaba por la situación de los niños vascos. Allí íbamos al colegio donde se hablaba flamenco, y en unos tres meses aprendí el idioma y casi olvidé el castellano. En el verano de 1939, me mandaron al campo donde estaba la familia Jansen. Pasé un verano muy feliz en compañía de los cinco sobrinos que había en la casa.

En ningún momento me sentí mal por estar fuera de casa de los padres, quizás debido a que tengo un carácter muy tranquilo. Tan a gusto me encontraba que cuando me dijeron que tenía que regresar a casa, me quedé muy apenada, tanto que les amenacé que me iba a esconder encima de un armario de la cocina para que no me encontraran y me devolvieran a casa. El 10 de octubre de 1939 regresamos a Bilbao poco tiempo después de que estalló la Segunda Guerra Mundial en Europa.

Pablo Valtierra Martínez

Ya una vez en tierra, nos llevaron a un tipo de campamento grande en el cual había instaladas muchas tiendas de campaña tipo militar, hasta nuestra distribución a diferentes colonias.

Estuvimos poco tiempo en North Stoneham, hasta que nos llevaron a la colonia de Langham cerca de Colchester. Yo tuve suerte porque me acuerdo que no me querían porque me peleaba con todos, pero gracias a la mediación de un chico que se llamaba Vicente, pude ir con ellos. Además varios de los que fuimos a esta colonia eran de mi pueblo Sestao y nos conocíamos.

A la llegada a la muy confortable Basque House, entramos todos los niños y nos metieron en uno de los salones que estaba llenísimo de todos los juguetes que te puedas imaginar. Esto ya nos llevó a pensar que no íbamos a ver a nuestros padres y hermanos por un tiempo. Todos los 20 niños nos peleábamos por los juguetes.

En nuesto grupo también había un grupo de chicas jóvenes de Bilbao que fueron piezas claves durante nuestra estancia aquí, como Rafaela, la cocinera, Marina, gran profesora, futbolista y pianista, y varias otras que no recuerdo, y como no el profesor, filólogo, y promotor de muchas cosas incansable, Mr Leonard Read, hijo de uno de los profesores de Oxford, que estaba allí en todo momento que lo necesitaras.

Revisaron nuestros ropajes y según las necesidades de cada uno, nos llevaron a la parte superior de la casa donde había como un pequeño cuarto, y en el interior había algunas personas que nos iban dando cosas. Se ve que casi todo el pueblo había donado de todo: juguetes, ropa nueva y usada. Nos miraban a ver lo que nos hacía falta, algunas veces zapatos, otras veces pantalones. Era un pequeño lío: a unos les sobraba medio pantalón, a otros los zapatos eran grandes, pero nos reíamos todos mucho con lo que nos daban.

Luego salimos y vimos los jardines, también a algunos jardineros y entre los empleados recuerdo a uno que se llamaba Otto y era alemán: este era zapatero y era el que nos arreglaba los zapatos. Pero luego descubrimos que también era un gran jugador de ping pong y éste nos enseñó a toda la colonia a jugar. Mr Leonard nos llevaba a los lugares de los alrededores. Había un bosque bastante cerca con grandes extensiones de terreno adonde luego íbamos por nuestra cuenta a cazar conejos. Solíamos poner unos lazos para cogerlos a la salida de las madrigueras, como también los cogíamos a campo abierto acorralándoles entre los que íbamos a cazarlos.

Nos tuvimos que adaptar a las señoritas profesoras que habían venido de Bilbao; puesto que los libros y todo estaba en inglés, era muy difícil. Estudiábamos literatura y matemáticas entre otras cosas, y también nos sacaban a dibujar en la calle y yo llegué a dibujar bastante bien. Finalmente empezamos a ir a la escuela pública que estaba cerca de la colonia. Allí estábamos con los niños ingleses. Hacíamos otros trabajos como por ejemplo hacer unas corbatas que luego traje a España. Estas cosas nos agradaban a todos nosotros, porque desconocíamos este tipo de enseñanza. Así que cuando regresé a España noté la diferencia. Hay que darse cuenta de la verdad, cuando nosotros llegamos a Inglaterra nos llevaban una diferencia de 30 años.

Los días transcurrían y también empezaban a venir muchos padres con sus niños. Siempre nos traían algunas cosas, por ejemplo caramelos y ropa. Yo creo que como es lógico les dábamos un poco de lástima al estar fuera de nuestras familias. Añadido a esto, España estaba con cambio de gobierno, algunos padres en la cárcel. El mío en particular fue condenado a pena de muerte, aunque al final se salvó. Yo no sabía mucho de él, alguna carta que yo escribía se la intentaban pasar cuando le llevaban algo de comida. Mi padre, al ir a comer el bocadillo, se encontraba con la carta dentro y eso le alegraba mucho.

Había unas grandes nevadas en Inglaterra en el invierno y eran muy bonitas. Nosotros en la colonia hacíamos entre todos los niños un Papá Noel enorme de nieve en el jardín justo enfrente de la entrada principal. Primero poníamos una gran bola de nieve abajo para el cuerpo, luego otra encima para la cabeza, y por fin venía el gorro rojo y la bufanda roja de Papá Noel. Además como era el clima tan frío no se deshacía nunca. Por lo demás todo el mundo tiraba bolas, las que más trompazos recibían como siempre eran las niñas.

Todavía me acuerdo como íbamos a la escuela en esa época y veíamos incluso trineos tirados por caballos con niños que los llevaban a la escuela porque ni los coches podían transitar por la carretera. También se veía algunas madres llevando a sus hijos en trineos pequeños de madera.

Algunos niños como yo también en el jardín cogíamos los nidos de los tordos, o sea los huevos y también veíamos esos mirlos totalmente congelados en el suelo. Recuerdo que en España nosotros nos comíamos los pajaritos pero lo que yo observé era que los ingleses los respetaban mucho.

En el verano nos llevaban al río y lo pasábamos muy bien. Aprendimos a nadar y a veces nos quedábamos a comer y pasábamos todo el día allí. También íbamos incluso cuando llovía: esto hacíamos cuando vivíamos en Bilbao donde llovía casi siempre. El trayecto de la casa al río era muy bonito, atravesábamos campos, había faisanes que iban con sus polluelos, el paisaje me recordaba al del País Vasco, siempre tenía un verde precioso.

También en las colonias teníamos actividades artísticas. Se formó un grupo de teatro musical. Este grupo estaba compuesto de niños y niñas y luego cuando venían los ingleses a vernos les ofrecíamos estos pequeños espectáculos. Se bailaba algo de flamenco y se cantaba: recuerdo haber cantado *Asturias patria querida*, también el célebre *Los cuatro muleros*, de García Lorca, y gustaba mucho, así como las canciones vascas. En esto nos acompañaba al piano la joven bilbaína que se llamaba Marina, gran artista y directora. Ofrecíamos estos espectáculos por los alrededores y a otras colonias.

Recuerdo que se formó un equipo de fútbol del cual el capitán era Vicente. Fue un gran capitán de equipo y gran compañero. También teníamos a la misma Marina que nos entrenaba y jugaba muy bien al fútbol. Con el famoso Otto, el alemán, jugábamos a *treasure hunts* en el bosque. Escondían figuras, nos daban como un croquis y pistas para encontrarlas.

En una época nos dio una erupción de sarna a varios de los niños y nos tuvieron que bañar en azufre amarillo. Nos aislaron del resto del grupo para no contagiarles hasta que estuviésemos completamente curados. El que nos cuidaba y preparaba el baño con el agua con azufre era Mr Leonard.

Recuerdo que todas las semanas nos daban una pequeña paga, unos peniques or *farthings*, y los íbamos a gastar en el pueblo de Dedham. Allí hacíamos travesuras: mientras unos estaban pagando los caramelos que compraban, había otros que los cogíamos y nos marchábamos sin pagar. Cuando volvíamos a la semana siguiente, tenían a alguien que estaba cuidando de que no nos marcháramos sin pagar. Eran buena gente y como éramos niños y sabían que no estábamos con nuestros padres nos dejaban hacer de todo.

Después de cierto tiempo en la colonia algunos niños, reclamados por sus padres, regresaban a sus casas. A mí no me reclamaron y un día llegó un señor a la colonia para adoptarme a mi y a una niña que se llamaba Petra Martínez. Este señor que nos adoptó era ingeniero en una fábrica de papel del condado de Kent. Allí vivíamos en una casa muy bonita. Había preparado un pequeño refugio en caso de bombardeo y nos llevó al ayuntamiento donde nos hicieron probar varias máscaras de gas en caso que los alemanes tiraran gases. Estaba prohibido salir sin los señores a la calle y siempre nos llevaban colgados del brazo.

Fue un gran cambio vivir con una familia, en particular los sábados y domingos que eran los días que nos sacaban a pasear en coche, y esto hasta entonces nunca lo habíamos hecho. Junto con su mujer y su hija salíamos al campo y comíamos a las orillas del Támesis. Era muy bonito y a veces alquilábamos una barca. Eso me gustaba mucho pues me recordaba a Bilbao que está al lado de la ría. Otras veces nos llevaban al parque zoológico. Allí el matrimonio y su hija se reían mucho, sobre todo cuando compraban cacahuetes para que les diéramos a los monos y en vez de dárselos a los monos, me los comía yo. En la casa no nos faltaba de nada, teníamos todo lo que queríamos aunque también lo pasábamos mal por el problema del idioma, ya que hasta ahora habíamos vivido con niños españoles en las colonias. La familia se esforzaba mucho para que estuviéramos contentos. Por la noche, antes de ir a la cama, jugábamos toda la familia a las cartas como al póquer y, en invierno a otros juegos chistosos al lado de la chimenea. Eran una maravilla de personas. No recuerdo cuánto tiempo estuve allí y fue una lástima perder el contacto con ellos.

Entonces mis padres pidieron que regresara. Aunque estaba contento de volver a España, también tenía pena de dejar a esta familia adoptiva que se portaron conmigo como verdaderos padres. Por dejadez nunca supe más de ellos. El regreso lo hicimos en un barco pequeño, y como todavía estábamos en tiempo de guerra, cruzamos el paso de Calais con las luces apagadas. Decían que podía haber algún submarino alemán y no podíamos hacer ruido así que íbamos muy preocupados. Nos imaginábamos lo peor. Por fín llegamos a Francia y de allí fuimos en tren hasta Irún y entonces Bilbao. Luego llegó el encuentro en Sestao. Fue una experiencia inolvidable: la alegría de estar otra vez juntos era enorme.

Fue duro adaptarse a esta nueva situación, ya que toda la familia había estado separada de alguna forma: mi padre, en la cárcel, mi madre y hermano en Francia y mi hermana en Suiza. Fue muy duro para mi padre, ya que al haber estado luchando en el bando opuesto a Franco, no le querían dar trabajo en ninguna parte. Sus amigos no le hacían mucho caso por miedo. En una ocasión, llamó a la puerta de una empresa y le abrió el director. Este había sido un comandante franquista que mi padre había conocido cuando él estaba preso. Mi padre cuando le vio casi se echó a correr, pero el otro le llamó por su nombre y fue el enemigo el que le dio trabajo y luego nos ayudó mucho a nosotros.

También me acuerdo de los que se quedaron a vivir en el Reino Unido. Y quiero concluir diciendo que los ingleses que nosotros conocimos fueron muy buenos.

Álvaro Velasco Luengo

La vida en el campamento de Eastleigh era muy regimentada, muy cansina. Un día, para acabar con el aburrimiento de nuestra existencia diaria, mi amigo Pedro Sáenz y yo jugábamos con la idea de robar un par de pantalones de ultima moda que habíamos ojeado en la cuerda de la ropa. La principal atracción de estos pantalones eran las mil rayas que demostraban la buena calidad. El plan salió como esperábamos, con precisión militar. Escondí el botín en el fondo de mi mochila: no lo usé nunca en Eastleigh por miedo a que los reconocieran.

Unos meses mas tarde junto a otros 80 niños me mandaron a la colonia de Brechfa, al oeste del País de Gales. ¡Por fin tenía la oportunidad de ponerme mis nuevos pantalones! Los planché con mucho esmero entre dos colchones de paja, entonces me los puse y me paseé como una estrella de Hollywood, orgulloso y recibiendo comentarios de admiración.

La verdad sea dicha, un compatriota de San Sebastián, Tomás, se fijaba mucho en mis pantalones nuevos. Miró la etiqueta en la cinturilla y eran suyos. ¡Que pequeño es el mundo!

En otra ocasión, en el terreno del deporte, la rivalidad entre los chicos de San Sebastián y de Bilbao era fanática en Laleham School, Margate, tal y como ocurría en España. Se organizó un partido de fútbol semanal entre los dos grupos. Se decidió que habría un gran premio de pasteles, lo que era un gran festín para los chicos. Por desgracia para mí siempre perdíamos ante los de Bilbao: nuestro equipo de San Sebastián no resaltaba ni por la técnica individual ni por la cohesión de grupo.

Como consecuencia, cada semana mi equipo y yo nos quedábamos sin comer a la hora del té. Frustrados por esta situación, concebimos un plan para burlar y quitarle el botín al panadero, el cual venía todos los días a las siete de la mañana.

El esquema tenía tres protagonistas. Pedro Sáenz, del Barrio de Aguea, era el vigilante, observando al panadero. Juan Cantalapiedra, mientras tanto, se encargaba de abrir y cerrar las puertas de la furgoneta del pan, lo que me permitía, el tercer vínculo, seleccionar los pasteles y el pan antes de salir corriendo y esconder el botín robado. ¡Los chicos bilbaínos se sorprendieron de que los de San Sebastián, derrotados, de alguna manera dieran la impresión de haber ganado! *

(Álvaro murió en 2009)

www.basquechildren.org